DIPLOMACY AT THE CUTTING EDGE

By the Same Author

Inside Diplomacy (2000 & 2002)

Managing Corporate Culture: Leveraging Diversity to give India a Global Competitive Edge (co-author, 2000)

Bilateral Diplomacy (2002)

The 21st Century Ambassador: Plenipotentiary to Chief Executive (2004)

Asian Diplomacy: The Foreign Ministries of China, India, Japan, Singapore and Thailand (2007)

Foreign Ministries: Managing Diplomatic Networks and Delivering Value (co-editor, 2007)

Diplomacy for the 21st Century: A Practitioner Guide (2011)

Economic Diplomacy: India's Experience (co-editor, 2011)

India's North-East States, the BCIM Forum and Regional Integration (co-author, 2012)

The Contemporary Embassy: Paths to Diplomatic Excellence (2013)

DIPLOMACY AT THE CUTTING EDGE

Kishan S. Rana, IFS (Retd)
Former Indian Ambassador to Germany

Manas Publications
New Delhi-110002 (INDIA)

MANAS PUBLICATIONS
(Publishers, Distributors, Importers & Exporters)
4402/5-A, Ansari Road (Opp. HDFC Bank)
Darya Ganj, New Delhi-110 002 (India)
Off. 23260783, 23265523, Res. 23842660
Fax: 011-23272766
E-mail: manaspublications@gmail.com
manaspublications@yahoo.com
Website: www.manaspublications.in

ISBN 978-81-7049-511-6
₹ 595.00

Cover Design by Ajit Rana

Designed at Innovative Processors

Printed in India at
Printways, Delhi
and published by Mrs Suman Lata for
Manas Publications, 4402/5-A,
Ansari Road (Opp. HDFC Bank),
Darya Ganj, New Delhi-110 002 (India)

Dedicated to my parents

Shivsinhji and Kusum Kunwarba Jhala
and
Mimi's parents
Vikram Singhji and Ratan Kumariji of Rohet

Contents

Preface

This book has been long in coming. I started to write a memoir in 1998, and then shifted attention to a different project, examining the working of the Indian diplomatic system, which emerged as *Inside Diplomacy*, 2000. Though my recollection shaped that and subsequent writing, a thought persisted that I should tell my full story.

I played a small role in the formation and execution India's foreign policy. It is a great honor to work in the Foreign Service (IFS), to receive the President's Letter of Commission as his envoy to a foreign state. Regardless of the work assigned to each person, we get to deal with an enormous range of issues in the course of a typical 30-plus-year career, from the day of entry into the Indian Foreign Service, right up to the date for 'superannuation'—a word we Indians have uniquely made our own, meaning the end of an official's working career. In India that used to happen at the age of 58, and I ended this career in July 1995 (that age bar rose to 60 in 1997). That relatively early age means that we get a chance at a second career, or a pursuit of a personal vocation. I have an allergy to the word 'retirement'; it implies an end of activity, which is increasingly inaccurate in our time, when people are active into their 70s and later—till that 'great retirement', to meet our Maker, or attain heaven, or whatever.

Friends, many of them Service colleagues, have seen and commented upon different chapters. I am beholden to Geoff Berridge, Chandra Chari, Kiran Doshi, Ranjit Gupta, and Suryakanthi Tripathi for their comprehensive assistance. Others that have read and helped to improve different chapters include: Kamal Bakshi, Avtar Singh Bhasin, Rajiv K Chander, Satish Chandra, Ramu Damodaran, Chinmaya Gharekhan, Vivek Katju, MK Krishna Kutty, Edward Marks, Aly Nazerali, MK Rasgotra, Sharat Sabharwal, HHS Viswanathan, R Yogeshwar, and some others that chose not to be named. All of them have helped to add vital details, fill out omissions, and correct the text. I remain responsible for the errors that have persisted despite these efforts.

I am immensely grateful to Chandra Chari for editing this book, not just for improving the text, but also offering many fine suggestions. My thanks are also offered to Manas Publications, the publisher of my first book, for helping with this book as well.

The immediate family has been an ally and source of inspiration in all my writing efforts. This time, they have also been active collaborators, and trenchant critics too, sometimes telling me, 'Surely you can't write that…'; or, 'Why have you left out…'. I have depended on Mimi's memory to guide me with facts and filling out incidents of which my recollection had turned hazy, besides setting me right on details. Ajit and Priya, who were with us at seven of our overseas assignments, have chipped in with their stories. Priya has also helped with proofreading, editing and text improvements. Deepika has joined them in critiquing the text. I offer profound thanks to them, as always.

Abbreviations

ACP	Africa-Caribbean-Pacific states, under the Lome Convention
APA	*Asia-Pacific Ausschuss,* a special business group created in 1993 in Germany, to focus on economic opportunities in Asia
ASEAN	Association of South East Asian Nations
BDI	German Association of Industry
BRIC	a political group consisting of Brazil, Russia, India and China
CARICOM	Caribbean Community
Cd'A	Chargé d'Affaires
CDU	Christian Democratic Union, a major German political party
CECA	Comprehensive Economic Partnership Agreement
CEO	Chief Executive Officer
CEPA	Comprehensive Economic Partnership Agreement (this is akin to 'CECA', where the word 'partnership' is replaced by 'cooperation')
CFL	compulsory foreign language
CGI	Consulate General of India
CII	Confederation of Indian Industry
CPV	Consular, Passports and Visa Division in the Ministry of External Affairs
DCM	Deputy Chief of Mission
DIG	*Deutsche-Indische Gesellschaft* (German-India Society), a cultural group in Germany

DIHT	German Association of Chambers of Commerce
DPR	Deputy Permanent Representative
EAM	External Affairs Minister
EPG	Eminent Persons Group
EU	European Union
FCO	Foreign and Commonwealth Office, UK
FDI	Foreign Direct Investment
FICCI	Federation of Indian Chambers of Commerce and Industry
FTAs	free trade agreements
G-77	the group of 77 developing states originally established in 1964, which now consists of some 130 countries
GATT	General Agreement on Trade and Tarrifs
HK	Hong Kong
IAEA	International Atomic Energy Agency
IAS	Indian Administrative Service
ICT	information and communications technology
IFS	Indian Foreign Service
IGCC	Indo-German Chamber of Commerce
IGCG	Indo-German Consultative Group
ILO	International Labor Organization
IMF	International Monetary Fund
ISI	Inter-Services Intelligence of the Pakistan Army
IT	information technology
ITEC	Indian Technical Cooperation Program, run by the Ministry of External Affairs
JEB	Junior Establishment Board, which at MEA handles postings of junior non-diplomatic staff
JS	joint secretary, a senior grade official, typically heading MEA divisions
LA	Los Angeles
LDC	lower division clerk
MEA	Ministry of External Affairs
MFA	foreign ministry
MHA	Ministry of Home Affairs
NAM	Non-Aligned Movement
NATO	North Atlantic Treaty Organization
NGO	non-governmental organizations

NPT	Nuclear Non-Proliferation Treaty
NRIs	Non-Resident Indians, i.e. Indians living overseas
OECD	Organization for Economic Cooperation and Development
OPEC	Organization of Petroleum Exporting Countries
PA	personal assistant
PDS	A political party in Germany, formed after Unification in 1991, with support mainly in East Germany, now called The Left.
PerM	performance management
PM	Prime Minister
PMI	Permanent Mission of India
PMO	Prime Minister's Office
PO	Political Officer (in Sikkim, up to 1975)
PR	permanent representative
PRC	People's Republic of China
RAW	Research and Analysis Wing (India's external intelligence agency)
S&T	science and technology
SAARC	South Asian Association for Regional Cooperation
SEB	Senior Establisment Board, which at MEA handles postings of attachés and personal assistants for missions abroad
SF	San Francisco
SIPA	Silicon Valley Indian Professionals Association
SPD	Social Democratic Party, a major German political party
TFAI	Trade Fair Authority of India
TiE	The Indus Entrepreneurs
UN	United Nations
UNEP	UN Environment Program
UPSC	Union Public Services Commission
WANA	West Asia North Africa
WHO	World Health Organization
WTO	World Trade Organization

Introduction

Several of my books describe the working of the diplomacy process, including a couple of textbooks; they draw from my experience, and recollections garnered from others. This present work is a complete personal narrative of my 35 years in the Indian Foreign Service. Academics sometimes lament that not enough practitioners recount their experiences in ways that might be of use to scholars, students and other professionals of this métier.[1] The Indian Foreign Service offers a rich collection of writing in this genre by our giants, among them in no particular order, KPS Menon, Apa Saheb Pant, YD Gundevia, Badr-ud-din Tayebji, JN Dixit, Rajendra Abhyankar, and others.

My earliest memory of a career choice is of an urge to join the Foreign Service, after I had got over a childhood hope that many young boys nourish, to follow in my father's footsteps. By 1948, around the age of eleven, when I began to think of such things, my father had become a banker; his civil service career ended prematurely after the integration of the Indian princely states at Independence. He had been the private secretary to the Maharana of Porbander, Natwar Sinhji, and in 1947 he was this state's acting *Dewan* (i.e. head of administration). Of course, I did not then understand my father's sharp rejection when I sounded him on a banking career; he told me that this was not much of a profession and I should choose something else. I did not then realize that my

---

1 Brian Hocking and Donna Lee, 'The Diplomacy of Proximity and Specialness: Enhancing Canada's Representation in the United States', *The Hague Journal of Diplomacy*, Vol. I, No. 1, p. 39.

father had taken up a bank job in a difficult situation, when his prospects for entering the newly formed Indian Administrative Service (IAS) were stymied; the IAS had accommodated several of his counterparts from other princely states in our region. He was amply qualified, with a BA from Edinburgh University, and uncompleted Bar-at-Law training at Lincoln's Inn, plus 16 years in the administration of Porbander State. Unfortunately, he faced personal hostility from a powerful neighboring maharaja, the Jam Saheb of Jamnagar, who became the first governor of Saurashtra, the state that emerged after 1947. He blocked my father from joining government service.

The why of that hostility is bizarre, yet typical of that age. Visiting Porbander in the mid-1940s in the company of several other maharajas, the Jam Saheb felt slighted at the seating order at an official dinner, and blamed my father for that gaucherie. Or, a land border between Porbander and Jamnagar, and my father's role in pushing Porbander's case might have been at the root of his contempt. He subsequently insisted that he would not visit Porbander if my father was in town. The Maharana of Porbander, a man of singular modesty and charm, gave in to that demand, and my father went away on the one or two occasions that the Jam Saheb thereafter travelled to Porbander, until Indian Independence rendered such princely tantrums irrelevant. But as governor of Saurashtra state (later integrated into Gujarat during the 1956 reorganization of Indian states), he had that blocking power. My father then found a lifeline in Dena Bank, run by a family that had close connections with Porbander. Let me add, however, that it was the same Jam Saheb who in 1945 gave me a scholarship of ₹1000 per year, which permitted my parents to send me to Rajkumar College, Rajkot; they added to this ₹500 of their own, to make up the annual school fee, as it was in those days. And some eight years later, my brother Nirmal benefited from that same scholarship to join this fine school.

My parents inculcated in me the values that have been a life guide. My father imprinted on me the imperative of integrity and upright conduct. From my mother I learnt the importance of determination and persistence. Rajkumar College was a crucible for learning and fellowship, as was St. Stephen's College, Delhi.

Approaching completion of school education at Rajkumar College, a dream took hold, that I should try and enter the Indian Foreign Service (IFS). Somewhere along the line, I had also developed a fascination with China.[2] I have been singularly fortunate that a higher destiny, or chance, allowed me to attain both these dreams. And when my time in the IFS was up at the age of 58 that same unseen hand guided me to an equally rewarding vocation, teaching, which has provided as much fulfillment as the Service. As granddaughter Suneira once told me, I have truly been blessed in this double indulgence.

I left school in early 1954 with a first class in the Senior Cambridge exam; in those days that test was the gold standard at the so-called 'public schools' in India, i.e. expensive private schools modeled on the British prototype. It sufficed to get a place at St. Stephen's College, Delhi, which was the preferred destination even for the alumni of my school, given that we were located in a relative backwater, the Saurashtra-Gujarat region of western India. Next to nobody had heard of my school at this elite Delhi institution, replete as always with students from more famous schools such as Doon, Mayo, and Sanawar. So at College, I was a kind of outsider; I also knew nothing of any region outside my own, having hardly traveled to any other part of India.

I sometimes felt as an outsider in the IFS as well, but that was not much of a handicap. Perhaps that is not a fair; I cannot blame others for the fact that I had no family, regional or 'community' clout in this Service. Many colleagues have massaged their particular affiliations and familial links in all our civil services, to considerable career advantage. A few have done this via marriage, i.e. support from a powerful father-in-law. My way of dealing with this reality is to acknowledge it, and add: that is just the way the cookie crumbles.

---

[2] This China orientation has been a joke among my IFS batchmates; Vinay ('Pondy') Verma often narrates his standing sally that these batchmates would take a bet among themselves as to how soon I brought each conversation around to this favorite theme; the usual time was less than two minutes!

Origin and Objective

My first book, *Inside Diplomacy*, completed in a year, was released in October 1999.[3] It was an outpouring of all that I had wanted to say after 35 years in the Foreign Service. That book had all the weaknesses of a first work, naïve in parts, and poorly edited, mainly as I overrode daughter Priya's advice; but it offered a holistic perspective on the functioning of the Indian diplomatic system. That book set me on a less trodden path, writing on the diplomatic 'process'. That work drew on personal experiences, leavened by experiences of Service colleagues. It brought friendships from unexpected places, and gave a spur for subsequent writing on diplomatic studies. In late 1999, it also introduced me to a small distance teaching entity based on the Mediterranean island of Malta, that soon became DiploFoundation, thanks to its visionary founder-director Jovan Kurbalija, who often says that as a Yugoslav, while studying in Malta in the early 1990s, he lost a country and gained a life vocation in connecting diplomacy to the internet. I immediately joined the faculty of this pioneering, non-profit entity, which in turn opened many other new doors. That book also brought a durable friendship with Professor Geoff Berridge, an outstanding diplomacy scholar, who has been generous and steadfast in his cheerful mentorship.

A pure memoir is of real use when it is honest and comprehensive, focused on essentials. A discursive diplomatic travelogue that conveys impressions of different corners of the world, or an ego trip of the I-me kind, describing personal encounters with world leaders and the narrator's role on major issues, just does not work for me. A combative personal compilation that tries to settle personal scores of the past also seems futile. In my Service years I profited from lots of unique opportunities, friendships and support; I also gained enormous personal satisfaction. My sternest critics, wife Mimi and the rest of my family, have urged that this account be 'humanized' with more personal stuff than initially intended; I have partly given in to that demand. The reader may judge if it lives up to its claims.

[3] Rana, *Inside Diplomacy* (Manas, New Delhi, 2000). A slightly revised paperback edition was published in 2002.

In this narrative of personal actions and recollections, I have tried to frame experiences in the context of subsequent knowledge. The goal has been to link those experiences with concepts and ideas that may interest professional diplomats and others. The penultimate chapter covers my efforts, while in Service and in later years, to try and improve the working of the Indian diplomatic system. In the final chapter, I have tried to sketch wider conclusions, thoughts that might apply to the delivery of foreign policy in any country. My goal has been to tell the story of Indian diplomacy as it was practiced in the years 1960-95, through the eyes of one individual, locating these experiences within a wider context. It is for you, the reader, to judge how far that has been delivered.

Some events narrated here also featured in *Inside Diplomacy*. I have tried to strike a balance between retelling these stories, and simply inviting the reader to check out details of a particular episode in that earlier book. I hope this compromise, i.e. an abbreviated account of the events already presented, with reference as to where fuller details are available, provides the reader with adequate explanation, while avoiding boring repetition.

I wish this book could be less about myself, even if that is unavoidable with any memoir. An alternative method might be to distill the material that emerges from oral history records of many individuals, and then find thematic episode clusters that could be strung together to make a complete book. But an author-compiler of that kind of a work would need a great deal of personal knowledge of the context of the events covered, to bring them to life, and avoid distortion. Someone could pick up this idea in the future, but at present rather little oral history material exists in India. A project that is being run by the Indian Council of World Affairs, New Delhi, now has on offer barely half-a-dozen oral history records; we need many more to produce a critical mass.

The *Bhagwat Gita* in a single stanza of two lines sums up the attributes of good speech. It sets out three essentials and two desirables: 1. Good speech should not hurt the listener; 2. The language should be precise; 3. It should be truthful. Further, if possible: 4. It should be pleasing; 5. It may also be of potential benefit to the listener. I think these injunctions also apply to good writing as well, especially to a memoir: to entertain, inform, and contextualize, avoiding negativity.

I have tried to avoid writing about episodes that depict individuals in a negative fashion, or respond to injury, real or imagined, I received from others. In a few instances I may have veered from that gold standard in covering some incidents that were essential to my narrative. I have tried to avoid raking over spent embers, which is unproductive. I have included my errors; perhaps some of these offer a moral. In a few of these instances it has been essential to name individuals in a less than positive fashion, for the sake of an authentic record; my apologies in advance if any of those named feel slighted, or if my depiction of their actions is less felicitous than what is retained in their memory or self-image.

In my first 15 years, I worked under four heads of missions abroad and one outstanding leader at MEA. Chronologically, they were: PS Kotdasangani, Jagat Mehta, KR Narayanan, N Krishnan, and Brajesh Mishra. I was singularly fortunate that all five were exemplars, in different ways, and I learnt a great deal from them. Three others I worked with at New Delhi were splendid mentors, Foreign Secretaries Kewal Singh and MK Rasgotra, and the PM's Principal Secretary PC Alexander. They guided me, and molded my understanding of diplomacy, and ways of dealing with people, vital in any job, but especially crucial at missions abroad that are always isolated outposts of one's national system.

Some of the biggest lessons come from the mistakes we make, especially in people management. My weakness has been impatience, compounded by a short temper. I generally demanded a great deal from those that worked with me; self-justification might be that I made the same demands on myself, but that would not satisfy those that felt that they had not been treated right. I regret my insufficiency of personal introspection. In my working days, we had no opportunity to learn through training—such programs simply did not exist at that time, though that does not excuse my lapses.

Mimi (Shivraj Kumari) and I married in 1966; she has been the resilient anchor and guide in my life, the perfect companion in a Service career, adaptable, genuinely enjoying and participating in all that came our way, and unfailingly 'diplomatic' at the eight foreign assignments where we were together. She built many friendships that gave us joy, and provided huge professional support for my work at all times. This involved extraordinary personal adaptation for her, and sacrifice as well. One example: in February 1994, during PM Narasimha Rao's visit to Bonn, she had to produce at home a lavish buffet dinner for over 250 guests at home, involving days of hard effort, albeit with a team of our two domestic helpers and others engaged temporarily; to cap it, when the PM opted to stay back at the end of that reception, she had to lay a full-scale Andhra dinner for the Prime Minister and his family, aided by the generous help of the wife of the naval attaché who was from Andhra Pradesh. The entertainment funds provided at the time simply did not permit us to outsource the catering.

We all have feet of clay. I have my regrets, perhaps the biggest is that I should have devoted more time to our children, Ajit and Priya, especially when they were at the edge of school graduation, and entered university, when we were at Kenya and San Francisco. I had imagined that passion for advancing Indian interests took priority over family affairs. That was a mistaken work-life balance choice, whose consequences were visited on them. My apologies to my family are inadequate for such neglect.

Career History

One question I have found impossible to answer is: which assignment was best, the most rewarding? Each place offered more than I had expected, and drew my family and I into its charms; each provided me with complexity, challenge and professional satisfaction. Example: in mid-1989, I received news of appointment to the high commissionership in Mauritius with unhappiness, and much trepidation. To put it bluntly, I thought at the time that I was 'too senior' for that job. On reaching that island-state, I quickly realized that I could not have been more wrong about the importance or the rewards of the assignment. And when my family and I left after two and a half years, we had some lingering dissatisfaction that a few things we wished were still undone, and the island of barely 1000 sq. km. had places that we had not been able to visit. I mention this simply to stress that one cannot judge a place at a distance. Provided one is open-minded and adaptable, every location offers its reward.

This chronology below lists the assignments handled in 35 years and three months.

May to November 1960	Joined the Indian Foreign Service on 15 May 1960, spending five months at the National Academy of Administration, Mussoorie (later renamed 'Lal Bahadur Shastri National Academy of Administration').
December 1960 to June 1961	After a few weeks of MEA training that had no real content, when my batchmates began to leave on their first assignments, I waited for the start of the academic year at the Chinese language institute, Hong Kong. I spent a week as 'Attaché (China)', and two months as 'Attaché (West Europe)' against vacant posts, before an 18-day journey to Hong Kong on the cargo ship *Sangola*, which carried a dozen passengers.
July 1961 to August 1963	Third Secretary (Language Trainee), Commission of India, Hong Kong; in effect a full-time student, handling occasional odd jobs at the Commission.
August 1963 to July 1965	Third Secretary, promoted after some months to Second Secretary, Embassy of India, Beijing.
July 1965 to July 1967	Under Secretary (China), Ministry of External Affairs, New Delhi; married Shivraj Kumari of Rohet on 23 November 1966.
July 1967 to July 1970	First Secretary, Permanent Mission of India, Geneva (also concurrently Consul in the Consulate General, Geneva); our children, Ajit and Priya, born at Geneva in 1967 and 1969.
July 1970 to August 1972	First Secretary (and No. 2), Embassy of India, Beijing.

September 1972 to August 1975	Deputy Secretary (East Asia), MEA; promoted as Director (East Asia) in August 1973; served as Director (North) November 1973 onwards.
September 1975 to November 1979	Ambassador, Algiers; concurrently Ambassador to Mauritania (until 1977, when this concurrent charge was transferred to our Ambassador at Rabat). This was my longest assignment.
December 1979 to August 1981	Ambassador, Prague; that was my shortest foreign assignment.
August 1981 to September 1982	Joint Secretary, Prime Minister's Office, New Delhi.
September 1982 to December 1983	Joint Secretary, MEA; from October 1982, Joint Secretary (Administration), MEA.
January 1984 to July 1986	High Commissioner, Nairobi; concurrently, Permanent Representative to UNEP and HABITAT, the two UN offices located at Nairobi.
July 1986 to September 1989	Consul General, San Francisco.
September 1989 to May 1992	High Commissioner, Mauritius.
May 1992 to 31 July 1995	Ambassador, Bonn; ended my career in the IFS on 31 July 1995, completing 58 years that month.

The Union Public Services Commission (UPSC) holds annual examinations for all the major public services. In my days about 40,000 competed for the 350-odd places in all the ten services of those days. Today those numbers of aspirants have grown to 400,000 and more. Thus the selection entails a large element of chance; behind each one chosen, stand hundreds that failed to make it, many of them not because they were notably less able, but because on a particular day, at an exam or interview, fortune favored the one.

I first appeared for the UPSC exam in the autumn of 1958, the very first year that I crossed the threshold of 21 years; I failed to make the grade, and was not called for the interview. At that point, I was at the start of my final year in the MA Economics course, and was ill-prepared for the exam. Worse, I had obstinately refused to offer a history paper. In those days, candidates had to select five optional papers (besides three that were compulsory); a person studying economics could offer only two papers in that subject, and a typical choice for the remainder was history and political science; I did write two papers in the latter, but for my fifth paper I settled on geography, not taught at Delhi University at the time. I paid for that obstinacy through poor marks, both that year and the next!

I appeared for the UPSC exam for a second time in autumn 1959, better prepared, with confidence resulting from a first division in the MA economics exam held a few months earlier. I made it to the interview and barely passed, owing to a silly mistake. That interview board included KM Panikkar, famous historian and former envoy to China; observing that I had offered a paper in geography, he asked if I knew where coffee originated. It was a classic interview ploy; I should have ducked it by confessing that I was unsure. Instead, confounding coffee with cocoa, I replied that it came from South America, and had then traveled across the world. Panikkar responded that I was inventive, but coffee originated in Arabia. I then clarified that I had confused coffee with cocoa, and had overlooked that a variety of coffee bore the name Arabica, confirming that connection. The result: I scraped through with the minimum pass mark of 140 out of 400![4]

The net result: I ranked on the UPSC merit list at number 37. In those days, when around 80 were take annually in the Indian Administrative Service (IAS), the traditional rival to the IFS; I was the last in the nine taken into the IFS, but a month later when a colleague changed her mind and chose the IAS,

[4] Since the 1970s the UPSC has abandoned a minimum passing grade in the interview; this acknowledged the argument of those who felt that a minimum requirement kept out those that the interview panel did not like on subjective grounds, and also allowed that board to tilt in favor of the well-connected. The Ministry of External Affairs has long urged that it needs an even more stringent interview standard, but this argument, including comparisons with other diplomatic services, have fallen on deaf ears, in the name of egalitarian standards.

one more joined the IFS, and I ceded that tail-ender position. In an extraordinary coincidence—some will call it elitism—of the nine in our 'batch' or cohort, seven were either graduates of St. Stephen's College, Delhi (which then barely had 500 students), or had spent at least one year at this institution; in those days our College typically contributed around 15 to 20 each year to the IFS and the IAS. This has changed radically; some recent batches do not have a single Stephanian, and the share of the other leading New Delhi institution, the Jawaharlal Nehru University has also gone down. This is part of a widening of opportunities, in terms of educational institutions, disciplines studied, and regional and family background that has taken place in the diplomatic services of most countries. Further, many new IFS entrants are graduates of engineering and medicine; those disciplines seem to train them better to tackle a very altered UPSC exam; more balanced representation is now needed for the liberal arts, which is offered by very few of today's successful candidates.

1

A Crowning Finale

Germany (1992-95)

My final assignment as ambassador to Germany (1992-95) was a paradox. How did a China-*wallah*, who had spent almost 10 of his first 15 years of Service dealing with China affairs, not speaking a word of German, end his career in Bonn? I had little experience in Europe, apart from three years handling multilateral and conference work in Geneva 25 years earlier (1967-70). Compounding the paradox, my only other foreign language was French, which I spoke fluently but with notable absence of grammatical rigor—a major sin in the Francophone world. Fortunately, Germany is not a country where diplomats unfamiliar the national language face active discrimination, as say in France. Officials and most others one encounters are fluent at English. But there is no gainsaying that without German one had no access to the print and electronic media; public functions, with speeches lasting an hour or more, were always in German, with no translations distributed.

Before the reader jumps to the conclusion that foreign ministries, like much of the government, are logic contrarians, let me explain that in early 1992, completing assignment as high commissioner to Mauritius, I suddenly found myself facing a wealth of choice. After careful thought I opted for Germany. How did that happen? That is part of my Mauritius story, narrated in Chapter 12. Let me commence this memoir with my final assignment, and then jump back to the very beginning of my service career, presenting the rest of my story in rigorous chronological sequence.

Prime Minister PV Narasimha Rao won the July 1991 election and formed a minority government; his government survived on the benevolence of the Left parties that gave support from outside, a formula not unknown in India. The treasury was empty, and the country's foreign exchange reserves were down to the equivalent of two weeks of imports. Having exhausted IMF credits, New Delhi physically sold a part of its gold reserves to Switzerland, to avoid default on foreign payment obligations; like orthodox families, countries do this only in situations of acute distress. For the Rao government, it was that grim scenario of near-insolvency that prompted the transformative policy measures that came to be known as India's 'Economic Reforms'. That story, how the unthinkable became the only option, is too well known to need retelling.

Barely three months later, PV Narasimha Rao embarked on his first foreign trip as Prime Minister, going to Germany for reasons that had little to do with strategy. The ostensible purpose was to launch a yearlong Festival of India. Through extraordinary coincidence, the Indian crisis had occurred at the same time that the Cold War ended and Germany found itself united with former East Germany (the 'German Democratic Republic'). Though the survival of the minority Narasimha Rao government was uncertain, German Chancellor Helmut Kohl somehow came to a personal decision that India's economic reforms might work, and that Narasimha Rao provided Germany a new post-Cold War opening in Asia. Chancellor Kohl decided to invest personal effort into the bilateral relationship; the consequences worked their way over the next several years. For us, that became a major breakthrough. Example: the two leaders decided to establish a joint 'consultative group' composed of eminent persons drawn from business, academia, journalism, culture and public life, to meet annually and recommend measures to enrich and diversify bilateral relations—more of this later. Kohl also decided to make an early return visit to India, which produced its own virtuous circles. For India, Germany became the launch pad for a transformed relationship with the West. Rapidly, Germany became India's strongest champion in Europe. Thus, thanks to a process that commenced before I reached Bonn in May 1992, I became a beneficiary of serendipity. That also created space for a push for stronger bilateral relations, my dominant task for the next three years.

An unusual hiatus had developed at the Indian Embassy in Germany after October 1991, when widely respected senior colleague Ambassador A Madhavan retired. Prime Minister Rao initially wanted to appoint, in a first, a major industrialist, recognizing Germany's economic importance. His choice was Russi Modi, who had just retired as chief executive of Tata Steel, but he turned down the job.[1] Thereafter, despite having known the IFS intimately through long years as External Affairs Minister, the PM took his own time to name a successor.

The German scene

Germany is the world's most decentralized large country, in political and socioeconomic structure. Its nearest comparison is the US, a continental landmass nation of different order, and possibly Switzerland that lies at the other end of the scale. Consider: Germany has no city comparable with London or Paris as a dominant metropolis, nor a business hub akin to New York, Chicago or Los Angeles. After Unification, Berlin became the German capital in 1998, but even today, nearly two decades later, barely 30 of the top 300 German companies are headquartered there. Major German enterprises are scattered across the country, in cities, and sometimes even in the tiny towns where they originated.[2] That partly results from a deliberate policy after World War II to avoid domination by a single city or region. Thus: Frankfurt is the central pillar of banking, and host to two of the world's biggest central banks, Germany's Bundesbank and the

[1] I imagine the late Russi Modi did not consider the appointment attractive, or worthy of his talent. In 1994, I spoke with him on the phone when he visited a mutual friend, an industrialist in the Düsseldorf area; I thanked him for turning down the job; he responded with a hearty laugh. Modi's reaction indirectly reflected the attitude of top Indian business figures to such appointments.

[2] Examples: media and publishing giant Bertelsmann is in the small town of Gutersloh; chemical giant BASF in Ludwigshafen, and Volkswagen in Wolfsburg.

European Central Bank; Hanover was projected as the initial locus for trade fairs; Hamburg had always been the center of trading companies since the Hanseatic days of the 16th century;[3] Munich and Stuttgart are the hubs for research and high-tech industry. The country's most prestigious national award, the annual Karl Prize, is given in the town of Aachen to a public figure contributing the most to European advancement; it was the seat of Charlemagne's 3rd-century empire. For embassy and consulate officials, this means extensive travel across the country, usually via a superb network of autobahns—and high-speed rail links—to meet with the heads of business enterprises, media companies, academia and others. In practice, I was out of Bonn an average of two or three days per week, on outreach, networking and promotion tasks.

After Unification in 1990, Germany became the largest state in the European Union, but its external policy underwent 'normalization' rather slowly. Kohl's political slogan was: 'Germany embedded in Europe', an assurance to neighbors that the country would not take recourse to aggressive nationalism, and that 'demons from the German past would not ride again'.[4] In consequence, Germany found itself inhibited from deploying its armed forces outside its borders; it was only in 1994, after a decision by the Constitutional Court that unarmed military reconnaissance aircraft were deployed in the Balkans, on a NATO mission, in what became a gradual process of normalization, morphing later into overseas deployment of armed forces.[5]

In the early years of German Unification, the largest challenge was internal, the integration of an economically deprived former East Germany into the high-income West German powerhouse. After 1991, annually several tens of billions of Deutschemark—

3 Such trading companies exist only in the Hanseatic cities of Hamburg and Bremen; for the great part German companies engage directly in the international market, not via trading companies.

4 Chancellor Kohl used this phrase during a live joint TV encounter with students at Sorbonne University, when he joined the French President in responding to questions in 1993, during the lead-up to the Maastricht Treaty referendum in France.

5 Germany moved very gradually to deploy armed forces 'out of area', meaning beyond Europe. Even in 2006 when German troops were deployed in Afghanistan as part of NATO forces, a relatively tranquil location was chosen in Northern Afghanistan.

and subsequently Euros—have been transferred to the five *Länder* (states) of the former GDR, to kick-start economic growth and reduce unemployment that ran to over 20%. But as it became clear even by the mid-1990s, bringing up the East to German standards was going to be a long haul. Helmut Kohl's 1995 assertion that 'green shoots of recovery' were beginning to emerge in that region, was both premature and over-optimistic.

The country also faced a politico-social challenge, in the mental divisions between the 'Wessies' and the 'Ossies', much of it the result of apprehension by the latter that joining West Germany had not produced an expected surge of immediate prosperity. The emergence of a new political party in 1990, the PDS, composed of former Communists, complicated matters further. It is a commentary on the paradoxical nature of human behavior that the PDS gained traction in almost all the Eastern provinces after 1991; today it is a significant minority party, calling itself 'The Left', and a ruling coalition partner in some provinces, despite much effort by the two dominant mainstream parties, CDU and SPD, to isolate and crush it.

A deeper problem was an inability of the German establishment to comprehend that in the process of swallowing East Germany, a new body politic had come into existence that was no longer the West Germany of the past; Bonn's rejection of all that the former GDR had represented also carried a price. For instance, all officials of the GDR diplomatic service were ipso facto excluded from the German Foreign Office, since they had been GDR Communist Party members; at one stroke the accumulated experience, especially area and language expertise on developing countries, was lost.[6] That story was repeated across professional sectors, including academia. Those shortsighted actions added to integration problems, as subsequent decades have shown.

New Openings for India

For India, Germany has always been a major economic partner, vital to strong ties with Europe. It was a country of choice for

6 A few of them ended up with employment in Japan and other Asian countries that valued their expertise and contacts. I used to meet a couple of them on visits to Berlin, and they were understandably bitter.

trade and investments, as also source for technology, the more so as unlike other advanced states, Germany had always been relatively open in transferring technology in India, to its subsidiary enterprises and to joint venture partners. That made it all the more important at the start all of our 1991 economic reforms, that we had to get the message out to German companies, business associations, and the *Länder* governments, that India was open for business as never before. German decision-makers had long been captivated by China, their top Asian priority. On the ground, this represented three distinct challenges. First, the major enterprises, such as Bosch, Daimler-Benz, Siemens and the rest, with powerful connections in India, had to be persuaded at the level of their top management that India was undergoing a paradigm change, which they may not have fully taken into account. The second task was to reach the small and medium enterprises, called *Mittlestand*, often family owned, to get them to think about India as a new business destination. Third, we needed to network much better with the powerful associations of business and industry, to harness them as our allies. The Embassy team had its work cut out.

The Kohl-Rao dialogue of September 1991 became the turning point. Germany opted to take a risk, that reforms launched by a seemingly fragile government, were credible, and that the country would find the political will to sustain itself on the transformation path. In hindsight, that decision does not seem novel. But in 1991, it represented a leap of faith. We may recall that even Indians needed to convince themselves for several years that the reforms were 'irreversible'; we may recall that few in Delhi believed that the Rao government might last its full term, or endure in the path of self-liberation from statist control and 'license *raj*'.

That new bilateral mood translated into a warm welcome at the Federal Foreign Office, the *Auswärtiges Amt* (AA). The Director of the Asia Division, Dr. Klaus Zeller and the head of the South Asia Section (*Referat*), Dr. Nobert Hall, quickly became trusted colleagues. I was initially puzzled by Hall's comment that India should no longer consider itself to be a developing country, but realized later, that behind such remarks was their assessment that India was moving to a higher growth path, and transformed economic status. By implication, they suggested it was time to move beyond old shibboleths.

A first concrete expression of this German reassessment was the crafting of the 'Indo-German Consultative Group' (IGCG) composed of about 15 eminent persons on each side, appointed by each government to meet once a year.[7] This 'eminent person' (EP) group was tasked to produce concrete suggestions to improve the bilateral relationship, and report back to the heads of government. In mid-1992 our task was to prepare for the first meeting in September 1992 at Bonn. On both sides, most participants were drawn from business, leavened with culture, education, science, and media personalities. The two ambassadors, plus a few officials from the foreign ministries and the head of government offices joined as observers.

German officials warned us that IGCG was 'an experiment'; if it did not work, it could be closed down. At the time, Germany did not have any comparable bilateral mechanism, other than a multi-track 'Atlantic Bridge' with the US, and another with the UK—both major allies and thus special. India's only experience was the India-Japan group that dated to the late 1950s, run by our Planning Commission, which functioned in desultory fashion (Chapter 3).

The first two co-chairs of IGCC were Dr. Ulrich Cartillieri, a board member of Deutsche Bank, and Prof. P N Dhar, distinguished economist and a former secretary to Prime Minister Indira Gandhi. They established quick rapport, helped by the outstanding individuals that both sides had selected as members. At the first meeting, held at Königswinter castle, on the outskirts of Bonn, several things became clear. First, the formula was a great success, but a one-day meeting simply did not provide enough time for the five themes: politics, economics, culture, science and education, and the media. Second, the method of producing a two-page document, summarizing the recommendations of the group, worked well, tightly focused on hard proposals; Cartillieri insisted on this. Third, the group showed its autonomy, refusing to be 'guided' by officials; that credit also mainly goes to the German co-chair.

---

7 See Rana, *Inside Diplomacy*, pp. 67-8.

A day following the meeting, Prof. Dhar and I were received by Chancellor Kohl. He conveyed personal support to the group, and showed his insights with detailed comment on some of the recommendations. My friends in the AA, seldom given to hyperbole, said that 'the group had exceeded their best expectations'. After 1992 Germany went on to create such 'EP groups' with several others, including Brazil, China, Egypt, Japan, and some more. In 1995, before my departure from Bonn, one high official remarked that the Indian group was the best one. I was then re-nominated to IGCG and attended its meetings till 1999.

By the time IGCG next met in New Delhi in late 1993, the meeting duration was extended to a day and half, with a 'warm-up dinner' the prior evening. The participants had developed personal friendships, and in several cases, this produced new academic and scientific cooperation between individual institutions, as well as deals among some businessmen. The real value of IGCC lay in its thoughtful proposals advanced to the two governments. For India, it also brought in a circle of well-informed non-officials into a quasi-advisory role to the MEA. In our age, where we acknowledge the legitimacy of multiple stakeholders in international affairs, this enriches the process, and engages them in mutually beneficial ties with foreign countries. I have always wondered at the reluctance of some countries, notably in Africa and Latin America, to use the EP mechanism.[8]

Germany showed its strong interest in India in other ways during my three-year assignment, by declaring India to be one of its three strategic partners in Asia, and in this process, 'de-hyphening' its South Asia connections, snapping the earlier practice of treating India and Pakistan more or less on par. As with the EP group, this reappraisal was reinforced by the summit level encounters during 1993 and 1994, as we see below.

---

[8] I have discussed this with participants in the distance learning courses taught at DiploFoundation, and have found them keenly interested, and equally unable to explain why their countries do not use the formula, of course in selective fashion. See, Rana, 'Building Relations Through Multi-Dialogue Formats: Trends in Bilateral Diplomacy', *Journal of Diplomacy and Foreign Relations*, Kuala Lumpur, Vol. 10, No. 1, December 2008.

Work at the Embassy

Within a few weeks of reaching Bonn I wrote a 3-page note summarizing my work tasks. This was sent to the MEA, evoking no response. Looking back, our priorities were:

First, to consolidate and deepen political links, reaching out to government personalities, the political parties, and the key provincial governments, not overlooking the parliament.

Second, to strengthen economic ties, concentrating on exports, especially in terms of new products and market niches, encourage higher German FDI flows into India, and network with key business partners.

Third, to sustain and extend existing solid cultural links, as well as institution level cooperation between academic and scientific institutions, and facilitate more Indian students to take advantage of scholarships and open education opportunities in Germany.

Fourth, to improve outreach towards the German media thinktanks and academia, improve our public image, and improve the efficiency of our consular services.

Fifth, to reach out to the diaspora, believed to number around 70,000, spread across the country, mainly consisting of professionals, plus some engaged in business, harnessing them in relationship building.

Sixth, improve our work performance, integrating the embassy more closely with the three consulates, and pursue high administrative efficacy.

The three other Indian offices in Germany differed in capacity and function. The Consulate General at Frankfurt was the largest, specializing in commercial activities, and handling a large flow of visitors, since Frankfurt was our only direct air link to Delhi and Mumbai (and later to Chennai). The Consulate General at Hamburg was the smallest; its partners were the trading companies in that ancient Hanseatic city-state. Berlin housed what we called an 'Office of the Embassy of India', technically senior to a consulate, successor to our former embassy to GDR, covering the five new *Länder* of unified Germany.

We had an outstanding long-serving honorary consul general in Stuttgart, Helmut Nanz, giving us splendid access; alas, he was winding up his business (including a supermarket chain), and gave up that office around the time I left Germany. In 1994 we proposed an honorary consul general for Munich; after persuasion, Horst Telschik, former foreign policy advisor to Chancellor Kohl, who had moved there as a board member at BMW, agreed to represent us. This was a minor coup, giving us fine access in the important state of Bavaria.

Three senior colleagues served with me as deputy chiefs of mission (DCM) in my three years and four months. The first was just a year junior to me, which made for a difficult situation; he moved out three months later, when his term ended. The second, a fine individual, had a work style that did not match mine; he left for a first ambassadorship after just over a year; his talented IFS wife, working as Minister (Information & Culture) left for her ambassadorship. The third was Shashi Gavai, outstanding in all respects, who moved in as DCM after serving as the counselor handling commercial and economic work; replacing him, Sanjeev Arora, preformed with distinction. Others that delivered much value included first secretaries Rajiv Chander and Suresh Chowdhry, and language trainees Tanmaya Lal and Dinkar Asthana. Military Attaché Brigadier Bhandari, Naval Attaché Commodore Subramanian, and counselor (S&T) Ved Mitra were equally outstanding. Among the local staff, Social Secretary Priti Fassman was an exceptional talent. At the MEA, HK Singh as Joint Secretary (Europe West) and his team provided exemplary support; embassies need understanding headquarters colleagues on whom they can rely. I preferred a trim ship with minimal 'baggage', turning down repeated offers from our Finance Ministry to send a minister (economic), to handle aid-related tasks. Adding to quasi-autonomous fiefdoms within a large mission is a recipe for strife and inefficiency.

Let me sketch the way we went about our work.

1. **Political** ties with Germany were in good shape. The end of Cold War had removed a legacy issue, i.e. doubt over India's links with the former Soviet Union; the Kohl government supported a reforming India. Our priorities:

- Adding to sound ties with the Foreign Office, we cultivated other major interlocutors, especially the

Ministry of Economics, and the Ministry of Economic Cooperation. At the latter, a special problem had arisen, personal antagonism that Minister Carl-Dieter Spranger developed following protocol and program snafus during the German President's 1991 visit to India.[9] Our friends in the AA made it clear that they sympathized, but in their system, one ministry could not interfere in the designated work area of another. I found an ally in State Secretary Hardtl, who received me in those early months for several rounds of discussion. Remember, in 1992-95, India depended on external bilateral aid, and Germany was by far the largest European contributor, a key player at the annual 'Aid India Consortium' meeting in Paris each June.[10]

- Sometimes things did not work out as planned, and this also offered its own lessons. A fine opposition SPD MP, Dr. Edith Niehuis, headed the Indo-German Parliamentary Group of the Bundestag.[11] I cultivated her, with mixed results; at a lunch that I hosted for this group early during my term, she described the operation of such groups in the German system and told me plainly that efforts to convert them into a lobby for closer relations with India would not work; they were not designed for an activist agenda. We remained good friends; in 1994 she invited me to address a community group in a small village in her constituency, located some 200 km from Bonn.

On a few issues, we differed with Germany. One was human rights; we resented a tendency, especially among some opposition SPD parliamentarians, to lecture us on our actions in Kashmir and detention of prisoners under Indian security laws. In late 1991, before I reached Bonn, at the annual bilateral aid talks, the

[9] The efforts undertaken to regain the support of this ministry, and its minister, have been detailed in *Inside Diplomacy*, p. 81.

[10] It was only in 2000 that this annual ritual was wound up, when India moved out of dependence on bilateral aid, though even today, we continue to receive multilateral aid from the World Bank and others.

[11] Unlike in the Indian Parliament at that time, these were official groups with adequate funding to permit them an annual visit to India.

Ministry of Economic Cooperation had tried to hand over a list of prisoners in Indian jails, at the behest of German Amnesty International and other NGOs; the Indian delegation handed back the list, adding that such issues were to be taken up through the Foreign Office, not at aid talks. That led to a suspension of the talks for some months, until that Ministry climbed down.

The Narmada project, under construction in my home state Gujarat, became a hot issue around the time I reached Bonn, principally at the behest of Indian NGOs, which urged German counterparts to block aid.[12] For me, it became a practical lesson in the working of open, multi-stakeholder diplomacy, of which I had no experience. At the Foreign Office there was much sympathy for the Indian position that this project was vital for the economic development of Western India, utilizing its only major river, to provide drinking water to a region that frequently suffered drought, besides irrigation and power generation. Familiar with the ground situation, I stressed that Gujarat had no alternative but to move ahead on Narmada, and that the Indian Supreme Court was monitoring implementation, to ensure that inhabitants on the land that was to be submerged because of the project, received alternate land in compensation.

The AA made it clear that with German NGOs embarked on a mass campaign, bombarding parliamentarians and the government with avalanches of fax messages, the Embassy had to counter this through its own efforts; this form of 'open' diplomacy then unfamiliar to India. We saw that the opposition SPD party was especially active, asking the German government to oppose World Bank funding. I met a number of MPs as well as government officials at the Ministry of Economic Cooperation, which handled German representation at the World Bank. I also sought support at the Chancellor's Office, but was told that they would not intervene; the German system leaves it to each ministry to handle such issues, unless they come up before the Cabinet.

The SPD party, nominally sympathetic to India, had a closed mind on this issue. Their Freidrich Ebert Foundation, working on public affairs, was not receptive to our suggestion that they

[12] See *Inside Diplomacy*, pp. 370-3.

organize a public debate on the project, inviting both the Indian opponents and the supporters of the project; they felt that the issue was 'too controversial'. The MEA was also unprepared for an external campaign, though the Gujarat government provided us with considerable publicity material on the merits of the project. Based on that, the Embassy produced a short brochure in German setting out our case.

We then invited to the Chancery several German NGOs that had led the campaign against Narmada. During a four-hour discussion, we presented our arguments, and urged them to take a balanced viewpoint. They in turn marshaled the counter-arguments of the Indian opponents. At the end, one of them told me that he wished our conversation had taken place earlier; at that late stage they could not change their stand, though they now understood that the Indian government also had a case.

In parallel, we pursued démarches at the Ministry of Economic Cooperation; a few days before the World Bank was to take up this issue, State Secretary Hardtl told me that they would be forced to vote against the project. I reported this to New Delhi; no doubt based on similar negative responses from a few other European capitals, India decided to drop its request for additional World Bank funding. Fortunately, at that stage, the international funds amounted to barely 10% of the project cost, and India could manage without this. In the process we learnt the methods of 'public diplomacy'.

We avoided pique or antipathy towards the Economic Cooperation Ministry; dialogue was the better option. Our Finance Minister guided this effort; when I first met him in June 1992, he had instructed that we had to rebuild connections with Minister Spranger. I focused on conversations with State Secretary Hartdl, and the director general dealing with developing countries, leaving it to Manmohan Singh to pursue Minister Spranger, during his annual visits to Bonn, and when they met at Fund-Bank meetings at Washington DC and elsewhere. That worked; in 1995 a transformed Minister Spranger accompanied Manmohan Singh to his hometown Munich after the official talks in Bonn, even personally escorting him for a full day. Hostility was transformed to friendship.

The other political démarches we made were felicitous. It became increasingly clear that official German agencies were receptive to an expanded cooperation agenda with India. Foreign Minister Klaus Kinkel, who was also 'Deputy Chancellor' as the leader of Kohl's coalition partner the FDP Party, continued his predecessor Hans-Dietrich Genscher's unusual practice of refusing to receive resident ambassadors for discussion, not even for a first call; Genscher had rationalized this in terms of his senior status, also as Europe's longest serving foreign minister. A month after presenting credentials, I asked embassy colleagues to send a note to the Foreign Office for a first call. Section head Hall told our DCM that perhaps the new ambassador did not know their practice. When I next met the Asia Director, I told the latter that I had heard of this practice, and of course it was for the Foreign Minister to decide on whether or not to receive envoys; for my part I would renew my request every six months or so. In parallel, we pursued this through backchannel contacts; after about a year Kinkel received me for a comprehensive discussion. But even on that occasion he warned that I should not expect to meet him on a regular basis. This was a small instance of evolving diplomatic practices; in recent years some more countries have begun to follow this baleful practice, which is of course contrary to established diplomatic conventions.

2. Creating new momentum in **economic** ties was vital, complementing and reinforcing our political activities. The fact that Germany was seen by Indian business as a trusted partner facilitated this; they preferred it to other European countries, apart from the UK.[13] In those early days of Economic Reforms, attracting interest in India was more uphill than today, when the 'India brand' more widely recognized.[14] We worked on a broad front.

[13] This was one of the conclusions of a survey carried out by the consultancy company Roland Berger and Partner; see Ulrich, Chaudhry and Rana, *Managing Corporate Culture: Leveraging Diversity to give India a Global Competitive Edge*, Macmillan India, New Delhi, 2000.

[14] In the 2000s, this produced hubris for Indian embassies, which were much sought by foreign investors, and I heard that some of them took the position that they no longer needed to market India. That now adds to our problems in mobilizing FDI for the 'Make in India' Modi era.

- Through six-monthly meetings with the three consulates, we privileged economic promotion, especially exports and FDI mobilization. The Consulate General in Frankfurt played a major role with their experienced staff, in harmony with the Embassy's Economic and Commercial wing. Our focus: supporting new product exports; preparing market studies in the identified niches; special promotion of software. Improving Indian participation in trade exhibitions was another priority, since Germany is home to the world's leading specialized fairs. Indian exhibitors had to improve and professionalize participation, in terms of pavilion design, display lighting, and personal behavior. The Indo-German Chamber of Commerce (IGCC) was a key partner in this, as many Indian companies used them as the point of contact.
- IGCC, led by its long-serving head in Mumbai, Gunter Kruger, had a special role. It belonged to the comprehensive German network of overseas business chambers, run by the national entity, DIHT (under German law, all businesses had to be members). From the outset, conversation with Dr. Kruger was forthright, sometimes producing disagreement. In our country, there was no counterpart, an '*Indian*-German Chamber of Commerce'—IGCC was simply too dominant (with 7000 members, it was the largest bilateral chamber in India, and also Germany's largest overseas chamber). I argued that notwithstanding its legal status, IGCC was also in effect also an *Indian* entity; it needed to be more proactive in defending the interests of its Indian members, who were in the majority in its membership. Alas, that line of argument had limited impact, but this did not block close friendship with Dr. Kruger.
- Parallel ties were built with the 'other' German business powerhouse, BDI, a national rival of DIHT, with the key difference that BDI is a voluntary organization, attracting the principal German industrial companies. It was Tarun Das, Director General of Confederation of Indian Industry (CII) in India and BDI's close partner, who urged me to

cultivate his counterpart Dr. Ludolf von Wartenberg, who became an invaluable ally; I met him regularly, to gain insight and to pursue economic opportunities. In 1994, BDI allowed CII to station an Indian representative at their headquarters at Köln for business promotion, the first time BDI accepted a foreign official at their office; it was a remarkable tribute to CII.

- A new business body was established in 1993, after Chancellor Kohl's Asia tour (see below), known by its initials, APA (*Asia-Pacific Ausschuss*). The dynamic CEO of Siemens, Dr. Heinrich von Pierer was persuaded to head it. Germans are wary of creating new agencies, partly due to their ponderous internal consultation process; commitments once made, are taken seriously. APA lobbied for close German-Asia links.
- For us, business promotion involved a sustained pursuit of German enterprises, in which the ambassador had a key role; in the German work ethic, that gave direct access to the company's chief executive, and opportunity for quality dialogue. I have written about this at some length in *Inside Diplomacy* (2000), so let me focus only on a few elements.[15] Singapore, one of the most astute economic diplomacy practitioners, and countries such as Ireland and Israel, as also the World Bank, have shown that investment mobilization works best by tackling the entire decision chain in the foreign company being wooed, to nudge them towards an investment decision. This sequentially involves: identifying a target company, as also the needed product or technology; an embassy or promotion body needs to reach out to this target; matching actions are needed from home, for sustained cultivation; when a proposal takes shape, one needs to track progress, and harmonize home actions, not just for project approval in the home country, but to also ensure that the intention is translated into action. India simply does not have such comprehensive mechanisms, so we opted for basic promotion, to raise awareness towards an India option

[15] See: *Inside Diplomacy* (2000), pp. 96-127.

at the highest level in the company, and offering them assistance as needed for prospecting the Indian market. This worked well with large German companies because they have their own contact network in India, including IGCC plus their own consultants. Getting India on the radar screen of the top management seemed to suffice. With medium-sized and small companies, the task was much harder, since they were daunted by the distance and cultural challenges of working in an alien environment. This has remained a key obstacle.

- I worked my way down the list of Germany's top 300 companies. Tackling those that had a presence in India, we sketched to them new opportunities arising from Economic Reform. Companies that had technology collaborations in India but no investment were a special target, and Consul General Alok Prasad spearheaded that particular effort out of Frankfurt; he had remarkable success in persuading some of them to invest. I travelled extensively to meet companies; in three years I probably visited about 150 companies, many more than once, other embassy colleagues took matching actions. Some outcomes: In 1994, when I met the CEO of one of Germany's largest retail chains, he asked: why should we think of India; it is sufficient that we import some consumer durables from there; three years later they became a pioneer investor in India. In at least three cases we found companies hesitant to give me an appointment; when I met them eventually they said that they were worried that somehow we had got wind of their desire to get into the Indian market. Some like Daimler-Benz were forthright; when in 1993 I suggested to the board member in charge of research that they might add to their three research centers around the world with one in India, they responded promptly that this was attractive, and within a year they established a small cutting-edge software center in Bengaluru.
- Another method was for officials of the embassy and the consulate to address business meetings hosted by the branches of DIHT—I probably visited 25 of their 80 offices

across Germany; we also found unconventional hosts for business meetings. That included German newspapers, banks, and even in a couple of cases the regional offices of political parties; all that we required was for them to bring together business enterprises interested in India.

- Business delegations traveled in both directions in greater numbers, raising awareness, and producing a wide catchment of enterprises that then took their interest to the next level, active prospection of markets for trade, investment and technology. We followed a simple principle: incoming delegations from India were treated as our key responsibility; besides framing their detailed program, embassy colleagues or I would accompany them to all their appointments for the duration of their visit. CII's annual 'CEO Missions', which brought heads of six to eight major Indian companies, played a major role; typically, in three days they covered three or four cities, and I accompanied them throughout. Similar proactive actions with German delegations going to India, whether from business organizations or from the *Länder*, helped win credibility. Some diplomats take the stand that such outbound delegations are principally the concern of the counterpart embassy in the home country, but that is a shortsighted view. Though we did not organize their program, we made suggestions and helped them via our Indian connections. I accompanied them when appropriate, as with a delegation led by Baden-Württemberg Minister-President Erwin Teufel.
- Not everything worked. Example: the 'Indo-British Partnership Initiative' launched in 1993, and sponsored by the two PMs, was a model of bilateral promotion. On a self-funding basis, the Confederation of British Industry and its Indian counterpart CII, established a sequenced monthly program of concrete actions (e.g. a machine tool delegation, a catalog exhibition of medical equipment, and a software marketing event, etc.), producing dramatic surge in trade and investments. We tried to interest the Federal Economics Ministry, where we had excellent

contacts, to try something similar; this was also pursued with APA, but Germans have an aversion to borrowed ideas.

My biggest failure in the economic arena was that no one in India showed any interest in learning from German experience in the training of technicians, i.e. its famous 'dual' system of vocational training; this was so obviously one of India's real needs. We pursued this with CII, and with our Industry Ministry. It was included as one of the recommendations of our eminent person group, but Germany took the position that unless India was really interested, they would not waste effort in trying to convince New Delhi. Similarly, we heard in 1994 that Germany was helping China to modernize its patent system; that too became an IGCG recommendation, and met a similar fate, thanks to New Delhi's disinterest. One of the first articles I wrote after leaving the IFS was on India's need to modernize vocational training and to use Germany's experience, published in 1996 in *Business India*.[16] Unfortunately, job-creation was not a real Indian priority at that time; nor had the jargon of 'skilling' entered the lexicon of Indian development planners. Indian business leaders, including CII, share in that failure to anticipate this major requirement, and profit from international partnerships.

3. **Culture, education, S&T:** all forms of intellectual discourse is integral to German DNA. Even in Bonn, a town that became the temporary national capital by virtue of its smallness, it was normal to get an audience of 200 for a lecture by a visiting personality.

- We cultivated thinktanks across the country; colleagues and I visited them in different cities. Partly, we projected economics, speaking of opportunities in a reforming India. Political discourse was also essential, presenting India's foreign policy perspective. One aim was scholarship on contemporary Indian affairs. For instance, a Hamburg thinktank produced a bimonthly economic compilation titled *China Aktuell*; we urged them to produce a similar compilation on India or South Asia, for the benefit

[16] 'Shaping a Workforce', *Business India*, Mumbai, 20 May 1996.

of corporate subscribers. Though the Foreign Office supported this idea, this thinktank was reluctant; they did not judge German business demand towards India sufficient. Years later such a compilation did emerge; it was a matter of timing.

- Our principal cultural ally was the *Deutsche-Indische Gesellschaft* (DIG), modestly funded by the German Foreign Office, with 40 autonomous branches across the country, in effect the largest culture promotional network available to any country in Germany. They typically hosted two or three annual cultural events, drawing on local talent and visiting Indian artistes. The Consulates and the Embassy supported them. In Bonn, Amresh Gupta and some others helped establish a small culture center named after Tagore and helped us greatly. Some remarkable German aficionados of India were our culture envoys. In Darmstadt, Hanna Paulmann, who headed the local branch of DIG, ran an annual 'Days of Indian Culture' spread over several weekends; through her contacts, she received top-ranking Indian dancers and musicians, funding this with ticket sales and local sponsorship from German companies and city agencies. In Nuremberg there was an equally remarkable German couple that hosted commercial events several times a year; making a special visit for their 10th anniversary celebrations in 1995, I asked how they managed to get house-full audiences of 500 and more, at DM40 per ticket, when the performing artiste from India was locally unknown; their simple answer: the audience know and trust us to deliver. This pattern was repeated in other cities. Unfortunately, other than admiration from embassy officials, the Indian system does not recognize contributions by such wonderful individuals. In theory, national 'Padma' awards are sometimes conferred on foreign nationals, but these are rare gestures. There also now exists an award that recognizes achievements by diaspora personalities. We miss a set of awards exclusively for non-Indians who have contributed to culture and understanding.

- In 1991 an Indian Cultural Center had opened in Berlin, then the only one in continental West Europe. Headed by an energetic Manjeev Puri, it played a key role in the Festival of India activities, in its final months when I reached Germany. In those pre-internet days, we found a new vocation for this Center, to act as an information multiplier for the scores of small cultural groups in different German and other European cities; they sought Indian performing artistes for their cultural programs. Increasing numbers of Indian musicians and dancers traveled to Europe on their own, pegging their visit to an invitation, or installing themselves with local friends; they sought performance opportunities. Commencing in 1993, our Center published a bi-monthly list of artistes coming to Europe, giving their contacts, availability dates, and performances terms. In effect the Center became a public service impresario. The circulation of our bulletin rapidly snowballed to several hundreds. Thanks to the internet such networking is easy today, but I wonder if it takes place.
- Student exchanges are major contributors to strong relations with foreign countries. The Indians that studied engineering in Germany in the 1960s and 1970s steered a preference for its technology. In contrast, we found that Indian applicants to German scholarships for international students were declining in the early 1990s, leading our energetic Science Counselor Dr. Ved Mitra to produce a 30-page brochure on higher education opportunities there, including its scholarship programs. One might reason that it is for each country to market its education, but in managing bilateral relations I have always held that the two countries should work in parallel. That exercise led us to examine the number of students coming from India for higher education; the total had fallen to under 500. That meant that leaving out the children of the Indians living in Germany (around 30,000), German universities barely attracted 100 students annually. Consider the background: First, continental European public universities are unique

in not charging differential fees for foreign students; the annual fees were barely DM2000. That did not take into account the living cost, but that was not higher than at other foreign locations. Second, learning German was a disincentive, but special language courses were offered, and most Indians man cleared these in six months, thereafter gaining language skills in parallel with their studies. Also, many universities were expanding their English language offerings. Third, the real disincentive to study was minimal opportunity for migration, and a perception that the country was not particularly friendly to foreigners. That was the nub. Overall, considering all the elements, there was sizable, untapped potential to 'marketing' Germany as an education destination. We raised this at the IGCG meetings for bilateral discussion to spur Germans to action.

- I took this up with one of the state secretaries in the Chancellor's Office, who became a valued interlocutor on different issues that needed to be flagged for Kohl's attention. Results were slower than one might have hoped. Eventually, in the late 1990s, German universities borrowed a leaf from Australia and Canada, and started annual visits to India by joint university delegations, to attract more Indian students. That, plus publicity and promotion effort by different German agencies has now pushed up the annual flow if Indians to German universities to around 4000. By 2015, the number of Indian students in Germany has risen to 12,000, but this is far behind much more expensive education destinations such as Australia and Canada.[17]
- Promoting S&T exchanges involved encouraging institutions on both sides to exchange visits and to aim at cooperation programs in fields of mutual interest.[18] This is long-haul work; results emerge after years. IGCG, attended by scientists from both sides, became a good forum to raise

[17] This remains a problem in other European countries too; Indian students in France are barely 4000.

[18] See also Inside Diplomacy (2000), pp.181-7.

this issue. Science Counselor Mitra developed exemplary contacts within the scientific community, proving the value of his appointments. Yet, even today, plans by the Department of Science in New Delhi to appoint science counselors to at least a dozen more Indian embassies wither on the vine; we have barely five science counselors in our network of over 120 embassies. We seriously lag behind comparable countries.

- India and France run a science center at Dehradun, established in the late 1980s. Our Department of Science found it useful and proposed similar cooperation with Germany. Taking this up with German agencies we encountered resistance. We urged them to check with Paris on the arrangement's utility; an informal response came back that the French were not much pleased with the joint center. We never figured out if that was a bit of disinformation from Paris, or whether Germany was reluctant to invest in this project. Years later, around 2012, a joint Indo-German science center had been established. Even good ideas take time to mature.

Two exceptional ladies were among our allies in Germany. Netaji Subhas Chandra Bose's daughter Anita Bose Pfaff, an academic, lived in Augsburg, Bavaria with her husband, an SPD member of parliament. She graced a Netaji commemorative event we organized in Bonn in 1993, and came again for a reception for Indians during Prime Minister Narasimha Rao's visit to Bonn in February 1994. She reflected grace and charm. Another special friend was Professor Gisela Bonn, who made her home in Stuttgart, was prolific author of books on India and South-East Asia, a highly respected friend to many in our country. Mimi took her to Rohet, Jodhpur in 1993 for the wedding of our niece; she came back enchanted.

4. **Media, image management, diaspora affairs and consular work**—all these fall within the rubric of what we now call 'public diplomacy', but that term was not in use in the 1990s.

- German journals welcome visits by foreign envoys to their editorial boards, and I kept up a round of regular meetings with about eight major publications in different cities, notably at Frankfurt, Stuttgart, Munich, Essen, Hamburg, and Berlin. At the Embassy, Deputy Chief of Mission Shashi Gavai supervised allocation of journals and TV channels to different embassy officers, for sustained cultivation; this worked up to a point, because not every official made the needed effort. Sanjeev Arora, for instance developed fine contacts with *Handelsblatt*.

- We faced a special problem with a couple of established German journalists that knew India well; they saw India's Economic Reforms as futile efforts by a country mired in its socio-economic morass. Conversation with one of the editors involved—who became a good friend—made it clear that the journal would not act against its own columnist. It was far better to work for positive publicity through other contacts, rather than try and influence these diehards. That paid dividend, when Shashi Gavai established dialogue with some journalists and encouraged them to travel to India; it was sufficient for us to play the role of facilitators for them, helping with meetings in India. This experience also brought home a point I learnt later in image management studies: when the reality in a country undergoes sharp change, perception of that change often lags behind; it takes much effort to play catch up.

5. For us the **diaspora** was more important than ever, given the huge changes underway in India, and our need for allies in Germany. The embassy and the consulates worked hard to cultivate the Indian community, while steering clear of their internal divisions and minor clashes over personal agendas of the main players. A simple method was to mingle with them and attend all the functions to which we were invited. Nothing like a single diaspora organization existed, and with different cities and regions vying for attention involved it was impossible to create one. We tried to get the Indian businessmen to work together on a limited promotional agenda, through regular meetings with community leaders at the Embassy, but that too produced limited result. Example: when Finance Minister Manmohan Singh visited Bonn in 1994, we persuaded some to host a dinner. That

was done through an ad hoc group, and over 100 attended, but the group subsequently fell apart. Further, some guests used the Q&A session to vent their anger over accumulated slights, over ill-treatment by customs officials, problems with bank accounts in India, and a generally unresponsive bureaucracy; they failed to use the event for insight into the economic reforms underway. Manmohan Singh, soft-spoken and serious, was displeased and told me that such functions were 'not necessary' on future visits.

Unlike in North America or the UK, the Indian diaspora in continental Europe faces a difficult environment. Language plays a role, but in essence the host countries are tolerant only up to a point; they do not treat migration as a natural process. That drives the migrant community inwards. Outside of work or profession-related connections, few Indians cultivated German with ease. That was especially true for first-generation Indian migrants. I came across only two prominent Indians who comfortably mingled with Germans and built solid friendships with them—Satish Batra in Aachen and the late Amarjit Bhamroyal in Munich. Both businessmen had splendid political, social and business connections, which they readily placed at the Embassy's disposal. Since then, we see in Germany second generation Indians active in politics and other walks of life, but confident engagement remains the exception. Example: Gavai once asked me if a young Indian running a small metal fabrication plant near Düsseldorf might be invited to a reception for businessmen, warning me that he only spoke Punjabi and German. We welcomed him cordially; he stayed till the very end of the function. Going out, he dragged me to his car, not to show the high-end Mercedes S Class, but his chauffeur: '*Sada* driver *gora hai*', he said with pride.

Consular work was our high priority, given its role in image building, diaspora relations, and public impact. The lessons learnt in San Francisco (1986-89) were fresh with me.[19] Our actions: In 1993 we computerized visa issue, including checking against the 'suspect index', taking the help of an Indian software company that we had helped win a contract for. Our project was funded

19 See Rana, *Inside Diplomacy* (2000), pp. 193-8.

through an optional 'rapid processing fee' of DM10, allowing applicants to obtain visas in 45 minutes. That involved stretching the rules. We became the first Indian mission to provide such services; the MEA offered neither approbation nor criticism. We also worked closely with the energetic representative of the India Tourism Office in Frankfurt, and I attended several functions for travel industry representatives he organized, offering our cooperation on visas. The three consulates took matching actions to improve consular services.

6. Sound **embassy and consulate management** is an obvious task for diplomatic missions. 'Management' also refers to the mission's proactive role in developing the bilateral relationship. Let us first consider the latter dimension.

- Embassies always have wide latent authority, to handle matters that arise in the assignment country, without seeking permission for every action; not all ambassadors fully understand this. Some basics are vital: first, one should be clear on policy objectives, and one's actions must be in conformity; second, always keep the territorial unit informed, even post facto; finally, sound judgment is crucial, to distinguish what is locally feasible, and that which needs home permission. The head of mission's credibility at home is crucial.

A couple of examples: With the capital to shift imminent, it became essential to find property at Berlin. At our Berlin Office, the former residence of the Indian ambassador to GDR was inadequate for future use; it was on lease, and located in an unfashionable area; we did not possess anything remotely suitable for the new chancery. That meant recourse to the Federal government, since prices in the open market had skyrocketed. In making our request, I invoked 'reciprocity', arguing that India had given Germany five hectares of the choicest land at Chanakyapuri in New Delhi on a 100-year lease, at a peppercorn annual rent of Rupee one. In mid-1992, I wrote to the Director of the Asia Division (and to the Chief of Protocol, coordinating the Berlin move for foreign embassies); Director Zeller told me in a friendly manner that the lease agreement for the New Delhi property, dating to the early 1950s, did not carry a reciprocity clause. I replied that there nevertheless existed a moral obligation to give us reciprocal help. This was reported to the MEA, and they supported out action. By chance, just at that time the MEA's Protocol Division asked us if we had any objection to a move by the German Embassy in New Delhi to purchase the former GDR chancery in Chanakyapuri—it is rare for the MEA to make such a back reference to an Indian embassy. We immediately urged Delhi to hold up approval; in Bonn we told the Foreign Office that we were linking action in Delhi with our request for land in Berlin. Surprised, they argued that there was no link between the two, but we maintained that in both cases embassy properties were involved.

Unfortunately, during the February 1993 visit by Chancellor Helmut Kohl to New Delhi, Foreign Secretary JN Dixit threw away that leverage; during an across-the-table discussion with his counterpart State Secretary Dieter Kastrup he granted permission, without upholding our reciprocal demand. I never figured out why, but suspect that a politically connected former princely family owning that property may have persuaded him.

Right up to the time I left Germany, we received no satisfaction over our request for land at Berlin, but my successor Satinder Lambah adroitly kept up our demand. On learning that an opportunity that might emerge to purchase a good land parcel, he obtained prior approval from Delhi. In the event, in 1996, he received an offer, with a 24-hour deadline, for a plot on Tiergartenstrasse, surely one of the finest locations in Berlin, and promptly sealed that deal. He finessed two important Western countries that had been vying for that same land.[20] I believe our 'moral obligation' case had paid dividend.

The second example relates to the German commitment to hold a reciprocal 'festival' in India, in return for our yearlong cultural manifestation in 1991-92. I took this up with the Asia Division in 1993, and received no response. A year later, at an informal Sunday lunch hosted at his residence, State Secretary

[20] See Rana, *Inside Diplomacy* (2000), p. 359.

Kastrup told me that high cost was a deterrent, and asked if in lieu, Germany could offer some additional scholarships for Indian students. I evaded a reply, knowing that this would be highly offensive to New Delhi. In 1990-91, when we were faced with a severe financial crisis, we wanted to postpone our festival; the Germans had invoked the sanctity of the joint Rajiv Gandhi-Kohl decision. The next morning, I sent a strong letter to the Asia Director, reiterating our request that the German festival be held in India at an early date, and the importance of reciprocity. I made no reference to Kastrup's offer; perhaps it was made informally with a view to deniability. I then reported the incident to the MEA. They were fully supportive.

We later learnt that the Foreign Office had been opposed to the scholarships-for-festival offer, but an official handling cultural issues who was close to Chancellor Kohl had forced their hand (he was reportedly a member of Kohl's inner circle, called the 'spaghetti club').

In books published after 2000, I have described such local actions as giving to the embassy a position of 'co-manager' of the bilateral relationship.[21] Some countries view this as an evolution in the MFA-embassy relationship; the concept is counter-intuitive, running against a superficial impression that modern communications have reduced embassies to mere messengers. Let me add that this new situation is nuanced; the embassy cannot overstep its intrinsic subsidiarity to the foreign ministry. What helps is the embassy's credibility at home, and its grasp of policy objectives.

Embassy management in the direct and literal sense involves presenting to the team the mission's objectives, enlisting their wholehearted commitment. Officials should be given worthwhile tasks, both as contributors to the shared goal, and to eliminate the potential for intrapersonal friction that comes from idleness. That means maintaining tight discipline, treating firmly all staff, home-based and local, with fairness and equity. We did a fair job at this, keeping our team productive and cohesive.

---

[21] See Rana, *The 21st Century Ambassador* (2004), pp. 91-2.

I remain beholden to the entire Indian mission team in Germany, the 40 home-based officials in Bonn, including our five security guards, and an equal number of locally engaged staff. A like number in the three consulates contributed this collective effort; I was especially obliged to their heads, Kamlesh Sharma and SK Uppal at Berlin, Sudhir Devare and Alok Prasad at Frankfurt, and Niranjan Desai and Madhu Bahaduri at Hamburg.

Our Life

In my first book I wrote: 'The diplomat's wife is perhaps the most unrecognized asset in the Service, all too often by the diplomat-husband as well!'[22] Mimi, the major asset in my life, worked the hardest at Bonn, offering superb hospitality at the large Residence, the renowned Villa Marienforst, site of an historic 11th-century ecclesiastical property, where Ludwig van Beethoven had played church music in his time. We were happy in this home, though by then Ajit was mostly at Mumbai and later at Bengalaru, on his first job, and Priya was away to university at Strasbourg, France. A stream of house guests was a blessing, among them the great vocalist Pandit Jasraj who came on two concert tours, sarod maestro Amjad Ali Khan, Gaj Singhji, former maharaja of Jodhpur, and many personal friends.

Our reception rooms accommodated up to 200 guests at the traditional Republic Day reception held each January 26 at noon. Since space did not allow us to welcome many from the Indian diaspora, we used the villa's extensive grounds for an 'open house' on 15 August, Independence Day, hosting up to 500 guests, funded with my regular representation grant, since a special national day grant was only available once a year for the Republic Day. Mimi's special effort was to provide a sumptuous buffet, as our regulations did not permit us to offer alcohol on these national days. Commencing January 1993 we held a gratis evening concert, on Republic Day, at the Museum of Modern Art, immediate neighbor to our Chancery; they cheerfully provided their 500-seat auditorium free of charge. Köln Radio helped us to

[22] See Rana, *Inside Diplomacy* (2000), p. 305.

invite a major musician from India, among them Pandit Jasraj and Amjad Ali Khan.

Mimi and I also sought to enliven our major dinner evenings with either a short dance performance by a German artiste, or something else to entertain 50 or 60 guests. This included single malt whisky sampling, run as a small competition, with the help of a Scottish couple that lived in the Köln region. At one Diwali dinner, Priya performed the Rajasthani *ghoomar* dance for our guests. The goal was to offer something different to the jaded Bonn officials and to our business guests and others; some took the trouble to come from neighboring cities, including Darmstadt, Essen and Frankfurt, driving 100 kilometers and more each way. It helped that Mimi, and our domestic assistant Prem Singh excelled at Indian and Western cuisine.

Mimi and the Indian Women's Association organized for two successive years an Indian Bazaar, as a fun public event, with all of us pitching in. She chose to hand over some of the money raised to a German NGO that worked for welfare in developing countries. They were intrigued, as it was their first experience to receive funds raised by a developing country embassy.

Rao-Kohl Summits, 1993-94

Today, leaders of major and emerging powers and other leaders meet several times each year, at regional, global and multilateral summits. Bilateral encounters have also grown. That was not the case two decades back, though the picture was evolving. For example, the opening week of the UN General Assembly in September had not at the time been transformed into an impromptu global summit. Regional and global encounters were also fewer.

At the end of 1992 the German Foreign Office began to plan for Chancellor Kohl's five-nation Asia trip, commencing with India. The initial plan was for Kohl to arrive one evening, and leave around the mid-afternoon of the third day. Towards the end of December, we were told that due to schedule commitments, the German Chancellor would reach Delhi on Thursday night, and leave on Monday afternoon, in effect adding the weekend to his stay. That meant four nights in India, rather longer than customary for busy leaders. It suited us very well; a second round of private discussions between the leaders at the PM's residence on Saturday afternoon was added to the program. We had offered to take the Chancellor to any place outside of Delhi as he wished. They considered Bengalaru, India's 'silicon plateau', but in the end opted for the rock cave paintings at Ajanta. That was based on Gisela Bonn's advice; a long-standing friend of Indira Gandhi and India's great supporter in Germany. She enjoyed favored access to Kohl and joined his delegation.

Kohl's India visit was unusual on several counts, and produced remarkable consequence. The first related to his entourage. We were told that Chancellor Kohl normally travelled with about two dozen 'special guests'—captains of business, parliamentarians, and figures from public life.[23] He preferred to stay in hotels with them, rather than at presidential palaces or guesthouses. (When Kohl reached Delhi, we also found him reluctant to travel in his limousine—for programs that included his special guests, he opted for their bus. That became a first for Indian protocol!) Kohl wanted them to meet the Indian Prime Minister jointly with him. New Delhi explained that there was no precedent for leaders holding discussions with accompanying foreign guests. I was then summoned to the Federal Chancellery by Kohl's chief of staff, Harald Nestroy, who told me that this request came directly from the Chancellor; our assurance that these guests would be invited to the official banquet was not sufficient. I replied that my recommendation might encounter fertile ground in New Delhi, if he could assure that our businessmen would receive reciprocal access to the Chancellor when our Prime Minister next traveled to Bonn. He readily agreed; New Delhi was then persuaded to drop its objections. The other unusual elements emerged later.

---

[23] We were to learn that complex jugglery was involved in drawing up the guest list for each foreign country visited. Besides the customary jockeying for inclusion (and one can easily imagine the 'visibility' and business advantage that such inclusion confers for companies that are negotiating business contracts abroad), some guests joined for a limited portion of the tour (depending on their business interests), while others were included for the duration. Political advisers rather than civil servants managed this entire process, exclusively from within the Federal Chancellery.

The visit was a success. On the main day, 3 February 1993, the two leaders, each accompanied by a dozen officials, first held 30-minute 'delegation-level' talks, across a conference table, making set-piece opening statements. They then withdrew for their *tête-à-tête*, accompanied only by interpreters, for some 60 minutes. (Simultaneously, Foreign Secretary JN Dixit and Foreign Office State Secretary Kastrup held official-level talks, deciding to reinstate this quasi-annual meeting series, which had lapsed.) Finally, the leaders moved to another hall at Hyderabad House, to meet the special German guests, with two official delegations attending. Chancellor Kohl began by telling the assembly that the Indian Prime Minister and he had decided to meet again after 10 to 12 months, when they would review progress on some action points that they had identified. The two leaders then invited the German businessmen and others to put forward their views. Well prepared as usual, the Germans raised problems that German investors encountered, plus trade issues, all connected with India's economic liberalization.

While senior Indian officials representing economic ministries responded to some of the issues, in an unscripted move, PM Rao invited German businessmen to send him a memorandum with all their suggestions on investment and business conditions in India, and promised to respond. That spontaneous gesture went down very well.

Lacking immediate access to the content of discussion between the two leaders, I assumed that the Germans would prepare a list of bilateral points that needed attention, and might hand this over to our PM when the two met at their 'informal' encounter the next day. Accordingly, I wrote out some six or seven points and handed these to Joint Secretary HK Singh; he improved on these and came up with a list of 10 'action points', i.e. issues important for us in Germany. As it turned out, the German side did not produce anything; our list became a kind of joint action agenda. This was a major outcome, and a first for a bilateral visit.

On the German side there were three direct results; Kohl's discussions with Narasimha Rao and other Indian leaders, and his dialogue with Indian businessmen at a working breakfast (besides a visit to the biennial India Engineering Fair where Germany was the partner country), reinforced his strong sense of the opportunity that India presented. First, as the Chancellor's aircraft took off from New Delhi on 5 February, he gathered the business leaders among his guests and asked them why Germany was so notably absent from India. I heard subsequently that he reverted to this theme several weeks later; those that had traveled with him were asked about their follow-up actions. Second, the two major German business associations, DIHT and BDI (plus Hamburg-based East Asia specialists, OAV) were nudged to create a new platform for business promotion, APA, as described above. Third, for the first time in his then 13-year chancellorship, Kohl asked the Foreign Office to prepare a paper on German policy towards Asia. This led to the publication at the end of 1993 of the '*Asia Koncept*' paper, where India was identified as one of Germany's three strategic partners on the continent, a prescient action at the time, much ahead of any other Western state; it took bilateral ties to a new level.

Exactly a year later, on 2-5 February 1994, Prime Minister Narasimha Rao made his return visit, spending four days in Germany, at Bonn and Berlin. That became the capstone to a new relationship, and gave us better connections in the German system. It also brought home to me the paradox that an envoy's real challenge is often in the home country—issues are easier to handle in the country of assignment!

One problem was that on foreign visits, Indian leaders and civil servants were reluctant to be seen with businessmen, and would not include them in official delegations.[24] Anticipating problems in New Delhi over a business delegation, I raised this directly with the PM during a consultation visit in October 1993; he confirmed that a business delegation would accompany him.

The PM chaired a large 'briefing' meeting that time, attended by key senior officials—the PM's Principal Secretary, the Foreign Secretary, and the secretaries heading key economic ministries—plus the Minister of State in the PMO, Bhuvnesh Chaturvedi.[25]

---

[24] It is customary now to have a business delegation present in the foreign capital visited by an Indian Prime Minister, but they never travel on the PM's special aircraft.

[25] Typically, Indian cabinet ministers did not attend such working meetings, leaving the running to their permanent civil service heads.

The PM began by declaring that he wanted to discuss issues relating to Germany some months in advance of his journey, so that advance action could be taken, rather than hold a meeting on the eve of the visit, to find that time was too short, as usually happened, he added. One pending item was the Indian response to the 20-page memorandum on economic liberalization that German businessmen gave immediately after the Kohl visit. He instructed us that a detailed response must go well before he reached Germany.

With each PM, internal meetings take a distinctive flavor. Unlike Indira Gandhi, Narasimha Rao held these often and spoke freely, sometimes giving a rambling discourse. He enjoyed foreign affairs, but an hour-long session sometimes produced no hard decision. As an outsider who been to few such meetings, I saw that the PM's remarks were sometimes rhetorical, greeted with silence by the 12 or 15 in attendance, unless of course a query was addressed to an individual. For instance, he might declare on an issue that the MEA should do something, and add: 'I don't know why this is not being done'. Our seasoned bureaucrats, including the Foreign Secretary, would treat this with quiet equanimity. At that October meeting, he said that Pakistan was going around the world, claiming that the Kashmir issue has become a major flashpoint; 'Is it a flashpoint?' With misguided enthusiasm I responded: 'Of course not!' That won me dirty looks from wiser colleagues; my remark became the starting point for another prime ministerial monologue.

As planning for the visit progressed, the business delegation became a problem. First, the German Foreign Office balked at including it in the Chancellor's program. I visited the Federal Chancellery, to remind Nestroy of his reciprocity promise. He readily acknowledged this and said that they would deliver. An excellent program then emerged: on the morning of the main program day in Bonn, after the customary Chancellery forecourt ceremonial welcome, the two leaders would proceed for their *tête-à-tête* talks, for which 75 minutes were provided; they would then have a working lunch, attended by six from each side, including the principals. Directly after lunch, they would meet Indian and German business leaders at the *NATO Saal*, after their own working lunch at the Chancellor's official residence (improving on the formula in New Delhi a year earlier); the leaders would spend about an hour with them. That became the first time that the Federal Chancellery hosted bilateral business delegations, which explained their initial hesitation.

Ten days before the visit, a senior MEA colleague told me that they had rethought this and did not like the idea of associating the PM with a business delegation. I was instructed to tell the Germans that the businessmen just 'happened to be' in Germany, and were not part of the PM's team. I protested, pointing to the challenges we had faced in arranging the Bonn program; New Delhi's line would undermine our stand. I added that the inclusion of the businessmen had been personally approved by the PM. At that point New Delhi produced an ostrich-like formula: they would say that the businessmen were coincidentally present in Germany, but I could act as wished, at my risk. As it turned out, the business meeting became a high point, with no further complications.

The March 1993 memorandum from German business also created problems, because economic affairs administrators in Delhi were tardy. Despite the PM's clear directive in October 1993 that our reply should go well before he reached Germany, his message to Kohl, enclosing a 25-page memorandum, reached Bonn three days before the PM's arrival, hand-carried by the advance security team. It was well received by Germany as a token of India's serious intent to carry forward liberalization. In a matter of days, the Indo-German Chamber of Commerce made it public, producing favorable editorial comment in India, in terms of responsiveness to foreign investors.

Other challenges came up. First, while the two leaders met for their private talks, how might the leading members of the Indian delegation be kept occupied? On our own, we arranged for five of them to be taken for one-to-one meetings with German counterparts, to be brought back after precisely one hour, to join the lunch. Thus the Minister of State in the PMO went to meet a senior CDU Party dignitary; the Principal Secretary met the Minister of State in the Federal Chancellery (I accompanied him), our Foreign Secretary met his homologue, the Foreign Office State Secretary, and the Finance Secretary was taken to meet the State

Secretary in the Economics Ministry. An embassy official escorted each; it went like clockwork.

Second, the chemistry established between Kohl and Narasimha Rao at earlier encounters flourished, to the point that the two leaders decided to take as read their standard positions on various issues, and went into a substantive discussion on international issues. They welcomed positive developments in bilateral relations; Kohl was especially appreciative of the work of the eminent person group (which had met twice by then). The Non-Proliferation Treaty, that hardy perennial in bilateral dialogue, was passed over. Footnote: when Foreign Secretary K Srinivasan briefed the Indian press on the talks, he told a questioner that the NPT had not been discussed. A little later, at a press briefing given by the German official spokesman, that Indian journalist posed the same query; the spokesman replied that the two leaders had stated their well-known positions. The next day's Indian papers presented this apparent discrepancy as 'an Indian denial'. We decided to ignore this, so as not to embarrass our German friends.

Third, we arranged a series of political meetings. Four German ministers, plus the leaders of three political parties (CSU, FDP and SPD) called on the PM, including the leader of the opposition. From Bonn we had urged that the rising Green Party be included, but the MEA turned this down. I mentioned this to the PM who readily agreed to meet them in Berlin two days later. The Greens leader, one Popov, began by posing five major questions on India's policy towards Pakistan, the US, Kashmir and other weighty issues. The PM gave comprehensive replies, to the point that we overran the 30-minute time slot. When word came that the next visitor, the Minister-President of Brandenburg was waiting for his appointment, the PM asked the Minister of State to keep him company, adding that important questions demanded proper responses. That became India's first high-level conversation with the Greens; they joined the German ruling coalition in 1998 and remained an important entity. It was a lesson in managing political contacts.

Fourth, we had organized individual meetings with several leading German CEOs, underscoring liberalized India's openness to business and foreign investments. Of the seven meetings held, the first was a disaster. I had not anticipated that all senior Indian officials would turn up. Some of them ignored the visitors and engaged in conversation among themselves, debating various points, leaving the German visitors baffled. Working with the PM's Private Secretary Ramu Damodaran, we quickly prepared a short list of Indian dignitaries to join subsequent meetings. As with the Greens, Delhi had turned down my suggestion that the Volkswagen CEO be included, on the ground that they did not have major investment in India.[26] This was true but the company was important, and the PM agreed; Dr. Ferdinand Piech called on the PM in Berlin; it marked a step towards Volkswagen's entry into India.

Fifth, the PM held a working lunch with Germany's India scholars at Berlin. We assembled 12 leading scholars of Sanskrit, history as well as contemporary affairs—Germany then had some 23 full professors in India studies; one of our concerns was that the number was slowly declining (today it is down to about 15). A large oval table facilitated serious conversation; I was the only aide present. Some good ideas came up, including one from the PM that since ancient Indian texts contained scientific knowledge in areas like medicine and mathematics, teams of scholars composed of linguists and domain experts should tackle such texts. Also raised was a hardy perennial: the persisting visa delays faced by foreign scholars coming for study visits. The PM sympathized with the scholars and said that the Home Ministry should be more liberal, and should be prompt in accepting or rejecting visits. I faithfully recorded these prime ministerial directives, and pursued them with the PMO, the Home Ministry and the MEA, but it produced no result at all; even today the problem remains.[27] A similar situation had arisen at a couple of the meetings with German industry leaders; the PM gave clear instructions to the officials present, including his Principal Secretary who chaired the powerful 'Foreign Investment Promotion Board', that a particular pending proposal should be cleared as it was clearly to India's

[26] Volkswagen had been one of the companies approached for India's original small car project in the mid-1970s, when it conveyed disinterest.

[27] The same point has been made in the US. The Indian Home Ministry retains a traditional bias against foreign scholars, to the point that such access to the interior is relatively easier today in China than in India.

advantage. But nothing happened, and the proposal withered away. India's long-persisting weakness has been a lack of will, or implementation capacity; almost any Indian agency can block action, unmindful of national interest.

Seasoned members of the Indian PMO held this visit among the best they had experienced. We were more gratified when a senior German official called it the best organized bilateral visit that he had known. Pakistan's PM Benazir Bhutto travelled to Bonn some months later, and her advance team asked for an identical program; they received the dusty response that each visit was handled on its merits.

Other Bilateral Travel

Other events kept up the bilateral momentum. In July 1994 Foreign Minister Klaus Kinkel traveled to India, the first by a German Foreign Minister in two decades, leaving out Genscher's attendance at the funerals of Indira Gandhi in 1984 and Rajiv Gandhi in 1991.[28] Kinkel took with him a business delegation that was qualitatively better than the one that had gone with Chancellor Kohl. It deepened mutual understanding, though Kinkel's host, External Affairs Minister Dinesh Singh was by then in very poor health, unable to engage in real discussions, despite brave efforts. Kinkel held good talks with Finance Minister Manmohan Singh and with our PM, and also opened the door for Lufthansa's direct Frankfurt-Chennai flights.

Air India strongly opposed Lufthansa going to Chennai, fearing loss of business for its nine weekly Delhi and Mumbai flights into Frankfurt. The notion that giving a major South Indian city direct flights to Europe might benefit the huge number of NRIs living in North America, fell on deaf ears. Just before Kinkel was ushered into the PM's residence, at the usual briefing that Indian envoys provide on the issues that the visitor might

[28] Genscher was known for his low interest in Asia, barring China. He continued this even after his retirement. FICCI pursued for two years a proposal to invite him to India on all all-expense paid visit to give a lecture at a time of his choice. I accompanied a senior Indian business leader to two meetings with Genscher, when we were received with exquisite cordiality, but that produced no result.

raise, I mentioned this to the PM. He responded: 'What is the difficulty?' I remarked that Air India was taking a dog-in-the-manger attitude. Kinkel did indeed raise the issue, and the PM told Minister of State Chaturvedi to look into the matter. Even then, it took six months for the Ministry of Civil Aviation and Air India to agree. Lufthansa later reported that Chennai became their most successful new destination.

For me Kinkel's visit is memorable for a hilarious episode it produced, involving the gift of elephants by Siemens in India to the lovely zoo in Munich; these stories are recounted in an earlier work.[29] In essence, in the course of an earnest discussion on a double taxation avoidance agreement with Finance Minister Manmohan Singh, an ever-serious Kinkel interjected: 'And what about the elephants?' This produced vast puzzlement, until Director Holl clarified that the reference was to two Indian baby elephants that Siemens wanted to gift to a zoo in Munich, for which permission was needed. We promised to do the needful, and that conversation got back on track. My gain for helping with the export of two elephants was nomination as godfather to Gajendra, now an adult approaching middle age; a plaque at the Munich Zoo Elephant House records this. On subsequent visits to Munich I have carried mangoes and *ladoos* for my godson!

Another productive visit was that by the Minister-President of Baden-Württemberg, Erwin Teufel. In the German system, the concentration of power in the hands of such provincial leaders is greater than found with anyone else, not only because the minister-president combines executive and some ceremonial functions, but also as he is personally a member of the upper house of parliament, the *Bundesrat*, and therefore a player in national law-making. This is a high innovation region, where industry combines with high-tech applied research. I accompanied him, and saw the strong impression India produced. It led to cooperation between the Steinbeis Foundation of Stuttgart and CII, aimed at joining researchers with problem-solving capability, with business enterprises as users. It led to a memorandum of understanding between CII and Steinbeis to benefit from the latter's technology transfer experience. But this did not produce the expected result, owing to a lack of an entrepreneur mindset

29 Rana, *Inside Diplomacy*, pp. 249-50.

among our researchers, plus deep reluctance within industry to entrust them with problem-solving. Even good experiences are hard to transplant.

A problem in the Indian system is that there is no one in New Delhi to engage provincial leaders in dialogue; an overburdened External Affairs Minister as the nominal host is not enough. I was not able to convey to the home authorities a need for special treatment in substantive dialogue with Teufel, the more so as he also ranked high in the ruling CDU party. Teufel and his officials were interested in providing special facilities for academic cooperation, to rectify the problem of a small number of Indian students in their state (and in the whole of Germany), in contrast to China, Indonesia, Malaysia and other countries. A good friend, Professor Dietmar Rothermund, head of South Asia Studies at Heidelberg University, had long urged that we should use high-level visits to seek more scholarships for Indian students. A difficulty is that unlike the Chinese and others, Indian leaders are reluctant to make such demands—call this a 'cultural' inhibition.

The Speaker of the *Lok Sabha*, Shivraj Patil, led a parliamentary delegation in June 1995, on a disappointing visit. He resented attempts to brief him on the situation in Germany and bilateral relations, telling me: I have already been briefed by the MEA. He opposed a suggestion that in his talks with the President of the Bundestag, he might explain the human rights situation in India, since German parliamentarians continually raised these in India, during their near-annual visits; he told me: these are nice people, and we should not provoke them with such issues. A top MEA official later told me that Indian dignitaries are usually reluctant to take up hard issues on foreign visits, especially if not connected with their direct responsibilities. This is an instance of lack of 'whole of government' thinking. In my experience, parliamentary diplomacy does not live up to its promise.

The Diplomatic Corps

The majority of Germans are not Catholic; after Unification, their percentage fell to under 40% (with Protestants in the majority). Nevertheless, the country has a *concordat* with the Vatican, giving the latter special status. One consequence is that the Papal Nuncio is automatically the dean of the diplomatic corps, the collective body of ambassadors, with its customary unwritten rules and local conventions. Despite the presence of 140 embassies, this dean has little time to lead the corps, since his main task is to act as the Vatican's link to the German Catholic establishment. The corps is left rudderless.[30]

This was visible in a relatively weak corps, vis-à-vis the host government. Incidents bearing this out are narrated in *Inside Diplomacy*, the most notable of which was a visit to Berlin to greet the Federal President in January 1994, marked by a total shambles in arrangements, probably on account of a hiatus between the protocol establishments of the Presidency and of the Foreign Office; anywhere else, the Corps would have protested loudly.[31] Another feature of a large Corps, say when the number of resident embassies exceeds 100, is that it functions mainly through its regional clusters, not as a unified body. This was much the case in Bonn. I have written of how Asian envoys established an exemplary arrangement that was unique at that time:

> At some places, by happenstance or through individual initiative, regional clusters of envoys become especially proactive.[32] In Germany in the 1990s, an 'Asia-Pacific group' brought together the envoys of countries from Pakistan to Mongolia and Japan, including also the Australasia and the South Pacific envoys; instead of a usual regional dean appointed on the basis of seniority, it selected a 'coordinator'. He helped the rotating host for the monthly lunches, where outside speakers were invited, and organized the group's two to three annual trips to different *Länder* and cities, hosted by the local authorities and by large companies; this became a means for the joint marketing of business opportunities. Other regional groups watched in envy.[33]

---

30 See Rana, 'Representing India in the Diplomatic Corps', *The Diplomatic Corps as an Institution of International Society*, Paul Sharp and Geoffrey Wiseman, eds (Palgrave Macmillan, Basingstoke, 2007), pp. 125-42.

31 The story is narrated in detail in Sharp and Wiseman, *The Diplomatic Corps*, p. 134.

32 Rana, *The 21st Century Ambassador: Plenipotentiary to Chief Executive* (DiploFoundation, Malta, 2004; Oxford University Press, New Delhi, 2005), p. 30.

33 See Sharp and Wiseman, *The Diplomatic Corps*, pp. 125-42.

Through consensus, I was appointed Asia-Pacific group coordinator, succeeding good friend, and a highly effective Tony Siddique, Ambassador of Singapore, when he left Bonn in early 1994. This was a rewarding task; we organized an average of three trips per year, to different *Länder*, including one to Bavaria, Baden-Württemberg, and another to Berlin, and to major companies such as BMW, Daimler-Benz, and Volkswagen. None of the other regional groups, even the Latin Americans, so well organized in most capitals, carried out such joint outreach. Since then, joint regional marketing by diplomatic groups has become customary. In India, ASEAN, Southern African SADC and others visit different states in groups, while the EU carries this to the next level with group tours by political and economic officials of different ranks.

Let me narrate two other experiences with the Bonn diplomatic corps. The British ambassador I met on arrival gave a splendid piece of advice. Germany, he said, was one of the few major countries where an ambassador could track a decision affecting his country, sometimes even influence it, if he found a way to make a timely intervention. I saw this in action in two instances. When the 'Asia Koncept' paper was under preparation, we learnt that the designation of India as a strategic partner was in the balance; our efforts may have contributed to eventual inclusion, with China and Japan. The other example is more direct, when we sought German help for the production of India's main battle tank, 'Arjun'. Diplomatic démarches seldom produce humorous situations, but the finesse with which a high German Foreign Office official received my request for the supply of a key tank component was outstanding. With a straight face, he replied that they were bound by an earlier decision to place India and Pakistan among a 'no armament supply' list, the tank's lower section or hull could be considered 'non-lethal', which meant that engines were feasible. But he warned that anything at the level of the gun turret was out. Some months later, when our Defence Production Department asked for the supply of the gun turret movement mechanism, my somewhat sheepish request evoked from that same official a wry comment that this entered a 'grey area', in terms of that earlier distinction. We persisted with our request and were told informally that this would come up in their national security group, a cabinet sub-committee, where Foreign Minister Kinkel would be obliged to oppose the proposal, but he was agreeable to being outvoted. Events played out as scripted, and we obtained the needed components. The British envoy's advice had shown a path.

Richard Holbrooke, US Ambassador in Bonn, presented a different experience when I paid a courtesy call on him around September 1992. With gratuitous abrasiveness that was sometimes his hallmark, he said: 'Mr. Ambassador, you will find that your country's relations with Germany will become monochromatic.' A photographer since the age of ten, I caught his allusion, but playing the naïve I asked him to explain. Holbrooke declared that Germany would insist that India join the Non-Proliferation Treaty (NPT), and that this would become a major issue in our relations. Our conversation wound down after that sally. I reported to the MEA that Holbrooke was both arrogant and clumsy in disclosing his presumably self-given 'India brief'.[34] In the event the German Foreign Office understood perfectly well the Indian position on the NPT, and in my three years, this subject did not figure once in Foreign Office discussions. Witness also the short shift given to the NPT in the Rao-Kohl discussions of February 1994.

Other Actions

Given Germany's unique political decentralization, it was always profitable to pursue contacts with the provinces and cities. Some were remarkably responsive. An example: the city-province of Bremen, with a population of barely half a million, is the smallest *Länder*. Somewhere in the past, this 'Hanseatic' trading port developed a special connection with the city of Pune; it provides funds amounting to DM1 million to pursue a series of activities with Pune's local authorities, education institutions and non-state agencies. That meant that in Bremen, visiting Indians were assured of a warm welcome. Other states with which special ties

[34] A deeper issue this raises is how US diplomacy takes up third-country issues in its bilateral exchanges, surely part of its notion of global responsibility. Sometimes the EU also acts in similar fashion.

were developed included Baden-Württemberg, Hamburg, Berlin, and of course the province in which Bonn was located, North Rhine Westphalia. It made sense to pursue economic contacts with them—as each handled its own FDI promotion activities—as also because of their weight at the federal level.

With the help of Ambassador AN Ram in Brussels, we developed a method of consultation that matched the EU style. The MEA was persuaded that it made sense for our ambassadors in major EU countries to meet once in six months, in the capital that held the rotating EU presidency, to exchange views on European affairs. We made a start with Bonn in December 1993; the Foreign Office state secretary dealing with EU affairs accepted an invitation to dinner with us, and in his short speech said that India was one of the few non-member countries that attempted such coordination among its EU envoys, and he had taken time off from a crowded schedule to join us to acknowledge this.[35] An unusual feature was that unless a senior MEA official happened to be in Europe, we met by ourselves, and discussed political, economic and other issues, and ways in which we could coordinate our actions, and of course report to the MEA. I heard that this practice ended subsequently.

Four of the then seven SAARC countries were represented in Germany besides us: Bangladesh, Nepal, Pakistan and Sri Lanka. As in some other capitals with such a critical mass, we met over dinner once a quarter, with a rotating host. When I became this group's senior envoy in 1995, we attempted something offbeat, a joint representation on an issue important to South Asia; the German Labor Minister had taken a rigid position on labor standards as a norm for international trade. On learning that the Pakistan ambassador would not attend owing to a 'prior commitment', I requested him to send a senior representative, and he was gracious enough to do so. Nothing came of our meeting with the Minister, who was cordial but unbending, but we did make a small point that SAARC countries could act jointly. This

[35] Unusually among European foreign ministries, the Germans have two state secretaries heading the Foreign Office, one exclusively dealing with European affairs.

local initiative was reported to Delhi, but drew no comment from our mandarins.[36]

Germany's political foundations run by all the major parties are unusual, especially in the activities they undertake abroad. In the German 'corporatized' manner of harmonious work, each has a specialized niche in overseas development activity; for example, the CDU's Adenauer Foundation supports entrepreneurship and economic liberalization, while the SPD's Friedrich Ebert Foundation works with trade unions.[37] Their overseas offices—and India hosts five German foundations—also in effect collect open intelligence on behalf of their parties, and guiding intellectual exchanges via the funding they provide to local thinktanks. This is a form of public diplomacy that flies under the radar in most of the countries that receive these representative offices. In Bonn, we were wary in our relations with these foundations.

A Balance Sheet

This narrative speaks for itself. Without claiming personal accomplishment, let me summarize at the end the useful things that happened in India-Germany relations, to which our team contributed. As always, our actions were in a continuum; we benefited from the work of predecessors, and passed the baton to successors who acted according to their context and vision.

First, extraordinary synergy emerged between a reforming India and a united Germany, enabling us to transform our bilateral relationship. Germany became our lead partner in Europe, the first to 'de-hyphenate' South Asia policy, abandoning an earlier Western mindset that always framed ties with India with an eye to Pakistan. This was serendipity at its best—not the product originally of a plan on our part, but we seized opportunity, facilitating it with calculated actions.

Second, the German economic powerhouse, especially its diversified business entities, large and small, plus its

[36] Our MEA does not care much for Indian initiatives on SAARC, as former secretary-general to this organization, Kant Bhargava has testified in KV Rajan, ed., *The Ambassador's Club* (2012).

[37] The foundations are funded through a formula that ensures equal treatment, within major and minor national party categorization. At home they work on voter education.

decentralized political actors, developed an 'India fever'. In Asia, China remained the priority, but interest in our country rose to new levels. Chancellor Kohl's 1993 visit strengthened his personal backing.

Third, within the inner councils of the EU, Germany began to speak of India, not challenging the UK, since Europeans traditionally defer to London as the fountainhead of wisdom on the subcontinent. Bonn now had its own assessment of where India was going. That helped us on the wide European canvas.

Fourth, in the same manner that the Rao government began to run out of steam in its domestic reform agenda, from about early 1995 onwards, nearing the end of its five-year term (when the Indian political calculus swings towards expediency), we also saw a reduction in German enthusiasm for India, especially among German business. That first golden phase of Indian reforms was ending. The world has much evolved since then, but Germany remains in the lead in Europe in its India actions.

Finally, I learnt useful practical lessons in bilateral diplomacy management, some of which were thought through only after some years. These became the foundation of my post-retirement academic work; I remained engaged with India-German issues for several more years.[38]

I also saw the limits to my action, and realized that not all that one wished could be accomplished. Even good ideas took time to mature; they could not take root if the environment was not conducive. Some of these are covered above, but let me end with a bittersweet story that goes back to the opening of this chapter, the Festival of India, 1991-92. The counterpart to that event was the German Festival in India, which almost did not happen (via a crude move to offer us a tradeoff through increased scholarships); this involved me in some actions. Two years after my service career ended, in an article written in 1997 on *Handelsblatt's* invitation I spoke out about the delay in holding the reciprocal German festival. That might have contributed to the holding of

[38] This took the shape of membership of the Indo-German Consultative Group in my personal capacity (1995-99), two articles that I wrote for the leading financial daily *Handelsblatt*, in 1996 and 1997, and a role in the Indo-German Chamber of Commerce, 1995-2010).

the event in 2000, though a German ambassador in Delhi called me a 'pain in the neck'. On the plus side, the bilateral eminent person group, IGCG, composed of prominent businessmen, supported this event, in a way that had not happened in 1991-92 during our festival in Germany. That was an evolution in diplomacy practices, bringing in non-state supporters.

Endnote: Three years after leaving the Service I learnt that my close working friendship with Dr. N Holl, head of the South Asia *Referat* had inadvertently created difficulty for him; Pakistan's Ambassador, General (Retd) Asif Durrani lodged a complaint at the Foreign Office around 1994 that this official was 'pro-India' and biased against-Pakistan. Such protest is extraordinary, the more so against a principal, working-level contact. Professional diplomats would shudder at painting themselves in a corner; it may have been a personal move by that envoy, former head of the notorious ISI (the military intelligence agency). That challenge to German professionalism received cold comfort from the Foreign Office. Dr. Holl went on to other assignments, ending his career as ambassador to Malaysia. I regret the inadvertent difficulty caused to him.

2

The Wonder Years

Training in India (1960-61), Hong Kong (1961-63), Beijing (1963-65)

In any profession, the salad years mold a career, ingraining first impressions and the early lessons that endure for life. I was lucky to get two bites at that apple, first in Hong Kong (1961-63) as a fulltime Chinese language student, on the periphery of our Commission there, and later in Beijing (1963-65) on a first substantive assignment. (I later went back to Beijing for another two years, 1970-72). But let me begin with the five months of training at the National Academy of Administration at Mussoorie, commencing 16 May 1960, with all the 300-odd young men and women, selected that year for India's top civil services; it was followed by 'district training' and some months of 'quasi-training' at the MEA, New Delhi. That added up to just over a year, to June 1961, when I left for Hong Kong.

In March 1960, as prospective IFS entrants, we attended a 'selection' interview at the Ministry of External Affairs. It was a formality; no one was ever rejected as far as I know, and that ended some years later. An MEA panel, composed of the Foreign Secretary and the two other secretaries, interviewed each one; the questions were innocuous. One question we all faced: how will you manage your children's education? I gave a safe answer: I would follow the example of others; a slightly combative response came from a batchmate who asked: is it obligatory to have children? We then had a joint meeting with Prime Minister Jawaharlal Nehru;

unusually, it lasted 50 minutes. We were arrayed at his shallow, V-shaped desk in our order of merit—I was at the tail end; Natwar Singh, then Under Secretary handling IFS officers, accompanied us. Panditji's first query in Hindi was: *Aap kaun se vishwavidhalaya se hain?* Salman Haider, the batch topper, seemed flummoxed by '*vishwavidhalaya*'; Natwar prompted him: 'university'. Panditji was not too pleased to find that seven of the nine were from Delhi University, and made a comment about a need for diversified representation. It was good that we did not mention that all seven had attended the same college, St. Stephens. His second query: why do you want to join the IFS? Haider responded: Sir, because there is too much political interference in the IAS. The PM was speechless for a moment. As Haider recounted many years later, he waited for Panditji's third eye to open and reduce him to ashes! That moment passed, and the rest of us stuck to banality—to see the world, work in different places, and serve the nation. Panditji then remarked: in the old days people joined the navy to see the world, but now they seemingly join the Foreign Service for this purpose. He went on to pose some harder questions, on what India sought in its foreign relations, the meaning of nonalignment, and East-West conflict. I butted in with a remark (from a book I had read), that the North-South issue was also important; that won for me the day's tough poser: what determines the country's foreign policy? I mumbled: history, culture and ethos; I was not smart or brave enough to mention 'national interest'. Panditji, evidently satisfied that this bunch of raw youth were marginally acceptable, then treated us a to 20-minute discourse on world affairs, and how China as a rising nation was bound to be assertive. None of us thought to take notes. Later, on hearing that Natwar Singh had recorded one, a batchmate asked to see it, to be told: Of course not—it is classified!

Training in India

We reported for duty on 16 May 1960, the first civil service entrants at the full 5-month training course at the National Academy of Administration, Mussoorie, that splendid hill station at a height of 6000 feet, overlooking the high Himalayas. The previous year's batch had moved from Delhi to Mussoorie in the middle of their 'foundation course'. It brought together entrants to a dozen civil services. This method is a huge asset, building friendships among officials across services.[1] These connections often endure, helping civil servants with informal networking; one can almost always locate a batchmate in any ministry or state capital, to find an informal path to deal with a problem issue, or get needed advice. Given that silo mentalities are almost universal among officials, this early joint training serves as a partial counterweight.

A wide range of lectures and training modules were offered, but after many years of academic study, not many took these seriously. We were herded into 'syndicate' groups to write papers, to examine an assigned issue in depth. We of the Foreign Service carried out a study of the India-China border, covering well-trodden ground. For most of us a paycheck was a novel first, inspiring lots of innocent fun and good-humored partying, including experimentation with alcohol. Bridge was another pastime, sometimes sessions held even during lecture hours. It sounds silly now, but a small group of us played bridge during class lectures, at the very back niche of one lecture hall, out of sight from the front.

AN Jha, one of the last giants of the famed Indian Civil Service, headed the Academy.[2] He was a walking repertoire of civil service lore and humor, holding court almost every morning at the lawn adjoining his office—one was free to join that cluster of a dozen and more, to be regaled with insightful real-life accounts, spiced with devastating wit. I recounted some in my first book, *Inside Diplomacy* (2000). His accounts of interviews at the Union Public Services Commission were both hilarious and audacious. He spoke of a candidate who appeared in a natty tweed jacket and spoke with a marked Oxford accent, appearing to show off, though that was unintended; when asked if he was

---

1 The Union Public Service Commission selects entrants to over 24 'All-India' and 'Central' civil services in what is called 'Grade I', the senior executive service. The services are the IFS and the 'Indian Administrative Service' (IAS), our long-time domestic rival, as also the Indian Police Service, and those handling income tax, customs, audits and accounts, and many more.

2 The ICS was the precursor to the IAS, famed for the high quality of its officials, and had provided the backbone to British colonial administration.

prepared to take off his elegant jacket to get down to work in India's rural areas, he responded: I will take off my jacket, but not my trousers—probably implying refusal to bow to political pressures. He received a zero in that interview, putting paid to his civil service hopes. Jha Saheb also spoke of another candidate who offered a devastating rejoinder to a quirky Police Service representative on the UPSC Board, who had berated all that had not opted for that Service; when faced with that query, this candidate replied: I have intellectual interests—the Board insisted that he get 10% extra marks for honesty. Our training included an extended 'Bharat Darshan' tour by special train, and a group meeting with PM Nehru.

Our 1960 batch, was a compatible group of nine; some among us, with several IAS colleagues developed a special bond that has now endured for 55 years. A small IFS cluster, consisting of IP (Munna) Khosla, Vinay (Pondy) Verma, SMS (Mony) Chadha and Kishan (Kish) Rana have been known in the Service for archaic 'Stephanian' humor: puns, limericks, practical jokes, and all the rest, some of which continues even today. It has been enormous fun.

At the end of those five months at the Academy, we were sent off on 'district training' for three months, to gain insight into how India is administered. The probationers were sent to areas far from their home states; as a Gujarati, I was sent to Aligarh in UP. I was fortunate in the District Magistrate there, DK Bhattacharya, a renowned administrator. He gave practical guidance and met me at least once a week; in those days UP was renowned for its excellent administration; like all young 'joint magistrates' (our designation as probation-officers), I undertook inspection tours of villages, checking land records and meeting farmers and their families. While that work did not directly relate to diplomacy, it gave a human face to the challenges of India's socio-economic development. After two months at Aligarh, I spent three weeks in the State capital, Lucknow, not a particularly enlightening or useful experience. Both at Aligarh and Lucknow, a bachelor civil service official drew sharp attention from marriage matchmakers; I managed to avoid a few traps laid by would-be in-laws; I had no plans to get married in a hurry.[3] One persistent individual pursued me through a series of letters after I reached Hong Kong, which frankly terrorized me for a while, alleging that I had made promises to his sister—whom I had never met; I was relieved when this correspondence died away.

On return to Delhi in early 1961, I joined the Ministry of External Affairs, but our batch was left in limbo most of the time, since no agency existed in those days to supervise training, or even draw up a program.[4] We shuttled from one MEA division to another, ostensibly to gain insight into their work. We also undertook a second 'Bharat Darshan' tour by train, and spent two weeks at 'Army attachment', divided into two groups, sent to army battalions deployed on the 'ceasefire line' in Kashmir; we went to the 6th battalion of the 5th Gurkhas in the Tangdhar sector. Army officers felt obliged to treat us civilians to military discipline: early morning physical exercises sessions were followed by long hikes up and down the mountain terrain to the forward posts, and field games in the evening. We relied heavily on 'Sloan's Liniment' to soothe our aching legs.

In March-May 1961, my batchmates left on their foreign postings, to study assigned languages at different embassies. Last to leave, I had to wait for the start of the academic year at the Hong Kong language school in August 1961, spending the interregnum working as an 'attaché', first in the China Division (for a mere two weeks), and then in the Europe Division, for two months. I remember well the bewilderment, even fright, with which I confronted the first few office files; one gradually learnt to

---

[3] Many Indian parents are anxious to get their sons and daughters married before they are exposed to the wicked world abroad, but my father and mother were fairly cool about that, as my father had spent over four years in the UK before marriage, first for BA at Edinburgh University, and then at Lincoln's Inn where he was pursuing a law degree when he joined the service of the Maharana of Porbander in 1933. In my batch, only one tied the nuptial knot before proceeding on a first posting.

[4] The Foreign Service Training Institute was established in 1985 (with the word 'Training' dropped from its title some ten years later); prior to that the Administration Division gave but limited attention to training of new entrants, though from about the mid-1960s, the Indian Council of World Affairs was entrusted with organizing lectures for probationers.

annotate simple observations: 'Deputy Secretary may kindly see', and 'For information'. In the process, one grasped the ropes of secretariat work. The best experiences came from three spells as a protocol officer, with a Hungarian prime minister, and with two other visiting ministers—these imprinted an enduring lesson that mastery over detail was vital in protocol and diplomacy. That also led to friendships with the young ADCs to the President; they were a fun lot, all six at the rank of Army captains or equivalent from the Navy and Air Force. I would sometimes drop in to the ADC Room at Rashtrapati Bhavan to meet them, and be treated to chocolate milkshakes and ice-cream, their staple food. One of the stories they recounted featured a Navy ADC (who eventually retired as a vice-admiral). He was walking along one of the long corridors with Pandit Nehru, escorting him to his car. Panditji pointed to a bust of GB Pant on a side table and asked: whose is it? Replied the ADC: Pantji, sir. Came back Nehru: That is obvious; who made it? Our friend had no response.

In July 1961 I boarded a slow cargo ship at Kolkata, *SS Sangola*, with accommodation for 12 passengers, for an 18-day voyage to Hong Kong, via Chittagong, Rangoon, Penang, and Singapore. In those days, the 'approved route for travel' for officials was by ship; travel by air was possible only on special sanction.[5]

Language Study

In the IFS, 'probationers' (an inelegant term for Service entrants) must learn a 'compulsory foreign language' as a precondition to confirmation in the Service. This is alotted on the basis of a list of needed languages prepared by the MEA's Administration,

---

[5] Though this jumps ahead in the story, in 1968-69 while at Geneva, I played a small role in getting the government to authorize air travel for all officials posted abroad. One member of our non-diplomatic staff was posted from Geneva to Rabat. He took over two months in travel time, besides his customary six weeks of home leave (in Kerala, I recall): he went by train from Geneva to Genoa, to catch a Lloyd Trestino ship to Bombay, via the Cape of Good Hope (the Suez canal was closed); he then went home by train from Bombay, for a total of 30+ days in transit, each way. On the return leg, he had to wait in Bombay for some days as the ship was delayed; on reaching Genoa, he took a train to Marseilles and then a ferry to Morocco.

mediated by the probationer's rank in his batch.[6] My rank in the batch limited choice to Chinese, Japanese and Russian. More glamorous French and German, with which went first postings to Paris, Brussels, Bonn or Vienna, went to those higher up the list. So I bit the bullet and asked for Chinese.

Two factors influenced that plunge. One was a childhood fascination with China described earlier. The other was Prof. VP Dutt (1931-2008); he had delivered a brilliant set of lectures on East Asian history at Mussoorie. He breathed life into a subject I had disliked; it fed my China urge. Prof. Dutt was then a young academic, fresh from his years in Beijing. He laughed when I asked him if it was really impossible to learn the language; he replied that both he and his wife were fluent in Chinese—it took hard effort, it was worth it. Thus, with tempered bravado, I became the first in the IFS to seek Chinese as a first foreign language preference; I never regretted that choice. It took me to a small school at Hong Kong University, patronized then by the diplomatic services of UK, Germany, Canada, Australia and some others, to learn Chinese (Mandarin, very distinct from Cantonese, spoken in HK).[7] In the wake of escalating India-China political discord, which made it difficult to continue with language training at Peking University, legendary *Beida*, New Delhi had chosen Hong Kong.

Each year one or two IFS probationers joined that two-year course. At any given time we had two to four at this School; after 1962, Indian Army officers joined, two in that year, and four more in 1963. Unlike us, they had learnt some Chinese at a language school at New Delhi, which meant that their knowledge of ideograms (written text) was sound, but they found it difficult

---

6 Over the years, MEA's language allotment policy has oscillated between focus on 'major' languages (as with our batch), to focus on neighboring countries, which meant in practice that some were saddled with languages such as Bhasa (Indonesian and Malay), Burmese, Tibetan, and Vietnames, spoken sometimes in a single country, with no practical prospect of specialization.

7 One of the paradoxes of China is a language, which in its written form is identical across the land, while the spoken dialect varies enormously, to the point of mutual incomprehension. Despite over six decades of teaching a unified national dialect (basically the Northern spoken form), even in 2014 I saw that taxi drivers prefer to speak Cantonese in Guangzhou.

to cope with the four tones, and the nuances of spoken Chinese. They added *joie de vivre* to our life.

Other IFS language trainees at HK, also bachelors, were Arun Das (1934-1994) of the 1958 batch who had spent a few months at Peking University before moving to Hong Kong, and CV (Rangi) Ranganathan of the 1959 batch; both were in their second year. I shared an apartment with Das, when Rangi moved out to spend a year as a paying guest with a Chinese professor.[8] Our apartment was at 1A Kotewal Road, barely a kilometer from the Language School, except that the School was about 300 feet below us on that steep hillside; the climb back was arduous, the more so if one was lugging a 10 kg tape recorder for the language lessons—the Walkman was not even a gleam in the inventor's eye! Das left in mid-1962 and his successor, my new flat-mate, was Bhupat Oza of the 1961 batch. We lived in relative luxury, with a cook-majordomo, Lao Phan, a Shanghainese, and two maids who did the laundry and cleaning. The only problem with that arrangement was that after paying staff and food bills, we were broke most of the time. In those days, the allowances paid to IFS officials were miserably low.

Many memories of those days crowd my mind. Some incidents stand out. Bhupat and I bought a car in partnership, and that produced several adventures. Impoverished as we were, neither could remotely afford a new car, so we looked around for affordable wheels. We first considered a large limousine, Armstrong-Siddeley Sapphire, a British car of the early 1950s that was obsolete even in 1962, going cheap mainly because it was expensive to run. We then considered a two-door coupé, a 1956 Nash Rambler convertible of which many were locally afloat at that time; its single sofa-style seat could accommodate three at a pinch, but that too was rejected as unviable. We finally chose a 1954 Volkswagen, and bought it for HK$3400 (for which we both took loans from our friendly Indian bank!). At the exchange rate of the time, that came to around US$700.

---

8 That arrangement worked well for Rangi's language studies, but he found himself rather underfed much of the time, making up with street food and cheap restaurants, which were plentiful.

Our credentials as car drivers were suspect. Bhupat could drive but had no license, while I had an Indian license but could not cope with Hong Kong traffic and its hill roads. So both took driving lessons. Alas, no one had schooled us in the nuances of car ownership. We were convinced that our Volkswagen Beetle needed neither water nor oil, so each time we went to a petrol station, we would disdainfully ignore the query from the pump attendant if the level of oil was to be checked. One fine evening, when Bhupat was at the home of an Army colleague, the car would not start. Our ever-resourceful Army friends then proceeded to check the engine, looking to the carburetor, the fuel line and the rest, eventually asking finally if the oil level was sufficient. They found that the sump was bone-dry, apart from a layer of sludge at the very tip of the oil-stick—a device we had never seen! After much laughter at our naivety, the car was oiled and started. We drove it to the Volkswagen garage the next day; the German manager was aghast at our neglect and warned that we might need a new engine! As it turned out, German engineering triumphed, and the car forgave our ineptitude. When I left Hong Kong for Beijing in August 1963, I bought out Bhupat's share in at the original price; later, in 1964, on buying a Triumph Spitfire, I sold the Beetle in Beijing at a profit of 40% over the original price. For many years thereafter Bhupat continued to ask for 'his share' of that profit!

Some of the friendships of those years have endured. John Boyd of the British diplomatic service and fellow-student, followed me to Beijing in early 1965, but I did not meet him subsequently until 1999, when as Master of Churchill College at Cambridge, he invited me to spend a week with him; we picked up the threads of that association as if we had parted just a month earlier. John and his wife Julia are among our close friends. Steve Fitzgerald of the Australian service was another; he was soon to quit diplomacy for academia and joined the Labor Party, and went on in the late 1970s to become Australia's first ambassador to China, while he was in his 30s. Steve and his wife Gay have remained friends with us. Patricia was a classmate, and we met again after I retired from the IFS; she had gone on to marry an Indian academic, become a distinguished professor of sociology and a China expert, and is now a colleague at the Institute of

Chinese Studies at Delhi, where we are both honorary fellows. Not all one's early connections endure, alas. My classmate for two years, good friend and competitor in language study, was an outstanding Canadian, Daniel Molgat. Daniel and I made a good team; he was the steady student, while I pushed for new avenues. Daniel owned an open-top Morris Minor, and had the quaint habit of trying to read the *People's Daily* while driving! One day, with a serious mien, he told me that his wife was annoyed with me; he went on to explain that they had been trying to have a second child and she attributed their lack of success to the hard slog he had to put in to keep up with me! I have not met him since 1965, and while we exchanged a few emails in the late 1990s, after our service careers, that old tie was lost.

A particular regret is that I did not keep up contact with the teachers at the language school, especially its outstanding Director, Prof. Ma Meng. (Similarly, connections with my school, Rajkumar College, Rajkot, and its outstanding Principal, Peter Rogerson, also withered away. After 1995 I have made several visits to the school, but that does not make up for the lost years). I enjoyed learning Chinese. Each class had just two to four students, so in effect we received intensive coaching. Once one crossed an initial threshold, the ideogram, with its arcane logic was fascinating (composed of a root 'radical', and 'phonetic' elements), as was the fact that each 'word' in common usage is composed of two ideograms, permitting an almost infinite variety of combinations, and thus a highly nuanced language. At the time of leaving School, my working vocabulary was around 7000 characters, sufficient for a university graduate.

Life in Hong Kong

For my first four months in 1961, De Mello Kamath (1907-82) was Commissioner at Hong Kong, a very proper and reserved official of the old school.[9] He was uneasy in dealings with the Indian

[9] India had opted for this unusual designation for its Hong Kong representative, rather than call him consul general or trade commissioner. Technically this gave him 'diplomatic' and not consular rank, though in practice it made no difference at all.

community, then numbering about 10,000, consisting mainly of businessmen; unwilling to cope with social competition among the leading families, he simply avoided all invitations to the home of local Indians, giving him an undeserved image of aloofness. His successor was PS Kotdasangani (1920-80), erstwhile ruler of a tiny Gujarat princely state; he had joined the IFS in 1948 under the ad hoc entry that also brought in several other former princes. Affectionately known as 'Raja Saheb', and as 'Prad' to close friends, he brought zest into the Commission, with his generous entertainment, and effervescent enthusiasm, besides active interest in the young officials under his charge. He plunged into local Indian social life without inhibition, telling us frequently that while he did not excel at elegant dispatches, he knew how to deal with people, and could take on any complication that the local community might throw at him. I learnt from him the enduring lesson that handling the Indian community is a proactive art, involving leading from the front. All that our diaspora sought was recognition from official Indian representatives, and when treated with respect, responded in more than equal measure. Much later, serving on PM Indira Gandhi's staff, during the course of a visit to Paris in November 1981, I had occasion to see the hard side of dealing with the diaspora. Indian leaders occasionally use well-connected diaspora members for personal gain and local outreach, sometimes producing headache for Indian envoys.

As language trainees, we spent virtually all our time at learning Chinese; this also involved pursuing contacts with the few North Chinese friends we could locate in Cantonese-speaking Hong Kong, to practice our blossoming language conversation skills. One of the most remarkable was Stephen Chou, a journalist friend, a person with an extraordinarily large heart, who became a kind of mentor to us. I remember once telling one of our teachers that we used him as a conversation ally; she replied: yes, Steve's accent is alright, though he was born in Tienjing (now Tianjin), and his family moved to Beijing only when he was eight years old. Consider this: Tianjin is barely 170 km from Beijing, but to a language purist, an accent originating there is just not the equal of the norm, the Beijing dialect!

Once in a while, the Commission assigned odd jobs to language trainees. One that fell to my lot in mid-1962 was to escort the visiting MEA Foreign Secretary, MJ Desai, who spent a couple of days in Hong Kong. He remarked to the Commissioner that the growth of the colony's textile industry seemed extraordinary; we should examine the factors behind its success.[10] That task, collecting data and writing a report, fell to me. I went around four textile mills, met managers and put to them some simple queries on their growth and business policy; despite a master's degree in economics (specializing in industrial economics), that was my first field study.[11] My report from that simple, even naïve, survey ran barely to four pages; one point that emerged was that these factories changed their production equipment every two and three years, to keep up with technology. When the Commerce Ministry in Delhi acknowledged my report, their only short comment was that Hong Kong's practice of buying new equipment every few years was strange, because in Indian textile mills the machinery lasted for several decades. In 1962, it was too early for us in India to understand the sins of technology obsolescence!

The looming border confrontation between China and India did not impact on our lives, though we occasionally took up for class study Chinese newspaper editorials on that theme, but the outbreak of hostilities in September 1962 produced shock. A few of our teachers showed reserve towards Indian students. Naturally, we were affected emotionally by the losses that India suffered, but at the language school, we remained isolated from the political and publicity process that engaged most Indian missions, though we tried to tell our side of the story to classmates and the teachers.

Hong Kong was a crucial observation post for events in China, in that it was the only land route open to the 'mainland'; there were no direct air links to any Chinese city from Asia, other than the flights from Mongolia, North Korea and North Vietnam. Many refugees, fleeing poverty and hardship in the aftermath

---

[10] Few may remember, but Hong Kong's economic success began in the 1960s with its textile industry, before it moved up the growth chain with other industrial products that led its export drive.

[11] In the 1950s, those in masters programs even at good Indian universities simply did not do any field work.

of China's Great Leap that had commenced in 1958, leading to economic crisis and starvation, crowded into the colony; the British rulers handed back to the Chinese authorities those caught, and there was virtually no outcry over their human rights. A few small groups of specialists, Chinese and foreign, attempted to piece together what was happening in China; their findings were published in periodic, under-funded newsletters. They painted a dire picture, but most of us lacked a frame of reference, and simply could not comprehend the scale of the calamity. The Chinese language print media of Hong Kong, polarized in their political hostilities, including allegiance or hostility to Beijing and Taiwan, spun out conflicting narratives that seemed to make no sense.

A key diplomat at the Indian Commission was First Secretary Vasant Paranjpe, an outstanding Chinese language specialist who had spent several years at Beida and joined the Indian Embassy thereafter. He had acted as interpreter with Jawaharlal Nehru and other leaders on their China visits, and knew China exceptionally well. He became a good friend and joined us at many evening parties, but he was reticent, and shared few of his China insights. It is a great pity that he neither recorded his personal experiences, nor produced any analytical work, perhaps because he became embittered over how relations with China turned out. Our paths were to cross ten years later, in less cordial fashion.

The Commissioner's Residence

It was in Hong Kong that I saw first hand the obtuseness of government decision-making. Officials based at the Ministry of External Affairs sometimes take financial decisions, including prolonged delay that amounts to refusal, without bearing any responsibility for their actions. In the bureaucracy, virtually the world over, the sins of omission are seldom punished. Around mid-1962, Commissioner Kotdasangani sent a proposal that the government should purchase the excellent rented residence where he was housed—a villa overlooking the Happy Valley Racecourse with a wonderful view of the harbor, located on a spur of land that measured about half an acre, huge by HK standards; the house included spacious reception areas and five bedrooms. The owner was willing to sell for half a million Hong Kong Dollars, which in those days worked out to barely ₹400,000. The government turned down the proposal, in part because the MEA had no established policy on purchase of property for Indian missions.[12] The Commissioner then persuaded one of the banks to lend the money, and resubmitted the proposal to the MEA, pointing out that the installment payments to the bank exceeded only marginally the monthly rent paid at the time. The government negated that as well. The Commissioner told us that he was seriously tempted to defy the government and go ahead with the bank loan, but he had run afoul of the MEA at his previous appointment as Consul General in Saigon, and feared that 'those SOBs will sack me if I act on my own!'

That story had an inevitable *dénouement*. In 1970, the then Commissioner sent a proposal to Delhi for the purchase of that same property, still our residence. The price had gone up to HK$5 million, and with the Rupee devalued, that worked out to ₹6,000,000 (i.e. 15 times the 1962 price). The government turned that down as well. Eventually, in the 1980s the government bought an apartment for the Commissioner at a cost of some HK$30 million. That old villa, by this time had risen in value to over HK$100 million; today, that property would be worth many multiples of that figure.

In many cities there are similar instances of opportunities missed for the acquisition of property, both official residences and embassy chancelleries.[13] This is partly balanced by a smaller number of instances, e.g. at Mauritius, Nairobi, and Tokyo, where determined heads of missions pushed through purchase deals despite obstacles, that worked to India's advantage.[14] It was only

[12] The why of that is shrouded in mystery, given that India had acquired some outstanding properties in the early years of Independence in major world capitals and at some other places. A simple reason perhaps was that no one at MEA had applied themselves to this issue.

[13] See *Inside Diplomacy* (2000), Chapter 15, pp. 351-61.

[14] In Mauritius, where the government owns a superb property, a South of France style villa on some three acres of land, the sum of money approved by MEA fell short of the final asking price by a small amount; the Indian High Commissioner despaired of getting MEA to approve an upward revision in the amount already sanctioned. Some of the leading Mauritius families of Indian origin came forward and made up that shortfall.

in 1980 that the government decided on a sustained program of property purchase. In its implementation, this ran afoul of another decision, which held that as a matter of principle, Indian architects should be engaged. While fine on paper, that decision had baleful consequences; embassy construction projects were delayed by many years, often because Indian and local architects wrestled over the regulations and building standards that varied in different capitals, compounded by geographic distance. For instance, the construction of the office-residence complex for the Permanent Mission at New York was delayed by a decade, during which time the building regulations changed, and we had to eliminate ten floors from the plans originally approved by the local authorities. In Oman, a legal dispute between the Indian and local architect blocked the chancery project by over 15 years. No one has ever been held accountable for such delay and cost.

Move to Beijing (1963-65)

In May 1963, as my language studies were ending, Foreign Secretary MJ Desai passed through HK, on his way back form Tokyo, spending an hour in the VIP lounge. The Chargé d'Affaires in Beijing, PK Banerjee had made a special journey to meet him, and when the Foreign Secretary asked if he faced any special problems, the head of mission in China replied that he did not have a single officer who knew Chinese.[15] The Foreign Secretary waved at us, the two MEA language trainees, declaring that one of us could go to Beijing for a short assignment while the Ministry located someone for a full term. In October 1962, I had already passed the New Delhi language exam, and had no excuse to prolong studies. I headed for Beijing in July 1963.[16]

I quickly learnt a basic government doctrine: nothing is more permanent than a temporary arrangement. I went directly from

[15] It seems extraordinary that since May 1961, right up to August 1963—that is all the way to the lead up to and immediately after the 1962 Border War, the Embassy did not have any Chinese-speaking Indian official. It also seems that the Embassy did not make an insistent demand to MEA.

[16] At that time this was a record and I scored the highest marks in that easy exam set by the Language School in New Delhi; that was of course overtaken by subsequent IFS language trainees.

Hong Kong to Beijing, without home leave (though that was my right), on the premise that my assignment was 'temporary', described as 'six to eight months'. Of course, at the end of that period I was told that I should stay on for the full two-year term (the norm at a 'hardship' assignment); in the event I stayed just over two years.

I traveled to Beijing by train from Hong Kong, which was then a two-day journey. Crossing into China was dramatic—passengers descended from the HK train and walked across a wood-and-steel bridge over a small river, while porters trundled one's baggage in large pushcarts; that village was Shenzhen, today renowned the world over as the heart of China's first Special Economic Zone, a thriving city of over 7 million. After an hour's wait, during which a simple lunch was served (included in the travel coupon), one boarded the train to Canton (Guangzhou), with its blaring loudspeakers broadcasting revolutionary songs; a hidden switch could give one relative peace, if one knew its location.

First Secretary AK Damodaran (1927-2012) was my traveling companion, coming to China from Moscow. Damu, as we all called him, belonged to the 1954 batch in the service, older than his cohort as a veteran of the Independence movement.[17] He was a gentle person, always supportive of young colleagues. I went as a third secretary, as the Administration Division had not notified my confirmation in service, nor found a vacant second secretary's post for me. In effect I was a successor to PTB Menon, who left a few months after I got there. A year later, Bhupat Oza arrived as the second language officer.

PK Banerjee led our embassy till the end of 1963. Holding the rank of minister, he had served in Beijing since June 1961, through the lead up to and during the 1962 War. Though holding a crucial charge, he was seemingly not much trusted by New Delhi, even treated with disdain. In a 17 September 2012 article in *Business Standard* I wrote:

> The treatment given to PK Banerjee by MEA is also perplexing. In June 1961, he was shifted from Tokyo to Beijing, without even a

[17] I much regret that we did not get around to recording AK Damodaran's rich experiences in MEA's Oral History Project, in which I have played a role since 2008.

few days in Delhi to meet the key decision-makers, even though he was specially selected to take over, in effect, from Ambassador G Parthasarathi, who left a month later (in fact immediately after RK Nehru's visit to Beijing in mid-July 1961). Even after tension grew over the next 18 months, he was not asked to travel to Delhi for consultations, before the outbreak of the October 1962 War; his first and only visit as CdA came in January 1963. He certainly felt, as his book shows indirectly, that he did not enjoy Delhi's trust; in his comments to us at the Embassy, some of his bitterness came through, even though he kept a stiff upper lip, and was a man of charm and wit.[18]

PK Banerjee was succeeded by Jagat S Mehta (1922-2014), like him in the rank of counselor, but with vast experience of China affairs, first as deputy secretary in the China Division, and later as the leader of the Indian delegation in the border talks that were held in 1960-61, the only concrete outcome of Zhou Enlai's April 1960 visit to New Delhi, which led to the publication in 1961 of 'Report of the Officials of the Governments of India and the People's Republic of China on the Boundary Question'; it consists of two parallel reports, Indian and Chinese narratives, with no shared conclusions.

My most vivid memory of the time with PK Banerjee is his farewell call on Premier Zhou Enlai, in mid-December 1963. I wrote about this in 1998, henceforth called '1998 essay':

> PK Banerjee was given the special favor of a personal farewell call, and took with him five of his embassy colleagues. Premier Zhou was suave and smiling, essentially repeating the message loudly proclaimed by China to Asia and to the world, that China sought a negotiated border settlement, that it was prepared to wait till India was ready for this, and that in the interim the two countries which had so much in common should improve relations in other areas. At that meeting we had a taste of Zhou's renowned alertness and charm. At one point he said something humorous, and noticing that I had smiled before the interpretation was completed, he

---

[18] See: PK Banerjee, *My Peking Memoirs: The Chinese Invasion of India*, Clarion, Delhi, 1990.

immediately remarked that I spoke Chinese. After inquiry as to where I had learnt it, he complimented me on my accent![19]

First Secretary Damodaran also wrote about that meeting and noted that the Chinese Premier expressed the hope to the outgoing Indian head of mission that 'he hoped that the present uncomfortable period would be over soon'.[20] Referring to the heavy exchange of protest notes between the two countries that was underway at the time, Zhou said that as the Premier, 'he had to scrutinize every single bit of correspondence between the two countries. "Can't we end this war of words", he said. It was a very important signal.' New Delhi ignored this, the same way it had ignored the secret message that Zhou had given to Banerjee in January 1963, which the latter had personally transmitted to PM Nehru when he visited New Delhi for the first time after taking over his Beijing assignment in June 1961.[21]

Beijing Life

For a young diplomat, work in Beijing was exciting, despite and probably even because of restrictions. One was engaged in a struggle to unravel 'a riddle, inside a mystery, wrapped by enigma'—to use Churchill's description of Russia. A common saying among diplomats was that you wrote your 'definitive' China book within the first six weeks of arrival; if you stayed for longer, the list of questions grew continually, while answers became elusive and perplexing.

At that time, the Chinese capital hosted barely 35 diplomatic missions. After France recognized the PRC in January 1964, some others followed suit and numbers surged to the 50s. We were in essence a tiny, incestuous community, in which group solidarity prevailed, and ranks did not matter; it was not unusual for first or even second secretaries to invite ambassadors, the more so if there was a shared interest such as bridge or photography.

---

[19] See: Rana, 'A Young Indian Diplomat in China in the 1960s and 1970s', *Looking Across the Himalayan Gap*, ed. Tan Chung, 1998.

[20] Damodaran, 'Diary of an old China hand', *Indian Horizons*, Vol. 43, No. 1-2, 1994, p. 166.

[21] See Rana, 'A message for Mr. Nehru's ears only', *Business Standard*, 20 October 2012.

I was a happy bachelor, sharing a comfortable, Western-style two-bedroom house within the Old City, with another bachelor officer—it had originally housed our Counsellor, a post left vacant after our post-1962 scaling down in diplomatic representation. It was close to the city's East Gate, in a *hutung* just off Zhangan Dajie. These *hutungs* were narrow twisting lanes in the Old City. After post-1979 massive reconstruction, rather few survive, which many, including Chinese citizens, view as a major loss. The traditional houses in the *hutungs* were built around central courtyards. Many were crowded, with several families sharing a large house. They were host to some iconic restaurants, including *San Jwor* ('three tables'), a reputed gathering place for intellectuals, like Les Deux Maggot in Paris. Like others of its ilk, it ceased to exist after the 1966-70 Cultural Revolution.

We had a Chinese staff of four; majordomo Lao Chang who had worked in our Embassy for nearly ten years, plus a cook and two maids; on the cook's off-day, Lao Chang produced for us Gujarati *kichri* and *kadhi*, dishes he had mastered when working with a colleague! Some months after arrival, I sold off the 1954 Beetle that Bhupat Oza and I had jointly bought; I ordered a Triumph Spitfire from the UK, and it arrived via Tienjing, white in color, with red interiors—it had a detachable hard top and a vinyl cockpit cover, but no soft top. Thanks to the young ladies of the Western embassies, I never lacked travel companions, to the frequent picnics and other outings that were our usual Sunday excursions; the travel restrictions simply meant that one partied harder at the places that were accessible, with the Ming Tombs and the Summer Palace being our standard favorites. Hyperactive social life was the norm, with parties featuring Scottish dancing, loud music, and other amusements that we found for ourselves.

Driving was a hazard in daytime, and perilous at night, owing to the sea of bicycles that surged in the main streets, but there were few automobiles, besides the ubiquitous buses. China had no vehicle insurance system, though Western embassies obtained cover through companies at home. If one was involved in an accident involving serious injury to a Chinese citizen, the norm was to invoke diplomatic immunity and leave the country, leaving it to one's embassy to negotiate a financial settlement. But that did not deter an occasional car race in late hours on the empty avenues. One could park just about anywhere. Many times I left cameras and lenses in the open Spitfire, parked on the principal shopping street Wangfujing, secure in the confidence that no one would touch the vehicle, even while it drew throngs of admirers. One night, after a dinner at the *hutung* home of a Western colleague, I drove home rather inebriated, revving the engine almost to the red zone, but sticking to first gear, thus avoiding mishap.

As foreigners we simply knew much too little about what went on inside the country. So we concentrated on the bits that were accessible, via the six daily newspapers that embassies could officially obtain, a handful of journals, plus the odd copy of a provincial paper that foreigners were not supposed to receive, but might pick up at an intermediate halt during a flight to Hong Kong on courier duty, or during a tour. We were restricted to a radius of 20 km from the center of Beijing, with three exceptions, the permitted section of the Great Wall, about 55 km from the city, the Ming Tombs that lay along that road, and the airport, which was about 30 km away. We could apply for travel to about six cities that were 'open', and were obliged to use the single official travel agency and its interpreter-guides. We could not visit any Chinese at their homes; contact with foreigners was dangerous for them. Food was in short supply; these were the years of recovery from the 1958 Great Leap and the ensuing famine. A strict coupon system operated for Chinese, which they had to hand over even at restaurants. Foreigners were exempt from this coupon system, but at restaurants it was almost obligatory to sit in special rooms, not in the main dining areas.

A major information source was fellow-diplomats, especially those that gained glimpses of real events during visits by their home dignitaries, plus other delegations, businessmen and others. Life in the diplomatic corps was one of intense information-sharing among embassies, and a few Western correspondents, representing Reuters, AFP, and the *Toronto Globe and Mail;* the East European journalists and others from communist states did not mix with us. The most colorful journalist was Jacques Marcuse, a Belgian, who represented AFP, who had lived in Shanghai and Chongqing in the 1930s, and had met many leaders of the Communist Party. He had a wicked sense of humor, with a collection of stories of his encounters with Chinese bureaucracy; his *bête noire* was an official in the Foreign Ministry's information department with whom he crossed swords many times, who figures prominently in the book that Marcuse wrote, *Peking Papers*.[22] Marcuse made up his own 'sayings' of Confucius; he boasted that no one ever challenged him, when he introduced these in conversation. At the airport bar, he maintained his own bottle of *Mao Tai*, the fiery grain-based liquor; his friends were welcome to call for it whenever stuck at the airport owing to delayed flights, which happened rather often; the bottle never seemed to run empty. *Mao Tai* then cost barely the equivalent of a few dollars; today it is a premium brand, a bottle selling at over $200; that liquor's crude Beijing cousin was *bai ga'ar*, which we sampled sometimes at the rudimentary Chinese bars.

In the information collection game, Indians were close to Western and fellow developing-country embassies; not many among the latter engaged in serious observation of the Chinese scene. We also enjoyed good friendships with the East Europeans, but information sharing with them was usually restrained, except in those cases where over time one was able to build some trust. Among the diplomats, I recall well Arjun Bahadur Singh of Nepal, Elmo Senaviratnam of Sri Lanka, Klaus Kapel of Denmark, Roland Van Der Berg of the Netherlands, and Igor Rogachev of the Soviet Union.

Soviet diplomats were savvy and many were fluent at Chinese, but they shared little by way of hard information, even with our Embassy, though Damu had good contacts with them; he spoke Russian and had come to Beijing from Moscow. The smaller Communist states were proxies in the escalating Sino-Soviet ideological debate; they projected a unified Soviet line, and were isolated from Western embassies. Enver Hoxja's Albania

---

[22] A Marcuse story: at one of the frequent official banquets he found himself once again with this information official. The conversation turned to Chinese traditions, and stories of dragons. The official said that Marcuse did not understand modern China where no one believed in such myths. Replied Marcuse: that is a disappointment because he wanted to call his book 'The Dragon's Feathers'. The official laughed and said that no one would believe him, since dragons did not have feathers!

enjoyed privileged status, receiving massive Chinese material support, in exchange for its complete identification with Beijing; they did not mix with anyone. North Korea and North Vietnam of that time were fence-sitters. The behavior of the diplomatic missions, in that rarefied atmosphere, became a side drama. Yugoslavia, much involved in the Sino-Soviet debate but for us a fellow-nonaligned state, was for us among our coolest friends, on account of the uniformly high professionalism of their diplomats.

It was in those days, especially guided by the astute professionalism of Jagat Mehta that the Indian Embassy built a reputation as one of the best informed in the Chinese capital, mainly because we worked hard, processing the bits and pieces of data we gained, to build a composite picture. We traded information, of course. But like everyone else, we were almost always groping in dim light, and often missed the real story, including the start of the Cultural Revolution in 1965, which produced turmoil on an epic scale.

I found myself working as a translator of odds and ends, keeping track of what appeared in the media (though we had a couple of Chinese translators who prepared summaries of articles of interest); I also took on economic reportage, since no one handled that area. We had no commercial exchanges to speak of, and I concentrated on writing in-depth dispatches on different themes. Jagat Mehta, an inspiring leader, gave ample latitude to his colleagues; I produced a study on the steel industry, culled from different journals, leavened with the data collected through observation during diplomatic tours. Another dispatch, on China's 'part-work, part-study' schools won approbation and was forwarded to the Education Commission in New Delhi.[23] Bhupat produced a fine study of demography trends.

A word on communication links: despite the importance of the Embassy in Beijing, we had no radio link to the MEA, unlike our Chinese counterpart in New Delhi.[24] Our cypher messages

---

[23] These schools resembled Germany's 'dual schools', perhaps at a lower level of technology, and produced semi-skilled workers. Such apprenticeship-oriented education has remained a weak point in India.

[24] The MEA was negligent in developing a radio communication network for its major embassies. Such links existed only at a few places such as Afghanistan, Bhutan, and Nepal.

were sent, after encryption, through the post office; they reached New Delhi after a typical delay of 24 to 48 hours. We received a daily news transmission from the MEA via a teleprinter, but principally depended on radio sets for the news; Indian radio broadcasts could rarely be heard in China, so BBC and the Voice of America were our daily staples.

The Chinese Foreign Ministry organized one major diplomatic tour each year. In 1964 the Commerce Ministry organized a tour to South China for commercial secretaries; the military attachés went on their own trips hosted by the Defense Ministry. I went on three tours. A description:

> The traditional pattern was that the Foreign Ministry invited the Head of Mission and spouse as guests, together with one accompanying diplomat. That gave junior officers a chance to visit far away places, not on the list of 'open' cities. Sometimes the tour covered places completely inaccessible, save under special arrangements, such as the lengthy car journey that took one group to the 'national model' agricultural village of Dazhai. This was also an opportunity to practice and utilize language skills, to ferret out some local information, which hopefully added to one's fund of knowledge, or gave a new insight, even while this was resented by the Protocol Department 'handlers' who were usually watchful to see that their charges did not stray too far. The group traveled mainly by special train, accompanied by a Foreign Ministry Vice Minister, the Chief of Protocol, and a bevy of officials. The hospitality was lavish, and the provinces vied with one another in offering to the foreign guests the best local cuisine. If Lawrence Durrell had been around, he would have found a treasure trove of amusing anecdotes and ego jousts within the diplomatic corps, given the fact that a week's shared journey brought out some of the rivalries and petty jealousies, already accentuated in the hot-house atmosphere of a restricted diplomatic post. During the car trips, the Foreign Ministry took scrupulous care to ensure that the assignment of vehicles was in the correct protocol order, with the Dean of the Corps in the lead, seated naturally in Car No. 1.[25]

[25] This led me once to wonder as to the number assigned to the Vice Minister's car, since he seemed always to be ahead, besides, of course, the escort and security convoy. His car bore No. 0, a perfect compromise!

Young diplomats established two informal 'clubs' in 1964. The first was a lunch group of diplomats from Western and developing country embassies, limited to second and third secretaries, starting with the six that met in my home for the first time, and slowly growing to our set limit of 12. One ironclad rule was that anyone promoted to first secretary rank received a ceremonial farewell, and was asked not to return. That became a hub for information exchange and produced some lasting friendships.[26] Jagat Mehta christened us a 'tails of missions lunch club'.

The second was a more informal group of Chinese speakers from Western embassies and I; besides six diplomats, it included language teachers and members of staff working in embassies and one or two others, all Chinese. David Wilson, then second secretary in the British mission (and later became Governor of Hong Kong), was the guiding sprit, and we met informally in restaurants that were remarkably inexpensive, and at opera theaters and cinemas, practicing our language skills, and sampling Beijing's offerings of cuisine, stage performances and films. Apart from Peking Opera, other opera forms and folk drama could be seen; one took the form of rapid-fire dialogue between two characters, in humorous couplets. Presented in run-down theaters, the tickets cost pennies. Our group took the name 'Yanjing Club', after an old name of the capital. Acutely conscious of the sensitivity in operating what was the only foreigner-Chinese group, we steered clear of political discourse, and curbed inquisitiveness vis-à-vis our Chinese friends. We realized that they had to report to some 'minder' on our activities. It was a wonder that we could meet; it marked a slightly relaxed political grip in China, during that quiet interregnum between the end of the 1958 Leap Forward phase, and before the storm of the 1965 Cultural Revolution. On return to Beijing in 1970, I learnt that none of those old Chinese friends were active; one among them, a teacher and sometime actor, was killed during the political tumult of the Cultural Revolution.

[26] That method of establishing professional groups has since become a custom in major capitals, where diplomats of different ranks working on political, economic, cultural, media and other areas come together on a periodic basis to exchange information. In Beijing, a number of such groups exist now, in a sense all of them successors to our group.

India-China Relations

In terms of people exchanges, India's bilateral relationship with China was virtually non-existent. We received no visitors from home, not even businessmen. A few Indians living in HK traveled to the two 'Canton Fairs' held annually, but we had no contact with them. Our consulate in Shanghai was closed; the one in Lhasa had closed down in the late 1950s. The Foreign Ministry or other official agencies did not treat us with hostility; dealings were correct, lacking in cordiality. My 1998 essay noted:

> The Indian Embassy received some petty slights, but for the main part the relationship was correct and the attitude of senior officials was constructive. When Asian or other diplomatic groups were received jointly, we were handled with perceptible coolness, but never in discourtesy. The Middle Kingdom has long practiced a finely turned method of subtle differentiation, and these habits were a great deal deeper than the patina of Communism. Seen with detachment, the Chinese manner of handling foreigners was a delight to watch, rooted as it has always been in profound self-confidence and a holistic vision of content and form.

In 1964, I traveled to Shanghai on my own, principally on a consular task, to meet an Indian trader who had unwisely opted to stay on in China, hoping to sell off his large stocks of bay leaves, as I recall. After the 1962 India-China border war he was jailed on a charge of rape—he had been living with a common-law Chinese wife. Embassy officials went to meet him in jail every few months with Indian magazines and a bottle or two of Indian condiments. He wept on seeing me, leaving me moved. The Chinese jail seemed grim, even frightening. That experience stayed with me for long, a reminder of the very human face of individuals caught in such issues, and the value of consular actions. I heard later that on completing his sentence he was repatriated to HK.

That train journey to Shanghai produced one of those bizarre coincidences that sometimes come up. I wrote in my 1998 essay:

> I vividly recall a journey made from Beijing to Shanghai by train sometime in 1964. In the "soft" class four-berth sleeper I had only one travelling companion—a professor of some sort (as I made out

from his conversation with his wife and teenage daughter who had come to see him off at the railway station). After the train started we began a conversation and I was delighted to have a distinguished academic as a companion. We had dinner together in the dining car, quite a fine meal. The professor gradually disclosed that he had in fact visited India and knew Gandhiji's secretary Mahadeo Desai, whom he had met in Poona. Respecting the circumstances and the context, I steered clear of political or sensitive issues, but got along very well with him. The next morning when I woke up I found that sometime during the night we had acquired a third travel-mate, a rather loud person who turned out to be an army officer. He engaged in a noisy conversation with the professor on international affairs, speaking of unspecified 'reactionary countries' and how China would deal with them. I ignored him, and some time later, when we were alone in the train corridor, the professor said in a soft voice that some people had not liked the idea of his conversation with an Indian diplomat. And it was better if we did not have lunch together on the train before it reached Shanghai. I replied that I understood, and hoped I had not inadvertently created difficulty for him. He laughed and said that it was a small matter. There is a footnote to that chance encounter. When I narrated the incident later to one of our senior China scholars, he said that the professor had been his teacher, and that he was also one of the distinguished India experts in the Chinese Academy of Sciences (later the Chinese Academy of Social Sciences). The professor had been too discreet to speak much about himself. It was inconceivable at that time that open and friendly contacts could be sustained between the Embassy and such personalities.

The weekly courier service to HK, at which we all took turns, including the head of mission, was a key lifeline, as much to get essentials and a few luxuries, as to get away from a rather dreary environment; each of us made two or three trips per year. Our neighboring missions, at Pyongyang and Ulan Bator were worse off then us, in terms of living conditions, and we also exchanged courier trips with them; I put off going to these places and in the end never traveled to either North Korea or Mongolia.

At that time, there was no real India-China dialogue. After the 1962 Border War it was simply too early for India. Mehta's memoir covers many of the political issues that he handled as our head of mission in China from 1964 to 1966.[27] But one omission in that account bears mention. In 1963, just months after the Border War, China believed that relations with India could rapidly be put back on track; witness Premier Zhou's 'confidential' message to Nehru, sent through Banerjee in January 1963 (see below). The realization of the extent of trauma caused by that war came very slowly to Beijing. In 1964, therefore, it was not surprising that China saw in Mehta's appointment a signal that an empowered envoy was being sent, to start the process of renewal, or at least commence substantive talks. I accompanied him to several rounds of talks at the Foreign Ministry, starting some weeks after his arrival. His interlocutor was Zhang Wenjin, long-serving Director of the Asia Division, who later served as China's ambassador to Washington DC, and as an assistant minister. Occasionally, Vice Foreign Minister Han Nienlong received Mehta. To the best of my knowledge, the Indian envoy did not get to meet Foreign Minister Chen Yi (who had shown himself to be rather hostile to PK Banerjee), much less meet Premier Zhou for substantive talks.

During those early contacts, Zhang probed Mehta on the ideas he had brought from Delhi, and how India thought the relationship might be set on an improvement path. There were no new initiatives—for the simple reason that New Delhi was not ready. Mehta responded to this with generalities; he could hardly expose that in those fading months of Jawaharlal Nehru's life (he passed away in May 1964), India simply had no new approaches to offer. Finally, during the third of those conversations, Zhang lost patience and asked plainly: 'Should I understand that you have brought no new suggestions from Delhi?' Mehta responded in gentle but indirect terms, affirming this, without saying so directly. Mehta does not allude to this incident in *The Tryst Betrayed* (2010). As note-taker, I prepared the draft record of discussion, but never saw the finalized version sent to Delhi. In the tight discipline of those days, such holding back of official papers from junior diplomats was common.

Jawaharlal Nehru died on 27 May 1964. I was away to Hong Kong that week, on courier duty, and missed the touching tribute

[27] See: Jagat S Mehta, *The Tryst Betrayed* (2010).

that Jagat and Rama Mehta organized to Panditji at the Residence; the condolence book was kept open for two days. Right up to the end of the second day no Chinese visited the Embassy, but towards the end of that day a message came that an important person would come to the Embassy, as Damodaran has written.[28] Premier Zhou came, accompanied by several officials, and stayed back for 10 minutes for conversation with Mehta; Zhou spoke of 'his long and eventful cooperation with Jawaharlal Nehru. There was not the slightest hint of acrimony'.

The real contribution of Jagat Mehta was that he prevented a downslide in relations, and observed events in China in a professional manner. But no substantive political dialogue took place. Premier Zhou's personal efforts to restart a dialogue ended with the departure of PK Banerjee, who between 1961 and 1963 had nine meetings with Premier Zhou, all but one of them of substantial nature.[29] After 1965, all the way up to 1970, China was in the throes of its hugely disruptive Cultural Revolution.

In August 1964 I had a remarkable, but unsubstantive, encounter with Chairman Mao. At the time, Congo was in the throes of a crisis, and China came out strongly in favor of President Mobutu. Foreign envoys were invited to a rally that was to be held at the Tiananmen Square in support of 'the struggle of the Congolese people'. Since India had not taken a stand on this issue, I was nominated to represent the Embassy. Anticipating that we would be at the tiered stand directly below the main rostrum-gate, I took with me my camera and telephoto lens. Much to my surprise, diplomats were guided to the main rostrum, for my first and only time. There, barely twenty odd meters from us was arrayed the entire Chinese leadership, including Mao, Liu, Zhou and the rest of the politburo. At the end of the rally, also very unusually, Mao walked down the ranked diplomats and in my turn, I shook hands with him; he did not speak with anyone.

[28] Damodaran, 'Diary of an old China hand', *Indian Horizons*, Vol. 43, No. 1-2, 1994, p. 167.

[29] Please see my three articles in *Business Standard*: 'Battle Lines of the 1962 War', 17 September 2012; 'A message for Mr. Nehru's ears only', 20 October 2012; 'The 1962 war—Where did India go wrong?', 31 October 2012.

Alas, my expensive 35mm camera had suffered a mishap and the rangefinder did not work, so that all the telephoto pictures were out of focus.

The enigma of China-watching, and Embassy life, is reflected in a couple of episodes. In an article in *Business Standard* dated 17 September 2012, I wrote:

> Around February 1964, rummaging through an old desk, I chanced upon a folder containing six or seven letters written in Chinese. None bore a receipt date or initials of any official. All but one, on scraps of paper, spoke of the terrible famine in China; they urged India to bring their plight to the attention of the world.
>
> One letter was different. Written in a particularly clear hand on a long, unused brown envelope that had been cut open to make a writing paper, the writer claimed to be a colonel commanding a PLA (People's Liberation Army) regiment in Tibet. He said that India was moving forward in the border areas into Chinese territory. If it did not stop these activities, the Chinese armed forces were ready to deliver a heavy blow to India to teach it a lesson. India should heed this warning. The letter ran to about 12 lines. It was seared in my memory. I prepared a full translation of that letter in a single copy, plus a summary translation of the others, and took this to JSM after showing it to First Secretary AK Damodaran, a sympathetic mentor. JSM, taken aback that such an important, even if enigmatic, communication had received no notice in the Embassy, asked that the papers be left with him. I never asked him at the time what happened thereafter. As JSM writes, we did receive the odd letter tossed over the tall solid steel gates of the old embassy complex, located on Legation Street.

Mehta wrote about this incident in his book, *The Tryst Betrayed* (2010):

> On the file, I found a letter written some months before 1962, with a specific warning that the Chinese were planning an attack on the Indian frontier. I felt this was explosive and so I removed it from the file and took it with me when I went home on consultation in 1964 and showed it to Foreign Secretary Gundevia. He recognized that it could be dynamite in its implications, as it should have been

transmitted to Delhi. Without much ado, he promptly tore it to shreds![30]

Was the 'colonel's letter' a deliberate, quasi-official warning, or was it a lone actor action by some well-meaning individual? The former seems more probable, but one simply does not know.

An Evolving Scene

Observing the scene in China was our fulltime occupation, stymied by the opacity of the system and scarcity of hard information, as narrated earlier. One useful source was the visitors that other countries received, and their conversations with the Chinese authorities. We tapped into them via our social exchanges, when they attended events organized by their embassies, and through the second-hand information conveyed by fellow diplomats. The weekly courier trip also gave access to those coming into the capital, since HK was the only viable air travel route. The flight, on an IL-14, cousin to the venerable Dakota aircraft, or its elder brother, the IL-16, involved three refueling halts on way to Guangzhou (then Canton), at Wuhan, Nanjing and Changsha; bad weather at any of these places meant an obligatory night halt. So fellow travelers had the opportunity to bond.

An example of the Beijing media: around mid-1964, rumors swirled in the diplomatic corps about an issue of the monthly journal *China Youth*, in which the back cover, a painting showing a farm harvest scene was alleged to contain a hidden message; a series of tiny red flags visible in the distance seemed to be flying in a direction contrary to the wind that played on the fields of wheat that awaited harvest. The hidden message was one of opposition to the Party. Such expression of hidden opposition through pictures and writing was an old tradition. True enough, a few days later all copies of the journal were removed from bookstalls, and embassies were requested to return the issue delivered to them. We complied, after photographing the back cover, in those pre-photocopier days.

---

[30] Jagat S Mehta, *The Tryst Betrayed* (2010), p. 138.

In 1964, increasing streams of Western businessmen had begun to visit China. The economy was on an upswing, as a result of easing of domestic controls, and Europe had discovered China. The Canton Trade Fair, held twice a year, was China's main commercial show-window, even while traditional commodities dominated Chinese exports. I visited one of these in 1964. Western countries began to organize their own trade shows in Beijing, displaying new machinery and technology; the billion-strong market tempted businessmen. China used these events in calculated fashion, to learn new processes and to access needed technology; it was yet to recover from the abrupt Soviet economic walkout in 1960. As one British businessman explained: a machine on display would attract well-informed Chinese engineers, who on successive days would come and ask about different aspects of the machine's construction and operation; those that came on following days evidently had access to the information given previously; on the final day of a typical four or five day exhibition, the questioners would seemingly seek to fill up missing gaps. Businessmen were torn between admiration for the thoroughness of this process, and anguish that their desire to sell also gave away crucial proprietary information. As a developing country representative I understood China's need for gaining access to industrial knowhow, the more so in its effort to break out of the isolation that came from past over-reliance on the Soviet Union in the 1950s, and their subsequent breakup. Even today, China continues to practice ruthless technology harvesting, in dealings with foreign companies.

At the beginning of 1965 we observed a great deal of cultural debate, what seemed to be a new kind of ferment, reflected first in the *Guangming Daily*, the leading publication in this domain, and subsequently in the *People's Daily* as well. My 1998 essay notes:

> ...an intense debate was emerging on cultural issues around early 1965. For instance, little could anyone imagine that the controversy, which suddenly erupted in mid-1965 over a sensitive film, *Early Spring* (which some friends and I managed to see in the few weeks it was screened, before it was banned), would herald the storm of the Cultural Revolution. No one could then decipher the complex and indirect signals. But even for those who were ignorant of the

master plan saw that an artificial controversy was being generated. Cultural objects like that film were being offered deliberately as scapegoats. The ulterior purpose was invisible till the time I ended my first tenure in China in September 1965.

> ...We had a couple of good friends who enjoyed dropping in on Sunday mornings, for coffee and conversation. One of them was a young colleague from an Asian country, which enjoyed significantly better relations with China than we did, and he was a useful source of information. One morning, probably in early 1965, this friend came and narrated his experience of a visit by their education minister, who ended his substantive program with a meeting with Chairman Mao, customary for foreign visitors of that level in those days. Mao asked the visitor about his travels and his impressions. The visitor responded with fulsome praise of the things he had seen, the institutions visited and the education system in general. To this Mao gave a curious reply, saying that the visitor should not believe everything he had been told, and that things were not as good as apparent outwardly. This was said in the presence of the Chinese Education Minster, and we could not figure out what the Chairman had meant. It seemed to go beyond the typical expressions of Chinese politeness, when after the foreign guest who offers fulsome praise is told, in phrases that are part of ancient syntax, that the praise is not merited. We could not believe that Mao was profoundly dissatisfied with the shape of the education system. Or that the entire polity needed a sharp cleansing action, to usher in a 'permanent revolution' as subsequently claimed during the Cultural Revolution. As in the case of the artificial—or rather guided—debate on culture, which unfolded at around the same time, we simply did not see the master design of the Great Helmsman.

That information seemed to tie in with critical remarks Mao had made to some other Western visitors of the time, especially the French. It seemed to suggest a return to a hard line, but none of us could imagine where it might lead.

1963 was the period of the great Sino-Soviet ideological polemic, which I did not follow in detail. While that fascinated many diplomats, some of us saw that dispute over Communist party orthodoxy, with its arcane idiom, as no more than a cover for what was a clash of national interests between the two 'socialist' giants; some of us held that China was first an inheritor to its ancient Middle Kingdom tradition, overlaid with a Communist or 'socialist' patina. Yet, many in the diplomatic community spent much time in attempting to decipher the complex language of that ideological debate.

Chiang Qing, Mao's wife who was to dominate political events during the frenzy and excesses of the Cultural Revolution, was still in the shadows even until September 1965, when I left Beijing, though her actions had begun to take shape. Liu Shioqi was China's President, very visible together with his elegantly attired wife. Mao, as Party Secretary General, lived in the shadows, visible only as a distant figure on the Tiananmen rostrum. Premier Zhou was the diplomatic face, attending many national day receptions, and hosting a cavalcade of foreign dignitaries, almost all treated to lavish banquets at the Great Hall of the People, the vast complex that makes up the western side of Tiananmen Square.

I left for Delhi in August 1965, to take up work at the MEA, traveling from Hong Kong to Mumbai on a fine Italian liner, MS Victoria. That ten-day cruise at government cost was most enjoyable. At a farewell dinner that he hosted for me in July 1965, Jagat Mehta recited a poem that he claimed had been found on my desk. Of course, authored by this remarkably energetic head of mission, identified even then by many foreign colleagues as a future foreign secretary, it serves as a fine endnote.

Much will I, in the Foreign Service, travel around

And many small and big capitals in duty pace,

Many Jaguars, Lincolns and Mercedes process and grace

(which now the tables of missions in the end the confound).

But when in Peking hero-worshiping children my buggy contemplate,

And hood down, onrushing winds the "hair-dos" mangle,

Then know I that never will such diplomatic success before me dangle

As when zoomed the single white Spitfire in front of the Heavenly Gate.

Can I forget how, when the diplomatic chariots all
In Great Tien An Men stood parked in marshaled line,
The choruses in ardour sang and minorities danced in thrall,
The unity of the world's workers and their triumphs to re-define,
Then the throttle spluttered and stopped short the surging blue multitude
And in silence from the Great Portrait their gaze on me and my Spitfire glued?
John Keats Rana[31]

[31] I have the original, duly signed by all Embassy colleagues.

3

Days of Comradeship, A Swiss Idyll

Ministry of External Affairs (1965-67), Geneva (1967-70)

Return to the MEA meant working as a desk officer and learning how headquarters functioned. This is a sound professional practice; all my batchmates were back by then. Midway through the two years in Delhi, on 23 November 1966, I married Shivraj Kumari (Mimi) of Rohet, daughter of Thakur Saheb Vikram Singhji (1921-72), of the Jodhpur Rathore clan. The marriage has been the most fortunate event of my life. Mimi is the sister of an old St. Stephen's College friend, late Manvendra Singh (1939-2014).[1] How this came about, starting one Sunday afternoon at the main bar of the Delhi Gymkhana Club, became a situation of hilarious miscommunication; I met Mimi that evening at a tea party, in the customary format of those days where young men and women were given a first introduction. That, and my subsequent pursuit of Mimi, to say nothing of the devious role played by our respective best friends, in 'engineering' that marriage, is worthy of a Bollywood melodrama script. Despite

[1] Manvendra was an exceptional individual, a person of charm and wit, enormously popular, who was responsible for converting the 300-year old family *garh* (fortified home), into a heritage hotel in the late 1980s, now the nucleus of a small set of exquisite hotels, part of the successful foreign and domestic tourism drive of Rajasthan. Manvendra also lived a life of genuine local and social service, playing a key role in the development of Mayo College, Ajmer, and the Choupasani School, Jodhpur.

temptation, let me put that aside, and say that I am beholden to my family and these friends, especially my parents, for putting up with my obstreperousness preceding that event.

Desk Officer in the Ministry (1965-67)

Work in the Ministry of External Affairs (MEA) in the mid-1960s was carried out amidst great comradeship, especially when 1960 batchmates congregated. We had all completed two foreign assignments; return to the home base completed the typical cycle. I was to follow that cycle twice again in my career, returning to the MEA in the 1970s and 1980s, each time after two foreign postings. We ended up in different MEA 'divisions', territorial and functional, working under joint secretaries or directors who headed these.

I was assigned as an under secretary (as the MEA desk officers are called) in the 'China Division', working under Director KR Narayanan (1920-2005).[2] The Division also had a deputy secretary, nominally my supervisor, through whom I routed some but not all files and drafts. He was ineffective, quiet and lacking political experience; he had been promoted to the IFS from our 'Information Service', which had been wound up in the early 1960s.[3] The other under secretary in the Division was batchmate BP Aggarwal, who dealt with Japan, the two Koreas and Mongolia. Major issues were reported directly to the Director. It was a heady experience, the more so when within weeks of reaching Delhi, the September 1965 India-Pakistan war broke out.

I enjoyed an easy, friendly relationship with KR Narayanan; he would sometimes give me drafts of papers on which he was

---

[2] KR Narayanan was a remarkable man, entirely self-made, who had participated in the Independence movement and had also worked as a journalist. He was a product of the London School of Economics, who after retirement went on to become the Vice Chancellor of the Jawaharlal Nehru University, New Delhi, and then joined politics, winning the election as a Congress candidate from Kerala, becoming a minister of state, and then Vice President (1995-99) and President of India (1999-2004). See: https://en.wikipedia.org/wiki/K._R._Narayanan

[3] This Indian Information Service, like the Historical Unit, were experiments of the 1950s that had not delivered the expected specialization, and these officials were absorbed into the MEA regular staff.

working, asking me to offer suggestions; I did this with a light pencil, and he was tolerant when I pressed my ideas in discussion. He also often gave me the drafts prepared by our deputy secretary, to improve the text. He was soft-spoken and hospitable, with a wry sense of humor. Within what was a rigid hierarchical system, he practiced collegiality. Typically, junior officials in those days were low down on the pole, with no access to the secretary rank seniors that headed the Ministry, bereft of opportunity to travel abroad—only senior officials traveled on the few delegations that went abroad.

Viewed from the China Division, the 1965 war was memorable for a strange 'ultimatum' that Beijing delivered, within two days of the outbreak of what turned out to be a 22-day clash, limited entirely to India's Western region; East Pakistan was not involved. A Chinese diplomatic note delivered on 16 September 1965 alleged that some Indians had abducted a small herd of yaks and sheep from Tibet across the border in the Sikkim region, and that if they were not returned within 72 hours, India would bear unspecified 'serious consequences'. That ultimatum was later extended by 48 hours, and fizzled out thereafter. KR Narayanan summoned the Chinese Chargé d'Affaires to the MEA after midnight, to coincide with that extended deadline; the meeting took place at 0200 hours in the morning. Owing to the war, for the first time at the MEA we had armed guards manning building entrances, and I remember alerting them at 0130 hours that Chinese diplomats were about to arrive and should be permitted entry, under escort. (In those days our division was located at the very end of South Block, adjoining Rashtrapati Bhawan, and we entered via Gate No.6, which also led to the PM's office. I shared an office room with five other under secretaries, located directly above the office room the PM used. Today that entire section of South Block is part of a tightly guarded PM's Office.) It was quite the most unusual of diplomatic meetings at the MEA; it degenerated into an exchange of accusations and counter-thrusts, and ended at 0340 hours, when both sides were worn out after that futile non-dialogue.

The deeper significance of that 'ultimatum' was that China had attempted to pressurize India, in the midst of India-Pakistan hostilities, through a rather absurd charade, without undertaking any action that might have opened a second military front against

India. Many in India, including Prime Minister Lal Bahadur Shastri, had apprehended that China would actually move military forces against us on the Tibet frontier. We now realize that at the time China was convulsed by the start of the Cultural Revolution; no one in Beijing had time to deal with foreign affairs.

China's Cultural Revolution, presented a bewildering kaleidoscope of events, which diplomats stationed in Beijing attempted to unravel, often at personal risk. This involved crisscrossing the city, to read wall posters, avoiding the increasingly aggressive Red Guards. Towards the end of 1966, foreign diplomatic missions and their personnel became targets, when Mao's distorted vision of a 'permanent revolution', degenerated into a power struggle at the very apex of that country's leadership. At the MEA we received a cascade of reports from an ever-active Indian Embassy, but for the great part we simply had no capacity to digest that material, much less evaluate what was a highly confusing situation. This was the time when second secretaries K Raghunath and Vijay were arrested and expelled from China, and the Indian Embassy in Beijing was surrounded by demonstrators and pelted with stones. That led to demonstrations in New Delhi against the Chinese Embassy.

Bilaterally, India and China were engaged in a paper war, exchanging protest notes and counter-accusations, alleging incursions across the disputed border by armed force personnel, and by aircraft. That flurry of diplomatic notes is captured in several volumes of the India-China White Papers. My task, as desk officer, was to draft notes based on information received from our defence and intelligence agencies, and to respond to Chinese protest notes and counter-charges. Much of that was reflected in our reports to Parliament, by way of replies to parliament questions, and other documents and statements that were presented there. It added up to much activity, mostly futile. The two countries could not engage in any substantive discussion in that atmosphere.

Relations with the Chinese Embassy were formal, lacking in cordiality, yet there was no overt hostility. I recall enjoying conversations with Second Secretary Li Danan, who often accompanied the Chinese Chargé d'Affaires as interpreter. Besides his excellent English, he was fluent at Hindi, having studied at Varanasi University in the early 1950s. When I once mentioned to him that this was surely an asset in Delhi, he wryly responded in chaste Hindi: 'Alas, no. The only people who speak pure Hindi here are the people at All India Radio!'[4]

Though I did not deal with Japan, a couple of events relating to Japan stand out. One evening in 1966, all the officials of the Division were invited to a formal dinner in honor of Foreign Secretary CS Jha, hosted by the Japanese Ambassador. He used the event to real effect. With a serious mien, he told the Foreign Secretary that every time he met Director Narayanan, he had to tell a lie to Gaimusho; his Tokyo colleagues would not understand why he visited so frequently the Director (China), when his country had no diplomatic relations with that country. His point went home; a few weeks later the division was renamed to a geographically more correct 'East Asia Division'. That was smart diplomacy.

In 1966, New Delhi hosted a meeting of a non-official India-Japan economic group, which brought together businessmen and planning experts from the two countries; this 'Track Two' group, was India's first experience with an eminent person caucus, set up in the late 1950s, following Nehru's visit to Japan. Its purpose was to share economic experience, improve mutual understanding and nudge the two countries towards closer economic cooperation. I was brought in to help with logistics and attended the meeting. An eminent business leader led the Japanese side, while Planning Commission officials headed the Indian side. The discussion was dominated by a Japanese concern over the possible nationalization of business enterprises in India; the Indian side was simply unable to provide assurance that nationalization might not be carried out in the future. Underlying that discussion, with its circumlocution and polite words, was a profound Japanese disinterest in India. This drove home disconnect prevalent between the two countries at that time. Subsequently that forum was wound up; there now exists a bilateral eminent person group. In the late 1990s Japan carried out an intensive study of South Asia, entrusted to several

---

[4] The context of course was that across North India the spoken idiom is Hindustani, a blend of Hindi and Urdu.

academic agencies, as a prelude to much deeper and expanding engagement with India today.

One relic of past connections with the UK was that the British High Commission sent to us from time to time reprints of outstanding dispatches from their embassy in Beijing. Printed on light blue paper, running to four pages, these were models of precision and professional craftsmanship, and to be honest, rather better than the material produced by Indian embassies. That practice subsequently withered away.

Life in Delhi

With the exception of IP ('Munna') Khosla, my batchmates in Delhi were bachelors, and we devoted a great deal of time to planning our evening parties; the organization effort was not commensurate with the outcomes, but it generated much discussion and activity. At the same time, we were wily enough to avoid elaborate maneuvers by older friends and MEA colleagues at matchmaking; IFS youngsters did attract a fair bit of attention. Given our college friendships, we enjoyed a degree of camaraderie that was perhaps exceptional. We played practical jokes on one another, and even today, in retirement, have retained some of those old friendships. We had joined the Delhi Gymkhana Club by then, and its bar became a favored watering hole, especially for 'liquid lunches' on Saturdays. In those days, when a five-day week was a distant dream, the practice of treating Saturdays as half-days had been replaced with a single Saturday as a holiday (the second one each month); consequently, we asserted a moral right to visit the Club bar on Saturday afternoons. The other great passion was bridge, with occasional all-night sessions.

I lived with my parents at their Jor Bagh flat for a year, and on the eve of marriage, moved to a house in A-Block of Defence Colony; the monthly rent of ₹390 was just about covered by my house rent allowance. After a delay of several months, my Triumph Spitfire reached Delhi, shipped from Beijing, and it became a special joy to zip around a traffic-free capital in an open sports car. After marriage, Mimi took to the wheel with verve, often with her black pet cocker spaniel Donna on the passenger seat, head out, ears flapping in the wind.

One afternoon around April 1965 Antony Menezes (1912-92), then Joint Secretary (Administration) walked into my shared office room—such personal visits by seniors were rare—and with a broad smile told me: 'We are sending you to Geneva for your honeymoon!' In those days of innocence I had not even suspected that I was up for a posting, much less made any effort to pitch for a choice European location. It was a fine gift.

Geneva (1967-70): The Environment

The mission at Geneva was officially a consulate general, headed by N Krishnan, a greatly admired official of the 1952 batch, who had served with distinction as member-secretary to the Pillai Committee that had examined the working of the MEA and had presented its report in late 1966. That meant that the Embassy in Berne, always headed by a senior IFS officer, usually in the rank of 'Secretary to Government' (Grade I ambassador), supervised the consulate general. By that time, most missions in Geneva functioned as 'permanent missions' attached to the UN Office, and to the several UN agencies headquartered in that city. Soon after reaching Geneva, I urged that we project that as our real role. The situation was complicated by the fact that the Ambassador at Berne was also named as the Indian representative to the UN Disarmament Conference, which typically met at Geneva on Tuesdays and Thursdays; this meant that Ambassador VC Trivedi, and after his reassignment, Ambassador Azim Hussain, were camped in Geneva for three days in the week. N Krishnan, while in full agreement on our real role, was too modest to push for his own elevation as 'permanent representative', which also implied a rank of ambassador. Over the next three years, we gradually redefined our work arena, focusing on permanent mission tasks, using official stationery with that designation. By the time I left Geneva, we were accepted in that role, though formal re-designation happened just a little later.

We were happy in Geneva. Mimi and I found a fine home in the village of Conches, just at the city limit and barely four km from our office, an old villa with substantive grounds, owned by a delightfully eccentric lady, who was an authority on medieval music. This 200-year-old villa was divided into three apartments, and we occupied the ground floor; at one edge of the property stood a small wooden chalet, housing a Vietnamese-Swiss couple. With Swiss precision, we received a map of the property, marking out the boundaries into which the garden was divided for the four tenants. Since this villa was close to a leading business school, it attracted tenants that came for its one-year management course; we thus encountered six different sets of fellow-tenants and over the subsequent 40 years, have retained friendships with three of them.

Both children were born in Geneva, at the *Hopital Cantonal*, son Ajit on 5 November 1967, and daughter Priya on 1 July 1969. For a while, Mimi was on the edge of fame, since she shared a gynecologist with Sophia Loren (who had suffered past miscarriages; she installed herself at the newly opened Hotel Intercontinental, placing herself under that doctor's supervision); her son was born a few weeks ahead of Ajit. We had taken with us to Geneva Mimi's nanny, Rajni Bai, whom we affectionately called 'Aji'. A family 'heirloom', she had accompanied Mimi from the first days of our marriage and traveled across the world with us till I left the IFS in 1995. She not only brought up Ajit and Priya but also instilled in them some of her earthy wisdom.

Multilateral Diplomacy

We worked along four main tracks at Geneva: Consular work was light, and handled by a First Secretary (Consular). Second, at the UN, the main regular activity was the Disarmament Conference, which occupied our Ambassador at Berne, assisted by N Krishnan, and a first secretary in our mission. Another priority was the annual session of the Economic and Social Council, in July for four weeks; different UN commissions that met in Geneva also engaged us. A third track was work relating to GATT, handled by a counselor representing our Commerce Ministry; RD Pradhan, who later rose to the high rank of Home Secretary. The final track was the work relating to the UN agencies based at Geneva, the most prominent of which were the International Labor Office (ILO) and the World Health Organization (WHO). I handled that, and supervised administration of the mission; in practice I spent half my time on ILO issues.

The ILO is a unique agency. It is the only survivor from the League of Nations, with a history of nearly 100 years. It has a 'tripartite' structure that has no parallel in the UN family, composed of the representatives of governments, trade unions or labor, and owners of business enterprises. In effect the 'International Labor Office' has its own assigned responsibility under its constitution.[5] This makes it the most 'political' of UN agencies, with the Office manipulating the tripartite structure to push governments in unusual ways. That gives special power to the ILO Director General. The 'cubbishness' of the ILO, i.e. its operation by an inner clique, was facilitated by another undemocratic practice; former holders of the annual presidency of the ILO automatically served on the 'bureau' that acted as advisers to the DG. While the presidency rotated on the traditional geographic principle common to all international organizations, it was only the Western countries that maintained continuity in their government delegation leaders over a long period, thus gaining undue advantage.

Robert Morse of the US was Director General, with Wilfred Jenks of UK as the Deputy DG.[6] They ran a tight ship as we saw when an outstanding director-rank Indian official, Aamir Ali, incurred the wrath of the establishment when a humorous novel he published in India, *Via Geneva*, (1967) was seen as a parody of the ILO. In consequence, a fine career unfortunately ran into dead-end.

The ILO's flagship event was the three-week International Labor Conference that met each June, besides three annual Governing Council meetings (excessive by UN agency standards, each bringing tripartite delegations from some 25 countries), and a series of industrial meetings covering different industry sectors, three per year, all tripartite. That added up to a hectic calendar. As happens often, participation was 'captured' by organizations with an inside track; thus, employer and trade

---

[5] This is also true of the UN Secretariat, which has special tasks of its own under the UN Charter. WTO, set up in the 1990s, is rather different; its secretariat has been given limited functions, because member-states did not want it to play the role of an autonomous actor.

[6] Jenks subsequently rose to the position of the ILO Director General.

union organizations based in Brussels dominated their segments, each with affiliated agencies in different countries. In India, it was the trade union INTUC, allied with the Congress Party that sent delegates. The employer organization was FICCI; the charismatic Naval Tata, of the eponymous business group, represented them. MEA took little interest and our Labor Ministry had the lead; their officials came only for the annual Conference, so that we handled most meetings. Given that issues of political import were few, N Krishnan only attended a few sittings of the Governing Body; that gave me early and enjoyable exposure to representing India at multilateral meetings. Over time I became fairly involved, and was rewarded with chairmanship at a couple of industrial meetings and committees. That taught me conference dynamics, which was to come in useful at Nairobi 15 years later.

We were not much involved with WHO affairs, for two reasons. Most of WHO work was non-political and highly specialized; the Indian Health Ministry dealt directly with WHO headquarters much of the time. The other reason was that the WHO Executive Board was composed of specialists, elected in their individual capacities, though in practice they also functioned as country representatives. The only time PMI became involved with this organization was each May, when the World Heath Assembly met at its annual session at the UN building, the Palais de Nations, attended by a six or eight strong delegation from India, led usually by the Union Health Minister.

One event that endures in memory is the Health Assembly session of May 1968, where the US and other Western countries came a cropper on their efforts to alter the composition of the WHO Executive Board.[7] At Geneva, we were unfamiliar with the lead-up to that session, but it transpired that a coordinated diplomatic strategy had been deployed by Western countries for over a year, to convert representation at this Board from 'experts' chosen in their individual capacity, to nominees officially representing countries elected to the Board. On the face of it, this was plausible; the elected members from the Soviet bloc countries, and even those from developing states conducted themselves as representatives of their countries; it was only the Board members

[7] This is covered briefly in *Inside Diplomacy*, p. 227.

from the West who sometimes refused to take direction from their national health administration. Formal designation as country representatives would end that anomaly.

Through quiet lobbying in most African, Asian and Latin American capitals, a draft resolution steered by the US and some of its allies, had mobilized over 50 co-sponsors. The WHO secretariat kept a low profile on the proposal, and it looked like a done deal. When this draft came up for discussion at one of the committees, in the midst of the Assembly session, a counter-strategy emerged for the first time, guided behind the scenes by the secretariat, which of course was loath to see itself hemmed in by an intergovernmental supervisory body. It also made sense that a highly specialist agency dealing with apolitical issues of global concern should remain quasi-independent. India, supported by a few fellow-developing states took up cudgels in presenting this perspective. Western states, which had not encountered any pushback during months of quiet lobbying, were completely taken aback, and appeared unprepared, though naturally, they forcefully argued their case.[8] During the course of dramatic debate that morning, the tide of opinion in that committee swung from overwhelming support for the Western draft, to strong resistance. To the dismay of the sponsors, some delegations, especially from Africa and the Caribbean, admitted that they had not fully considered the implications of the proposed changes. After a couple of hours of discussion several of them formally withdrew their names from co-sponsorship. Very quickly that became a cascade. The US and its allies saw that the resolution had no prospect, and withdrew the proposal. That drama had a singular consequence; the Executive Board retained its specialist character, which has since remained unchanged.

The other entity where we saw significant action was the UN Narcotics Commission, based in New York, which held its annual meeting in Geneva in September each year. In the years 1967-70, it had on its agenda a new subject that loomed as a growing new threat, 'substance abuse', via the new manufactured pharmaceutical substances that produced dependence and

[8] This account is based on personal notes I made on that day.

addiction. Sweden led the move to persuade the international community to apply new controls to these substances, collectively called 'psychotropic' drugs, consisting of amphetamines, barbiturates, hallucinogens, and tranquilizers. Their difference from the traditional narcotics was that they were manmade, and not derivatives of natural materials like opium, cannabis and cocaine, the traditional remit of the Narcotics Commission.

Remember, the late 1960s were the days of 'flower power' and Woodstock. The world was only slowly waking up to the age of synthetic drugs, LSD and other fashionable addictive substances. At the Narcotics Commission, composed of some 30-member states, Sweden led the battle for a new regime of international controls. It was opposed by all major drug-manufacturing states, notably France, Germany, Switzerland, the UK and the US. They did not deny that the new substances were liable to abuse; their argument was: as with alcohol, it should be left to individual countries to establish their own regulations and restrictions. Sweden contested this, asserting that most developing countries were not sufficiently aware of the dangers posed by these new substances, and it was at the point of manufacture that controls were needed.

DK Anand, Chairman of the Board of Excise and Indirect Taxes, whose remit included narcotics control, led the Indian delegation to this Commission. Ambassador Krishnan and he saw the logic of Sweden's arguments, and decided on the spot to support the move for a new regime of controls. It was an example of an Indian policy decision that was motivated not just by national interest but as a sense of global responsibility. Among the other delegations, we found an ally in the Ghanaian drug expert from Accra—they did not have a permanent mission in Geneva. For three years, our three delegations battled against the Western countries that wanted to bury this subject, supported by a compliant secretariat, and a Narcotics Commissioner, a Yugoslav national, who gave in to them. The Western drug industry was the principal hidden actor.

Gradually, the tide of public opinion in Western countries swung in favor of action, with the media flagging the dangers of abuse of new drugs, in effect challenging their own manufactures. By 1970, Western governments were beginning to shift their position, mainly under domestic public pressure. These trends culminated in 1973 in the passage of the 'International Convention Against Psychotropic Substances' at Vienna. I do not know if the full story behind that Convention has been told, but it was Sweden, supported by India and Ghana that hastened that Convention by a few years.

The Economic and Social Council met for four weeks at Geneva each July. As it was based at New York, the missions in Geneva had limited knowledge of the issues in play. One topic that figured prominently was coordination among different UN agencies, and the role of the UN 'resident representative' at different capitals. I developed skepticism over the real contribution that some UN agencies make to the welfare and advancement of member-states. My subsequent exposure to the work of UNEP and Habitat at Nairobi, both small agencies (though UNEP was gaining prominence in consonance with rising global awareness of environmental issues), did little to remove that impression of the relative inefficacy of the UN system, and the preoccupation of many UN officials with their comfortable lifestyles. The hiatus between the lofty aspirations of UN agencies, and their ground footprint, deserves attention. Be that as it may, discussions at ECOSOC seemed full of empty rhetoric. In 1969, the UN at Geneva set up its 'Inspection Unit' composed of eight senior personalities holding the rank of Assistant Secretary General, who were charged with monitoring the performance of the UN system. It seemed to be one more expensive ornament on a top-heavy system, bereft of value.

Finally, let me mention the 'International Lead and Zinc Study Group', which also annually met at Geneva for a few days. It was a quasi-official entity; Raj Bagri (later Lord Bagri), a businessman based in London represented India. While discussions involved marketing and price issues, what it showed up for me was the fact that India, while a major developing country, had more in common with most Western countries that did not possess these minerals but were prime consumers. In today's language, our real concern was access to important industrial resources, but out of solidarity with developing states, we were inhibited in our actions. This is part of a deeper paradox in India's situation vis-à-vis the G-77.

Indian Community Affairs

Geneva was home to some 30 Indians, most working in UN offices, GATT and other agencies. The 1960s were the time when Indians began to migrate to the US; my sister Dilhar and her husband Manhar (accompanied by their two children) were among the professionals who went to the US in those years, for advanced study and then to work at attractive jobs. North America, and to a lesser extent the UK were the main draws, while some moved in smaller numbers to West European countries. 'Indian Associations' came up in different cities, bringing together these migrants, for fellowship and cultural activities, such as celebrations of Indian festivals. I represented our mission on the executive committee of the Indian Association at Geneva and watched with interest the way this putative diaspora saw itself and reacted to Indian events. Some networking was emerging among these groups, and in 1969 I attended a small conference they organized, over a weekend, in the Swiss university town of Freiburg. The diaspora saw India in dichotomy: they took pride in Indian culture, wanting to learn more of their heritage, concerned that their children should hold fast to it; at the same time, they felt shame and despondency towards India's poverty and social ills, and its misgovernance. These contradictions have persisted.

But all was not gloom. The cluster of Geneva Indians came together on festive occasions and we enjoyed their company. They gave us real insight into the institutions where they worked. It became clear that at any assignment, they were a key resource. All that an Indian mission needed to do was respect them, and help them on consular and other issues where they connected with the home country. That exposed me to the fascination of diaspora affairs, producing a deep personal interest that has endured over the years.[9]

---

[9] See: Rana, 'India's Diaspora Diplomacy', *The Hague Journal of Diplomacy*, Vol. 4 No. 3 (2009), pp. 361-72.

Other Events

All manner of Indian dignitaries passed through Geneva. Ambassador Krishnan bore the brunt of hosting them to meals and receptions, but as his deputy, I did my bit and in the process met fascinating individuals. Many friends and personal visitors also came, and we accommodated them as houseguests in our small apartment as feasible. Relations with our villa co-tenants were uniformly cordial, to the point that in 1968 we hosted a joint party for some 70 guests, with a live band and champagne that became the talk of the town for a while. We also traveled extensively through Europe by car. Once, going away on a week's trip to Italy, Austria and Germany, we left a six-month old Priya with an American neighbor, taking with us Ajit and his nanny. Returning across the Swiss border we phoned her to say that we would reach Geneva around nine at night and would then pick up our daughter. She replied sternly: Of course you can't; she will be asleep, so you better come tomorrow morning. That too was intercultural learning!

Geneva offered exposure to uncommon activities. The Friends Society, i.e. the Quakers, was active at different UN centers, on the premise that improved dialogue and understanding among diplomats should contribute to world peace. In August 1967, barely a month after reaching Geneva, Mimi and I attended a three-day seminar they organized at Clarence, close to Lausanne, on organizational, human resource and other foreign ministry management issues. It drew diplomats from Geneva and officials from European foreign ministries, from some 30 countries. It sparked in me a lifelong interest in this subject. In early 1970, on the eve of moving to Beijing for a second assignment there, I attended at Vienna a fascinating discussion they hosted on the state of China studies in different parts of the world. These kindly Quakers were part of the Geneva scene and we enjoyed many social encounters with them; I regret losing subsequent contact with them.

Even in those days, the Genevese thrived on, and at the same time detested the hordes of foreigners that had taken over their Calvinist city nestled at the downstream end of Lake Geneva, in the midst of the Alps and surrounding hills. Few of them mingled with foreigners. A notable exception was Prof. Gilbert Etienne, and his charming wife Antoinette, who were hospitable and have remained friends ever since. Gilbert is a unique academic, an India scholar who speaks both Hindi and Chinese, studying development economics, including comparative study of the two countries. It was at his home that I met the legendary Edgar Snow, author of *Red Star Over China* (1933), which introduced Mao and the Chinese Communist Party to the West. I encountered Snow later in China.

My final memorable event in Geneva, barely three weeks before departure, was the visit of President VV Giri in early June 1970, at the invitation of the ILO, for the inauguration of that year's International Labor Conference.[10] The visit involved us in innovative protocol arrangements. It was the first occasion for a high Indian dignitary to go abroad without a country host; the ILO simply did not have the resources to provide the comprehensive hospitality that heads of state typically receive; the Geneva authorities were blasé, with too many high visitors to Geneva. I reasoned with Ambassador Krishnan that the Indian government would have to act as the host; that meant giving full hospitality to the visitors, meeting their meals and incidental costs, paying them only 25% of the daily allowance (this is a standard Indian formula, when officials receive state hospitality). The Ambassador, an administration veteran laughed and said the MEA would never accept that; I responded that without such an arrangement, we would be saddled with large bills for meals and personal incidentals, laundry and the like, with no viable means to cover these. In the event, we sent off a request to Delhi on this, and in a matter of days received back a telex in approval. A major faux pas was avoided; the delegation list from Delhi mentioned the President's son and daughter-in-law, but did not specify if they were a couple; they turned out to be halves of two different couples! Imagine the consequences if we had assigned to them a single hotel suite.

The President's spouse had a formidable reputation as a demanding prima donna, unlike her mild husband, but this

[10] I described some of these events in *Inside Diplomacy*, p. 237; this is a fuller account.

proved untrue. We managed to avoid any major disaster. A few small innovations helped, like ferrying the President and his entourage across Lake Geneva by boat, for a reception at Parc des Eaux Vives, avoiding the evening traffic jam at the bridge linking the two halves of the city; that boat trip became a novelty. It involved organizing two sets of vehicle convoys, but that was easy. The simple lesson was: plan well, master detail, and anticipate potential difficulty.

Around February 1970 I had learnt of my next assignment, to the Embassy at Kathmandu as First Secretary (Information). That did not seem enticing. I heard that the position of First Secretary (Political) at our embassy in China was falling vacant around the same time. When Jagat Mehta passed through Geneva I mentioned this to him. Foreign Secretary TN Kaul (1913-2000) happened to be in town at the same time and at an evening function, I told him that he had a volunteer for Beijing. The Foreign Secretary readily agreed, and in a matter of weeks, I received from the MEA my orders for Beijing. The five of us, Mimi, Ajit and Priya, accompanied by Rajni Bai, left for Beijing, via Delhi almost exactly after three years in Geneva.

4

Return to the Land of the Dragon

Beijing (1970-72)

In July 1970 I returned to a transformed Beijing, accompanied this time by my family. China was recovering from the tumult of the Cultural Revolution. The little color that had existed in the pre-1965 era had all been washed away. Everyone dressed alike in indigo blue tunics and jackets and trousers, in dark or lighter shades; in the bitterly cold winter these were padded with cotton. That was not radically different from five years earlier, but the flashes of color that women sported had disappeared. All rank symbols and decorations had also vanished from military uniforms, which were now rather shapeless, with a subtle difference that jackets worn by officers had four pockets, while ordinary soldiers made do with two. Many of Beijing's restaurants of the mid-1960s had closed; some began to open gradually after 1970. China was on slow recovery from the torments of another dark, dreadful night, though officially the Cultural Revolution ended only in 1976.

Embassy Life

As before, our Embassy and the diplomatic corps was the hub of our life. Our chancery had moved to East Beijing's Waijiao Talou area, with the Chancery and the Residence in two large buildings that shared a compound. By then, the Sanlitun area, located another four km away, had emerged as a second diplomatic enclave; our apartment was in one of its seven-storey buildings. India had been forced to abandon the chancery and embassy residence on what used to be called Legation Street, which had hosted all foreign embassies in pre-1949 China. Even countries that had owned their buildings were made to leave (we had bought our two buildings in a small courtyard from the People's Republic of China government in 1951; they had housed the Hong Kong and Shanghai Bank). Foreign embassies were told that this location was associated with the era of China's subjugation to foreign powers, and they could not remain there. Even China's favored friends, like Myanmar and Romania, were not exempt.

Brajesh C Mishra (1928-2011) headed the Embassy, as Chargé d'Affaires; like his predecessors, he was the head of mission in full measure, and treated as such by the diplomatic corps despite lack of ambassador rank, exchanging visits with other ambassadors as a matter of course.[1] He was an outstanding diplomat, son of a Congress party leader, DP Mishra, former Chief Minister of Madhya Pradesh; he enjoyed personal access to Prime Minister Indira Gandhi, exchanging correspondence with her that was not shared with MEA; he would sometimes tell me of the content, but did not show any of his reports to PM, though I was his deputy. In essence, Indira Gandhi wanted to normalize relations with Beijing, but felt compelled to move cautiously, in part owing to her conservative advisers, as we see below.

The Embassy had two first secretaries; First Secretary N Iyer handled consular work. Lt. Colonel, PD Sherlekar was the Military Attaché—both outstanding colleagues. We also had two young second secretaries, fresh from the Hong Kong language school, GS Iyer and Vijay Nambiar (in 1971 Harsh Bhasin joined the embassy), plus three attachés handling different jobs, including one supervising our six Indian security guards. The total strength of home-based staff was nearly 20, with a like number of local staff. A young and highly efficient PS Shahdadpuri, who went on to become a second secretary in Libya, assisted me; he was on his first foreign assignment; he wisely opted to quit the service in the

[1] India had withdrawn its ambassador from China in mid-1961, when bilateral relations deteriorated, and China followed suit. Ambassadors returned to their posts in 1976 when a measure of normalcy was restored in our ties; China insisted that since India had been the one to initiate that withdrawal, it must send back its envoy first, and they reciprocated thereafter.

late 1980s, and is now a leading businessman in Dubai, remaining a good friend.

Mishra was a disciplinarian; his management methods were somewhat domineering. Once he felt that each official under his charge accepted his primacy, things went smoothly, on his terms. A small example: he would not write annual reports on officials in the Embassy, till their final departure; he perhaps rationalized that this provided a hold on them, and that he would not be in the position of having to give a low grade to someone that he had earlier considered satisfactory.[2] The Embassy worked harmoniously, with none of the petty sniping or internal tension among officials or staff that crops up in missions of similar size. All the wings of the Embassy acted to a shared purpose, as had also been my experience in Beijing under Jagat Mehta several years earlier, with the difference that this time the Embassy team was larger. The onset of the Bangladesh crisis in early 1971 reinforced our sense of commitment, a conviction that we were guided by a national purpose.

Spouses were kept busy at the embassy school that had started around 1969; it operated out of a section of the Residence. All the wives of officers, and other Indian staff spouses that were qualified, were expected to teach, with Smt. Mishra as school principal; they were unpaid.[3] This school accepted children from other embassies, attracting a total of 50 students: with low fees, it provided a needed service to the foreign community, especially drawing students from African, Asian and Western embassies, to the kindergarten classes.

The Beijing diplomatic community was much larger compared with the mid-1960s, with over 60 resident missions, and the number grew continually. The Canadians arrived in 1971, followed by others, and that brought an infusion of fresh faces. There were many more foreign correspondents as well, including Japanese, widening the range of source material for observation

---

2 It is a commentary on our system that no one in MEA demanded that he should comply with annual reporting rules.

3 In subsequent years teachers received a stipend; the Indian Embassy School was closed in the early 2000s, when a number of regular new schools were established in Beijing.

of China events. But the opacity of the Chinese system was undiminished, with a sense of abiding enigma deepened by the traumatic memory of the Cultural Revolution. Mishra enjoyed close friendships with some ambassadors to the point where on occasion they would show him their cipher telegrams reporting events such as visits by official delegations, or give a detailed account of what had transpired.

Political reporting was our staple work; for India, virtually no direct commercial or other economic exchanges took place. No tourists or visitors, or even scholars or journalists came from India; a few Indian Communists might have come to China, but typically they would not contact us. There were few foreign students in China, and none from India. A handful of Indian businessmen had begun to visit the biannual Canton Fair, mainly those based in Hong Kong, making a tiny contribution to India-China trade. Consular work was slender, consisting mainly of giving visas to Chinese officials and to fellow-diplomats. A few Indians that had stayed on in Shanghai were fully integrated into their local ethos. A small incident lightened our mood; the consular assistant told me that the date of birth given on the passport of a Chinese diplomatic courier going to India was 'wrong' (First Secretary Iyer was away on leave); I gave him a short lecture, to the effect that he could not possibly know the applicant's real birth date.[4] He heard me out and said: he could not have been born on the 31st June, as the month only has 30 days. Fantastic, I told him and proceeded to phone the Foreign Ministry, making the same point to their protocol division that had sent us a visa application under the cover of a diplomatic note. That official gave me the same spiel that I had delivered to our assistant, adding: you have never met this applicant, so how can you know his date of birth. I then gave out reasoning; this produced a long silence, after which he said: we will send a messenger to pick up that passport and application. I guess that poor courier found himself transferred to some remote outpost.

As earlier, the Indian Embassy was acknowledged by its peers to be among the best informed, mainly by virtue of deft

---

4 China, like the UK, is among the countries that use diplomatic couriers to hand-carry to embassies their most sensitive papers.

trading in information, and exchanging news within a wide circle of counterparts, based on our own analysis of the media, and material collated from diverse sources. The Xinhua bulletin issued twice a day was our official information source, besides the six daily Chinese language journals that we were allowed to receive, supplemented with occasional provincial papers picked up during travel, as in the 1960s. I developed useful contacts with some East European diplomats, and regularly met two of them, one an ambassador. I learnt a salutary lesson on naming information sources, reporting to Delhi a conversation with this ambassador. A senior MEA colleague, reading my report, decided to cross-check with that envoy's counterpart in Delhi; some weeks later, my ambassador friend asked me if I had named him as the source while reporting our conversation. Sheepishly, I confirmed this. He said that his Delhi counterpart had reported this to his foreign ministry, which had taken him to task for sharing information with me. A simple moral: do not name sources, even if this might appear to diminish the credibility of the information.

We enjoyed easy friendships with Asian and African embassies, the latter moving into Beijing in growing numbers. Relations with Western counterparts were always cordial and productive. What we missed greatly was access to universities and to academics; no thinktanks existed at that time, and as far as I know, no embassy had real access to Chinese scholars at the universities. Personal meetings with locals, other than officials we met in the course of work, were impossible, even dangerous for ordinary Chinese, thanks to the pervasive street and local 'work committees' that kept meticulous watch in what was a vast big-brother society. Sometimes, little nuggets of information came our way through the Chinese staff that worked in our homes, all supplied by the ubiquitous Diplomatic Personnel Service Bureau, the single official agency for embassy services. For instance, when our cook at home exhibited many small wounds and scabs on both his forearms, Mimi learnt through gentle questions that his wife had inflicted these, resisting an abortion when she was carrying her second child, in violation of the country's one-child diktat; it was a revealing instance of the suppressed stress of Chinese life.

China Vignettes

As foreign observers, we believed that by 1970 China had emerged from the dark night of the Cultural Revolution. Outwardly, some normalcy had been restored, compared with the chaos of 1966-69. Politically, it was Mao's wife Jiang Qing, and Lin Biao, the squeaky-voiced People's Liberation Army marshal, veteran of the Korean war and designated heir to Mao, that held center stage. After Mao's death in 1976 and the arrest of Jiang Qing and the 'Gang of Four', that epoch came to be viewed as the second phase of the Cultural Revolution. That lay in the future.

China was visibly different from much I remembered from 1965. Some of the restaurants that I had frequented earlier had closed, among them 'San Jwor' ('Three Tables') Restaurant, an old gathering place for intellectuals, famous for its freshwater eels. Our 'Yanjing Club' of 1964-65 was a distant memory; we heard that one of our Chinese friends from that group had been killed, and all the others had also suffered. Those informal exchanges between diplomats and Chinese personnel that worked in embassies or taught diplomats, were now impossible. Similar restrictions applied to foreign journalists, who relied upon their interpreters and staff, who were of course used by the authorities to keep a close eye on their activities. Prominent among them were Jim Pringle with Reuters and Jean Leclerc du Sablon of AFP. *The Toronto Globe and Mail* and *The New York Times* were also represented. Events relating to the Cultural Revolution were taboo subjects, and most discussions with officials produced boilerplate responses.

One evening in early 1971, after visiting a diplomat friend in a Sanlitun building that adjoined the one where our apartment was located, I ran into Lao Chang, who had been the majordomo at my house for two years in 1963-65, and so good to me in my bachelor days. He had aged; I was moved to see him, and was also very happy that he had survived the political storm, when so many connected in any way with foreigners became targets of the Red Guards and mob frenzy. I lingered back when our lift reached the ground floor, and expressing delight at seeing him, asked about his welfare. With a weary smile, he said he was well, and added that it was not good for him to be seen talking to me, because others would report this. I bid him goodbye and left with tears in my eyes. Sadly, I had no further encounter; I did not dare contact him again.

The culture scene, under the personal supervision of Jiang Qing, remained hostage to the legacy of the Cultural Revolution. The revolutionary musical 'Red Detachment of Women' was one of her prime offerings, staged specially for the diplomatic community at the Great Hall of the People, and during visits by high foreign dignitaries. Many remember it; beautifully staged, with stirring martial music, it remains the epitome of that era. Most traditional opera was in ruins, its leading performers hounded during the upheaval. Gone was that panorama of the Chinese performing arts; it underwent revival only after 1976. Films too were dreary, heavy with political themes, presented in inartistic fashion. The famous Lama Temple to the north of the old city, a major repository of Tibetan Buddhism, located close to the city's North Gate was closed, having been ransacked by Red Guards. The revival of religion that we witness across China since 2000 reflects the history and resilience of spiritual belief. Today, the Lama Temple, like temples in other cities, is a thriving hub, crowded even with young Chinese devotees. Streets adjoining the Lama Temple attract hordes of foreign tourists looking for artefacts.

India-China Relations

Three months before I reached Beijing, at the 1970 May Day parade, Chairman Mao had shaken hands with Chargé d'Affaires Brajesh Mishra on the Tiananmen rostrum, and had told him: We cannot go on quarreling like this. China and India are old friends and should restore that friendship. That full story has been narrated by Mishra in an oral history interview, how a few in New Delhi, acolytes of strong friendship with the Soviet Union, transformed that political opening into a caricature, an empty 'Mao smile'. [5] At the Embassy we were unanimous India had failed to grasp an

5 See: Brajesh C Mishra, '"Mao Smile" Revisited: Sino-Indian Relations During an Important Period', *Indian Foreign Affairs Journal*, Vol. 1, No. 4, October, 2006.

opportunity to improve the bilateral relationship; trivializing that significant initiative by China's leader was a needless error that put back even limited normalization of relations by several years.

In consequence, there was little content in the bilateral relationship. We received almost no visitors from India, be it businessmen, journalists, or others; the country was not yet open for foreign tourism, save for a few hardy adventurers. The Foreign Ministry treated the Embassy with cool correctness. It was against this background that I had an interesting encounter, detailed in my 1998 essay:

> A small instance of the quality of the evolving India-China relationship of 1970 was the visit to the Embassy by the renowned Mao biographer Edgar Snow, who was on what was his last visit to China. I had met Snow a couple of years earlier, at the home of Professor Gilbert Etienne in Geneva (inviting me to that lunch meeting, Gilbert had warned me not to get into an argument with Edgar Snow over India-China relations; I had replied that one could not argue with a legend!). Reading in the Chinese press around October 1970 that he was in Beijing as Mao's personal guest, I tried to phone him...He telephoned some weeks later and said that he had been travelling in the provinces, and that he would come and meet me at the Embassy. He turned down my offer to call, and some days later drove up in his official limousine, for about 40 minutes of general conversation. He was too wily to give away any hard information and spoke in general terms of his positive impressions of the changes in the country. He also pumped me for information on some new document, which had emerged in the Hong Kong press about events on the mainland, relating to Chinese personalities, if I recall correctly. There was nothing of substance in the meeting. The significant aspect was that it took place at all, and that Snow made it a point to visit the Indian Embassy. It was a straw in the direction of normalization.

A rare 'normal' event in our bilateral relations was the visit of an Indian table tennis team that came to Beijing in October 1971, for the Afro-Asian Games. This was invested with political meaning, though again, the political mood of the Bangladesh crisis did not permit any follow-up at that time. The entire Embassy team, led by the Chargé d'Affaires and his wife, went to the airport to greet them on arrival. It was an Indian foray in 'ping-pong diplomacy'. Mimi recalls a comment made by some members of the team: their Chinese guides spoke such fluent Hindi that they felt embarrassed at their own 'Hinglish' style of speech, in which sentences in Hindi are seeded with English words.

In the four years I spent in Beijing on two assignments, no MEA official visited us, even on an internal inspection tour. I do not recall a visit by any government official to China in that time. Nor did we receive family visitors or friends. Academic contact was non-existent. This added up to deep isolation.

1971 Bangladesh Crisis

From early 1971 onwards, the escalating Bangladesh crisis preoccupied the Embassy; our concern was China's role in support of Pakistan's repressive actions in what was at that time 'East Pakistan'. Mishra worked hard at keeping up regular dialogue at the Chinese Foreign Ministry, conveying to them India's apprehensions over the escalating crisis, and the burden that India bore with an influx of millions of refugees, fleeing repression. I accompanied him on most of those visits and prepared the summary records of discussion. The purpose was to convey the rationale of India's policy, and our concern that the situation was becoming unmanageable, especially when the influx approached ten million in number (the UN High Commissioner for Refugees headed a small underfunded entity, and did not furnish material support to India). Mishra transmitted to the Foreign Ministry two letters that PM Indira Gandhi wrote to Premier Zhou, explaining India's concerns; the second one was delivered in July 1971.[6] True to his style, he held that exchange very closely; I knew nothing of it at the time, though I did sense that some discussion at the Chinese Foreign Ministry was afoot, from which I was kept out. In a talk at the Indira Gandhi Centre in 1998 Mishra said: 'I was received only once by the Vice-Minister of Foreign Affairs

---

[6] This information comes from a compilation of India-Pakistan documents put together by AS Bhasin, *India-Pakistan Relations 1947-2007: A Documentary Study*, 2012.

in charge of Asia, Han Nianlong, and that too in 1971, i.e., two years and many months after my arrival in Beijing. Kishan Rana had joined me by that time, and China had gained her rightful place in the UN. Indira Gandhi wrote letters to heads of state or government explaining our case...(including) a letter for Premier Zhou Enlai, which I delivered to Han Nianlong. That was the only time he received me.'[7] As best as I know, Zhou did not reply to either of these messages.

In mid-July 1971 Henry Kissinger made his secret visit to Beijing, facilitated by Pakistan. When news of that encounter broke, I was at a national day reception; the foreign diplomatic corps was shocked that the unthinkable had happened—a direct, empowered China-US dialogue had been launched. No one, in Beijing or elsewhere, had anticipated this rapprochement. The transcript of the Zhou-Kissinger discussion now reveals the extent to which Kissinger pushed buttons on the Bangladesh issue, in effect provoking the Chinese Premier into harsh comment about India. Far from making any attempt to defuse the escalating crisis in Bangladesh, Kissinger was intent on provoking China into direct involvement in what was becoming a major crisis. On his next Beijing visit Kissinger attempted the same and found Premier Zhou unresponsive ('we will discuss that later...').[8] The new element was the Indo-Soviet Treaty of Peace and Friendship, signed in August 1971. That episode does little credit to Kissinger.

In keeping with escalating East Pakistan developments, the Chinese media became strident in its criticism of India. This was also reflected in speeches by Chinese dignitaries at national day celebrations by embassies and at state banquets in honor of visiting foreign delegations (as before in the 1960s, foreign embassies were customarily invited to banquets for visiting heads of state or government, and foreign ministers). Mishra made it clear to Chinese interlocutors that he would walk out of functions if India came under attack in speeches. After the first walkout, it became standard practice to instruct the flag-car chauffeur that he should stand by with the car at the main entrance, in anticipation

---

7 Brajesh Mishra, 'Walk out of the dinner and eat it', Chapter 46, *Across the Himalayan Gap*, ed. Tan Chung (1998).

8 See: http://nsarchive.gwu.edu/NSAEBB/NSAEBB66/#docs

of a likely walkout. That worked smoothly. Sometimes the speeches were delayed till the meal was over—not delivered at the start of the function, as customary—which led to comment in the diplomatic corps that the change was to ensure that the Indian Chargé finished his dinner before making his exit! A footnote: this routine ended around the middle of 1972, when for a change India was not criticized in the Chinese speeches. As it happened, that particular reception speech attacked the Soviet Union, at which the Soviet Ambassador, accompanied by the East European phalanx, walked out. That dramatic effect was spoilt when on descending the People's Palace complex steps, they were greeted by the Indian flag-car, but alas, not their vehicles. They were not amused at the delay in mobilizing their cars!

When the Bangladesh War broke out on 3 December 1971, as had seemed inevitable in those final weeks, China's reaction was one of the unfathomable elements. Many in India thought it might intervene in some fashion, confronting New Delhi with a second front. The Indo-Soviet Treaty of Peace and Friendship, probably gave pause to Beijing, much as it favored Pakistan. We saw redoubled Chinese support to Islamabad in public statements, but no overt action against India, nor expression of threat. One conclusion: China is perhaps more cautious in actions than its words might have us believe.

At the Embassy this was a tense time, and we prepared ourselves for a difficult situation. All of us were glued to radio sets, listening to BBC and Voice of America. All India Radio was hard to receive, and truth to tell, in that rapidly changing situation Indian official statements were part of 'public diplomacy', often slow to report hard developments. Fortunately, rapid success on the ground by the armed forces of the Bangladesh *Mukti Bahini* and India crushed the opposing forces, and this greatly energized us. On 14 December Mishra accepted my suggestion that with a winning hand, we might suggest to New Delhi a 'unilateral ceasefire' as early as possible, to counter the insinuations that after triumph on the Eastern front, India would attack West Pakistan.[9]

[9] That was a canard afloat in Western circles, and led Kissinger to dispatch an aircraft carrier from the US Seventh Fleet into the Bay of Bengal; that gratuitously hostile gesture, born of a total misreading of Indian intentions, remains fresh in Indian memory, after all these years.

That borrowed a leaf from China. I have no idea if our 'Crash' cypher message to MEA with that suggestion reached Indian policymakers in time, but we were on the right side of history, and had anticipated events. India did indeed declare a unilateral ceasefire on 16 December 1971. That evening the Embassy team, including our chief, were at a reception at the UK mission, flush with euphoria; late that evening, Mishra invited us to the Residence for champagne. A first bottle and the toasts led to many more, in what became an exuberant, convivial mood; very many hours later, when we drove home, a rather tipsy Mimi—a real first for her—asked: what are so many Chinese doing on the street, so late at night? 'They are on the way to their day's work,' I replied.

A footnote to that crisis is the manner in which East Pakistan diplomats made their personal arrangements to shift allegiance to Bangladesh, and our unusual role as facilitators. At the very start, Mishra met twice with the Bengali Agricultural Counsellor of the Pakistan Embassy—Obeidullah Khan—at the residence of Second Secretary Vijay Nambiar. In my 1998 essay on China I wrote:

> The Bangladesh war also produced for us the melodrama of assisting the then Pakistani diplomats of Bengali origin to establish contact with their own new government-in-the-making, since in the politically charged atmosphere of Beijing there were none but the most formal contacts with Pakistani diplomats—mainly I should add at the preference of the latter, who may have found that even routine courtesies, or return of courtesies to Indian counterparts, detracted from their self-image of victims of Indian machinations. This was my only exposure to the cloak-and-dagger style, as roundabout means were mutually used to make soundings and first contacts, often via the spouses, since the latter often had their own friendships and equations! The establishment of these first links with the Bangladeshis, who became major players in their new nation, was a heart-warming experience. It also provided relief and a counterpoint to the tension generated by the war.

China remained hostile to Bangladesh for many more months, but as pragmatists, they gradually accommodated themselves to reality. They did see that *dénouement* as a loss of face, and it pushed back for some time normalization of India-China relations.

Observing China

As during my earlier assignment, the influx of visitors to China provided a useful recourse for insight. Our weekly courier trip, made in rotation by all India-based officials, gave one opportunity. Most were businessmen; they came laden with hopes of winning in a huge unknown market. They usually went away with small orders. The China boom, via Deng Xiaoping's economic reforms was almost a decade away, but an uptick in foreign trade and other economic exchanges was taking shape. By chance I became involved in a small political adventure:

On the way back from a routine courier trip to Hong Kong I traveled with a Chinese-speaking American academic, who seemed interesting; we got into a conversation. She gave her name as Roxanne Witke, and she spoke of her interest in meeting Chinese leaders—rather a difficult task for an unknown visitor. A couple of weeks later I read in the Xinhua news bulletin that she had met Jiang Qing, someone who seldom met foreign visitors. I tracked her down at the then premier lodging in the capital, the Beijing Hotel, and invited her to join my wife and myself for dinner at the Mongolian restaurant on Hou Hai lake, at the back of the Forbidden City. She accepted and, over the meal, she proceeded to unfold her extraordinary experience. This is narrated in her biography of that complex and, of course, controversial leader of the Cultural Revolution. The difference was that she spoke fresh from her first meeting with Madame Mao, at a point when Witke did not know that on her way out of the country through Guangzhou (still the only viable entry-exit point, even though direct flights to Shanghai from the West and Addis Ababa had commenced), she would be summoned back by the imperious lady for a series of additional meetings. The story of how later on attempts were made in the mid-70s to stop the publication of her book, at a time when Jiang Qing was under political attack and headed for downfall is well known.

> The striking aspect for me in that dinner meeting with Witke was the tale she unfolded, and her unerring prescience. She had earlier met Deng Yingchao, the spouse of Premier Zhou Enlai. Witke narrated the meticulous manner in which she had to prepare

herself for the audience with Jiang Qing, listening to unpublished speeches where she could take notes but not see the text or record the readings on tape. She recounted that Jiang was truly concerned that she was not viewed with sympathy by the outside world, and felt that Witke could help in depicting a more human picture of her. Witke remarked that someone was trying to make her into a latter-day Edgar Snow, and perhaps she was not displeased at the prospect. Jiang told her that Premier Zhou had urged her to go ahead with this meeting. Witke also spoke of the thorough investigation made into her academic and family background, plus the ways in which different Chinese interlocutors made this known to her. Then she went on to add her initial conclusion based on that first meeting that someone was giving Jiang a long rope to hang herself with. Witke also felt that she had unwittingly become enmeshed in China's internal politics, and might be used in the maneuvering by various personalities.

This proved to be remarkably close to the truth, as the world learnt subsequently, when some of the inside stories on the events in China of the Mao era began to emerge. But to go back to that evening in the Mongolian restaurant, Roxanne Witke told a story, which gave insight into the inner workings of a land of enormous secrecy, and she seemed credible for the reason that the account was vivid in personal detail.[10]

Roxanne Witke's book *Comrade Jiang Ch'ing* was published in 1977, despite Beijing's strenuous effort to block its release. My encounter with her does not figure in it; possibly, she regretted sharing so much of her initial information about Jiang Ch'ing. At Jiang's trial, revelations in this book were part of the indictment.

As before, travel by resident foreigners was limited to a radius of 20 km, the three permitted exceptions being the Great Wall, the Ming Tombs and the airport. Other trips required Foreign Ministry authorization. The list of 'open' cities expanded

---

[10] An MEA colleague was kind enough to locate for me a copy of my 1972 report on the conversation with Witke, after this account was published. I was glad to see that all the details I recalled conformed to that report, except that I did not mention in my original report Witke's first impression that someone was trying to make her into a latter-day Edgar Snow.

gradually, when places like Chongqing in Sichuan were made accessible. New travel privileges first went to 'friendly' countries, in a subtle political hierarchy of favor dispensation. That was the traditional way of dealing with foreigners.

In 1971 that old staple of Beijing diplomatic life, the annual diplomatic tour hosted by the Foreign Ministry, was revived, having been suspended during the Cultural Revolution. As before, each head of mission and spouse were invited, together with one embassy official. I went on two tours, once accompanying Mrs. Mishra when the Cd'A could not join, and taking Mimi with me on the second one. The latter, in 1972 took us to Loyang and Sian, both steeped in history—the army of clay warriors had not been excavated at Sian at the time, but the collection of artefacts offered on show was no less impressive.

At Loyang, visiting a museum of steles, I strayed from the guided group, as was my habit, to speak directly with local officials. In the midst of all those stone tablets commemorating the deeds of Song dynasty figures, I paused to admire an unusual inscription that was in both in Chinese and Sanskrit, recalling Fa Xian's journey to India. A museum staff member whispered to me: 'With such a shared history, how can we persist with our current problems'! It was heart-warming to find that even in that harsh political climate, some were brave enough to affirm our friendship.

A major, dramatic event was the flight and demise of Lin Biao on 13 September 1971; gaining prominence during the Cultural Revolution, Lin had emerged in 1969 as the anointed heir to Mao. That news broke in Beijing like a thunderbolt. It was completely unanticipated for the simple reason that no real information about China's leaders percolated to the outside world. The world of China watchers had access only to photos and lists of personalities attending events and commemorations, to decipher shifts and trends. When Western leaders visited Beijing, reports on their meetings with high personalities slowly percolated within the diplomatic corps. Photo analysis was another favorite tool. The ranking of personalities was often revealed in these, and in official press reports. And if someone was purged, the photo was often physically cropped to eliminate that individual—remember, in those days electronic image manipulation and 'photoshopping' were unknown. I remember the utter delight with which I once located during my first assignment a leadership lineup photo from which a purged official had been eliminated, but the tip of his shoe had been overlooked in the reworked photo!

News about Lin Biao seeped out gradually. The British manufacturer of the Trident aircraft that crashed in Mongolia with Lin and his small retinue asked anxiously if their plane had developed a defect, as a vital matter of public safety. A couple of months later they were told authoritatively that their plane had not been at fault. It slowly emerged that Lin had attempted a coup and fled. Or it could be that he had lost in a power struggle, and that the plane had run out of fuel. Neither Mongolia nor the Soviet Union, despite all their differences with Beijing, has ever disclosed any hard information. We gradually learnt that Jiang Qing was the winner. Even today, little more is known with certainty, though theories abound.

Premier Zhou Enlai appeared frequently at receptions for visiting foreign leaders. It was his custom to walk down the lineup of foreign envoys, shaking hands with each, and their spouses. He was invariably alert and perceptive, and would lock gaze with each person; we used to say that the warmth of that handshake was in proportion to the bilateral political relationship of the day. The evening the news broke of the People's Republic of China gaining its seat in the UN, he was at an embassy national day reception. Clutching a glass of *Mao Tai*, he went to every table to clink glasses with each guest. At my turn, I said to him in Chinese: 'Congratulations on China's success, Excellency'; he responded with an expansive gesture with an arm and shoulders. Zhou has remained the most enduring of Chinese leaders, in the perception of its people.

China's Opening to the US

The July 1971 visit of Kissinger, which marked a major turning point in world affairs, was followed swiftly by President Richard Nixon's visit to Beijing and Shanghai in April 1972. In hindsight that reconciliation seems logical. Consider China's situation at the time: emerging from the chaos of the Cultural Revolution, an aging Mao wanted to seize the initiative on the world stage. He sought dramatic transformation in foreign relations, and by that token, in China's external economic options. Yet in fact no one anticipated this, much less put forward predictive analysis even considering such a possibility. That is a revealing commentary on the imagination of diplomatic and scholarly observers.

Even the US was not prepared to believe that such transformation was possible. We now know from Chinese and US sources that Mao's October Day 1970 gesture, publicly receiving Edgar Snow on the Tiananmen rostrum, was intended to signal to Washington DC that it was ready to move forward, but this diplomatic signal was completely missed, by the US and by the world media. That gesture was seen only as the expression of an old friendship with someone who in the 1930s, had eloquently revealed Mao and the Chinese Revolution to the outside world.

Nixon's visit to China in April 1972 became the most discussed event in the Beijing diplomatic corps. Paradoxically, we depended on news that came via radio broadcasts from the US, for an event that took place in the capital where we lived, barely 15-odd kilometers from the venues where the events were taking place. Our location gave us no special insight.

Our Return

In March 1971, Mimi and I and our small children had traveled home on emergency leave, when my father was struck with leukemia. When he passed away a year later, I was holding charge in Beijing as Mishra was away to Delhi; he knew of our bereavement (since the news had come to me via MEA); I waited till his return before traveling alone to India, at my cost, as no further emergency home passages were available, and I could not afford to take Mimi with me. The very day I reached home at Porbander, traveling by air via Mumbai, news reached me that Mimi's father, aged 51, had tragically died of a heart attack at distant Gorakhpur, in eastern UP. It was impossible to even phone them from Porbander to convey grief; after dispatching a condolence telegram, I left the next day for Beijing, to be with Mimi and the children in that acute crisis. Years later, in 1988 and 1992, Mimi and I were similarly to miss the last rites of our mothers as well.

Consequently, with my two-year term drawing to a close, I sought a transfer to headquarters. After five years abroad, we were ready to return home, and the double bereavement of March 1972 made that imperative. We reached Delhi in August 1972.

Ajit and Priya were aged five and three when we left Beijing. Ajit had attended the Embassy school, while Priya had joined the kindergarten in our final months. They both were fluent at Chinese, and Priya's Beijing accent was bell-like in its clarity. For anyone who has struggled with this tough language, such an accent is like manna from heaven. Alas, small children retain neither their accent nor foreign language skills when they leave that environment. Endnote: At Hong Kong airport, the flies hovering in the waiting lounge puzzled and frightened Priya—she had not encountered such creatures in Beijing.

5

East Asia and the Himalayan Kingdoms

MEA (1972-75)

Returning from Beijing, I joined MEA as deputy secretary in the East Asia Division, and some months later was promoted to the rank of director.[1] I was deputy to Vasant Paranjpe, joint secretary heading this Division; we had been together at Hong Kong. Alas, our past easy relationship was lost. While working in that Division continued my career specialization, the situation soon became impossible. Paranjpe was insecure, understandable given his 'outsider' position in the IFS; he was reluctant to entrust anything important to me. A deeper problem was our differences in policy towards China. He had enjoyed exceptional past insight into that country in the 1950s, the heyday of *bhai-bhai* friendship, and viewed China's subsequent actions towards India as a betrayal; this produced in him deep antagonism towards Beijing. In contrast, fresh from my second China assignment, I felt that it was vital for India to locate a pragmatic reconciliation path, and work for a solution to the border dispute, starting with normalizing relations. That involved sending back ambassadors to the two capitals. I was influenced by the political value of Mao's May Day 1970 gesture, and Mishra's analysis of this. Further, the end of the

[1] In the Indian system, this used to be an 'automatic' promotion, coming on the completion of 13 years of service, though it went into effect only when posts were available, but such staggered implementation did not affect the seniority. Now some selectivity is applied in giving this promotion.

Bangladesh crisis had left India in a much stronger political and psychological mood, giving political elbowroom for initiative.

China Affairs

In those days, the full range of MEA's China papers were accessible to an official at my rank, including those marked 'Top Secret', handled by the NGO Section, the super-efficient entity that handled our most sensitive files. I went through the papers of the 1950s, and saw that the inside story of this bilateral relationship was rather different from the self-image that we had nurtured and projected, i.e. that India was the victim of a huge deception, and that China was the unvarnished aggressor against India. Immediately after Independence, we had viewed the India-China border in the Western sector, i.e. Aksai Chin, as 'undefined'; the maps issued by the Survey of India in the early 1950s had carried that inscription. Just a couple of years later, we had somehow changed our minds, deciding that the border was clear-cut and ran along an alignment that we asserted as our definitive border. A precise picture of how that had happened was not evident from the MEA's papers.[2] But even in the late 1950s, some doubt persisted over the legitimacy of our assertion, evident in comments by officials on the files. It was only in the mid-1950s that India became aware that China was setting up a string of new border outposts along the border, many of them much within what we asserted was our territory, notably in Aksai Chin. This was clearly aggressive action by China. Through alchemy that was not explicit, India then decided to respond with a 'forward policy', by setting up our own border posts.

At the same time, we were inhibited in directly taking up this issue with Beijing. Was this due to China's evasive responses in the early 1950s, when China had been dismissive of its cartographic aggression, placating us that these were 'old maps, not yet revised'? We knew the danger of that imprecise situation, but opted not to press for early resolution, not even when the 1954 Tibet agreement was negotiated. What seemed missing from the

[2] It is possible that papers that are held in the PM's Office contain more information on this vital point.

MEA papers was the larger picture of reportage by our intelligence agencies, and the role they played in steering that forward policy. In the papers I saw, the imprint of Jawaharlal Nehru loomed large; he was concurrently the foreign minister and treated the MEA as his own ministry. Notes written by deputy secretaries traveled up to him in routine fashion; he occasionally drafted messages that were sent to our Embassy in Beijing and to the Consulate-General in Lhasa over the signature of the MEA officials of different rank, including cipher telegrams, ostensibly sent by deputy secretaries.

The above rough summary does not do justice to all the nuances and details of issues in what was to become a full-fledged border crisis, leading to war in 1962. Also, I rely on memory in writing of this. But even without access to papers in the PM's Office, there was sufficient material in the MEA to show that Prime Minister Nehru had been ambivalent about our border claim, right up to the late 1950s, contrary to popular belief, and that different officials had pushed for a more assertive stand. One episode sticks in memory: sometime around 1957, when our intelligence reports showed that some new Chinese border posts had been built in Aksai Chin, the MEA officials debated India's response, i.e. how to take up the issue with Beijing. The papers traveled to the PM and back again to the MEA. After much cogitation, the action approved by Nehru was that a copy of India's map should be sent to the Chinese Foreign Ministry. One wonders if anyone in Beijing understood the import of that simple action, much less recognized it as a form of subdued protest.

As the number two in the East Asia Division, I undertook two actions. In 1973, I wrote two policy notes, urging that we should initiate a political dialogue with China. Since Paranjpe would not let such notes travel upwards, I waited till he was out of Delhi, and then sent out my suggestions to several senior personalities, the Foreign Secretary and the private secretary to the External Affairs Minister. A displeased Paranjpe told me that I had exceeded authority; I argued that it was my right to offer suggestions, and he was welcome to counter these with his own thoughts, so that such an important issue could be debated from all relevant perspectives. Very possibly he did this, but those papers were not shown to me. In a few other instances, when I took decisions on files without consulting him, he took a similar stand, saying in personal conversation that I did not have the authority for such action. I responded that we could show the papers to the head of administration to determine if I had exceeded a permitted ambit of authority; he dropped the matter, but remained resentful.

The other initiative taken after going through the China papers was to prepare a handwritten selection of material that portrayed the evolution of that crisis, and the comments that different personalities had recorded in the key period 1955 to 1961 (with precise references to the files from which the material had been culled). That was explosive material; in those days when photocopiers did not exist, and almost no official handled a personal typewriter, I could not dictate these sensitive extracts to a personal assistant, and hence reproduced them in a handwritten note, in my crabby handwriting. That document, which ran to a mere four pages, was handed over to the IFS colleague who worked on the PM's staff as a director; I urged him to show this to the PM. I have no idea if he acted on that note, or simply destroyed it.

In hindsight, these actions were probably quixotic. As a middle-ranking official dealing with China affairs, my effort was to mobilize serious attention to this issue, but seemingly that did not interest those in authority at that time. Perhaps we were too inhibited to take initiative. The complex story of India-China relations includes many missed opportunities, as also erroneous actions, in Beijing as also in New Delhi. Prime Minister Indira Gandhi wanted to approach China, but was also hesitant, as Brajesh Mishra had told me in Beijing. Some of the archival documents of that time have begun to emerge in India, but we know much too little of what went on in China, and almost all of their authentic official papers remain locked away.

Relations with Japan

I also dealt with Japan affairs, and two episodes from that time remain in memory. The first involved negotiation with the political counselor in the Japanese Embassy concerning a visa exemption agreement, based on a draft that had come from Japan.[3]

[3] This incident has been narrated in detail in *Inside Diplomacy*, pp. 191-3.

It provided for visa-free travel for genuine tourists, provided they did not take up work; on our side the Consular, Passports and Visa (CPV) Division, the Legal and Treaties Division and the Home Ministry (MHA) were the key players. Matters proceeded smoothly, and inter-ministry exchanges took place on file; Japan went along with most of our suggestions, until MHA threw a spanner in the works. The Indian media carried stories in those days of young women from East Europe that came as tourists and ended up working as cabaret dancers in Delhi. MHA insisted that all visa exemption agreement must mention that cabaret dance was prohibited employment for tourists; they were unmoved by the argument that this was covered automatically, when tourists were prohibited from *all* forms of employment. Japan balked at that explicit language, saying that Japanese cabaret dancers did not go to foreign countries; mentioning this in our agreement would imply that a problem existed. MHA refused to climb down and we were forced to abandon the project. The losers of course were the citizens of the two countries. That was also the first of my experiences with the obduracy of the Foreigners Division of the Home Ministry.

I received a verbal invitation from the Japanese counselor to spend two weeks in Japan, under their 'young visitor' program, as a guest, all expenses paid including air travel. I replied that it would not be ethical to accept, since I dealt directly with Japan at the MEA. He was taken aback, and said that this was the first time he had heard of anyone turning down such an invitation. I was probably idealistic, and not sufficiently practical.

By the middle of 1973, it was evident that I could not continue in the East Asia Division owning to breakdown in relations with Paranjpe. By good fortune, prospects opened up in the Northern Division, when a colleague was posted abroad; I moved to that job in October 1973. Before describing that phase, let me sketch the atmosphere in the MEA and our work style.

Life in the MEA

Lunch clubs are an old institution in the MEA, as informal gatherings of colleagues, typically of five or more, often batchmates or those close in seniority, where officials gossip, laugh and joust with one another, and develop camaraderie. A few in our group brought food from home, but most resorted to the third-rate but often quite palatable canteen food. It was over innumerable cups of tea that discussion flowered for an hour or so. A sociologist might view such gatherings as informal horizontal communication. Lots of professional ideas, and analysis of international issues of the day, emerged from these gatherings. On occasion, useful work information was exchanged, and new actions took shape. Such lunch clubs remain a hallowed institution in all ministries, especially in one peopled by a small Service, and close personal affinities.

In the mid-1960s, when I was an under secretary, we met at similar gatherings as raw, young desk-officers, but serious discussion was rare. That changed as we moved up the career ladder; as deputy secretaries and directors, we were typically second to the division heads, much preoccupied with professional issues, not just relating to our own work domains but also the manner in which the entire system worked, and what ought to be done to improve matters. We saw ourselves as the 'Young Turks' of our system, ambitious and motivated, itching to contribute to the Service improvement. One might say that this was a typical response of ambitious young officials who had lots of ideas but not the means to project these to senior personalities, much less act on these. That produced interesting consequences.

For one thing, several of us took an active interest in the affairs of the IFS Association, our official 'trade union', which by custom is always headed by the Foreign Secretary as President; over the years this Association has worked in fits and starts. In 1973-74, I served as Secretary of the Association. With no set periodicity, it typically met a few times a year, not counting meetings held to condole the demise of leading officials, or bid farewell to senior colleagues; annual dinners were also customary. Following our efforts, the Association began to hold informal tea meetings once a week, on Fridays, when seniors and juniors might drop in for conversation, absent of hierarchy. Such good ideas only worked for a while. One persistent problem was that foreign secretaries had little time or interest in the Association, and this set the tenor for other seniors as well.

Our group of Young Turks found an ally in Saad Hashmi (1935-77), of the 1958 batch, Director (Coordination), and close to Foreign Secretary Kewal Singh (1915-91).[4] With Saad's encouragement, two actions took shape. MEA sent out cipher telegrams to all embassies (also distributed to all senior officials) on major developments affecting India, to inform missions abroad; that provided material for their démarches to foreign governments. But an analysis of issues that were not of prime importance did not go out, either for circulation in the Ministry, or to missions abroad. We developed a new method: on a weekly basis, some of us working as number twos in the key territorial divisions would meet each Tuesday to discuss shaping events, to produce a 'Coordination Brief', consisting of short paragraphs on events of interest to India; each Friday, this two-page summary was distributed in the MEA, and sent to missions via the bag. I became the group convener. That worked well for a couple of years, mainly because we were compatible, keen to overcome a hiatus in information sharing in the MEA. Later, this initiative withered away. In hindsight, such collective analysis of what might be called secondary or emerging foreign affairs issues should be an established practice in any serious foreign ministry, not left to the mercy of episodic individual actions. The MEA has remained weak at horizontal communication.

The second action was more ambitious. We sought an outlet for our ideas on how the working of the MEA might be improved. Perhaps that responded to the wishes of Kewal Singh who was a new Ministry head (he became Foreign Secretary in mid-1973). Around the end of 1973, Saad told us that we could produce a set of actionable ideas, but with no official sanction; all he could promise was that the Foreign Secretary would consider our proposals. Our lunch club was energized into a brainstorming group; in early 1974, we came up with a short note consisting of 20-odd proposals (the full text is in Chapter 13). Implementing one of our proposals, the Foreign Secretary appointed KV Rajan (1965 batch) as his special assistant. In June 1975, this exercise was repeated, and a second note was produced. I was the coordinator.

---

4 Saad Hashmi died at a very young age in 1977 while serving at the Permanent Mission in New York; the IFS lost an outstanding official who had a brilliant career ahead of him.

This has been the only time in the MEA when middle rank personnel undertook such a task, aimed at systemic reform. Over the next several years, some ideas we had advanced were implemented, mainly due to the logic of circumstance; few remembered our efforts. For me, that action became an education. After leaving the Service, I have carried out research on foreign ministries. In any foreign ministry a major obstacle to reform is the entrenched establishment, which views change as a threat. In late 2013, Foreign Secretary Sujatha Singh undertook a reform effort, getting young officials to come up with suggestions. That encountered a similar fate. Reform works only when it is accompanied by strong will among decision makers to implement that change.

Northern Division

On 12 October 1973, I moved to the Northern Division as Director (North). That date is etched in memory because for the first three days, each morning the NGO section sent a steel box filled with five or six bulky Top Secret files, dealing with major, sensitive issues; on each, my predecessor had scrawled: 'Put up on 12 October, 1973'.[5] I was puzzled; the NGO assistant dealing with our papers clarified that they had another 15 or 20 files bearing that same notation; my predecessor was clearly a prevaricator of a high order, who had evaded taking action on all those papers. Some kindly soul in the NGO decided that I should not get them all in one cascade!

This Division dealt with Nepal, Bhutan and Sikkim; it also looked after the Dalai Lama, installed at the hill station Dharamsala, in handling the arrangements, assisting with his Delhi visits. Uniquely among territorial units, the Northern Division handled aid disbursement for Nepal and Bhutan; MEA's other aid activities were centralized in the Economic Division. Initially, NB Menon (1921-96) was the joint secretary, concurrently also heading the East Asia division; in early 1975, Gurbachan Singh

[5] The MEA's NGO Section deals exclusively with 'Top Secret' papers. It is formidable in efficiency, with a capacity to track down old papers, and find interconnections between different issues. It is an invaluable institutional memory resource.

(1923-2012) took over from him; both were respected colleagues. As a recently minted director, I took a rather unreasonable stand—that I should be in full charge of this division. That did not happen; Foreign Secretary Kewal Singh (who held oversight of the Northern Division) laughed away my demand, saying simply that I had been working in a relatively autonomous fashion, and that should continue. It is to the credit of these two fine senior colleagues that they gave me latitude, even if we did not always agree. Major issues always went to the Foreign Secretary for decision.

Sikkim

Sikkim was a major preoccupation at the MEA; it was handled at a policy and implementation level directly by Kewal Singh, who maintained exclusive, tightly restricted communication with the Political Officer (PO) in Gangtok, initially K Shankar Bajpai, who was succeeded in mid-1974 by Gurbachan Singh. I saw little of those exchanges. Sikkim was a dependent entity in a quasi-autonomous relationship with India, under the 1948 India-Sikkim Treaty. Under British rule, unlike Nepal and Bhutan, which had always been regarded as independent entities, Sikkim had been a member of the Chamber of Indian Princes. That it was not integrated into India in 1947-48 along with over 500 other princely states was one of the anomalies in the history of that period; in 1973-74 Sikkim was under delicate transition.

In March 1963 the Chogyal had married an American, Hope Cook; she may have played a role in his push for a more independent role for Sikkim. Around that time, the complex ethnic mix of Sikkim, composed of the small but indigenous Lepchas and Bhutias, and the more numerous Nepalese, also became a factor in its local politics, primarily the result of growing awareness and education among the people. They realized that they were caught in an anachronistic time warp, missing out on development, unlike the rest of India. For India, the choice became one of watching a hereditary Sikkim leadership distance itself from India, or working with the majority of the local population that sought closer ties with India. In geopolitical terms, the prospect of a third kingdom nestled in the Himalayas, going its own way, was unpalatable. The essence of Indian policy was to support the people of Sikkim, vis-à-vis the Chogyal, and assist them in their desire to integrate with India. Moves were accordingly initiated that took Sikkim into a closer relationship with India. This policy was implemented under the direction of Prime Minister Indira Gandhi, who personally oversaw coordinated actions with the Ministry of External Affairs, and the intelligence agencies.

I had no role on major political issues. In Gangtok, besides the PO, the head of the local administration was a senior Indian official, initially BS Das, who was succeeded in mid-1974 by BB Lal. The Foreign Secretary directly corresponded with them. Around May 1974, on the eve of K Shankar Bajpai's departure from Gangtok, I accompanied the Foreign Secretary on a three-day visit to Bhutan; on the way back we traveled from Thimpu to Gangtok by helicopter, and stayed for two days with the PO at his lovely residence.[6] I did not attend the meetings with the Chogyal, at which the PO accompanied the Foreign Secretary. One consequence of those discussions was a referendum, in which the majority of the people opted for closer association with India. That led to a constitutional amendment in October 1974 that gave Sikkim 'associate state' status.

Some months later in March 1975 the Foreign Secretary and I made the same journey, first to Thimpu and then to Gangtok; by this time Gurbachan Singh was the PO. I was given informal word that I might have to stay on in Gangtok for a week or longer, depending on events. The morning we were to leave Sikkim for Bagdogra by helicopter (to take a special aircraft to Delhi), Kewal Singh told me that I should remain at Gangtok until ordered to return; when I asked for my brief, he said simply: you are to help in carrying out the MEA's wishes. Events were moving towards an endgame.

I stayed at the PO's Residence, as a guest of Gurbachan Singh, for over two weeks. During that time I made two hurried visits to Delhi, traveling via Bagdogra and Kolkata, departing at 0500 in the morning from Gangtok and reaching Delhi at 2000 hours, for a late night meeting at the Foreign Secretary's residence (at which

---

[6] That residence, with its luxuriant gardens filled with varieties of orchids that are local to Sikkim, is now the Governor's Residence at Gangtok.

some others, including top intelligence officials attended), and then leaving early next morning on the return journey. The issues covered included evolution in local events, and the mechanics of a second referendum that was to be carried out in mid-April 1975, on the heels of the first one of October 1974, to ascertain again the wishes of Sikkim's people on their future.

After that first referendum, intense political activity had continued in Sikkim, leading to some disturbances. On 8 April 1975, the Indian Army carried out the disarming of the Sikkim Guard, a 250-strong armed force that had been trained by the Indian Army, which had also provided some officers. The Sikkim Guard owed personal loyalty to the Chogyal, and had become an object of controversy during the political upheaval, as a praetorian guard. Forcible disarming of any armed unit is fraught with danger, and the Indian units that carried out this difficult action handled themselves with restraint and abundant caution; one member of the Sikkim Guard was killed. Meticulously planned, the action was timed for the lunch hour, to minimize risk.[7] I was present during this operation at the Political Officer's office at the Residence, which became a communication nerve center; the Chogyal made frantic phone calls to the PO, who responded with calm, repeatedly advising him to adjust to the events underway. The Chogyal accepted the inevitable with a blend of anger and resignation.

This second referendum was held in April 14, 1975 and led to the full integration of Sikkim into India. With that, responsibility for its affairs passed into the hands of the Home Ministry; Chief Executive BB Lal assumed office as the first Governor of the state; what had been the Political Officer's Residence became his base, as Raj Bhawan.

India faced domestic and international criticism over the events in Sikkim, but this was a situation where 'reason of state' became the determining factor for India. Political upheaval in that sensitive region was simply not acceptable. The Chogyal's miscalculations lay at the base of the escalating difficulties that his regime faced, leading to an inevitable outcome. In retrospect, if

---

[7] The choice of that time, in broad daylight rather than during the night, was a kind of double bluff that worked well.

that time had been missed, other major political events underway in India would have precluded New Delhi from giving serious attention to Sikkim, especially the Allahabad High Court judgment of 12 June 1975, which two weeks later led to the declaration of a National Emergency on 25 June.

Bhutan and Nepal

In dealing with Bhutan, our task was to sustain and reinforce a special relationship in a manner that accommodated Thimpu's growth and development, and its international aspirations, matching evolution in its personality. King Jigme Singye Wangchuk, who had ascended the throne in 1972 at the age of 17, was wise much beyond his years, managing effectively both his personal control over his country's affairs, and stability in relations with India. He made two major visits to India during my time in the Division; I accompanied him on his travels outside Delhi. I also traveled thrice to Thimpu. Three decades later King Jigme showed much sagacity, guiding his country towards democracy in careful stages, eventually abdicating in favor of his son in 2007. Such dual transition, from monarchy to people power, and abdication in favor of his young heir while he was still in his 50s, is without precedent.

Annual discussions on Indian aid support to Bhutan, like all other bilateral discussions, were conducted in an atmosphere of open cordiality, free of tension or disagreement, and produced harmonious outcomes. The presence of a few middle rank Indian administrators in Bhutanese ministries also helped. It was the finalization of the Chukha Hydroelectric project, through a bilateral treaty signed on 28 March 1974 that became the most important action of that time. This was the first major river project in Bhutan. Thanks to that country's vast Himalayan water resources, it became the precursor to other hydro-projects.

Since it was the Planning Commission that decided on aid to Bhutan, with fund disbursement by the MEA, that same mechanism was used for discussion on the Chukha project; it involved the diversion of the river waters through an underground tunnel leading to a subterranean power station, to produce 375 MW. This was a run-of-river project, meaning that it did not involve a dam or water storage. DP Dhar (1916-75), Deputy Chairman of the Planning Commission, a senior member of the Cabinet, led the Indian team at the discussions, and took the key decisions. He enjoyed strong clout as a confidant of PM Indira Gandhi. Some international experts believed that the Himalayas were not geologically stable enough for the project; Indian experts were confident that it would be safe.

India was to provide the entire project funding, 60% as grant and 40% as a soft loan. The central issue was the pricing of the power, and the manner in which the revenue should accrue to Bhutan, rising over time. DP Dhar insisted that India had to be fair and long-sighted in this pricing. The others concerned, including Finance and Power Ministry colleagues suspected that we were being over-generous. I was in this latter cluster, while Joint Secretary NB Menon favored the liberal approach. DP Dhar prevailed, and the treaty was finalized accordingly. RC Bhargava, an outstanding senior IAS officer, then a director in the Power Ministry, provided the power cost escalation formula, using a complex mathematical formula that gave expression to DP Dhar's wishes.

Matters came to a head at the Political Affairs Committee of the Cabinet that met a few hours before formal signature, to give final Indian approval to the treaty text. That is a quaint method, since by the time a draft treaty comes before the Cabinet, negotiations have been completed, and it is too late to make changes. Equally, only a finalized document can be taken to the Cabinet, not a draft that is still open. This is one of the idiosyncrasies of the system, but real government approval comes during the negotiation process.

In the relaxed atmosphere of those days, a mere director could attend such a meeting; I was one of five or six officials present, seated at the back row, while the Cabinet Ministers (or the Ministers of State deputizing for them) sat at a long table, with the Cabinet Secretary to the PM's left. Since the External Affairs Minister was away on a foreign visit, our Minister of State, innocent of knowledge of this treaty, represented him; the Foreign Secretary was similarly out of Delhi. Prime Minister Indira Gandhi, who had been kept informed of the internal controversy, asked pointed questions at that meeting, but held her counsel, though it became evident that she did not like the terms offered. Halfway through, Joint Secretary NB Menon, the senior MEA representative, sought the PM's permission to speak; he offered an eloquent case for treating Himalayan neighbors with sensitive generosity, comprehensively defending the treaty terms. Expressing a classic liberal standpoint, he described the mountain people as simple and worthy of our trust. The PM heard him out, and moments later launched into an outburst, rare for her. She said that her concern was not so much over the terms of this particular treaty, but over the mindset with which India had handled relations with its small neighbors. We were inconsistent in actions and had often imagined that by giving away all that was demanded of us, we would win friendship. The MEA had been especially negligent in Sikkim and Nepal in the past, right from the time when her father had been Prime Minister. She emphasized that India should act with clarity in promoting its interests, in a consistent manner, treating small neighbors with fairness, but not over-generosity. Simply giving away whatever was demanded would not win lasting results or enduring friendship. DP Dhar, the target of the PM's comment, did not respond. Our Minister of State looked hapless, and kept silent. With that the treaty was approved. That evening, at a dinner to celebrate the treaty, I remarked to the Cabinet Secretary that the PM had delivered a clear set of directives on neighborhood policy, and asked if he would write on this to the ministries concerned. He smiled and turned to some other subject.

Subsequent events have proven DP Dhar entirely right in the *fair* terms offered to Bhutan in that first deal covering its hydropower resources. These terms were further improved in the mid-1990s at Bhutan's request. Chukha became the template for other power projects, starting with Chukha II. Today, these India-Bhutan projects deliver nearly 2000 MW of vitally needed power to India; the two countries are implementing several other major projects that will take the total to around 9000 MW. Already, power sales to India contribute over 20% of Bhutan's GDP, and in the near future, over half of its GDP will come from this resource.

This cooperation with Bhutan provides a stark contrast to the situation in Nepal, which is endowed with a vastly larger hydropower potential, of which around 45,000 MW can be harvested. That has remained completely unexploited over more than fifty years; Nepal has viewed the Kosi and Gandak projects of the 1950s as exploitative and unfair to their country.[8] Now, since 2014 we may be moving beyond that legacy; new India-Nepal hydroprojects are under development, but we have lost over 50 years. If even 20% of Nepal's potential hydropower capacity had been exploited, it would have transformed the destiny of that country, and provided huge benefits to India as well.[9]

Over the years, ties with Nepal have been marked by inconsistent Indian actions. This has been matched by obstinacy and distrust from Kathmandu. As the larger country, which should be capable of relatively easier adjustment in its actions, India carries the larger part of the blame for a bilateral relationship that has seldom been smooth, and almost never mutually productive. Failure to move forward on any of the India-Nepal hydropower projects is inexplicable, even indefensible. This includes not only the river projects in the interiors of Nepal, but also the projects on our shared rivers, such as the Pancheshwar.

To the best of my knowledge, we have never carried out a comprehensive examination of the India-Nepal relationship, setting out our objectives as a prelude to deciding upon both strategy and tactics. I am sure the Policy Planning Division of the MEA has written fine papers on this subject from time to time, but these have not been used as a platform for a thorough examination, across the government. We might argue that this is not the way Indians function. Proof of this lies in the collections of archival papers that have been published in 1997, covering bilateral relations with Nepal.[10]

As a director in the Northern Division in 1973-75, I carry some of that blame. It was simply not the practice in the MEA to carry out a holistic examination of major bilateral relationships, much less to produce a forward-looking set of objectives, and

---

8 See Jagat S Mehta, *Negotiating for India* (1992), p. 252.

9 In theory, Nepal's hydropower potential is estimated at 80,000 MW. About 50,000 MW of this is estimated as capable of relatively easy exploitation.

10 The India-Nepal papers have been published by its compiler-editor, AS Bhasin in five volumes. See: *Nepal-India, Nepal-China Relations Documents, 1947-June 2005* (2005).

set out the ways in which these might be attained.[11] Yes, 'policy notes' were written from time to time, by ambassadors and by the territorial divisions, but these were linked with episodes or specific circumstances. They were not guided by a comprehensive vision; equally, they did not incorporate contributions from the other key ministries and agencies directly managing bilateral issues in different functional domains. Further, it never occurred to us at the MEA that the Indian States that bordered Nepal, i.e. Bihar and UP, ought to be consulted, and brought into the bilateral relationship management process. It is to the credit of the Modi Government that after May 2014, 'cooperative federalism' has been deployed in neighborhood policy, starting with Bangladesh. That needs extension to Nepal.

Highly regarded senior IFS colleague MK Rasgotra took over as our ambassador in Kathmandu in early 1974. He has always been a strong-willed and effective individual, and initially, he projected a policy stance that was accommodative of Nepalese concerns and demands. Ambassador Rasgotra maintained an easy and open style with MEA officials at all levels and used his charm to get what he wanted; he was one of the few senior ambassadors who dealt directly with desk officers. On my visits to Kathmandu, he did not let me stay at a hotel, saying that there was ample room at India House, and that we should discuss issues informally. He was a gracious host. Rather few Indian envoys use their official residences in such a manner. After about a year in Kathmandu, he changed his line to one of rigidity towards the Nepalese. I am not sure as to the origin of that, but a factor may have been his assessment of the mood at the top levels in New Delhi, especially that of Prime Minister Indira Gandhi. For Nepal it became another instance of Indian inconsistency, and produced matching rigidity from them.

The tenor of discussion with Nepal was always friendly during that time, but a miasma of suspicion was often discernible in the way they saw us. When I paid my first visit to Kathmandu

11 Thailand is one of the few developing countries I know that carried out such a forward study of its relations with about 25 to 30 countries, during the time when Thaksin Shinawarta was Prime Minister, in the late 2000s. One may well ask how important bilateral relationships can be managed without such a master plan.

around May 1974, the Foreign Ministry organized a small excursion for me outside the capital to see a road project being built with Indian aid. At one point, my car was stranded for about an hour at a construction site, blocked behind an earthmover, which 'inconveniently' ran out of fuel. The point of that charade was to drive home to me the hardship Nepal was suffering at that time owing to a shortage of fuel, resulting from a quota regime imposed by India, after the global oil price crisis of 1973. Then, as now, all the hydrocarbon fuel to the two Himalayan kingdoms has been supplied by India as part of its domestic arrangements; in October 2015 China has become a second supplier.

A notable event was the coronation of King Birendra in July 1974. Vice President BD Jatti (1912-2002) represented India, and I was in the small team that accompanied him; high delegations from some 30-odd countries attended. China sent a vice premier, while the UK was represented by Prince Charles and Lord Mountbatten. Arrangements for so many foreign dignitaries, unprecedented for Kathmandu, were cheerfully chaotic, which everyone took in good spirit. After every public function, it took some 30 to 45 minutes for the dignitaries to leave the venue to return to their hotels and guesthouses; since each VIP limousine was escorted by several open vehicles carrying armed troops, they moved in convoy even for pickup, taking much time to assemble and depart. Lord Mountbatten, ever punctilious, visited India House, without prior appointment, and signed the guest book. Later that day, India's last Viceroy and first Governor General waved away Ambassador Rasgotra's apology for not having been at hand to receive him, saying that he still regretted that that particular stellar property could not be transformed into the British Ambassador's Residence. India naturally inherited the former British Residence at Kathmandu when colonial rule ended. The British Ambassador is housed in one of the smaller houses located at the entrance of the sprawling India House complex.

The evolution in Sikkim during 1974-75 became a factor in Kathmandu's view of India. Both Bhutan and Nepal were worried if they too might be subject to a kind of retroactive assertion of sovereignty curbs, and toughness from New Delhi. A few in the MEA might have preferred that, but it simply would not have worked. In any event, Indian policy towards both these countries remained unchanged, even if New Delhi became a little more assertive than before.

Other Activities

The Northern Division handled the arrangements for the Dalai Lama's stay at Dharamsala, a small hill station in Himachal Pradesh, the higher section of which had been transformed into a 'Little Tibet' thanks to the installation there of the growing collection of dignitaries and officials that had surrounded Tibet's spiritual leader, and the trappings they had adopted, as a 'government-in-exile'. India did not recognize any such entity. We were steadfast in acknowledging only an 'Office of the Dalai Lama', but that did not prevent the emergence of an elaborate apparatus, including a so-called *Khashag* (parliament), and a series of office-holders, all of them using Tibetan hierarchy titles. Thanks to the growing influx of Western funds that supported development, social, and educational activities, these Tibetans have become increasingly prosperous, and Upper Dharamsala is replete with foreign acolytes of the Tibetan way of life. The MEA maintains a 'Liaison Office' at Dharamsala, headed by an under secretary-level official. I made one visit to Dharamsala in 1974, to call on the Dalai Lama and meet Tibetan officials. It gave an insight into what was even then, an increasingly prosperous life enjoyed by the Tibetans there, and the influx of Western visitors that thronged to meet them, some settling in Dharamsala, for study, meditation, as well as business.

One of my jobs was to receive and see off the Dalai Lama on his visits to Delhi, and to escort him to official meetings with the President and Prime Minister, without attending any of these. That gave opportunity for conversation with this great man, full of good humor, sometimes even a little mischief. He loved to recount anecdotes, in a self-deprecating style. One story related to his visit to the British Parliament, where the Speaker hosted him at lunch. Before leading him to the dining hall, the Speaker remarked that they had prepared a special vegetarian meal for him, and was taken aback when the Dalai told him that he is not a vegetarian. 'Do you know what happened?' he asked me. Like a good counterfoil in such conversation, I responded: 'No, Your

Holiness'. 'They ate my lunch, while I ate theirs,' he replied with a loud guffaw. In a more serious vein, he spoke sometimes of how the gradual migration of some young Tibetans to Western countries that gave them refuge, say Canada and Switzerland, posed challenges to keeping alive their Tibetan heritage. Once, after meeting a high Indian dignitary he remarked how he missed the towering figures that he had met when he first arrived in India in 1959, and that one did not now find people of that stature. I replied that it could also be that one's own perspective changed over time.

I did not presume to discuss political issues with the Dalai Lama. In dealings with other Tibetan officials, we acted with sympathy, providing them with the facilities they needed, without encouraging any of their larger ambitions. This also meant holding firm to their status as honored refugees, without condoning, much less encouraging, Tibetan political or international activities. The Research and Analysis Wing (RAW), had its own network of contacts with Tibetans, and pursued their policy; at my level we had no connection with that, and the only bits of information that came to the Northern Division from RAW were routine reports of little value.

At the MEA I handled an extracurricular task. For over a year, in 1974-75 I headed the 'Junior Establishment Board' (JEB), which selected the junior-most non-diplomatic officials for postings abroad, including assistants, clerks, as also drivers to the embassies where we sent home personnel. By tradition, this Board was chaired by a director from outside the Administration, to show impartiality in these selections that were of much importance; a posting to the high-demand 'A+' assignments determined university study opportunity, subsequent employment and migration for their children. Thus, North America, the UK, Australia and New Zealand were in huge demand; our challenge at JEB was to maintain equity and impartiality; well-connected officials did their utmost to secure the best berths. JEB's recommendations went to one of the MEA's ministers of state for final approval. I insisted that we maintain the integrity of the process, and in effect ignored all recommendatory notes, and framed a slate of postings openly at the meeting in the presence of the members of the Board. That experience was to serve me well on return to the MEA Administration seven years later.

I left the MEA for Algeria in September 1975 accompanied by my family, for a first ambassador assignment. The story of how that came about is covered in the next chapter.

Endnote: Paranjpe wrote a willfully distorted 'Annual Confidential Report' on my work for 1973; the Administration Division brought this to my notice (under civil service rules adverse comment has to be shown to the affected official). While I pondered over what to do, Secretary (East) Vishnu Trivedi, supervising the non-China segments of the East Asia Division, told me that he would write a detailed repudiation of that annual report. Secretary Trivedi was a fellow-Gujarati, but that act of kindness owed more to his gentle nature than regional affiliation. Thanks to that, I was able to maintain a personal record of never having submitted a formal 'representation' or complaint to the MEA. Months later, when I encountered Paranjpe at a party at a colleague's home, I asked him why he had been so vindictive. His response: 'You may find for yourself some time how difficult it is to work with a brilliant deputy.'

6

First Ambassadorship in the Maghreb
Algeria (1975-79)

By 1975, Indian euphoria over success four years earlier in Bangladesh had evaporated; political tensions had grown within the country. Following a judgment by the Allahabad High Court that threatened to unseat the Prime Minister from her parliamentary membership Indira Gandhi proclaimed a 'National Emergency' on 26 June 1975, ostensibly to deal with a major subversive threat. The Emergency sent a shockwave through the bureaucracy, as it did across the nation. In our peer group in the Ministry, it made us cautious, as rumors swirled concerning arrests and detentions of political figures and many others. Close friends became prudent in discussing political events, though in the MEA we were largely insulated from the domestic storm. For instance, my 'car pool' colleagues, composed of close and old friends living in the Vinay Marg housing cluster, which included IAS batchmate PR (Ranga) Chari, eschewed political conversation.

I was approaching three years at the MEA and was due for an assignment abroad. Noting that Syed Shahabuddin at Algiers, two years my senior, was due for transfer, around April 1975 I made it known to Foreign Secretary Kewal Singh that I was interested in that job. A number of officials with barely 13 or 15 years in the IFS were being appointed ambassadors to new missions in the Gulf region, part of India's diplomacy drive after the 1973 oil price surge, but Algeria, a leading nonaligned player, was a bit of a stretch. I guess my performance in the Northern Division worked for me and this appointment was approved by the PM. That was a big favor, when my substantive rank was that of counselor. An unusual problem emerged as I began to prepare for this job.

The Algerian Scene

Algeria was relatively unknown in India. Under President Houari Boumediene, it strode tall on the international stage. It had hosted the 1973 Non-Aligned Summit, and showed itself adept at socialist rhetoric, which was the dominant trend within this Movement at the time. It was a mid-ranking oil producer, but played a lead role in OPEC, the oil cartel, becoming virtually its ideologue. Algeria also possessed vast reserves of natural gas, which it was in the process of valorizing, building trans-Mediterranean pipelines to Italy and Spain, and setting up gas liquefaction plants for transport to distant markets, Japan and the US. Unlike other oil states that squandered their wealth in ostentation, it was building a diversified industrial base, though that too represented a misallocation of resources, of a different kind.

Algeria won independence in 1963 after a harsh, protracted armed struggle against French colonialism, from 1954 to 1962. It was estimated that out of a population of 10 million at the time, upwards of half a million lost their lives, and around three million were uprooted from their homes and land, mainly owing to a French policy of creating broad *cordons sanitaires*, stretching along the land frontiers of Morocco and Tunisia. Virtually no family was untouched by this epic struggle, which had reshaped the Algerian psyche. In the developing world, other than Vietnam, no other country had paid so much for its independence.

The film *Battle of Algiers* (1966) graphically captures the pervasiveness of this war, in which schoolgirls acted as couriers and planted bombs.[1] At its root was the French myth that Algeria was not a colony, even while located across the Mediterranean Sea, but was a part of 'metropolitan France'. It was home to over one million 'colons', migrant Frenchmen who ran the country, not only as overlords but also as its workers, restaurant staff, petty civil

---

1 Alistair Horne's book *A Savage War of Peace* (1978) gives an excellent account of the Algerian struggle for independence.

servants, farmers and taxi-drivers. Unlike British colonies where locals were co-opted in running the country, and therefore had to be educated in administration and the professions, the colons played all these roles. Consequently there were no institutions of higher learning, and rather few schools. As Minister of Heavy Industry Mohammed Liassine once told me, at independence, the country had six graduate engineers—he was one of that cluster.

After independence, Algerians gained a reputation for dourness and rigidity, and were considered to be difficult negotiators, forever suspicious of foreigners, and rooted in leftist ideology. The writings of Franz Fanon provided their worldview. The country practiced socialism in which the private sector was largely decimated, apart from small enterprises and a few businesses run by those who were well connected. After Colonel Houari Boumediene overthrew the leading architect of independence, Ben Bella in 1965, a cabal of seven colonels, each heading a vast military region, ran the country through the 'Revolutionary Council'; with one or two exceptions, they remained in the background. The ministers were mostly technocrats, and President Boumedienne headed the cabinet. Abdelaziz Bouteflika was the effective and articulate foreign minister.[2] The offices of vice-president or prime minister did not exist; nor was there any constitutional provision for an interim head of state, which led to complications in 1978.

An Unusual Incident

Ambassador Shahabuddin landed himself in a bizarre incident in July 1975, when he and his family received bullet injuries at the hands of a soldier guarding a villa in the rural vicinity of Algiers.[3] Driving his personal car, accompanied by his wife and daughter, he had gone on a Sunday drive. Seeking a place for a picnic lunch, they chanced upon a side road that led up, curving behind a hill, with no structure visible from the main

---

2 He has proved to be a great survivor, and is currently Algeria's President, having held this office since 1999.

3 I wrote a full account of this incident in a series of three articles published in *Asian Age* in July 1998, then published out of Delhi and London.

road. The gate was partly open, with a standard 'route closed' road sign. Shahabuddin chose to ignore this and drove up. As he rounded the bend, he encountered a barrier blocking the road, guarded by an armed soldier, who told him that he had entered a restricted area and must await an officer he had summoned. The Ambassador identified himself, producing his diplomatic identity card, and attempted to turn back. The soldier said that he did not know anything about that identity card, and the visitor must wait for his superior officer. When Shahabuddin argued that he enjoyed diplomatic immunity and could not be stopped, the soldier pointed his sten gun and said that he would open fire to prevent the Ambassador from leaving. The Ambassador ignored this threat and began to turn his car around; the soldier shouted a warning and when he did not stop, he opened fire. Some bullets hit the roof of the Ambassador's Peugeot 504, and small metal fragments of hit Shahabuddin in the head; his daughter was wounded in the neck. They were then transported to the main military hospital in Algiers and the colonel heading the military region and other officials visited the Ambassador to assure him of the best of treatment. True to character, Algerians expressed regret at the incident, but did not apologize, or openly explain the situation. Of course, the tightly controlled Algerian media carried no news, and the incident did not leak in the world press.

That secluded residence to which the Ambassador chanced upon had unusual significance, but no one was willing to speak of this. Many years later my Algerian friends privately confirmed what had long been suspected, that Ben Bella was being held there. It transpired that the former president was moved from one location to another during his two decades of house arrest. That time he happened to be at that unmarked villa.

For reasons unknown, Shahabuddin reported the incident to New Delhi via an open cablegram; a cipher telegram was more effective and would automatically have gone to the top authorities, including the Prime Minister. His open, commercial channel message took two days to reach its recipient, the Additional Secretary (Administration). Shahabuddin had earlier surrendered the Embassy's telex link, as a quixotic gesture of economy; a direct phone call to India was difficult and was not attempted.[4] Consequently, the news filtered to Delhi indirectly, via our Embassy in Paris and the Algerian Ambassador in Delhi. Lacking our Ambassador's report, an immediate reaction of outrage over the shooting had passed by the time his message reached India; by then the mood had changed to treating him as partly culpable. An enduring professional moral: getting one's story to headquarters, accurately and honestly, is crucial. Failing to do that, one cannot hope to control subsequent developments.

By chance, the MEA's instructions to seek my *agrément* had reached Shahabuddin a couple of days prior to this incident, but he had not taken action. After he was released from hospital, Shahabuddin took the stand that to show disapproval towards the Algerian government, the post should be left vacant for several months after his departure. New Delhi did not agree, pointing out that the shooting incident was not a willful gesture. Nor did it support the Ambassador's contention that the subsequent contretemps over his hospital treatment merited such action. Shahabuddin dragged his feet over the *agrément*; the MEA then took the unusual step of forwarding my nomination through the Algerian ambassador in Delhi; Algerian approval came in a matter of days. Such a move is contrary to custom, and often signifies disagreement with the envoy who is at his post overseas. Thus, my predecessor left in late-July 1975; I reached my post in mid-September.

Preparation

I undertook the customary pre-assignment *Bharat Darshan* tour, accompanied by Mimi, travelling to Mumbai and other cities, meeting business chambers and others, but found that few had real connections with Algeria, given the limited bilateral trade, and even less by way of education or cultural connection.[5] One of the entities I met in Delhi was the Association of Indian Engineering Industry, headed by Tarun Das; one could then anticipate that it

[4] Ambassador Shahabuddin could have easily telephoned the Indian Ambassador in Paris and requested him to urgently transmit news to New Delhi. It remains a mystery why he failed to convey news of this shocking event to the MEA with the required urgency.

[5] In those days, our annual two-way trade was less than $10 million.

would undergo remarkable growth, to become a powerhouse of Indian business, and that over the next 20 years it would become a prime source of support in developing economic partnerships at all my foreign assignments.[6]

In a recent work, *The Contemporary Embassy (2013)* I described my meeting with the Prime Minister, before leaving for Algiers:

> Prime Minister Indira Gandhi gave me [instructions] in September 1975, at my pre-departure interview for newly appointed ambassadors that was customary in those days.[7] She was in the midst of reading some papers, which she put down, turned her attention to Algeria and said:
>
> I have warm recollections of my visit to Algiers for the Non-Aligned Summit (held in 1973). President Boumediene is an important leader, and we enjoy good political understanding. But that is good as far as it goes. Your task should be to work to develop an economic relationship that is commensurate with that.

For me, that clear advice on primacy to economic work, and its link with political relations, became a guiding principle for the rest of my career.

Because of the delay in moving to the new post, I had ample time to study the few dossiers and limited data in Delhi on this assignment. The Algerian Ambassador in New Delhi, Omar Oussedik, became an invaluable information source; he was a veteran of the independence struggle and I spent several hours in conversation with him, besides attending a customary welcome dinner. I learnt from him especially the value of treating the counterpart ambassador in the home capital as an ally, even a resource, for building strong relations in the assignment country. At subsequent appointments that proved to be useful;

---

6 AIEI of those days is today's Confederation of Indian Industry (CII), a major promoter in the internationalization of Indian business. Tarun Das has been a key figure in India's economic diplomacy. See: Das, *Crossing Frontiers* (2015).

7 In those days, junior ambassadors were not given a fixed appointment or listed on the PM's schedule, but were simply asked to come on a particular day, to 'take a chance'. Since then the practice of all ambassadors designate meeting the head of government has withered away, not just in India.

the counterpart can give insight, and is often helpful to overcome blockages in his country.[8]

First Impressions

Initial appointment as a head of mission, even to a small embassy, is a huge challenge and opportunity. All of a sudden there is no one available to discuss one's doubts, or use as a sounding board; one cannot locally find a peer who can be trusted. And of course, events seem to unfold relentlessly. This dilemma is acute in a first ambassadorship. Communications to one's headquarters improve continually, and yet isolation is not eliminated. The analogy of a ship's captain first came to me at that time; the home establishment is available for counsel, but they are always busy with their own affairs, and cannot visualize the local context. Any tempest in that country mainly becomes one's own affair.[9] That does make for quick learning.

Algeria was a highly politicized country, steeped in the ideological idiom of Franz Fanon. I used to go to a barbershop opposite our chancery, which was on the 4th floor of a building of some 10 floors on Rue Didouche-Mourad, an arterial road that led to the commercial district and the *Kasbah*, the old town, but got tired of the barber's political lectures, and usually opted for a hair trim from Mimi, after she mastered that skill with our children. The country saw itself as a natural leader of developing states, and internationally punched above its weight. Its attitude towards France was ambivalent; it profoundly distrusted Paris, given its colonial experience, but was at the same time entrapped in that milieu. Example: Algeria is the largest French-speaking country that has opted to remain outside Francophonie. But despite Boumediene's efforts to promote Arabic, French remained the language of usage; *Le Monde* was widely read among the intelligentsia. The Soviet Union held a privileged position, but did not dominate. China was in a favored position; India was much admired, but mutual exchanges were limited. Boumediene never

---

8 This interplay and direct relationship between counterpart envoys is one of the under-studied aspects of the diplomatic profession.

9 That analogy with a ship's captain is a central theme of my book *The 21st Century Ambassador: Plenipotentiary to Chief Executive* (2004).

visited India, though Foreign Minister Bouteflika had traveled to Delhi.

The Indian Embassy in Algiers was small, consisting of a first and a second secretary, and two attachés, besides five home-based staff and five local staff. When I arrived, Arvind Dave was a first secretary and had held charge as Chargé d'Affaires; his father had taught at the Rajkumar College. An outstanding IFS colleague Satish Chandra came in 1976 as counselor. We also had a fine Indian interpreter, K Balakrishnan, exceptionally helpful. I had a smattering of French when I reached Algiers, thanks to three years in Geneva, and quickly realized that speaking it in Algeria was a matter of survival. I also found that taking Bala with me to interpret at social receptions led to embarrassment; much older, he was often taken to be the ambassador and I his interpreter!

The Residence was in the tony El-Biar district on the hillside, an elegant but small Moorish villa with extensive grounds; its main drawback was its tiny salon, into which one could just about fit in 12 to 14 guests, as long as they did not move about; in contrast, the dining room was comparatively spacious. The courtyard could accommodate 200 at a reception.

I was received in Algeria with special cordiality, affirming indirectly that the shooting incident was a closed chapter, and that we should move forward. That welcome was tempered with typical Algerian idiosyncrasy. When I asked for a customary first call on the Foreign Ministry Chief of Protocol to hand over the initialed copies of my credential papers, the response was: 'That is not possible, since the ambassador has not yet presented his credentials.' (In my four years, I never met him, not even at a social function). I met the Deputy Chief of Protocol, and had an especially cordial meeting with the Director of the Asia Division, who also looked after nonaligned affairs, Abdurrehman Bensid, who became a close friend. One of his first remarks: You seem younger than me! He was relieved to find that though we were both 38, he was younger by a few months. He warned me of secretive working style that Algerians practiced, dating from their liberation struggle; an official would typically not even tell his wife where he was headed when he went out. The indirect message was: go slowly, do not expect too much.

It was easy to meet ministers and the secretaries-general heading ministries. Dr. Taleb Ibrahimi, Minister of Culture and Information, gave an exceptional welcome. He spontaneously offered that if I ever ran into difficulty in Algeria, he was available for assistance; I did not have occasion to redeem that blank check. He had much warmth towards India, partly because an Indian scholar had taught his father, a notable figure in his day.[10] I benefited much from all these early encounters, and understood that the environment was conducive for a transformed bilateral relationship. With political ties excellent, economic cooperation had to be the first arena for action.

During the customary calls on diplomatic colleagues, I learnt how foreign envoys perceived Algeria. Some chose to keep a distance from officials, whom they perceived as arrogant, even reclusive. It was the British ambassador who provided trenchant advice; reiterating a widely held view that Algerians were suspicious of all foreigners, he said that a new envoy should expect to be under scrutiny for about two years, while they made up their minds if he could be trusted. Passing muster, he would then find all manner of doors opening up. That turned out to be accurate. While it was possible to initiate useful actions in that first period, it was almost exactly after two years that real personal friendships with officials began to flourish, with invitations to their homes, and convivial *Ramadan* receptions where one made many new contacts. I also observed that at the first few of those social gatherings one usually met a captain or major from the Army, silent and watchful, but that scrutiny ended after some months. That made our fourth and final year in Algeria, my longest foreign assignment, especially productive.

Indians in Algeria

The Indian community was miniscule, but became a source of much information and indirect support. That experience drove home the message that the size of a diaspora is not important; in different situations, it has potential for support to the Embassy.

---

10 When Dr. Ibrahimi visited India in 1977, he specially requested a visit to Lucknow, to visit the final resting place of his father's teacher.

Three Sindhi families had made their home in Algeria some 20 years earlier. Among them, the Mirpuris and the Budhranis became our good friends. Rani, just moving out of her teens, daughter of Roopchand Mirpuri, adopted Mimi as her elder sister; that friendship remains evergreen after 40 years. Another key ally was a lady doctor, Dr. Vengaswami from Pondicherry, unmarried, who had for long made her home in Algiers. An invaluable source for understanding the economic dynamics of the country was found in Altaf Nazerali, originally from East Africa, now a Canadian citizen; he headed the Algiers office of a major US company that was executing a massive project to set up a TV and consumer electronics plant. He gave valuable insight into the working of state enterprises and the country's economic system, and saved me from errors as well.

By the time we left in 1979 there were nearly a thousand Indians in Algeria, doctors, teachers and other professionals who came on individual employment contracts or to execute projects, but that gets ahead of my story.

Economic Activity

State enterprises dominated the Algerian economy; the private sector was confined to small retail commerce and distribution of some materials, but engaged in little by way of manufacture, except through small enterprises. The country had adopted a socialist model in its own fashion. Each state enterprise exclusively dominated an entire industrial sector; for instance, SNS was the steel monopoly, while SNMetal handled all other mineral products. Besides manufacture or processing, these monopolies also handled all imports for their sector, which meant that their inefficiencies in manufacture and services could be hidden under the huge profits from imports. The Soviet Union was the model, though Algeria also had extensive dealings with Western companies.

The windfall gains from the 1973 oil price surge were ploughed into an ambitious plan for rapid industrialization, unlike other countries where oil income went into prestigious building projects, or directly into the pockets of the leaders and their coterie. Corruption existed in Algeria, as in much of the Arab and developing world, but it was largely a '10 percent' country—its officials were highly competent and were committed to the country's advancement. Another feature: their paranoia over being cheated by foreign partners produced delays in decision-making, a situation rather familiar to us Indians.

In practice, the Algerian model showed another facet of the danger of petrodollar-inspired wealth. The technocrat elite hated their dependence on foreign business partners, and thought that they could buy their way to mastering technology for the country's advancement. In its own way, that produced an illusion that was not radically different from what other countries were trying to do with their grandiose mosques and public projects. Astute Algerian negotiators did manage to get access to both modern equipment and technology in their foreign contracts, but they simply did not have the technical infrastructure, nor professional human resources in the required numbers and depth, to shift out of reliance on borrowed technology. One simply could not buy one's way to industrial self-reliance.

SONATRACH was a giant company that straddled the entire hydrocarbon sector, from prospection of oil and gas, to production, refining, distribution, and export. SONACOME handled the mechanical industry in its entirety, as did SONELEC for the entire electric and electronic industry. SONELGAZ was the power, water and consumer gas supply monopoly. Competent professionals ran them, proud of their technological savvy; they tended to be aggressive, even domineering with foreign partners, driven by their political conviction that Western enterprises were out to exploit the 'Third World', a favorite expression of those days in the Francophone world. By 1978 Indian enterprises were in close association with all these four companies.

My predecessor, Ambassador Shahabuddin had worked hard to finalize what was to become India's first project in Algeria, the supply and installation of two electric sub-stations. Tata Exports, the international arm of the Tata group had pursued this for some time with the Algerian state monopoly SONELEC; unusually, he had relied upon his private secretary, Ranjit Singh, an Attaché, as the point of contact with junior officials in that local company; this had worked well; he saw the task as special, and tackled it with zeal.[11] I learnt later that around the same time in Libya, Ambassador Arjun Asrani had relied upon my old colleague Shahdadpuri, then an Attaché, for vital economic outreach to Libyan state enterprises. I continued with that arrangement and occasionally used my representation grant to cover Ranjit's entertainment. After much delay, that contract was signed in 1977, when the Indian side overcame two major obstacles.[12]

In late 1977, after the Tata Export contract had been signed, I visited Mumbai as their guest (with the MEA's approval), to discuss other business prospects in Algeria. I was invited to lunch at Bombay House, seated opposite JRD Tata; this lunch, attended by the heads of major Tata companies was a daily practice. Observing that discussion was forthright, and that I might not get such a chance again, I said to JRD: 'Sir, viewed from a remote corner of Africa, one gets the impression that often the Indian public sector is more dynamic than private enterprises.' JRD interjected: 'Do you mean the private sector in general or the Tata enterprises?' I then responded in detail, explaining how Tata Electric almost pulled out of the project because the Algerian client had decided to purchase circuit-breakers in bulk (a major chunk of the contract) from Merlin Gerin, rather than from Tata Merlin-Gerin. It would have been a disaster for India if this first industrial contract had been abandoned. The powerful head of Tata Electric was present and heard me out in silence. Alas, that did not prompt the Tata group to undertake further efforts in my time to enter Algeria, but they moved in well in subsequent years. The real problem was the prevailing ethos in India, a relative passivity to international business opportunities. The moral: to gain market entry, one had to be satisfied with a cake that might turn out to be smaller than initially anticipated. After the pain of learning all the hard first lessons in a new market, one had to persevere, winning larger contracts down the road, and not give up.

---

[11] Details in *Inside Diplomacy* (2000), pp. 109-10.

[12] See *Economic Diplomacy: India's Experience* (2012), pp. 109-10.

Industrial and Project Cooperation

HMT, the Indian state enterprise that straddled a product range from machine tools to agricultural equipment, even wristwatches, was one of the stars of the public sector. A few months after reaching Algiers, I received a cable from its charismatic CEO, Dr. SM Patil, asking if the Embassy would support their efforts to gain market entry; our telex connection had not then been restored, and I replied immediately by cable; when this reached Bangalore, Dr. Patil is supposed to have said: let us work there, the Indian Ambassador seems to be our kind of person. R Yogeshwar, HMT's director based in Luxembourg, a person of remarkable wit and drive, came to Algiers, and that launched a transformative relationship.

Our economic marketing took off earnestly with our first-ever participation in the Algiers Fair of October 1976. Yasmin Saifullah (*née* Khan) was the energetic director of the Indian pavilion; she ensured that the HMT lathe on display received its required high-voltage power connection, working as a demonstrator for our visitors. President Boumediene chose the Indian pavilion as one of the few he saw. Algerian friends observed on seeing that lathe: India is clearly a serious industrial player. After the Fair, we sold the first Indian machine tool in Algeria; today, HMT's machine tool population in that country has crossed 500.

HMT won our first industrial contract in early 1977, to provide technical management of a machine tool plant that SONACOME had bought from Germany, which it found difficult to operate. HMT dispatched 15 engineers from India, to work alongside Algerian counterparts; the overall management remained with the latter. That kind of deal could work only if the two sides had mutual confidence. A year later, SONACOME asked HMT to provide similar services for two more industrial plants; by then Dr. SM Patil had retired and the new management lacked vision. Possibly, HMT found it difficult to locate the requisite talent to take on these project assignments, but we lost the opportunity to scale up our Algeria engagement.

In parallel, HMT began work in 1977 on a turnkey project bid for SONELGAZ (a utility provider, with no manufacturing experience), for a plant to manufacture electricity, gas and water meters. That complex deal involved four Western companies: two providing technology, another building the gas meter plant, plus a consultant acting as adviser to SONELGAZ. HMT, at that time, had never even bid for an international project; they decided to treat their offer as a training exercise, with little expectation of success. NK Krishnan Kutty, an exceptional technocrat, led that team. HMT ended up winning the contract. Their project execution was meticulous and added luster to India's reputation. HMT even helped the client on issues outside its contract. At one meeting with all the foreign partners, SONELGAZ declared that while they were all performing their contractual obligations, it was this Indian company that had uniquely shown commitment to the success of the entire project.

Engineers India Ltd (EIL) was another state enterprise that shone in Algeria, and that came about by accident. I was on a visit to the port city of Arzew, which was the site of SONATRACH's first gas liquefaction plant, where two more massive plants were planned. At the site, I mentioned to the Director that India had a major hydrocarbon consultancy company that employed about 1000 engineers (I was wrong; the figure in 1977 was 1700). He replied: 'Why have I never heard of it?' I replied that our countries had been victims of two different colonizers, and inhabited different language worlds. He could not believe that no one in India read *Le Monde*; their advertisements seeking consultants for the LNG-2 and LNG-3 plants had escaped our notice. He pulled out from a desk drawer the bid papers for LNG-2; I sent these to EIL. Cutting short that story, EIL ended up winning; its task was to help SONATRACH with quality of engineering and cost control on the project. The lead partner was Foster Wheeler, being paid on a 'cost-plus' basis, which made cost monitoring critical. Two months after work began, an elated SONATRACH official told me that whatever the outcome over the next 22 months, they were already winners, as EIL had saved them much more money than the value of their contract. EIL managed this in harmony with Foster Wheeler, discreetly giving them space for corrective measures, as needed. That laid for EIL the foundation for a succession of contracts in Algeria, plus a burgeoning international reputation.

Not every economic bid worked. Two actions were unproductive, despite much effort. A steel industry consultancy enterprise, MECON, held several rounds of discussion with SNS, the steel monopoly, and at the Arab Iron and Steel Union, based in Algiers. The chief executive of MECON's repeat visits produced no results. Another Indian state enterprise that failed was the Mining and Allied Machinery Corporation (MAMC), headed by a dynamic CEO, PC Luther. They pursued a thin-seam coalmine project in the interior of the country; when it became clear that this would be a deep-shaft mine, to win high-quality coal in seams barely 70cm wide, it became obvious that the project was unviable; MAMC's hopes of selling mining machinery proved futile.

The key point in the above narrative is that these Indian enterprises gained the confidence of Algerian clients, in a charged and difficult atmosphere. India drew the attention of Western enterprises; they were not pleased at the arrival of a developing country competitor, not a member of their 'club'. This produced blocking effort by leading Western companies to undermine the reputation of Indian companies. Little was openly in evidence, but disinformation was the name of that game. I also saw this later in Kenya and Mauritius. On the flip side, developing states saw the value of giving contracts to companies from fellow developing countries, provided they had the requisite competence; they could not claim special benefits. This has remained a practical dimension of South-South cooperation.

Indian Cinema and Culture in North Africa

India's relative ignorance of North Africa was a limiting factor beyond the economic arena. Yet, we found that even in the 1950s, a few Indian films had somehow breached the geography and language barrier, and reached these states; in Algeria such films had provided cultural and *political* inspiration to a people then immersed in a relentless liberation struggle. In those days, no organized export of Indian films took place; perhaps no one saw much value in it, in that pre-TV, pre-NRI diaspora age.[13]

[13] NRI refers to 'non-resident Indians' the catchall term by which India refers to its diaspora, though in the strict sense, it should not include the descendants of those who migrated out of India some generations back, either as sugar plantation workers or as business entrepreneurs.

Virtually by chance, a few Indian film prints reached the Lebanon, where they were sub-titled in French and Arabic; they went on to Egypt and the Maghreb countries; later, the sub-titling shifted to Morocco. Perhaps these were pirated prints, but in those days of rigid Indian foreign exchange controls, no one could be sure.

For the Algerians, then immersed in their brutal war against French colonialism, these films were a breath of fresh air, proof that former colonies could enjoy lives of normalcy that gave full play to universal human emotions, beyond the quotidian atrocities they faced—remember, Algeria in the 1950s saw the first modern liberation struggle in which bombings of cafés and cinema halls filled with civilians were a legitimate activity in the wisdom of the time, though suicide-bombers lay in the future. Thus the Indian classic *Aan* became a blockbluster, across North Africa, with the only difference that the film had been re-titled *Mangala,* after its heroine.

For Algerians of that age, that particular film evoked unique nostalgia. I was told on good authority that if I could get a print of that movie, even the reclusive President Boumediene would come to a screening. Alas, my efforts to obtain a copy through the MEA proved futile; I guess no one in Delhi saw mileage in making that effort.

Another film that had almost equal impact was a 1960s low-budget, medium success of the Indian industry, *Aa Gale Lag Ja,* starring Shashi Kapoor and Sharmila Tagore; in its North African incarnation, the film became *Jaane Tuu,* after its lead song. Again, the chance arrival of this film produced an incredible hit in Algeria, and only to a slightly lesser extent in the neighboring countries as well. When sari-clad Indian embassy ladies went to the Central Market to buy vegetables, they frequently encountered youngsters not only chanting the film's songs, but on occasion, even lines of dialogue, parroting a language that they did not understand one bit!

Our efforts to get Delhi to pay attention to the small Algerian market produced response. In 1977 we received a film delegation, led by Dharmendra, then at his career peak, and the splendid director of humorous movies, Basu Chatterjee. Alas, none of Dharmendra's films had reached the Maghreb, so he was an unknown quantity to the locals. The films they brought were successful, but failed to reach mass audiences. Dharmendra seemed bemused to find himself at a place where no one seemed to know him.

We had better luck with dance and music. For three successive years we received weeklong visits by composite 10 and 12-member Indian classical dance and music groups, as part of their tour to Europe and North Africa after a customary annual tour of the UK. By the time they reached Algeria, these groups, composed of dancers in the Bharatanatyam, Kathak and Odissi idiom had honed well their integrated performances and Algerian audiences received them with much enthusiasm, in the capital and other cities. Several have gone on to become our present-day icons, including Madhvi Mudgal, Leela Sampson, Aditi Merchant, as well as musician Madhup Mudgal.

The Indian Emergency and its Echoes

A day after I reached Algiers, Mohammed Yunus (1916-2001), Special Envoy of PM Indira Gandhi, arrived carrying a message from the PM addressed to President Houari Boumediene, explaining the rationale of the Emergency. As an ambassador-designate, who had not even handed over the initialed copies of credential papers to the Foreign Ministry, I was invisible in that rather *protocolaire* capital, with its rigid rules.[14] It was Chargé d'Affaires Arvind Dave that accompanied him to his meetings, including a call on the President. In India, Yunus evoked respect, even fear, given his proximity to the Indian PM, besides his blunt and brusque manner; in those Emergency days he rode high. I got along well with him, and he enjoyed recounting his tales of early days in Algeria, in the mid-1960s, when he had served as ambassador, playing the role of mentor-guide to a brand new

[14] In most capitals the custom is that once the initialed documents are handed over (usually within a few days after reaching the new assignment), the 'ambassador designate' can call on officials of the host country, but not ministers or personalities of higher rank; that must await formal presentation of credentials. Today, most countries have relaxed these provisions, in part because credential ceremonies can be delayed by several weeks, even a few months.

ambassador. I also enjoyed his fund of humorous stories, about his family, and the Nehru days when as a young well-connected MEA official, he was lodged at the PM's residence.

At our isolated oasis in North Africa, we were far removed from the harsh reality of the Indian Emergency; the Algerian government, with its tightly state-controlled media, was solidly in favor of Indira Gandhi. Yet, a flavor of the Emergency reached us during the October 1976 meeting of the Club of Rome held in Algiers, at the luxurious coast-side *Club du Pins* convention center, built for the 1973 Non-Aligned Summit. In those days, that international thinktank evoked much attention, having just produced its apocryphal report, 'The Limits of Growth', which later came to be seen as both alarmist and unsound.[15]

An odd collection of Indians turned up for this event. There was a government-sponsored delegation from India; some economists and others were also invited in their individual capacity, including Prof. Sukhomoy Chakrabarti, former member of the Planning Commission, who had opted to go to the Netherlands for the duration of the Emergency. Ideologically and politically poles apart, this group came together during lunch and recess times at the three-day event, to chat informally and gossip, and I spent much time with them. One question posed to me was: how was it that the Algerians, not known for intellectual achievement, had managed to entice the Club of Rome to come to them for an annual session? I replied that they had great organizational capacity, and worked together for such events. Remarked one Indian interlocutor—it is the latter quality that is always scarce at home.

Anticipating New Delhi's anxiety over how India might have been portrayed at this gathering, at a time of pervasive Western criticism of the Emergency, I sent off a detailed report on the conference by cipher telegram the evening it ended. True enough, my message crossed with an urgent query from Delhi. As it happened, India had not figured at all at the conference discussions.

---

[15] For an account of this meeting, please see: http://www.itnsource.com/shotlist//RTV/1976/10/27/BGY510090417/?s=*

In January 1977, I attended my first and only conference of ambassadors held in New Delhi—25 of us, located in the capitals of West Asia and North Africa had been summoned.[16] PM Indira Gandhi opened the meeting, feisty in spirit, defending the Emergency which was 'forced' on her by the campaign organized by the opposition; I do not recall if Jayprakash Narayan was named, but that was the official line, repeated endlessly by the government at that time. Foreign Secretary Jagat Mehta echoed that theme. After the PM's impromptu remarks, ambassadors were invited to state their concerns, from the perspective of their locations. One ambassador, I think it was Ashok Chib (1930-2002), spoke of the difficulty in projecting our official line in the face of criticism that democratic India had compromised on its values; he urged that early elections were important. Three or four ambassadors found the courage to echo that, mostly in gentle and elliptical fashion. I spoke up to suggest that one problem we faced was that the different ministries did not fully appreciate the value of engaging with foreign countries; an example was the limited attention that All India Radio gave to its external services, which could not be received in North Africa. Indira Gandhi heard us out, and responded in good humor. She said that some of the concern in foreign countries was understood; India had not abandoned democracy. Turning to those that spoke of early elections, she asked if it was necessary for her to announce elections at this conference! As it happened, the general election of March 1977 was announced on the evening of the last day of our conference.

A footnote to that conference: at the end of the first day's working session, I put forward a suggestion that we should come up with our recommendations as a group, for consideration by the MEA and the government. When Jagat Mehta heard about this move at the evening's dinner, he asked: who suggested this? Given my name, he said: I thought as much. Nothing came of that; those in authority in India have institutionally been averse to new ideas and feedback.

---

[16] In December 1992, I was among the envoys invited to another ambassador's conference in Delhi. Unfortunately, it coincided with the destruction of Babri Masjid; on the opening day we were all instructed to return to our assignments, to deal with its aftermath.

Indira Gandhi's election defeat and the appointment of the Janata government produced limited turbulence in the Indian diplomatic establishment. In Algeria, our friends were bewildered at the sudden defeat of an iconic figure they knew so well. They were also surprised that an entire community of officials, including ambassadors, who had represented the previous government, could so easily 'shift loyalty' to the opposition that was now in power. The notion of civil service neutrality was completely alien to them. To be honest, that was also India's first experience with such a transition.

About a year later in 1978, Sikandar Bhakt (1918-2004), Minister of Works and Housing, visited Algiers as a special envoy. Receiving him, President Boumediene said: 'India is a great country and we have no intention of interfering in your domestic affairs; but Indira Gandhi has been an outstanding leader not only of India but of the Third World, and we hope she will be treated with the respect she deserves.' Bhakt responded that there were domestic political issues being pursued against her regime, but there was no question of her arrest, as some had speculated. Directly after the meeting, he came to the Residence for a cup of tea, and listening to the BBC, our indispensible news source, we heard of her arrest. Bhakt let out a string of choice oaths, lamenting the timing of that move in New Delhi.

For the great part, neither the Emergency, nor its end, and the arrival of the first non-Congress government in New Delhi affected life in embassies abroad in any significant manner, apart from transfers of a handful of ambassadors and others closely identified with the former regime. The MEA did send out politically motivated instructions on the line that embassies were to project to the country of accreditation, but most of us soft-pedaled this, for the simple reason that rather few countries were deeply interested in India's internal politics. Western capitals, especially in the Anglo-Saxon world, were the exception, because of feverish reaction by journalists and others that saw themselves as India experts, but I did not observe that first hand.

Cooperation Actions

In 1977 I wrote a first 'annual action plan', a collection of some 15-odd bullet points, setting out what seemed to be worthy objectives to pursue, in political, economic, cultural and other fields, over a 12-month horizon. I sent this to the MEA, but it drew zero comment. At the end of that year, an evaluation was written out, candidly setting out the things accomplished and those that were not, with brief comments, and that too met with silence from New Delhi. I rationalized that this did not matter, as the object was to keep our focus on needed actions.

By then a number of dossiers on project proposals initiated by Indian companies were in play; I wrote a report every six months, summarizing developments on each significant proposal, plus listing new activities underway, excluding anything commercially sensitive for any of the companies. This was prefaced with an overview of economic developments in Algeria and the outlook. It typically ran to four pages. Initially these were sent to the ministries involved, and to state enterprises, but subsequently we also sent copies to the private Indian companies that were main actors, on the premise that they had every right to useful contextual information. It may surprise some, but neither the official agencies, nor the companies mentioned in our reports, objected to such information sharing. I continued with that practice of producing a six-monthly summary of bilateral economic activities at my subsequent five foreign assignments.

As these reports focused on bilateral activities, an edited summary of the main dossiers, especially proposals that were in the pipeline, was also handed over to the Algerian ministers directly involved. One of them looked at the list of 10-odd projects and remarked that if by the time I left, if even three or four were realized, I should be satisfied. As it turned out, I stayed longer in Algeria than intended, and when I left, about 12 projects on the first two lists had reached fruition, and were under implementation.

During 1977 we became involved at the Ministry of Heavy Industry with an over-ambitious project. Under the inspiration of Soviet advisers in that ministry (the total number of such advisers was unknown), a big project was drawn up, called *Complexe Electro-Mécanique Lourd*, with the acronym 'CEMEL'. It involved the replication of what the Soviet Union had persuaded Indian planners to implement in the 1960s, through our state-enterprises BHEL, HEC, MAMC and others, to manufacture heavy industrial equipment. The key difference was the size of India and Algeria, to say nothing of the domestic engineering and professional expertise to support such massive undertakings. Lachmi Boujemeline, Secretary General of the Heavy Industry Ministry, who by then was a close friend, first mentioned this project to me. My straight reply to him was that Algeria did not possess the market demand to support such an ambitious production complex, nor the requisite abundance of technical expertise; their Soviet friends were leading them up the garden path.

In mid-1978, Heavy Industry Minister Mohammed Liassine visited India; we sent a formal invitation when we were told of his interest, to visit Indian enterprises and hold discussions. We refused their request to bring with them a couple of Soviet advisers, saying that we treated such exchanges as strictly bilateral, and not open to any third country, however friendly. They had not anticipated such a response, but accepted it in good cheer.

The Algerian Minister's discussions with his counterpart, Industry Minister George Fernandes were uneventful, but one small incident revealed to me the awe this Minister inspired. I asked Industry Ministry officials if senior Tata officials, who had come from Bombay to meet the delegation in Delhi, had been invited to our Minister's dinner for the Algerians; no one had the gumption to put them on the guest list, and even the Secretary asked me to take this up with the Minister; the reason was the Minister's strong aversion to private business. I made the request to George Fernandes, adding that India's first project contract by Tatas was under execution. He glared at me briefly, before agreeing to their inclusion.

I accompanied the delegation to different places, including Bangalore to visit HMT, Ranchi, where we visited HEC and MECON, and Durgapur where we went to a major MAMC plant. At Ranchi after spending a morning at the massive workshops that made heavy castings and forgings, and the huge machine shops, Minister Liassine posed a simple question to the HEC chief executive: if the choice was to be made again, should India opt for another HEC? The reply was blunt: it was a mistake to build such a complex plant as a single entity; it was impossible to obtain orders to keep it working to capacity; it was better to have several plants of different sizes, at different locations, to meet the realistic requirements.

I have no idea of the internal impact of that India visit on its ambitious CEMEL project, but during the year or so I remained in that country, till the end of 1979, I did not again hear of it. My friend Boujemeline seemed to agree with my quip that their project was too big a 'camel' for Algeria to digest. Behind that story lay the tragedy of Soviet planning, i.e. its conception of repeat orders for massive machine projects, failing to make allowance for technology innovation.

Our bilateral cooperation advanced extremely well in the deployment of Indian expert manpower. The first major breakthrough came at the Health Ministry, when the Minister, Ait Messadoune, who had just shifted to that charge from another ministry, invited me to his office and asked if I would work with him to bring doctors from India. That was music to my ears. He pointed to a fat dossier on his desk and said that this idea had been considered over many years, but each time it came up for decision, objections were raised over some key truths: that the Indian doctors did not speak either Arabic or French; they did not know the French 'conception of medicine'; and of course they did not know Algeria. He wanted to make a serious effort, in the conviction that the project would work. I immediately agreed that our authorities would fully cooperate.

We made it clear that while we would help with recruitment, Algeria should offer attractive terms to Indian doctors, and sign individual contracts with them. In the event, thousands of doctors applied; the first batch arrived after a few months. That group of 15 underwent the travails that befall pioneers. At the end of their first week they came in a group to meet me after and said: they had anticipated that it would take them time to adjust to local foods, but they had not imagined that even normal bread would be unavailable ('all we get are sticks of bread, but we don't like them' one said, referring to *baguettes* that were the Algerian norm); most were vegetarians, primarily from Andhra Pradesh and Karnataka, and found nothing palatable; the working environment was unfamiliar, as were the medicines; no one spoke English so that they had become 'deaf-mutes'; that was the final straw. Several asked that they be sent home; one or two were in tears.

I heard them out and replied that most of the problems they faced could be handled. We would ask the Health Ministry to improve food arrangements, and they too should guide their cooks. The other issues involved familiarization; they needed to realize that as pioneers, they faced a sharp culture shock. I reminded them of the garlands and *tilak* they had adorned on leaving home; did they want to go back and disappoint their families and friends? It was essential to go through the first month as a tough adjustment process; after that, they could review their position. The Health Minister had given a personal assurance that anyone who wanted to return home would be given an air-ticket, without any question asked.

The doctors accepted this, and in effect mentally accepted their adaptation process. None opted to return. That first group alerted their successors on the conditions to expect. The Algerians also learnt from that experience, and made special arrangements, also ensuring that those that had come earlier guided the new arrivals. One doctor suffered a heart attack and passed away on the taxi ride from the airport; since the contract document was signed only on arrival, his friends agonized over what might happen. The Health Ministry showed real compassion in ignoring formalities, taking care of all expenses for repatriation of his body and paying sizable compensation. Their simple comment: we honor the brother who came to help us.

By mid-1979, about 800 Indian doctors were at work in Algeria, most in the interior. Unlike French or Soviet doctors, they did not mind working in rural areas, since for them the entire country was a novel experience. At the public health centers, the queues were longest outside the rooms of the Indian doctors; despite language barriers, Algerians found them sympathetic. By 1979 we were operating about 25% of the public health services. Our doctors stayed in Algeria right up to the early 1990s; after internal upheaval following the elections of 1991, and escalating violence, most Indian doctors left. By then over 4000 Indian doctors had worked in the country and gone home with sizable savings that they used to set up their own clinics and diagnostic centers. Algeria had changed the lives of these doctors and their families.

A similar process, on a smaller scale, was at work in the universities and institutes; professors and scientists recruited in India began to arrive in Algeria from 1979 onwards. Recruitment in India matched their policy to expand English medium instruction at the tertiary level. Other technical experts were also brought from India.

Another area that Algeria identified for Indian cooperation was modernization and expansion of their rail network. Initial discussions were held in 1979, though most of the real action took place in subsequent years. Our public sector enterprises IRCON and RITES were major beneficiaries, and one entire segment of Algeria's network was reserved for Indian cooperation. That translated into large contracts after I left the country.

In 1978 and 1979 two Indian missile-corvettes purchased from the Soviet Union made friendly visits to Algiers, which made a pleasant change for us. Algeria was a purchaser of the same class of vessels, but we learnt at the time of the second transit visit that the Soviet Union had objected to our showing the 'war room' to Algerian naval personnel, owing to the fact that there were variations in the electronics equipment supplied to the two purchasing countries.

Our Life

We traveled extensively in Algeria. Ghardaïa in the South, in the Sahara, was an enchanting oasis village, home to the M'zebite people, a minority Islamic sect with a unique lifestyle adapted to desert conditions. They are a social anthropologist's delight, especially in the way centuries earlier they had permanently divided their limited, seasonal access to irrigation water. The towns and villages inhabited by the Kabyle people, located along the Atlas mountains, were closer to Algiers and gave access to another way of life.

Mimi established her own network of contact and friends, and this also helped me to understand the country better. Some were her tennis-playing friends, mainly women professionals, lawyers, doctors and others, which gave us contact with a wider Algerian group, through the social entertainment that followed. That became the way in which we worked at different posts, as a team projecting the best we could for India, profiting from our varied and sometimes overlapping connections. Wives of diplomats of most countries feel that their role is not acknowledged or valued as it ought to be, and they are entirely right in this. A single diplomat is handicapped, in social, as also in broader eco-political outreach.

Three friends in Algiers deserve special mention. Yasmine Belkacem was a schoolgirl during the peak period of the Algiers battle of 1956-57; both her legs were blown off when a bomb she was carrying exploded prematurely. She was a person of great courage and fortitude, treated as a national heroine; the government took special care of her. A charming hostess, she organized frequent receptions for her diplomat friends. She went each year to the US for treatment, and around 1978 she was fitted with prosthetic limbs, which moved her out of a wheelchair to which she had been confined for so long. Another special friend was Marie-Claude Radzeweski, a French national and lawyer who had long made her home in Algiers, living with her father. She was another gracious hostess, and a great contact builder. Among our best Algerian friends, besides Boujemline mentioned earlier, was a senior Interior Ministry official, Meziane Chérif, who later went on to be the governor of a province, and in the 1990s a cabinet minister.[17] We enjoyed many convivial evenings with them.

Events in Algeria

President Houari Boumediene died on 27 December 1978, after lingering in a coma for 39 days. In mid-November he had gone to Moscow for treatment, and on return, appeared on national TV, looking gaunt and frail. That same night he went into a coma, from which he never awoke. That produced a national crisis. The constitution did not provide for any temporary arrangement for this high office, and the Revolutionary Council took charge. Three countries, France, Germany and the US flew in CAT scanners, at

[17] Meziane Chérif, in his youth was one of the nationalists responsible for blowing up the refinery at Marseilles in 1960, a well-documented incident. He was captured and condemned to death; he was saved by the negotiations that led to independence.

that time cutting-edge equipment that was not available in Algeria. They, and several others, including China, the Soviet Union and the UK flew in teams of doctors; a few medical press conferences were televised, and resembled an international symposium, with translations from multiple languages. Such a prolonged crisis and uncertainty involving a national leader was unprecedented.

An Indian cabinet minister traveled to Algiers for the funeral of the President. Algeria had never seen a state funeral and this showed in the arrangements. Boumediene had a powerful hold over his people, and the public outpouring of grief was marked by hysteria and some chaos. The coffin was transported to the cemetery on a low gun carriage, pulled by an armored vehicle; at one point the crowds broke through security barriers and almost toppled it to the ground. At the cemetery, the surging crowds pushed at the gates, and as the simple interment took place, a huge roar could be heard amidst traditional Arab ululations. It was a remarkable experience.

Col. Chadli Benjedid, who had been Defence Minister, succeeded as President; he was a little-known person who lacked Boumediene's mass appeal, though he held office till 1992. As it turned out I got to see much more of him than was possible with President Boumediene, who simply did not receive ambassadors, apart from their brief credentials ceremony.

Atal Bihari Vajpayee visited Algiers in July 1979, in what was to be his final foreign trip as External Affairs Minister; Jagat Mehta, by then a long-serving Foreign Secretary, accompanied him. The visit went smoothly and advanced our bilateral relationship. An incident at the reception I hosted for the Indian community remains with me. Speaking in the Residence courtyard, in the presence of some 200 guests, I spoke in Hindi, in deference to Vajpayeeji's attachment to the national language. But he was more astute than I. Noting at a glance that most of the audience, composed mainly of our doctors, were from South India, he quipped: I don't know why the Ambassador has spoken in Hindi. I will address you in English. Speaking candidly of the crisis within the Janata party coalition government, he said: I do not know how long I am going to be a minister, but I am delighted to meet all of you, fellow-citizens advancing India's cause in this friendly country. He demitted office a few days after his return to New Delhi, when Charan Singh took over as Prime Minister.

In October 1979, Algeria celebrated the 25th anniversary of the launch of the Revolution that led to independence. India sent newly appointed Vice President Mohammad Hidayatullah, former Chief Justice of India as its representative. In those days our vice president traveled overseas by commercial aircraft, and he came accompanied by just three persons. We found him very simple and charming, who spent much time in conversation with Mimi and 10-year-old Priya, at informal meals at the Residence. Because of his age, he asked me to accompany him to the social functions, and in the process I saw President Chadli at close quarters, as well as some of the Arab and other leaders that had come for the event. This was the only occasion when I saw a military parade in Algiers, and a fly-past by its array of sophisticated aircraft, all acquired from the Soviet Union.

We left Algeria at the end of November 1979. At the airport, the Foreign Ministry surprised me with a large bundle as a gift, which turned out to be a fine Berber carpet, measuring about 6 by 9 feet. I was told that they gave such a present only to some departing ambassadors. They took care of its transport to Prague, my next assignment—I write in the next chapter how that came about. At Prague I gifted the carpet to the Embassy, and when I re-visited the Chancery in 1995, saw that it continued to adorn the Ambassador's office.

7

Socialist Paradise, Iron Curtain

Czechoslovakia (1979-81)

The assignment to Prague came about as a kind of consolation prize, though fine in its own right. In March 1978, much before I completed three years in Algiers, I was posted as deputy permanent representative (DPR) in New York, considered to be a career-enhancing job. I did not seek this; it came about because someone in the Janata government (after Indira Gandhi's election defeat in March 1977) decided that the incumbent DPR, Salman Haider, who had worked with the former PM, must be moved out. I protested gently; I did not like the reasoning behind that decision, and because in Algiers a real task needed to be competed. Foreign Secretary Jagat Mehta bluntly replied that it was not for me to question the decision. I then prepared myself for the transfer, sold off my small personal car (a Peugeot 104), and told colleagues in the diplomatic corps that I was to leave in June 1978. I even received my farewell gift from the Papal Nuncio who was then Dean of the Algiers diplomatic corps.

In May I was told that the transfer was postponed by six months; before the end of 1978 came a second six-month deferment, and in May 1979 a third one. In hindsight, Foreign Secretary Mehta seemed indulgent to Haider, who had worked with him in the Policy Planning Division in the late 1960s. I did not resent this much, because Algiers was rewarding; I stayed there for four years and two months. It equaled Germany as a productive assignment. I missed out on the New York job, but had no rancor over that.

When External Affairs Minister Atal Bihari Vajpayee and Mehta came to Algiers in July 1979, I sought a change of assignment, requesting Minister Vajpayee that I had waited long enough for New York and hoped he would send me elsewhere. I mentioned three embassies in my seniority zone that were falling vacant at that time; after reflecting for a moment he said: 'Go to Prague.'[1] That move took place in November 1979.

The Czechoslovak Scene

In the 1970s and 1980s, this country was under a firm Soviet yoke; the 'Prague Spring' of 1968 was a distant memory. A standing joke was that Czechoslovakia was the world's perfect non-aligned country; it did not even interfere in its own affairs. What sealed that compact was Soviet economic indulgence that produced for the Czechoslovaks relatively high prosperity, compared with other East European states. The regime feared above all defections to the West; as in other countries of East Europe, anyone departing, including diplomats, needed an exit visa. Travel out of Prague by train to the immediate Western neighbors Austria or Germany was a chilling experience, thanks to the hour-long inspection at the border by several groups of armed border guards, with machine-gun toting soldiers supervising a comprehensive search of the train carriage, besides manned overbridges and more armed guards along the rail track. Menacing guard dogs, used to sniff out defectors hiding anywhere inside or under the train carriages, completed that spectacle of socialist bliss.

Yet, in its own way, Prague was a happy place. The city, especially the old town is one of the most beautiful European cities, with a rich collection of architectural gems from the 10th century onwards, that suffered no damage from conflict or war. Even World War II had left the city unscathed. An outsider could discern differences between the Czech and Slovak people, in

---

1 Atal Bihari Vajpayee, who went on to serve as a successful prime minister (1999-2004), was perhaps the only External Affairs Minister to enjoy independent control over the MEA. In India, the appointment of heads of mission is seldom in the hand of this minister.

their way of life and temperament. The Czechs enjoyed a good life, manifest in a plethora of museums and the performing arts. Restaurants were plentiful, and the food relatively cheap. Wine and beer flowed freely. Culture and awareness of heritage had steeped deep into the people. It used to be said that Prague was one of the few places in the world where one could discuss culture and art with a taxi driver. We imbibed some of this; Ajit and Priya, then 13 and 11, came to understand, in an easy and natural way the distinguishing features of Romanesque, Gothic, Baroque and Rococo architecture. Ajit, then at Mayo College, during his 1980 summer holidays pursued a photography project, resulting in an album of his own impressions of Prague, with an accompanying text; this was at my instigation, but with his total enthusiastic enjoyment. He roamed up and down the city with a basic Asahi Pentax K-1000 camera and took lots of photographs. He learnt to develop the films and printed the enlargements, with just a little guidance; I had converted a basement room at the Residence into our darkroom.[2] Ajit retains an abiding interest in photography, now transmitted to his son Karnavir.

Our Life

We reached Prague at the beginning of December 1979. I was lucky to be included in a batch of envoys that presented credentials to President Gustav Husak within two weeks of arrival, before the year-end holidays. It was the most spectacular credential ceremony in which I have been privileged to participate. Entering the main gate of Prague Castle, the official cars drove into the first inner courtyard, and I disembarked at a small podium, facing an array of some 300 presidential guards. National anthems of both countries were played, and then facing the guard, I loudly spoke out the required word of greeting, as coached by the Chief of Protocol a day earlier: *Nazdar*. To a man, they shouted back: *Z'dar*.

---

[2] That had an unexpected outcome at Mayo College. Apparently it was the first time that anyone had turned in a summer vacation project, and Ajit tells me that it led the School to institute a system of summer projects for all senior students. My guess is that this move was on the cards, and Ajit's work may have speeded up that process.

That particular element, a dignitary receiving a guard of honor speaking out a greeting, is unique to that country. Two incidents involving that ritual had entered local legend. Ethiopia's Emperor Haile Selassie, on a state visit in the 1970s was requested to speak out that greeting, but he was taken aback when the guard shouted out their response. He then said again: *Nazdar*, and they cheerfully shouted back their programmed reply. Legend has it that this went back and forth a couple of more times! The other story involves an ambassador who forgot the word of greeting. Undaunted, he dredged his memory and came up with a mnemonic, *Budwar*. That was the name of Czechoslovakia's second most popular beer, and the honor guard collapsed in laughter.

In Prague, we developed some deep friendships, with Indologists and others. A few invited us to their homes, which was never easy for locals in Communist states, as they surely needed prior permission from security 'minders', and of course had to report on outcomes. We did not use these contacts for political discussions—that was not on the Indian agenda, and we respected their sensitive circumstance. We were occasionally invited on weekend outings to resorts, on rivers and on lakesides, belonging to one or another state enterprises. Sometimes friends invited us to picnic outings, but on most weekends we traveled around on our own. That entire region is so rich in historical heritage that at every turn one came across old castles, museums and historical buildings. That kept us busy on weekends.

Other attractions were the music, opera and stage performances at a multitude of theatres in Prague. Diplomatic missions could always obtain tickets, and these were cheap. We enjoyed a profusion of music, opera and ballet. Czechoslovakia was also remarkably inventive in the performing arts—one example was 'Laterna Magika' which blended projection of a film, with live stage acts, in a fascinating, seamless combination. Another major draw was the mime theatre of Ladislav Fialka. Someone had even produced a film that was projected in three segments; after the first one the audience voted, via a special gadget given to each viewer on how the movie should progress—as a comedy, melodrama or a tragedy—and for the final segment a further choice was offered on the ending. Since we did not know

Czech, we did not have access to other stage forms and plays that were presented, but these too were rich in content and diversity.

The Indian Chancery was located in a stately mansion in Mala Strana ('Little Town'), at the foot of the Prague Castle, a few hundred meters from the historic Charles Bridge that led to the Old Town. And right along that way was U Fleku, a delightful beer-hall located in the basement of what had been a famous monastery, producing its own caramel-flavored, strong dark beer. On my first visit, I did not muster the courage to tackle a one-liter stein of that seductive beer, and asked for a small glass, drawing a look of astonishment from the waiter. It did not take long to get accustomed to the full-size beer-mug.

The Residence was in a lovely villa about four km from the Chancery, close to the U-Bahn, on the way to the airport. That spacious building is located in sprawling grounds with a sloping driveway; it had ample public salons and a dining hall that seated 20 guests at a long table. Wisely, the Indian government bought that property in 1991, after the exit of the Communist regime, when it became possible to make such purchases from the state, which owned most buildings in Prague. But I am told we lost much of the antique furniture, when it was claimed back by the original owners.

Embassy life was different in comparison with Algeria in several respects; in some ways it evoked memories of Beijing. For one thing, we depended on our Czechoslovak staff owing to the complexity of the Czech language, and the fact that even Embassy long-timers—those that had stayed in Prague for almost the full length of their three-year term—did not manage more than a few words and phrases. Embassies were expected to bring their own interpreters to official meetings, except for those held at high levels; an exception was the Foreign Ministry (where host officials either spoke English, or provided their own interpreters). We had a team of three interpreters, led by a cool, unflappable Mr. Jaroslav Stareck, who had by then been with the Embassy for nearly 30 years; he was a source of information and sound advice as well. Of course we knew that all the local staff were required to report on us, and that they attended daily meetings at the start of the working day; we simply adapted ourselves to that reality.

Priya once asked our fine, dignified flag car driver Mr. Rehak who had long served the Embassy, if he was a spy. The poor man was shocked at such a blunt query, but in response to Priya's rigorous questioning he is said to have pointed to a couple of places in the car where listening devices were implanted! Ever discreet, Priya did not recount this to us until much after we left Prague.

A peculiarity of life in that country was that foreign exchange was in high demand, and a vigorous market existed for 'unofficial' transactions. As best as I knew, Embassy officials did not normally use that 'market' route. Since we were paid in US Dollars, and needed to convert some of that into local currency, transactions carried out through the bank also gave us a coupon currency called 'Tuzex', which could be used to buy scarce imported products at special shops, or sold off on the unofficial market for the local currency. Officials from most embassies cheerfully participated in such transactions. A virtually identical situation existed in other East European capitals; the local authorities turned a Nelsonian eye to these practices.

Our small embassy had four officials on the diplomatic list. Initially, the deputy was First Secretary HHS Vishwanathan, who came to Prague from Zaire; dynamic and highly efficient, he provided exemplary support. BB Tarei, Second Secretary was a pleasant individual and helpful. Since India bought sizable quantities of Czech defense equipment, and needed to keep track of developments on that arms market, the Embassy had a military attaché, Colonel HB Kala, who was a great asset.

Czechoslovakia has always had a great hunting tradition, and the government carefully sustained it, principally for the benefit of its senior party and government officials, and foreign guests.[3] Diplomats interested in this pastime ended up as incidental beneficiaries. An annual tradition was a pheasant shoot organized at the nominal invitation of President Gustav Husak (though he did not attend); all ambassadors were invited to Konopišt Castle, on the outskirts of Prague; it was one of Archduke Ferdinand's residences. That hunt amounted to culling of carefully reared

[3] After the end of Communism, both the successor states, the Czech Republic and Slovakia organize hunts for foreign guests, who pay handsome fees for this privilege.

birds, and ended with a banquet; each hunter was rewarded with a brace of pheasant.

Foreign Minister Ch oupek was an avid hunter and he would invite a small group of ambassadors to join him on duck shoots, and an occasional wild boar hunt. Having just a smattering of experience, thanks to the Rajasthan traditions of my wife's family, I joined that group, and enjoyed splendid excursions into the interior, to the many lakes and forests that abounded in Czechoslovakia. Especially memorable was a wild-boar hunt at the Topo ianky castle, in what is now Slovakia. Held in the dead of winter, with several inches of snow on the ground, we tramped up and down the hills for several hours; lunch consisted of a hearty goulash soup and bread, accompanied by two rationed small glasses of fiery liquor; it was an exhilarating experience. In the course of seven rounds, the beaters drove the wild boar towards the hunters arrayed in a fixed line. I ended up with the lead trophy, having shot a large, dangerous animal in my assigned zone, after my neighbor's gun misfired. One feature at all these hunts was the tight safety protocol, with each gun accompanied by a seasoned expert who made sure that the norms and traditions were fully observed, including disciplined handling of firearms.[4]

The Prague diplomatic corps was fairly small, with some 60 resident embassies. The Soviet bloc embassies were aloof, most headed by political personalities that cared little for the niceties of protocol among envoys; I recall the Polish ambassador, whose chancery adjoined ours in Mala Strana keeping me waiting for a first courtesy call for 25 minutes, after which I left—I received no apology from him. But among the rest, relations were convivial, and we enjoyed splendid dinners and soirées. We also formed a bridge circle with some of them.

Unlike Algiers, Prague was on the travel track of our friends and family, and we received lots of guests in the short time spent there. This was a blessing, and all our family became good guides for these visitors, including Priya. She joined the French school, and ended up with a total of six years of French medium

[4] Some may recall the tragic incidents in former Yugoslavia involving hunting accidents in the 1980s, including one in which an ambassador lost his life.

school education, up to an age of 12, which gave her a permanent grounding in both that language and its heritage. Ajit had joined Mayo College midway through our Algiers term, and spent four years there, till we returned to Delhi, when both shifted to Modern School. New regulations that allowed officials to send children to local English-medium schools went into effect only in 1981.

Our Bilateral Relationship

In 1938, Nazi Germany had made an irredentist demand for a part of Czechoslovakia that they called 'Sudetenland', based on the historical ethnicity of its people. That was the first flexing of Nazi muscle in Europe. Jawaharlal Nehru, ever attentive to world affairs in the midst of India's Independence struggle, made a special journey to Prague, accompanied by a teenaged Indira; he was on his way to Switzerland where his wife was undergoing treatment for tuberculosis that took her life just a year later. In Prague, Nehru met with the leaders of Czechoslovakia, and expressed solidarity with them in the face of their neighboring Nazi menace. That is a small, unremembered episode in European history, but the Czechoslovak people have not forgotten it, the more so as they received precious few affirmations of support at that time. India has since basked in the reflected glory of that solidarity gesture.

As with all the other countries of the Soviet bloc, India's relations with Czechoslovakia were excellent, with a good level of trade and industrial exchanges. The country's dominant state enterprises dealt with India through their long-established network of Indian agents and importers, in relationships that were 'cozy' and not amenable to scrutiny. India imported a range of capital equipment and defence supplies, through these established arrangements. The downside was that close familiarity did not encourage new actions, and this meant for me putting aside my Algeria experience; I understood the adage that teaching new tricks to an old dog is always harder than the other way round.

I made extensive visits to state enterprises, meeting chief executives, and visiting manufacturing plants in different parts of the country. It became clear that they knew India well, and were not easily persuaded to re-examine or deepen links with

India, either to add new products to the exchanges, or to take into account India's own growing prowess as an industrial partner. For them, familiarity had produced a kind of mental block towards the changes taking place in India. This was in sharp contrast to experience in Algeria, but as always, personal discussions and visits were useful in giving me insights, and prompted some reexamination on their part. Limited progress was registered at widening economic links.

No major political exchange took place in my time in Prague, in terms of visits by high personalities. The bilateral joint economic commission held a session in India in mid-1980, and I traveled with them; that was a strictly *sarkari* format, with only state enterprises on the delegation, though Indian businessmen were at the periphery at each of the cities we visited; they could be spotted in hotels, 'looking after' their Czechoslovak friends. The Minister of Trade led the Czechoslovak delegation, and he proved to be a delightful raconteur of black humor of an intensely self-deprecating kind, in much the same way as I had seen in Algeria—proving again that socialist societies are masters of this genre. An example:

> President Gustav Husak decides to go on a month's summer holiday to the Crimea, but is reluctant to entrust his job to anyone in the cabinet, for fear that he may turn out to be an usurper. He drives around Prague to locate a trustworthy person. After several false starts, he finds a young man he deems suitable, agreeable to accepting this temporary job. He takes him to the airport and on the way says there are three problems which the young man might help him resolve: Prague has a terrible housing shortage that blocks young people from getting married and they often have to live in cramped apartments with their parents; further, there are long queues at shops, owing to chronic shortages; finally, despite all his efforts, people still throng the churches. Can you deal with these problems? Fine, says the young man, I promise to do my best.
>
> Wanting to take his temporary successor by surprise, Husak returns from his holiday a day earlier than planned. As he drives into town, he finds every second apartment complex adorned with signs, 'apartments for rent'; at the shops, the queues have disappeared; unable to believe his eyes, he stops his limousine at

a church and finds that though it is a Sunday, the place is almost deserted. He then rushes to the Prague Castle and confronting his successor, exclaims: what magic wand have you used to solve all my problems? The young man replies: It wasn't a big deal. I closed the borders to the East, so that all the goods we used to send out to our big brother in Moscow are now retained at home, and the shops are full. I also opened the borders to the West, so that half the population has left; abandoned apartments available for others. Wonderful, exclaims Husak; but what did you do with the churches? Simple, replies the young man; I replaced all the old pictures of Jesus and Mary with your portraits, so now no one goes to church!

On a more serious note, a major Indian problem in Czechoslovakia and other East European states was that we often pandered to their prejudices, as narrated below. That was symptomatic of a tendency to treat this group of countries on exceptional terms. Indian foreign policy clearly leaned in favor of Moscow in those days, for all our protestations of non-alignment. Yet, since the Soviet Union dominated this bloc, there was little appetite for political dialogue with the smaller East European capitals; with them we were uncritical, and often supine. A few in our Service acted as sycophants of the Soviet Union, owing to personal conviction, and in response to the favors they received. Of course, there were others that showed their bias in favor of the US and the West. That story largely remains untold, though a few like JN Dixit have mentioned this in their writing.

The Chief of Army Staff, General OP Malhotra visited Czechoslovakia in 1980. He brought a sizable delegation; the lavish scale and the number of gifts he brought for his hosts struck me. This seemed excessive, more than what is customary with visits at the level of our important ministers, or even prime ministers. I understood that this had become a kind of tradition for our armed forces; equally impressive return gifts were carried back home. The visit was uneventful and proceeded smoothly.

Our state enterprise Indian Tourism Development Corporation (ITDC), which ran over 30 hotels across India at the time, collaborated with a Czech counterpart to open an Indian restaurant in Prague in 1980 named 'Mayur', supplying cooks and technical help. With two state-run entities joining hands on such a small venture, commercial viability went out of the window. We learnt, for instance, that the 'norms' set out for special ingredients for Indian cuisine were inflated; four portions of chicken curry stipulated 1 gm of saffron—a quantity that might be used in a normal Indian household over several months. It made the project unviable, doomed to failure. The restaurant closed down some years later.

Across Europe, new consular problems were emerging, owing to an influx of hopeful Indian migrants, mainly from North India, attempting to reach West Europe, in pursuit of jobs and their dreams of a good life. Germany was the destination of choice. Agents in India and Europe masterminded this human trafficking; they fleeced the intending migrants, charging large sums of money, providing them with false documents and travel papers, and exploiting their dreams. Czechoslovakia was one transit route, with groups brought into Moscow or Warsaw, taking advantage of easy availability of visas to these places, then moved in closed vans to Germany. Some were intercepted at border check-posts. One group was caught up in a horrific traffic accident not far from Prague in which several young Indians lost their lives. Our consular officials were hard pressed to obtain authentic identification from them, and help out the injured survivors, in a situation where they had sold all their belongings and land to win that migration lottery; they often gave false addresses, as they were most reluctant to go back home. That human drama has played out over succeeding decades, even while the transit methods and modalities have evolved.

Another feature of our local activities was outreach to Indian students, of whom there were about 50 in Prague. We hosted for them at occasional music and dance evenings, providing beer and Indian snacks. That kept up their India connections. There was no resident Indian community, apart from a couple of people that held modest jobs with the radio services.

Marketing India

In the 1970s and 1980s culture diplomacy and marketing an image of a new India was one of our external priorities. Notions of 'soft power' (*ã la* Joseph Nye), and the pursuit of public diplomacy via information exchanges lay in the future. As it turned out, we did some things rather well, while some other favorable developments just happened, in consonance with the law of unexpected consequences. A few events illustrate this.

A good practice at any new post or job is to go through *all* the files of the sections or the mission that the official supervises. One reason is that the 'handing over notes' that are required to be written by departing heads of missions, are usually not nearly as comprehensive as they aught to be; the MEA does not supervise this process.[5] It is seldom necessary to actually read all the 'bumpf'—a rather euphonic word that often sums up the value of old files—just skimming through these gives a flavor of the issues that reigned in the past; sometimes this can alert the newcomer on the time bombs and hidden mines at that assignment. One such file was a juicy extended argumentation between my predecessor, Surendra Singh Alirajpur (1923-96), and the Ministry of Information and Broadcasting, with the External Affairs Ministry a bemused spectator; in contention was the status of the envoy, vis-à-vis a visiting film delegation at the 1978 Karlovy Vary Film Festival.[6] In brief, that delegation was led by the Secretary, Information and Broadcasting (i.e. the top civil servant of that Ministry); at Karlovy Vary, the Ambassador insisted that as the President's representative, he outranked the Secretary. The latter, conceding this in the abstract, argued that at the film festival, it was the leader of the delegation who should stand first at the customary on-stage lineup, prior to the Indian film screening. Such protocol jousting, absurd from afar, is the very stuff of formal diplomacy for some! As I recall, nothing conclusive emerged from that dispute, but it warned me.

We brought a powerful delegation to the 1980 Karlovy Vary Festival. Famous film director Mrinal Sen was on the Jury, while the official delegation was led, as usual by the Secretary (I&B), a very urbane and gentle AK Dutt. Others were film director

5 See Rana, *21st Century Diplomacy: A Practitioner's Handbook* (2012); a template for handing over notes is on pp. 298-301.

6 The Karlovy Vary Film Festival is held in alternate years at this elegant spa resort city, and remains one of the major events on the European cultural calendar.

Buddhadev Bhattacharya, and doyenne film critic the late Amita Malik. Mimi was a big hit with the delegation; at a dinner we hosted in Prague, Dutt nicknamed her 'the princess', and even Amita, known for her sharp pen, wrote some flattering things about us and the Embassy. The next day, at Karlovy Vary, waiting in an anteroom to be ushered on stage for the introduction preceding the Indian screening, Amita asked me with a twinkle in her eyes, 'Ambassador, surely you are going to stand at the head of the line, as protocol demands?' I gave a non-committal reply, and quietly stood behind her. When she asked again, I told her that this was an event for film professionals; as the local Indian representative, it was my duty to honor them. That single gesture built friendship, even trust, with that group; later, back in Prague, as we bade them farewell, Mrinal Sen paid a slightly left-handed compliment: 'You don't behave like an ambassador'!

It was the Indian entry in the Festival that became the object of my correspondence with both Information & Broadcasting and MEA. Simply put, *Ek Din Pratidin* ('A Day Like Every Other') was a stark, leftist, ideological portrayal of the downtrodden, pouring into Kolkata from the rural hinterland, and the misery they encounter. Mimi, usually mild, was so shocked by the film that she blasted its director, Buddhadev Dasgupta (possibly expending some of the goodwill built with them); the director then promised her that his next work would be a comedy—a promise he has not kept! My problem was not with that film (which won a 'Special Mention' from the Jury), but the fact that India only chose such depressing, essentially negative narratives of India for festivals in the socialist East European countries. Writing to the MEA and to the Information Ministry, I argued that this was dishonest, as it pandered to the ideological bias of the receiving countries, and reinforced their stereotype view they had of India. Such an unbalanced film selection was also unfair to the country's film industry; there was much more to India than 'art' cinema.

Nothing came of that correspondence; Secretary Dutt, an old-school civil servant to the core, sent pleasant but evasive replies, and the MEA was not interested. That episode underscored the extent to which we in India had bought into the ideological baggage of the socialist countries, not from conviction, but out of practical convenience—why not offer them that which pleased them? I know that many in the Indian public service who went along with such policy were not leftists. Most simply saw that as low-cost pandering to the 'socialist' countries—how quaint that term sounds today! India appeared mired in impossible social conditions, with an ineffective economic policy, doing little for its masses. That was lousy public diplomacy.

We had better success at the Prague Spring Festival, one of Europe's major annual music event; more than 80 classical music performances are crowded into 20 days in April. Long back, Pandit Ravi Shankar had performed at this event, and I wanted to get Indian classical music back. Discussion with different officials led nowhere; they essentially said it was an event for Western music. The only option left was to raise the level of the discussion; at a meeting with Deputy Premier Luchan, who held charge of cultural affairs and information, I mentioned to him that I was surprised at prejudice towards Indian culture. He was shocked at that; I explained to him our problem. The outcome was an invitation from them for a leading Indian musician, to present a concert in Prague; I conveyed that offer to our good friend Pandit Jasraj, the classical vocalist. We have known Pandit Jasraj and his talented family for about 50 years, from the days when as a young musician he spent a month at Mt. Abu, staying at the resort home of the former Maharana of Sanand, Jaywant Singh, one of his gurus. Every evening he sang an informal *baithak* in a spacious drawing room at Sanand House. He was to visit Italy in mid-1980, and extended his trip to Prague, staying with us for several days, accompanied by his family. The Czechoslovak authorities organized a concert in a small Renaissance hall, for an invited audience. They were delighted with the event and invited Pandit Jasraj to the April 1981 Prague Spring Festival.

The 1981 concert took place in a beautiful Baroque hall in one of the grand palaces in Mala Strana, for a ticketed audience of 400. It was a great success; several European connoisseurs told us that owing to unfamiliarity with Indian music, they initially found it 'unusual' and 'strange', but after a few minutes, it became just great music, whose language is universal. We felt that India's re-introduction to the Prague Spring Festival was an important action.[7] I left Prague on transfer to New Delhi in August 1981, and heard that sitar artist Debu Chaudhary was invited to the 1982 Festival. One might have expected the Indian Council of Cultural Relations (ICCR) to privilege India's entry to such events, but alas, that organization has long been a handmaiden to its ruling chieftains and their favorites. Subsequently, the Indian Embassy did not persist in its support; after 1982, no Indian musician has been invited. Consider: a country like Poland instructs its embassies to find openings for their artistes at major festivals, since this helps project their country's attractiveness, which we now call 'soft power'. For India such opportunities that cross cultures should be treasured even more, but few in New Delhi seemed interested. Thus an important cultural window to Europe closed again.

When we negotiated a 'cultural exchange protocol' in 1980, we encountered another facet of the Communist dogma. These protocols are designed to flesh out the overarching cultural agreement, signed earlier; they set out program activities, to exchange artistes and performing groups, exhibitions, film weeks, and other actions. On the way to the Ministry of Culture for a preliminary discussion, I sounded our chief interpreter Stareck on a demand we often received from local India enthusiasts for yoga teachers. He told me that it would not be acceptable to the host government. I went ahead anyway and put that proposal on the table, and met with a polite but firm refusal. Later I asked Stareck as to the reason; he explained that Communist ideology saw yoga as subversive, because behind the physical and health benefits it provided, lay a deeper philosophy, which was not acceptable to their regime. Today, thanks to an action that originates with PM Narendra Modi, the UN and the world celebrate the summer solstice as World Yoga Day.

[7] I have subsequently learnt from other Indian classical musicians and dancers how they cannot gain access to the grand festivals, be it Salzburg or Bayreuth.

Departure

I narrate in the next chapter the curious manner in which I was selected for an assignment in the Prime Minister's Office (PMO). In mid-July 1981 the Foreign Secretary told me that I should immediately join the PMO. With some difficulty I obtained four weeks to wind up my affairs and pack for that unanticipated move to New Delhi. We left Prague around 12 August, ending my shortest overseas assignment.

8

Heady and Instructive
PM's Office (1981-82)

One Sunday morning in February 1981 at Prague I received a phone call from Foreign Secretary Ram Sathe, rare for a young ambassador in a post of modest importance, and a first for me. He asked if I would join the PM's Office (PMO) as a joint secretary, since Kamal Bakshi (a good friend, 1961 batch) had suffered a heart attack and could not resume work. We were in our bedroom when the call came; I asked him if I could consult my wife. Her instant response was: 'Oh, no!' Impulsively, I lifted my hand from the phone mouthpiece and said yes to the Foreign Secretary. For sure, Mimi was wise. Yet, a chance to serve on PM Indira Gandhi's staff was not to be missed. I had then been in Prague for barely 15 months, and had never imagined myself in such a job.[1] Despite subsequent travails, I have no regrets.

Immediately after that call, reality set in. My doubt was practical. I had met the Prime Minister but briefly before proceeding to Algeria (described earlier), and had an even shorter meeting after I took charge in Prague. As a note-taker, I had attended meetings in Delhi when visitors from Nepal or Bhutan called on her, in 1973-75 as Director (North) in MEA.[2] What might

[1] Around 1974, while serving in the MEA as a director I received word that I might be asked to join the staff of the Minister of External Affairs, but nothing came of it, and I did not lose any sleep over that.

[2] It used to be the custom in the 1970s that mere Directors and Deputy Secretaries in the MEA could attend such meetings as note-takers, often alongside the PMO official who performed the same duty.

happen if I landed up in Delhi to take up the job and was then told that I was not acceptable? It seemed silly to abandon an attractive a capital like Prague after barely a year; the prospect of drifting at a loose end in the Ministry was abhorrent! The next morning, I sent an elliptically worded cypher message to the Foreign Secretary, asking if I should come to Delhi for an interview. That had evidently not occurred to anyone, but was readily accepted.

A Job Interview

I reached Delhi three days later, and called on Foreign Secretary Sathe with trepidation. I did not known him, save as a senior colleague encountered in Ministry corridors, but he had a reputation for exceptional generosity, fairness and consideration. He put me at ease with his opening words and said that I should immediately seek an appointment with Principal Secretary PC Alexander, who would guide me on what was to be done. He added singularly pertinent advice: if the assignment went to me, I would need to keep my 'political antennae fully deployed'. Adding that Mrs. Gandhi had her own likes and dislikes, it would be part of the job to steer away from her those who were in the latter category, and that I had to be exceptionally alert at all times. Failure to heed this advice cost me eventually. But that was in the future!

I had met PC Alexander only once, five years earlier in Kuwait in February 1976, at a two-day meeting of ambassadors and commercial officials from Indian embassies in the West Asia & North Africa region, when he was Commerce Secretary. Commerce Minister DP Chattopadhyaya had chaired that meeting. I dare say that the offer to join the PMO came from positive impressions from that encounter. Two incidents from Kuwait remain vivid. In my brief conference statement, I spoke of the way Indian public sector enterprise operated in North Africa; instead of acting as commercial enterprises, they behaved like ministries. Commerce Minister DP Chattopadhyaya interjected: 'Is that a bad thing?' Straight off and without thinking, I replied: 'It was widely recognized that ministries are one of the least efficient organizations created by man.' The 30-odd officials present held their breath, wondering if I would be struck down for impertinence. But after a moment the Minister cracked a smile, and the others felt it was safe to offer a gentle titter of amusement! The second incident was a long session of gossip and after-dinner drinks with colleagues in the room of PMS Malik (1962 batch, then in the Commerce Ministry); we stayed till 5 AM, when Malik threw us out, Ranjit Gupta and I; Ranjit said some blunt things to me that night, but we have remained good friends.

My meeting with PMO Principal Secretary PC Alexander was brief. He told me to go and see the PM's Special Assistant, RK Dhawan, in effect her personal secretary; ranking as a director he held enormous clout, controlling most—but not all—access to the Prime Minister. I was to learn later that Indira Gandhi gave distinct zones to those most proximate; each had a designated space, but no one was exclusive. Alexander was insistent that immediately after meeting the PM I should see him and give a full account of all that transpired.

A day later I found myself facing the PM, for my 'job interview'. After a few words asking where I was posted, she fell silent, leaving me nonplussed. How can one be interviewed, if the interviewing authority poses no question? On the spur of the moment, I decided to handle this impasse as if I were being asked a series of questions about my career track, and gave a short monologue about what I had done, first as a China-*wallah*, and then in Algeria and in Czechoslovakia. She appeared interested, and asked a question or two, about President Boumedienne and his successor President Chadli Benjedid; before long, I ran out of steam. Finally, she nodded saying I could leave. The meeting had lasted under ten minutes.

I hot footed to PC Alexander's office, down that corridor, and gave a full account. 'But what did she say at the end?' he asked, more than once. 'Nothing, Sir', which left him puzzled. He said finally that he would check with the PM and that I should phone him the next day. He subsequently told me to return to my post; they would decide later on.[3] I went back to Prague, none the wiser.

---

3 Kamal Bakshi reminded me after reading a draft of this chapter that on the day of my interview with the PM, I went to see him in the evening, both to wish him speedy recovery (he was subsequently posted to Sweden, and recovered fully). He heard me out and advised that he too had faced an equally enigmatic interview, and suggested I should begin to pack my bags for a move to Delhi.

After several weeks of silence I assumed that the issue was closed. With no means to check further, I erased the episode as perplexing, and beyond my ken. In mid-July I was astonished to be told to 'immediately' come to Delhi. I took over the new job on 16 August 1981.

I never learnt the full story of what had happened. Chinmaya Gharekhan, two years my senior, working as Joint Secretary (UN), had taken over when Kamal Bakshi fell ill in February 1981. For reasons unknown, PC Alexander wanted someone else, on a regular basis, and I was the first among a half-dozen that were interviewed. No one seemed to make the grade until July, when the PM decided that I was acceptable. When I left the PMO in September 1982, Gharekhan took over from me, and served with much distinction, all the way till the end of 1985, including the first phase of Rajiv Gandhi's primeministership. Possibly PC Alexander had initial hesitation over Gharekhan, but he became Indira Gandhi's choice. His successor Ronen Sen, wielded exceptional influence, serving three prime ministers, till July 1991.[4]

PMO: Structure and Role

In 1981, the PMO barely had eight executive-rank officials, and even today the numbers remain small, around 20. The job given to me had started at the rank of deputy secretary and was later held by directors. The first incumbent was Natwar Singh (1954 batch), starting in 1966, for five years.[5] MM Malhotra (IAS, 1959) followed in 1971-73, and then Salman Haider (my batchmate), in 1973-76. The job had no template, or guidelines; each incumbent found his own way. In essence, it involved assisting the PM on external

4 After Rajiv Gandhi took over as the PM in November 1984, Ronen Sen, then in the MEA's Administration Division, who was close to the new PM, handled some special external affairs tasks (in the 1970s he had looked after Rajiv and Sonia Gandhi when they had visited Moscow when he was a counselor at the Embassy). He formally took over as Joint Secretary (PMO) in January 1986, and stayed in that job up to July 1991, serving also PMs VP Singh and Chandra Shekhar. That is the longest assignment in the PMO for any IFS official.

5 Natwar Singh has covered this in detail in *Walking With Lions: Tales from a Diplomatic Past* (2013).

affairs related tasks, handling visitors and dealing with logistics; policy matters were not a significant remit in my time, but that varied at different times. The PM's key foreign affairs adviser was the secretary heading the PMO. On appointment in early 1980, PC Alexander was elevated to 'Principal Secretary' (ranking him on par with the Cabinet Secretary, who heads the entire civil service). Alexander handled policy issues, as the PM's main adviser; for long G Parthasarathi had been a powerful *eminence grise*, but by 1981 his influence was on the decline.

PC Alexander was firmly in the saddle.[6] The others were: HY Sharda Prasad, in the rank of Secretary, the PM's information adviser and speechwriter from her earliest days. He was the soul of modesty, with affable, deadly humor. One of the few pieces of advice he gave was that the PM had much respect for people who contributed ideas for her speeches. I offered a few suggestions, but failed to treat that gentle hint with the respect it deserved.[7] Arjun Sengupta, economic adviser, was an additional secretary (promoted to secretary in 1982); he handled all matters relating to the economic ministries; Arvind Pande (a director, IAS), assisted him. Two other joint secretaries, both from the IAS, were: Vijay Tripathi, handling issues relating to the Home Ministry and intelligence, as also major appointments, and had direct access to the PM;[8] R Rajamani handled the scientific ministries, education and social affairs, and supervised the PMO administration—a model of civil service rectitude, he was invariably generous. Three more were at director rank: Salman Khurshid who handled legal issues;[9] and Usha Bhagat, Social Secretary, who had assisted Indira Gandhi for many years, took care of some of the PM's

---

6 PC Alexander joined the PMO after he retired from a distinguished IAS career, when Indira Gandhi returned to power in January 1980; at the time he had been in Geneva as executive director at the International Trade Centre in Geneva.

7 In the mid-1990s, much after he retired, he wrote an article: 'Why I shall not be writing my memoir.'

8 Vijay Tripathi died in office in early 1986 after an extended illness.

9 Salman Kurshid quit the PMO in early 1982, to work in the Congress Party, and resume his legal practice. The scion of a distinguished politician, he told the PM that he would be of greater utility in political affairs. He clearly felt stifled in the bureaucracy. He served as External Affairs Minister in 2010-14.

personal correspondence, including letters from the public, plus sundry personal tasks; RK Dhawan, director, sat in the PM's outer office and controlled access and appointments, also running her personal office; a complex individual, he was the PM's confidant, with much political clout, and the only one with a second office at the PM's residence, besides a third one at Parliament House; when the House was in session, Indira Gandhi shifted base there. ML Fotedar ran the PM's party office at 1 Akbar Road, which adjoined her residence (1 Safdarjung Road), but never visited South Block.[10]

I came to know that PM apportioned direct access, and her confidence, in measured degree to several individuals. None held primacy; they acted independent of each other, namely, PC Alexander, RK Dhawan, Vijay Tripathi, and ML Fotedar. Sharda Prasad and Usha Bhagat, less powerful, also dealt directly with the PM. Others, politicians and officials, given specific tasks from time to time, enjoyed some personal trust; they supplemented the four as access and information points. Group meetings were rare in the PMO. Ministers typically met her by themselves, and she listened to their advice, but kept her own counsel. For instance, I never saw External Affairs Minister PV Narasimha Rao at a joint meeting. Some believed he did not have much clout, but that may not have been accurate; she met him frequently. G Parthasarathi advised on foreign affairs, but his role was on the decline. The PM met the heads of internal and external intelligence, IB and RAW, each week, again one-to-one. Some foreign secretaries enjoyed that privilege, but not all. Towards the end of 1981 Foreign Secretary Ram Sathe had fallen from favor, for reasons unknown; consequently, he reported through the Principal Secretary. When MK Rasgotra took over from him in May 1982, he was given a standing fixed-day appointment for personal meetings; the PM also told him that she did not like long notes or files, and preferred him to raise matters at these meetings.[11]

On my first day at the PMO, PC Alexander laid down the ground rules, saying: I was no longer an MEA official while at

[10] Indira Gandhi was assassinated by two of her bodyguards as she walked from her residence to this office, along an internal walkway connecting the two compounds.

[11] MK Rasgotra disclosed this in a conversation with me in 2014.

this job; my full loyalty must be to the PM. He added: that might sometimes put you in the position of acting in a manner that may not suit the MEA, but that could not be helped. I replied: as an ordinary official I had no political ambition; this appointment was an extraordinary privilege. I did not see it as any kind of right, and would naturally give complete loyalty to the PM; I would gladly go back to the MEA anytime my services were not required.

Indira Gandhi chose in her own way to signal to those around her that she had a new staffer. In those days, the PM traveled to the airport to receive and see off high foreign dignitaries; their aircraft would come to the 'technical area', i.e. the section controlled by the Indian Air Force. Ministers, the diplomatic corps and officials gathered at a small, shabby building that opened directly to the tarmac; they usually milled around in clusters. Through a ritual perfected with long practice, the PM would arrive a few minutes before the dignitary's aircraft landed. A couple of weeks after I joined the PMO, at one of these events, she directed me to a sofa, sat down and spoke with me of some trivial matters—I think she mentioned how at lunch geography games were her favorite, and that afternoon when everyone else ran out of rivers that began with a 'T', she still had two names up her sleeve! She also mentioned that daughter-in-law Maneka was 'like a teenager' and it was good to have her in the family. That was a rare direct glimpse into her personal life.

My Tasks

I found that there was no guidance, but the nature of my work became clear in a short time.

- All MEA cipher telegrams marked to the PM (and that in our system meant virtually all telegrams, other than those designated as 'personal' by the sender or those classified as 'Top Secret', which went directly to her personal office), came to the Joint Secretary. I had three options: those deemed important would go to the PM, typically with major points sidelined; those of peripheral value were initialed and consigned to the archives; and those in an intermediate middle category were put aside, to be summarized in a daily or once-in-two-day summary. A copy of the summary went to the Principal Secretary. Since there was no style guide, early on the job, I asked the PM if use of 'telegraphese' was permitted in these summaries; her good-humored response: 'Not permitted, encouraged!'

- Another task was to examine the files that came addressed to the PM from the Ministry of External Affairs, and put them up to the Principal Secretary, who then decided what was to go to the Prime Minister. By the 1980s, it became standard PMO practice that the examination and noting on such files in the Office took place in separate note-sheets that were marked 'Internal', which did not go out of the PMO. Thus the only notation that went back to the MEA—or any other Ministry—on their files, was the final decision, on behalf of the PM.[12] That way, the 'processing' remained within the PMO. I should add that most MEA files went directly to the Principal Secretary (usually from the foreign secretary or other MEA secretaries); he obtained a decision from the PM, and conveyed that to the Ministry. Sometimes the Principal Secretary passed these papers to me for examination, often by hand, to be returned to him the same way. Internal PMO noting summarized the issue, focused on the points for decision; such noting had to be in double space and was not to exceed one-and-half pages. It was surprising how complex issues could be distilled to their essence!
- A regular task was to receive the Prime Minister's foreign visitors at Gate No. 6 at South Block, or at the portico leading to her Parliament House office, and escort them into her office for the meeting, take notes and finally see them off, right up to their car. The requests for appointments usually went directly to the PM's Special Assistant Dhawan, but some also came to me, to be passed on to Dhawan. I was involved with only the official foreign visitors; there were a few other foreign guests that met her, including personal friends, of whom I typically

[12] In the mid-1970s, when I was in the Northern Division, the PM's decisions were often given on the files we sent to the PMO; clearly, working methods had been formalized by the 1980s.

knew nothing.[13] No one advised me on the way in which these records of discussion were to be written. I surmised that such documents had historic value and opted for detailed summaries, rather than relatively short notes highlighting only the main points. My reasoning was that a fulsome note gave flavor of the meeting; the records were of long-term value. I found later that different incumbents in my post had followed their own inclination, and some opted for short summaries. In the beginning I sent drafts of such records to the PM for approval, but after a couple of months decided to finalize them on my own; it seemed unreasonable to burden the PM, the more so when she seemed to accept such drafts without correction.[14] But if the visitor was of special importance, the draft note was indeed submitted to the PM for approval. Copies of the finalized notes went to the Principal Secretary, the MEA, and the Indian Embassy concerned.[15] By chance, one of those records is published in a massive collection of India-Pakistan archive documents, compiled by AS Bhasin. It covers Pakistan High Commissioner Abdul Sattar's farewell call on the PM. Reviewing Bhasin's compilation for an Indian journal I wrote on 30 July 2013:

> Mr Sattar wanted from Gandhi a word of praise; she was loath to being manoeuvred. This note reads: "[The PM said] ... it was high time that we put an end to confrontation. She was always a little sad to hear comments in Pakistan that she had

---

[13] Trawling through the internet I came upon a fascinating account of Indira Gandhi's meeting with a major Australian Jewish leader, Isi Leibler, former Chairman of the Governing Board of the World Jewish Congress, who met the PM at her residence on 21 December 1981; such meetings did not figure on the PM's official program, copies of which were sent daily to the senior officials at the PMO. In this particular case, what was intended to be a short meeting became a very substantive discussion that went on for half an hour. For details, see: http://jcpa.org/article/a-1981-meeting-with-prime-minister-indira-gandhi/

[14] I learnt later that some others that handled this job opted to send draft discussion notes to the PM for approval.

[15] I learnt subsequently that in later years, this method was modified, and sometimes portions of discussion records were left out of what was sent to the MEA. That may have been rationalized in terms of sensitivity of issues handled, but it did not make for effective foreign affairs governance.

not reconciled herself to the creation of Pakistan. Here in India she was often blamed for the opposite." When Mr Sattar waxed eloquent on his efforts to rectify distorted comments in the Pakistani press about India, and his help to Indian journalists to visit his country, Gandhi wryly observed: "...despite this there were frequent press statements, and also statements by leaders".[16]

- We needed quick reports on the meetings held by visiting foreign dignitaries with other personalities—since the meeting with the PM was typically at the end of the dignitary's substantive agenda—and this sometimes led to problems. Indira Gandhi was relaxed about the format in which such information reached her; a brief hand-written note was acceptable. Often there was simply no time to get from the concerned Ministry a discussion record or the points the visitor might raise. Sometimes MEA colleagues were reluctant to give this, even on the special secure phone system. I probably should have used greater finesse in making these demands; that contributed to my reputation as a demanding and 'difficult' PMO official.
- Indira Gandhi did not need briefings on international affairs, or on relations with major foreign countries. But she needed hard current information, say the volume of trade and trends, FDI flows and major bilateral projects in the pipeline. It was my task to provide such data, as relevant.
- A huge amount of effort went into preparing the program and detailed arrangements for the PM's overseas visits. This is detailed below.

On occasion, PC Alexander showed to me a list of ambassador appointments proposed by the Foreign Secretary and asked for suggestions, or comment on individuals. A couple of times I was told a suggested name was not suitable and that I should come up with someone else. This was handled in direct conversation, and the papers were returned to him in person. The Principal Secretary submitted his recommendations to the PM, via personal discussion.

I did not offer suggestions of my own on external issues, save on two occasions. Around December 1981, when Pakistan had

[16] Book review published in *Business Standard*, 30 July 2013.

persisted with its proposal for a 'no-war' pact with India, I sent a note to the PM, through the Principal Secretary, suggesting that we might propose a 'treaty of peace and friendship' to Islamabad, not because it had the slightest chance of acceptance, but as a counter-move. That note came back to me some days later, with a 'Seen' scrawled on it, over the PM's initials. About a month later, the PM announced in a speech that rather than sign a no-war pact, India wanted Pakistan to join in a treaty of peace and friendship. Thereafter, India did not hear of that no-war proposal.

In early 1982, I suggested in another note, again sent via the Principal Secretary, that we should set up a 'department' in the MEA for non-resident Indian (NRI) affairs, and gave the example of several other countries that were closely managing their diaspora policy. I received back that proposal after a while, with an inscription by PC Alexander that he had discussed this with the PM, who suggested that the MEA set up a division to handle NRI affairs. That advice was forwarded to the MEA. Some months later in 1982, the MEA created a 'cell' for overseas Indians, later raising it to a division. A new 'Ministry of Overseas Indians' was formed in 2004. In the post-May 2014 Modi government, this has now come back to the MEA as a department.

Papers sent to the PM usually came back in 24 hours or less. She dealt with most material sent to her desk as it came, with a rapidity that matched that of Jawaharlal Nehru; I saw from old papers that Panditji dashed off long notes the same day that someone—usually the Foreign Secretary—sent him a paper. A key difference: Indira Gandhi virtually never wrote long notes, handwritten or typed.

A footnote: since during parliament sessions the PM used her office in Parliament House rather than the one in South Block, in my first week at the PMO I asked my personal assistant for a staff car to go there, as a foreign dignitary was to call on the PM. With some amusement, he said that the PMO had no staff car! Surprised, I checked with Joint Secretary Rajamani, who said that we were expected to use our personal cars for such duties.[17] I found that there was a shortcut one could take to get from the PMO end of South Block to the PM's Parliament office, via the central core of North Block, but it involved a brisk 12-minute walk!

---

[17] This became a problem only when Mimi hijacked our Volkswagen Golf.

PMO Work Ethos

On the PM's staff, we learnt quickly that excellence was an expected norm, and merited no special recognition, except perhaps via an occasional, gentle signal from the PM. Deviations from this norm were not acceptable, and that too was made clear in its own way, rather more directly.

In my first months at the PMO, I proposed to Sharda Prasadji an interview with a Western journalist representing a major journal based in Delhi; I forget the name of the journal, but my motive was to help with the PM's international projection. When a first attempt was unproductive I mentioned this again; Sharda Prasadji told me bluntly that I should not push this idea, because the PM did not like that journalist. It seemed strange that a 'like' factor operated in such a manner. Subsequently I saw that among the foreign ambassadors too, the PM seemed cool towards a few, including one or two representing major powers. Indira Gandhi was very clear in her dislikes, and that sometimes impacted on Indian diplomacy, as described below.

Indira Gandhi put extraordinary effort into her prepared speeches, and this meant a huge amount of work for Sharda Prasad; he gladly tapped different sources, and spent much time with the PM to sense her thinking and to bounce ideas for major speeches; producing a succession of drafts was his exclusive task, one that could not be delegated. In those days before computers or the internet, he relied on his personal collection of reference material and multiple contacts across the media, academia and the civil service, for inspiration. Many speeches were finalized on the run, relying on teams of typists.

As Shardaji often explained, Indira Gandhi's thinking was linear, reflected in her speeches. Each sentence contributed to a tight, logical and sequential structure, without repeating points, nor providing 'connectors' between sentences and ideas. This made the speeches dense, and full of nuanced content. On a few occasions, speeches were finalized much in advance of the delivery date; one of these exceptions was her Sorbonne speech of November 1981, of which more later. Once in a while it happened that the PM either had to abandon a finely honed text, or was left without a prepared speech. Both these happened at the

Philippines in early October 1981; no one could doubt the capacity of the Marcos couple to surprise.

During that 24-hour visit to Manila, at a formal black-tie dinner banquet at Malacañang Palace, President Marcos delivered a witty, impromptu after-dinner speech that was elegant and very personal. Indira Gandhi abandoned her prepared text and responded in like manner; the evening was a great success. The next day Imelda Marcos hosted a lunch; during visit preparations, we had simply been advised that 'some ladies' would be invited; our ambassador did not furnish detailed information. The lunch was held at a large new convention center, featuring 600 Filipina lady guests, all in colorful traditional long gowns, with their puffed sleeves. It was like a festival of multihued butterflies. The only men present were some six of us, members of the PM's delegation; perhaps to give us solace, apart from PC Alexander and the Indian Ambassador seated at the high table, we were placed together at one of the round tables, close to that high table. After the first course, Imelda Marcos strode to the podium and delivered a tightly researched elocution on the historical panorama of India-Philippines connections, starting with maritime voyages several centuries back. Indira Gandhi raised an eyebrow at Shardaji (her eyebrows were mobile, highly expressive!), and the latter gently shrugged his shoulders to signify that we had been blindsided. No one had told us that speeches would be delivered at the lunch. She then got up to deliver a scintillating address of her own, entirely off the cuff. There was no fallout; the PM took it in her stride.

After I had been on her staff for a few months, I ventured to ask the PM if impromptu speechmaking was demanding; it probably took much effort. No, she responded, it is not so difficult. Getting into deeper waters, I then ventured the observation that it might be worthwhile to use that impromptu method more often, since it seemed to work so well. That bordered on the limit of the permissible, under what could be called an unwritten *lèse majesté* code, but she responded with a smile.

Producing any draft for the PM's approval was never easy. She loved to edit texts, and improved any draft presented to her. On one occasion, immediately after her April 1982 visit to London, when she established an extraordinary rapport with British PM

Margaret Thatcher at what was their first substantive meeting as prime ministers (they had also met briefly at Tito's funeral in May 1980).[18] I had put up a rather dull and routine draft message of thanks, and earned a massive reprimand, whose words are etched in memory. In large letters she wrote: 'Never, NEVER put up to me such a trite and cliché-ridden draft.' She then evidently sent a personal message to the British PM, which I never saw. True, my draft was terrible; that occasion merited a personal message from her, which I did not anticipate. That was a low point.

Personal Correspondence

Indira Gandhi carried out extensive personal correspondence with some world leaders, besides exchanges with her personal friends. None of this traveled down to PMO officials, and as best as I know, virtually nothing has been published; her interlocutors included Zambian President Kenneth Kaunda, Tanzanian President Julius Nyerere, British PM Margaret Thatcher and others; again the details are unknown. Since these touched on foreign affairs, and revealed her thinking, it is a pity that these archival papers remain locked up. After 30 years, it is time to act on the premise that the public has a right to these papers.[19] As

[18] Former foreign secretary MK Rasgotra gave the following important information in a 2015 conversation: 'Margaret Thatcher's first meeting with Indiraji was in 1972. I was Acting High Commissioner in London from April or May 1972 till the end of 1973. Margaret Thatcher was Education Minister in Prime Minister Edward Heath's cabinet. We had a long friendly chat when I paid a courtesy call on her. I had sensed a potential PM in her from her performance at the Conservative Party's Convention, which I had attended earlier. I had asked her whether she would like to visit India, and her quick spontaneous response was: "High Commissioner, I would love to visit India provided you can guarantee a meeting for me with Indira Gandhi." I had then sent a hand-written personal letter to Indiraji saying that Margaret Thatcher, a young Conservative star, possibly a future Prime Minister, was interested in visiting India provided PM would grant her a meeting. Indiraji's consent came promptly. In the event the two leaders met for an hour and half instead of the scheduled half-hour!'

[19] At the demise of Panditji in 1964 and Indira Gandhi in 1984, all papers were bundled together as 'personal' and transferred to family control. The same thing happened with Winston Churchill's papers after his death in 1965, with the difference that he had worked out the disposition of these documents in his lifetime. In reality, the bulk of such archives cover official matters, and should be under government control. In 2015, some of the Nehru papers have been opened up, at the Nehru Library.

for personal correspondence, one of her friends for many years was Gisela Bonn, author and Indophile; she lived in Stuttgart and became a good friend, till her demise in early 1995; I never ventured to ask Gisela about these exchanges.

Usha Bhagat, Social Secretary, handled all the hundreds of letters that came daily to Indira Gandhi from people across India and the world. A selection from these, about 30 or 40 per day were put up to the PM. She read these and sent out replies to about four or five each day. It may be hard to believe, but each of those pithy, direct responses came from her, dictated to a personal assistant, with no drafts put up by officials, not even Ushaji. Around June-July 1982, I went through a portion of this collection, which were typically filed together with the relevant incoming letter. Believing that they provided fresh insight into the thinking of a great leader, I prepared a short compilation, running to 30-odd typed pages. I discussed this with Sharda Prasad, and he seemed to agree that a small publication should be brought out. Before I left the PMO, in September 1982, I handed over these papers to him, but heard nothing further. I am sure copies can be found at the PMO.[20]

At this distance in time, I recollect only a few of the replies that Indira Gandhi wrote. One frequent refrain in the incoming letters was sympathy over the death of Sanjay in June 1980, and she was asked how she handled such a tragedy. Several of her replies used near-identical words to say: one never 'gets over' such loss; all that one can do is to absorb it within oneself, and get on with what needs to be done, rebuilding one's life around it. As always, her writing style was terse; many replies consisted of one single substantive sentence. She also employed humor. When someone asked her if the white streak in her hair was natural, or assisted with lotions, she simply replied: it has now become a kind of trademark! Long before social media, Facebook and Twitter emerged, that was Indira Gandhi's quiet way to connect with people.

PM's Foreign Visitors

Accompanying foreign visitors to meetings with the PM

[20] It did not occur to me to keep a copy of that compilation; doing that would have violated an ingrained work ethic.

produced remarkable insights. Some discussions were especially memorable. Indira Gandhi seldom engaged in small talk. If a visitor showed nervousness or was tongue-tied, she would maintain silence, perhaps twiddle a pencil, or even arch a mobile eyebrow. When I was Director (North), I vividly remembered a 1974 visit by a prince from one of the Himalayan kingdoms; he ran out of conversation after a few minutes. That led to prolonged spells of silence. Haider, Director on her staff and I, as two note-takers, struggled almost in pain to keep a straight face, until after some agonizing minutes, the prince decided to take his leave.

Most visitors spoke to the point; the PM expressed herself concisely, with no casual chatter. But she could also signal her mind through her mood and gesture. One of the most awkward meetings, around October 1981, was with Jeanne Kirkpatrick, US Permanent Representative to the UN, who held cabinet rank. The visitor commenced her remarks with an expression of sympathy at the tragic demise of Sanjay Gandhi, which for some unfathomable reason came across as gauche and insincere. The PM froze her out, responding to the visitor's subsequent remarks in monosyllables. Perhaps this had something to do with the PM's reservations at that time towards the Reagan administration, but more than that, it was just bad personal chemistry. The meeting ended in barely ten minutes, and the visitor left in deep embarrassment, literally quivering with emotion.

Soviet Defence Minister Marshal Dmitriy Ustinov visited India in March 1982, at the head of a large delegation that included 30 general-rank officers. The high point was his meeting with the PM, which was singularly unproductive. He suggested that Indian and Soviet navies should conduct joint exercises. This idea, floated often by Moscow in the past, was intrinsically unacceptable to India, which cherished its autonomy, the more so when efforts were underway to better ties with the West for economic and other reasons. The PM simply ignored this suggestion and proceeded to respond to the other points that the visitor had made. The Soviet visitor repeated the idea of naval exercises, and Indira Gandhi ignored that for a second time. She did not want to be drawn into that discussion. I asked myself if anyone, say Western observers who saw India as beholden to

Moscow, could believe that an insistent Soviet suggestion could be so finessed by an Indian leader. Later, I wondered if the PM held an additional private meeting with Ustinov at her residence; that seemed possible.

When Iranian Parliament Speaker Rafsanjani came to call on the PM in early 1982, Hamid Ansari (then Chief of Protocol at MEA, who became India's Vice President in 2007) was concerned that she might inadvertently hold out her hand for a handshake; this would have been against post-Revolution Iran's custom. The meeting was to take place at Parliament House; we chose the Cabinet Room as the venue, taking care that the Iranian delegation was ushered in and seated across the large table, before we brought in the PM. The conversation was unremarkable, but what sticks in memory is a note she scribbled out and handed to me, seated at the back row, while an interpreter was at work: 'The picture on the right wall is crooked. How can one sit in a room with crooked pictures?' Her sharp eye for detail and humor went together. I wish I had retained that note!

Among the more bizarre encounters was one with a US public figure with a checkered history, who harbored strange theories on global international finance. He held that the Jewish community, Swiss bankers and the British Queen were all involved in a plot to manage global affairs. He called on the PM in early 1982. This individual also ran a private intelligence network, funded by like-minded people. Part of his myth was his contact with world leaders, and he has subsequently spoken of 'meetings' with Indira Gandhi, and that he was in touch with her till her death in 1984. I learnt subsequently that this appointment was given on the recommendation of a Congress Party MP. A day before that meeting, two of his American acolytes, tough-looking minders claiming to be an advance team, met me to ask about the format. They might have not bothered, as the actual conversation on the set day became farcical; the visitor gave a short interpretation of how he saw world affairs, manipulated by that 'unholy trinity', Jews, Swiss banks and the UK Establishment. The PM tried to steer the conversation to other issues, but the visitor kept coming back to his bête noire. Thereafter, the PM mocked him gently, saying at one point: 'We should not forget the Queen.' That was one meeting where I gave up taking notes and struggled to keep a straight face.

Foreign Ambassadors in Delhi

Indira Gandhi received foreign envoys posted in New Delhi quite frequently, unlike leaders in most world capitals. In New Delhi, newly appointed foreign ambassadors made a customary first call on the PM, within a few months of presenting credentials. Subsequent access was not limited to the representatives of great powers; hardly a week passed without one or more ambassadors coming to meet her, either to hand over a communication, or to raise an issue deemed important by that country. She demonstrated clear likes and dislikes. Two of her favorites were the Bulgarian Ambassador Tocho Tochev, especially gregarious and cheerful. He had a smile for everyone, and addressed every Indian official as 'excellency'. I suspect Tochev was used by the PM to convey messages to Moscow, and he had access to her residence as well; I was not involved with most meetings held there. Another favorite was the Colombian envoy, a lady who spoke little English but got along famously with the PM—she was the only one Mrs. Gandhi received in her office on her sofa set; all others met her across her worktable, the same shallow, V-shaped table that Pandit Nehru had used (I remembered it from the 'interview' that our batch had with him in March 1960). Some envoys were visibly nervous at such meetings. For instance, the PM's meetings with the Soviet Ambassador Vorontsov always appeared formal.

A few European envoys, not belonging to major powers, were invited socially to the PM's home. I was not involved; these engagements were handled by her personal staff, and did not appear on her daily official calendar, copies of which went to the principal PMO officials. One in that favored cluster was the Cyprus High Commissioner, who later told me that when he was leaving at the end of his assignment in 1982, the PM told him that she regretted not having been able to fulfil her promise to visit his country, but he should tell his government that she would make the trip a little later. In fact she traveled to Cyprus in 1983.

One of Indira Gandhi's innovations, which later fell into disuse, was to annually invite all foreign ambassadors in Delhi to a series of tea parties at Hyderabad House; this state guest house was the PM's location of choice for official entertainment; it is run by the MEA, used exclusively by the PM and the External Affairs Minister, and sometimes by the Foreign Secretary and by other MEA secretaries.[21] All the ambassadors, then numbering about 90, were received in three batches in alphabetical order, with Chief of Protocol Ansari as the organizer. After the PM greeted the assembled guests, each was given an opportunity for a few minutes of private conversation with the PM, who was seated at one of the sofas. It was not always easy to signal to the envoy to make room for the next one in line, and that task fell to me, to hover around and gently urge the envoy to make way. I recalled this in Germany, where the system was different; each January, at the Chancellor's New Year reception for the diplomatic corps, entirely a standup affair, four or five envoys were selected for a tête-á-tête conversation (I received this honor in 1994). There, the Chief of Protocol stayed close by to remind the ambassador to make way for others. Indira Gandhi also received Muslim ambassadors at an *Iftar* dinner during the Ramadan month.

The access enjoyed by foreign ambassadors in New Delhi had a footnote. Indira Gandhi sometimes remarked that Indian ambassadors did not seem to meet with the leaders in their assignment countries. On two occasions I responded to her remarks to say to her that most foreign leaders did not meet with ambassadors resident in their capital; in the Arab world and in East Europe, of which I had experience at that time, such meetings were not permitted. 'Why is that? I meet ambassadors all the time,' she replied both times. It seemed pointless to explain.

Official Entertainment

The PM's official functions for visiting foreign dignitaries (usually a lunch for a president, since he would attend an evening state banquet at Rashtrapati Bhavan, or a dinner for prime ministers),

[21] The state-owned Ashok Hotel, provided the catering and services, and made a special effort to maintain high standards; Indira Gandhi did not offer any official entertainment at her residence, but after 5 and 7 Race Course Road became the PM's permanent official residence, after 1989, other prime ministers have held dinners and receptions at this official residence.

were held at Hyderabad House. Once in a while, the lawns were used for receptions. Official functions were not held at the PM's Residence.

Hamid Ansari worked assiduously on the PM's guest lists; he bore the main brunt for suggesting 'interesting persons', which was her standing demand. Sometimes we brainstormed together. He suggested the menu to the PM, proposed by top chefs at the Ashok Hotel, and drew up a seating plan. Indira Gandhi preferred a formal long-table format; the more casual format of round tables of 10 or 12 was not in vogue. She often changed the seating for the principals ('these two will have nothing to say to each other,' she might remark); she also took into account the language preferences of foreign guests, and bent protocol norms for their convenience. Behind all that was the PM's formidable attention to detail, plus consideration for her guests.

I cannot recall a single significant lapse at any of the dozens of lunches and dinners I attended while at the PMO, and that is a tribute to Hamid Ansari. He also steered a major change that was implemented in late 1982, in the official arrival ceremony for visiting heads of state and government. It meant crafting a brand new arrival ceremonial at the Rashtrapati Bhawan forecourt. This had its origin in what the PM observed during visits to foreign countries, in 1980-82, especially the manner in which Western countries had simplified ceremonials. It also meant dropping airport rituals. The PM's concern was that we should not tilt in the direction of oversimplification, when many developing countries retained airport ceremonials. Hamid Ansari worked out detailed options and carried out mock drills to hone our new ritual. Even after this, the PM delayed a final decision for a few months. This is the background to the current practice of an arrival ceremony at the magnificent forecourt of Rashtrapati Bhavan. With that, New Delhi also dropped the departure ceremonial, as had existed before 1982.[22]

22 Right up to mid-1982, Indian leaders traveled to the airport to see off visiting presidents and prime ministers; now it is the 'minister in attendance' that represents the government at both the airport arrival and departure of these dignitaries.

One day at lunchtime in March 1982, I received an urgent phone call that I was required at Hyderabad House, where the PM was hosting a lunch for personal guests. I found some 30 guests seated at the table and the PM asked me to take a vacant seat at the table end. A little while later she summoned me to phone her staff about some other personal guests who had gone sightseeing, to check if they wanted to go to Agra on a special flight that was to leave that evening with some foreign dignitaries. I went off to the ground-floor office—remember, mobile phones did not exist—and brought back to the PM an interim response. Some minutes later I was sent off on another phone errand, with one more to follow; it transpired that those guests had other plans and did not want to go to Agra. At the end of the meal, when I escorted the PM down the steps at the circular rotunda of this fine building, she remarked: 'He cannot even organize a simple lunch and wants to be an MP.' I could only guess the target of that unusual criticism. She then added, referring to the phone calls during lunch: 'Well, sometimes my bright ideas do not work out.' I replied: 'Perhaps, Ma'am, but they do keep us on our toes!' She took that sally with a cheerful smile.

The PM's Visit to the Commonwealth Summit and the Asia Pacific

After the demise of Sanjay Gandhi in a private aircraft crash on June 1980, Indira Gandhi did not travel abroad for over a year. Commencing on 23 September 1981, she embarked on a 17-day Asia journey, a centerpiece of which was a week in Melbourne, for the Commonwealth Summit (known by its acronym CHOGM).[23] She made six trips abroad in the 13 months that I spent on her staff. I traveled on five. As usual, no norms or template for planning the PM's visits existed (I developed the first version of a guidebook in early 1982); one learnt by doing, with all the errors this entailed.

Besides Australia, that trip included Indonesia, Fiji and Tonga before the CHOGM, and the Philippines directly after. An official delegation list of just 10 persons (besides personal staff

[23] The jocular unofficial meaning of this acronym is 'Commonwealth Holiday On Government Money'.

and security officials), was named in a note I received from RK Dhawan; no one from the MEA was included. I took this up with Principal Secretary Alexander. His response: You are from the MEA and represent them. I gently remonstrated that I was a PMO official; it was not right that no one from the MEA was included. He laughed and said that was the PM's decision. That pattern was replayed on four of the subsequent five visits. No minister joined her delegation, though External Affairs Minister PV Narasimha Rao came to Paris in November 1981, traveling directly to France for that leg of the visit. It also meant that senior MEA officials traveled in advance to these countries on commercial flights, not on the PM's aircraft, which could comfortably have accommodated several. In those days the PM traveled abroad on an Air India Boeing 707, leased for each journey. The Indian Air Force VVIP fleet did not have aircraft for long distance travel.

The 707 aircraft was modified. The entire front section became a private suite, with a bathroom, a sitting area for four persons across a table, and a bedroom section at the end. A narrow corridor along the side of the plane led to the next two sections, an executive class with wide seats in 2+2 configuration (with the Principal Secretary occupying the first row), for about 20 persons, seldom fully occupied, and an economy class section for the support staff, security personnel and the eight or ten journalists that were carried on the plane. Air India executives sat at the front of that section.

We reached Jakarta around 1700 hours on 23 September, and spent 25 hours in the Indonesian capital. That presidential complex, much like the one in the Philippines, is set in a luxuriant park, and is self-contained; it includes the presidential residence, a banquet house, a guest residence for high dignitaries and a host of ancillary facilities. A state banquet, with dancers and music, was held that evening, while the two leaders held official talks the next morning. The PM gave a press conference before departure that evening. Rather little of that visit remains in memory, except that the protocol arrangements were meticulous. Example: when delegation members searched for their pre-assigned cars, they found the chauffeur holding up a placard indicating the car number in that car-cade. The devil is always in the details.

The next stop was Fiji, the first visit by an Indian PM to the island-state, so closely connected with India; just over 50% of Fijians were descendants of indentured sugarcane workers. Ratu Kamisese Mara was long ensconced as prime minister; the internal instability that arose after 1987, with a succession of four coups by the armed forces, lay in the future, but tension was palpable between the two communities, the native Fijians and the Indian community, known locally as *girmitiyas*.[24] Those events showed the limit of India's capacity to help its overseas ethnic communities. The moral: New Delhi had to manage political complexity in ways that precluded those kinds of breakdown.[25]

The formal arrival ceremony took place in a stadium, amidst dance, music and traditional gifts. The high point was the ritual drink *hoqona*, offered as a liquid potion in a large shallow wooden bowl, made by ceremonially grinding roots and other vegetative material. We had been advised that the PM needed only to take a sip, to meet custom, but instead, in respect for tradition she took a deep draught, leading to spontaneous applause. On travels, Indira Gandhi relished local foods and customs; that was her personal hallmark, admired by all that saw it in action.

Tonga, the next stop, was an extraordinary experience; that South Pacific paradise was little touched by modernity at the time. The villages we passed on the way to our hotel were abuzz with activity; we were told they were readying their contribution to the King's banquet. Tongans are tall and heavily built; their women are statuesque. The King was a towering figure; he used a New York Checker Cab as his official limousine. At that evening's banquet, guests sat on cushions under small thatched roofs in the open, in clusters of six, around a five-foot wooden tray laden with fruit and other eatables; the pièce de résistance at each was a medium sized roasted pig suspended from an elaborate frame, all the food draped under a gauzy mosquito net. Each village contributed several trays, and immediately after the banquet the trays went back to the villages for their own feast. We ate

---

[24] That name came from the 'government permits' that these migrant laborers held.

[25] The expulsion of 'Asians' from Uganda by Idi Amin in 1972 had furnished that same lesson.

sparingly, careful not to disturb too much the elaborate décor of each tray; most of us did not touch the roasted pig.

The PM held a private discussion with the King of Tonga and the Crown Prince the next morning. We later went sightseeing, and visited a seaside site where the sea had cut under the rocks, creating vent-holes on the surface; ocean waves burst forth from these in sprouts of seawater. That evening the PM offered a return banquet, held at the residence of one of the princes. (Under Tongan custom that could not be held at her hotel, or another location; any place that the King visited for social entertainment then became taboo for others, unless it belonged to a member of the royal family.) Air India, our indispensable ally, had flown in cooks and food ingredients for an exquisite, authentic Indian spread that the Tongan guests relished, surely for the first time on their land.

Australia had made outstanding arrangements at Melbourne for the Commonwealth Summit, held from 30 September to 7 October 1981.[26] CHOGM met in a custom-designed, wood-built convention center put up for the event, deploying state-of-the-art technology, to be demolished afterwards. For instance, all delegates other than the heads of government were issued with electronic chip-embedded passes that were essential for entry. The objective was to automatically produce a complete entry record. The British Foreign Secretary forgot to bring his pass one morning and had to send someone to the hotel to fetch it, while he cooled his heels at the entrance. The facilities included a large plenary hall for the opening ceremony, a chamber accommodating 170 persons, with the 50 leaders seated around a large round table. Only the delegation leader could attend, accompanied by two others holding 'float passes', which automatically recorded each entry.[27] Officials met separately in another hall, to hammer out the joint statement, the customary end product of each CHOGM. Larger-than-life Shridath Ramphal of Trinidad, the PM's friend, heading the Commonwealth Secretariat, was a key player.

---

26 See Rana, *Inside Diplomacy* (2002), p. 242.

27 This is increasingly the method at major summits, to ensure that leaders speak among themselves in unscripted form; the Commonwealth lays special emphasis on such direct dialogue. At one point PC Alexander lent me his pass so that I could see the event—and I was promptly put at work by the PM to deliver verbal messages to some of the leaders.

The Commonwealth has long been in search for a role; this was evident in this elaborate but rather empty CHOGM biennial gathering, a one-week affair in those days, with a two-day 'retreat' in the middle, when the heads of government (or delegation leaders) met by themselves for frank, unstructured discussions, at a secluded venue.[28] Australia held its retreat at Canberra, at their Prime Minister's official residence. High Commissioner KD Sharma managed to be the only person other than the head of delegation to attend this retreat on a fulltime basis; this was a minor coup. Indira Gandhi appreciated that she had an aide at her disposal; it won for KD Sharma an unexpected bonus, an appointment in 1982 as India's High Commissioner to Islamabad. I was among a small Indian group that traveled to Canberra, to be available if needed. On the first Retreat day, I visited that venue briefly, to deliver an urgent telegram to the PM. I found Commonwealth leaders seated in clusters in the main salon in complete informality, chatting away.

Several episodes from CHOGM remain fresh. Just before leaving Delhi, the PM received a request from an Australian aboriginal organization for a meeting. All her advisers, including the MEA, the High Commissioner in Canberra and Principal Secretary Alexander advised against a meeting, but the PM wanted to see them. This went back and forth several times, and in the end, after reaching Melbourne, she agreed that a meeting would hurt relations with Australia. But she made it clear that she had declined with great reluctance. It was a classic dilemma between right action and the expedient. Had she received this group, she would have been on the right side of history. We may recall that General KC Cariappa, sent as India's High Commissioner to Australia in the early 1950s, after he had headed the Indian Army (before his elevation as Field Marshal), had ruffled many feathers by speaking out in favor of aboriginals.

The PM hosted two dinners for leaders at the Melbourne hotel where all the heads and about ten from each delegation were housed. She was the sole host at these dinners; I attended for the first 15 minutes or so, while she greeted the dozen-plus

---

[28] Since that time, CHOGM meetings have become slightly more businesslike, but still stretch over five days, with the Retreat in the middle.

presidents, prime ministers and spouses that attended each dinner, and then withdrew; not even PC Alexander joined the dinner. Indira Gandhi also held private meetings with select leaders, again, not attended by anyone from the delegation; High Commissioner Sharma played a role in arranging some of these. For some reason, Mrs. Gandhi was unwilling to respond to a request we received for a meeting from Sri Lankan Prime Minister R Premadasa; when I reminded her about this pending request, she replied that he was invited to one of her dinners and that was sufficient. This was evidently a consequence of personal dislike, which was unfortunate. Such slights are remembered for long.

It was at Melbourne that the PM finally decided that India would host the 1983 CHOGM, overcoming her initial reluctance on account of cost. Secretary General Ramphal had long pushed for this decision. On her instructions, I sent a note to all senior Indian officials to observe Australian methods, to identify those relevant for ourselves. Not one response was received. So much for advance planning! On the return leg to Delhi from the Philippines, I gave a handwritten note with several suggestions to the Principal Secretary, and later chaired one preparatory meeting for the New Delhi CHOGM, before this task was passed to the MEA.

The Philippines was the last stop, on 8-9 October 1981. Besides the state banquet on that night and the lunch hosted by Imelda Marcos described earlier, a high point was a tour by bus across Manila (in an elaborate motorcade) on the morning of 9 October, with the PM and the Indian delegation seated together. Imelda Marcos acted as tour guide, microphone in hand. She pointed out many new buildings and complexes constructed during the Marcos regime, most of them 'built by me, with help from my friends'. The previous evening, as delegation members sat around before dinner, while the PM and President Marcos were engaged in tête-à-tête talks, she walked into the salon; introducing herself (as if that was needed!), she proceed to chat with us. Imelda came across as the real force in that tandem political couple.

Of the four Indian heads of missions that the PM encountered on that visit (including High Commissioner KD Sharma in Australia), one of them received a rare personal letter of thanks that the PM dictated on the return flight, while two incurred her displeasure. On return to Delhi, PC Alexander sent a note to the Foreign Secretary asking that a written reprimand should go to both and that this should be shown to him in advance; he sent back the first draft sent by Foreign Secretary Sathe, and asked that a stronger message be sent out. In my time at the PMO, this was the only occasion that such reprimands were given to Indian envoys; the reason was the PM's personal impression of inadequate performance.

Other Foreign Travels

In 1981, India faced a serious financial crunch and needed foreign loans and concessional credits to implement development plans. This led to a situation where North Block (i.e. the Finance Ministry) dictated India's external agenda, and guided some of the PM's foreign travels. Indira Gandhi hated to ask for aid; one of her favorite expressions at that time in conversation with foreign leaders visiting New Delhi was that India needed some support to 'get over the hump', i.e. temporary assistance. It was left to others accompanying her, usually Principal Secretary Alexander to elaborate on that request; sometimes this took the shape of discussions with foreign leaders in her presence, where she would remain silent.

In October 1981, the PM traveled to Mexico for the Cancun Summit, stopping in Romania on the 18-19, for two nights. That capital showcased the grandiose plans of President Ceausescu, especially his massive razing of homes and buildings in the center of Bucharest to make space for a huge plaza facing the presidential palace, evoking Beijing's Tiananmen Square. On the return leg, from Mexico, the PM halted in London for a day, to informally meet Prime Minister Thatcher, and also take in a musical show, which was one of her loves. I should add that the PM's Boeing 707 aircraft had to make a refueling halt between Europe and Cancun, and she was emphatic that this should not be the US; thus on both legs the aircraft halted at Montréal.

The Cancun Summit was held on 22-23 October at this seaside resort; its two co-chairs were Mexican President Jose Lopez Portillo and Canadian Premier Pierre Trudeau.[29] It was an

[29] See Rana, *Inside Diplomacy* (2002), pp. 240-1, 244.

extraordinary event on several counts: the leaders of 22 countries attended, among them 14 developing states; for most it was a first opportunity to take the measure of President Ronald Reagan. Prior to the summit, a preparatory meeting was held at Vienna, but only to settle logistics. The Soviet Union and its bloc partners did not attend. The summit's goals were primarily economic, to see if leaders could agree to give new impetus to economic growth; Algeria had suggested an action plan to eradicate hunger in the world by 2000. The meeting atmosphere was relaxed; most of the discussion took the shape of direct, unstructured exchanges among leaders, with virtually no set speeches, but it produced no concrete outcome. No pre-cooked joint statement had been prepared, and remarkably, officials did not meet in parallel, much less draft a communiqué; it was left to the two co-chairs to sum up the discussions. The central Cancun premise, that leaders by themselves could come up with solutions, proved to be a chimera.

All the 22 leaders were housed in what was a vertical matchbox-shaped resort hotel; each delegation was allotted eight to ten rooms, besides a small suite for the leader.[30] That hotel was also the conference venue. The building only had two lifts, which meant that during the rush hour—immediately before and after meetings and for much of the day—the lifts were packed. Imagine, with each leader moving with a small phalanx of officials and escorts, when doors opened at different floors, those packed inside cheerfully waved to the waiting leaders, in what became a kind of holiday mood. I am sure the service staircase adjoining the lifts had never seen the likes of Mitterrand and Trudeau puffing up the stairs.

The PM's aircraft landed in the morning, a day prior to the summit; from the time we reached our hotel, around noon, till early evening, I was engaged in trying to line up the PM's meetings with other leaders, via their staff, working the internal phone and using the room list provided to us. Before leaving Delhi only two meetings had been fixed, with the US President and Chinese Premier Zhao Ziyang. The unspoken question, to

[30] Even the Indian Ambassador to Mexico could not be accommodated in this hotel; those in other hotels faced delay and security checks to get to the conference venue.

be handled gently, was: 'Who will call on whom?' Indira Gandhi preferred to have leaders call on her, but we could not insist that a president call on a prime minister. That was no problem with someone such as President Nyerere who cheerfully declared that he would come across to the PM's suite, but others like Algerian Chadli Benjedid's staff, were clear that the PM should come to meet their President. One of my minor coups was to tail the French President in the reception area on the first conference day and get from him a personal response that he would come to the *apartment* of Indira Gandhi.

The individual discussion with leaders was one of the real outcomes of Cancun. At the meeting with Ronald Reagan, the PM in effect moved beyond the legacy of the Emergency and the ensuing India-US antipathy. When the two leaders stepped out on the terrace of Reagan's penthouse suite (naturally the largest in the hotel) for a private chat, the assembled journalists and photographers hemmed them in, but they did manage to speak directly to one another. This produced for Indira Gandhi her decision that she 'could do business with Reagan' (as PC Alexander told us afterwards), and culminated in her July 1982 journey to the US.[31]

Only the leaders participated actively in the conference discussions; each delegation was given two 'float passes', to enter the conference room, which meant that most accompanying officials sat around in the ample lounges. PC Alexander, who was in the conference room much of the time, gave me his pass on day two, saying that I should go in to watch the proceedings for a few minutes, to witness an incomparable event. The leaders were in informal attire, and addressed one another by first names; discussion was amiable, but seemed to be going nowhere.

UN Secretary General Kurt Waldheim joined the summit. His single-point agenda was to solicit support for a second term in his job. For reasons not evident, the PM did not support his re-election, and would not give him an appointment, though G

[31] Foreign Secretary MK Rasgotra told me in a private conversation that right up to March 1982, the PM's key advisers were adamant that she should not take up the US invitation, for fear of offending the Soviet Union; this is to figure in his memoir that is in the works.

Parthasarathi, on our delegation, pressed for this. On the first day of the conference, while we were in the lounge, he told me in peremptory fashion that I should arrange the Secretary General's call on the PM. Aware of the background, I responded that this was beyond my ability and that he might like to do this himself. 'Don't be impertinent', he snapped back. In the presence of others, I explained that since the PM had shown reluctance to meet Waldheim, it was unfair to ask me to get her to change her mind. He did not pursue this further.

The PM had decided to host a lunch for the leaders on the first day, since there was no competing event at that time; invitations had been sent out from Delhi just before our departure. It became one of the major events, drawing 17 leaders, though President Reagan and the Chinese President did not attend. Only the heads were invited, and Air India provided a scrumptious banquet, prepared by chefs flown in from India; about five top personalities from the Indian delegation joined that lunch.

The return journey via London involved a private meeting between the PM and Margaret Thatcher; perhaps the decision on a festival of India in the UK was finalized at that time. We were to leave for Delhi at about 2330 hours, just before Heathrow's nightly curfew on late night flights, but left earlier. The PM's plans to attend a musical were abandoned owing to a bomb scare at the theater.

The next foreign trip was from 6 to 15 November 1981: three days each were spent in Bulgaria, Italy and France. An unusual amount of planning went into this particular trip for several reasons. For Rome and Paris, the PM wanted a minute-to-minute breakdown for each activity. I was asked repeatedly, by Dhawan and also by the PM, if the journey time from one location to another could not be reduced, to give her more latitude. In Paris, the PM and her delegation were to stay at Hôtel de Marigny, the official guest house in the center of Paris, and it was left to the super-efficient *motards* of the Gendarmerie to whisk the PM's motorcade through dense city traffic with an elegant series of brief roadblocks that permitted rapid movement with minimal traffic disruption. But it was the Sorbonne University speech that became the visit's preoccupation.

Ambassador MK Rasgotra obtained from Sorbonne—technically, University Paris 1—the offer of a doctorate *honoris causa* for the PM, not an easy accomplishment; he was adamant that the PM should speak in French at that prestigious function. The PM was equally determined that she would not subject her rusty language skills, acquired during schooldays in Switzerland, to a rigorous test in front of a discerning French audience. The issue remained unresolved; Shardaji told me, as we set out from Delhi on the trip, that the Ambassador would have to climb down. The first evening in Sofia, five days before reaching Paris, PC Alexander phoned Ambassador Rasgotra from the PM's suite at the Bulgarian guesthouse, to tell him that the speech would be in English, though the PM would make initial remarks in French. Rasgotra responded that the Sorbonne doctorate was predicated on the assumption that she would honor that important audience in their language. Finding that he had made no headway, PC Alexander simply told the Ambassador that he was handing over the phone to the PM.

The PM gently repeated what the Principal Secretary had said, but Rasgotra stuck to his guns, adding that this decision was connected with all we had tried to achieve with France. He also explained that he had arranged for a professor of French at Rome University to come to the PM's hotel at Rome and help her with the French text, which had been translated and would by waiting there. She finally relented. Rasgotra showed courage. He knew the PM fairly well and that episode, in a way a foundation to that successful French visit, clinched his appointment as foreign secretary some months later.[32]

Rome was marked by the smooth elegance of Italian arrangements, including a splendid lunch hosted by the Italian President in a pavilion-like salon that sits atop Quirinal Palace, the historic residence that has housed popes, kings and presidents; it is approached by a staircase, and gives a 360 view of the Rome skyline. The visit was marred a little for the PM by the need to

[32] During the Paris visit, I was struck by the ease that Ambassador Rasgotra reflected, and asked him about this. His response: we have rehearsed all the arrangements, and things are now on autopilot. I have confidence in my Embassy colleagues.

prepare for her Sorbonne speech. As the only member on her delegation who knew some French, I sat with her at a round table in her hotel salon, as she methodically went through the 15-page speech with the lady professor. It was a tribute to the PM's patience and determination that she showed no resentment that over five hours were spent in three days, repeatedly going over the text. In effect she sacrificed private family time, which she would have spent with Sonia's parents and family, who had specially come to Rome. When the aircraft took off from Rome for Paris, I was summoned to the PM's cabin and she again went over the text, reading it aloud; I offered small improvements to the pronunciation as needed. In fact her French was excellent, as was the accent—what was missing was her connection with the language, and confidence over how some words were pronounced. At Sorbonne, she delivered a flawless speech that won her much acclaim, and became the centerpiece of the visit.

The Paris visit was packed with activity. The PM prepared carefully for that visit. One evening, some ten days before she set off on that trip, I received the French Ambassador at her Residence, the only such call by a New Delhi-based envoy during my year at the PMO. She discussed some issues that were then current, and halfway through, told me that I could leave; she had another ten minutes of private conversation with him, the only such exchange that I recall. Paris was also the only foreign destination where External Affairs Minister PV Narasimha Rao joined her, having traveled direct from Delhi. President Mitterrand reciprocated the high importance she gave to reshaping that relationship; I believe this became a landmark in bilateral relations.

A conference of Indian heads of missions in West Europe was held in Paris, and the PM spent one morning with them, though I do not recall any special outcome from that discussion (the External Affairs Minister and senior MEA officials guided much of the discussions with our ambassadors). The PM also found time to meet with the Indian High Commissioner in London, who had come to seek instructions on some points connected with the Festival of India that was to be held in the UK in 1982-83. A leading Indian businessman in London, who had become an unofficial personal representative of Indira Gandhi, was also present at the brief meeting, which at one stage descended into a squabble between the HC and the businessman, till the PM spoke sharply and told both of them to focus on the event and not their personal differences. This was the only time I saw firsthand the power enjoyed by such private individuals. Indian leaders have tended to develop their own allies and friends among the Indian diaspora; a few have played a role in bilateral relationships with countries, especially in the UK and the US, though not on the European continent—even arranging political meetings for Indian visitors to these countries. Such actions undermine our envoys, but it is a fact of life that some diaspora businessmen command much local influence.[33]

This was the only visit in my time at the PMO when both of the PM's daughters-in-law traveled with her; Maneka Gandhi left Indira Gandhi's residence some weeks after that Europe tour. Two small incidents remain in memory. I heard that at Sofia, Maneka sought to meet a famous Bulgarian lady fortune-teller, and may have made prior arrangements for this purpose; it was said that Usha Bhagat was tasked to keep Maneka company, perhaps to try and ensure this meeting did not come about. In the event, that did not work and one heard that the meeting took place. The other incident involved a famous French photographer who had sought an appointment for a photo session with the PM at Paris; after consulting Shardaji, I had informed our Embassy in Paris that this could only be decided after the PM reached Paris. On the first day of the visit, hearing that the photographer was waiting at the Marigny entrance, I went out to meet him, to tell him I would check with the PM. At the Paris Opera that evening I found an opportunity to inquire, and the PM agreed; as for the photographer's request that Sonia and Maneka join her for some photos, she told me to check with them. Sonia agreed readily, but when I mentioned this to Maneka, she simply looked away. The next morning, the photo session was held in the main salon of Marigny, and in the garden; those striking photographs, depicting a regal Indira Gandhi, were subsequently carried in a leading French pictorial journal.

---

[33] A few Indian heads of missions or their deputies that have served in places such as London and Washington DC have spoken of this; the Indian media have not focused much on such activities.

After the visit to Italy, Ambassador Jagdish Ajmani took a fine initiative to write out a draft note for the guidance of Indian embassies on handling the PM's foreign visits. That seemed excellent, and after discussion with the Principal Secretary I worked on that first draft to produce a detailed guidebook. That became the first of such guides, which have undergone elaboration over the years. One weakness of the Indian system is a lack of such 'SOP Guides', setting out key procedures.[34]

It was on the way back from the long trip to Mexico that I had another taste of PMO undercurrents. The PM's personal major domo at her house was one Nathu Ram, a short round figure, who commanded a measure of influence of his own. It was said that ministers and others who wanted a good word put in for themselves, cultivated him. He was a permanent fixture on foreign trips. As he waddled down the aircraft aisle, coming back from the front section of the aircraft, he stopped to chat briefly. It may have been the PM's physician Dr. KB Mathur who introduced him, and after a few remarks, Nathu Ram said to me in Hindustani: 'You used to be Jagat Mehta's man, is that not so?' Astonished at his impertinence, I replied with equanimity that I was a simple civil servant, and owed no special allegiance to any of my seniors. Why that query? I guess it was a kind of shot across my bows, to demonstrate his proximity to the PM, i.e. that he was influential. It showed once again our feudal ways of functioning, and also unfortunately, how sycophants operate in proximity to leaders.

Festival of India in UK

The idea of organizing a yearlong presentation of Indian culture in its multiple forms and idiom, through the plastic arts, exhibitions, lectures and intellectual discourse, may have originated with Pupul Jayakar, longtime promoter of Indian arts and crafts,

[34] The phrase 'SOP' comes from the armed forces, where standard operating procedures are a fact of life. What we do tend to have are elaborate 'do and don't' guides for the food preferences of most of our leaders—ranging from the whimsy of a Morarji Desai, to the strict vegetarianism of many others. Indira Gandhi had no such food guide, and was happy with the cuisine of the lands she visited.

and a friend of Indira Gandhi. The PM readily supported this innovation in diplomatic exchanges, and in turn persuaded Margaret Thatcher to receive in the UK what was called a 'Festival of India', with each side taking care of its own expenses. During those 12 months, India sent over 30 groups of artistes, many different exhibitions and other cultural manifestations; UK's task was to receive them suitably and to organize all the local facilities, typically covering multiple cities and venues. No country had hitherto presented itself to a foreign partner in such an extended and multidimensional fashion.[35] We launched what has become a key cultural diplomacy blitz method.

Even with the UK covering all the host country's costs, the Festival cost India over ₹20 crore, an unprecedented sum for those days. It was only the PM's personal clout, and the assertive organizational talent of Pupul Jayakar that ensured cooperation of the varied Indian agencies that had to be cajoled and pushed into mobilization, including different Indian museums that have never taken to the notion of sending abroad their prize exhibits.[36] PC Alexander instructed me to attend some planning meetings that were held at Pupulji's residence and to report back on the discussions. After one of these, I asked him if we should not link these cultural events with some economic promotion activity. He responded rather sternly: stay out of making any suggestions of your own; you have a listening brief, to report back to me what transpires at these meetings; we are not to interfere with Pupul Jayakar's plans. Naturally, I complied. But, we did ourselves a disservice by failing to make the culture-economic connect.

The Festival was inaugurated in London on 22 March 1982; Indira Gandhi made for that a special five-day visit, her longest

[35] India organized such festivals subsequently in the USSR in 1983 and in the US in 1985-86. This is now a standard cultural diplomacy method, with presentations that range from a month to a year.

[36] After the first three Festival rounds (UK, Russia and US) stories emerged in the Indian press of small damage suffered by a few priceless Indian exhibits; it was never clarified how and where this occurred. Comparable art exhibits go around the world, from China, France, Italy and many other countries, without damage. One has the impression that Indian reluctance to exchange art exhibits is more an act of conservatism, and unwillingness by official agencies to pursue such cooperation.

to any single country in those days, besides a nine-day trip to the US in July 1982 when she traveled to several cities, including Honolulu. The glittering Festival inaugural at the Royal Festival Hall featured the melodious vocal Carnatic classical music of MS Subbulakshmi; Pandit Ravi Shankar performed jointly with the London Philharmonic Orchestra. Buglers of the Indian Presidential Bodyguard played a short fanfare with flourish. In London, the PM's hotel of preference was the Claridges, where she had stayed with her father. It was at this venue that she had her meeting with intellectuals, which drew amused comment from British journals, as noted below.

The substantive highpoint in London was the discussion at 10 Downing Street on an issue that had become *the* key deliverable. In essence, a round of fund replenishment for the soft-loan window of the World Bank, the 'International Development Association' (IDA) was due; the US, under Reagan had decided not to contribute. The question: could Europeans and Japan, the other contributors, be persuaded to go ahead? Naturally, it suited most finance ministries to keep away, claiming they could not act without the US. India, a major IDA beneficiary, was anxious to persuade London to keep up the concessional fund flow. That morning, a drama played out in two acts at the British PM's residence. While the leaders held their tête-à-tête, unaccompanied by anyone, Principal Secretary Alexander and a British FCO Minister of State held prolonged, inconclusive official-level talks. After over an hour, the two prime ministers joined UK officials; Mrs. Thatcher opened the second act with a breezy remark: 'What have you chaps been doing while we have been solving the problems of the world?' That produced contradictory summaries from the two delegations, first an anodyne piece of obfuscation from the UK, followed by a politely dissenting version from Alexander. Mrs. Thatcher declared that she did not understand the problem, and turned to Foreign Secretary Lord Carrington, who gave a succinct summary, a model of precision. Mrs. Thatcher decided on the spot that not only would the UK contribute to IDA, but would also try and persuade other European states to follow suit.

Now, after more than 30 years, it would be educative to find out from the UK archives the real story of that episode. Was it superb play-acting by the Iron Lady, or did she really not know about this key issue on the Indian agenda? In any event, it left Indira Gandhi and the Indian delegation deeply impressed with Mrs. Thatcher's sympathy, and decisiveness.

Much after I left the PMO I learnt that the one thing Indira Gandhi cherished was an opportunity to meet intellectuals and high achievers from different walks of life, especially foreign nationals.[37] Looking back, clearly I did not offer up any suitable candidate for such encounters.[38] During foreign trips to major Western countries she sought out intellectuals, consisting of scientists, authors, Nobel laureates and others. Both in Paris in November 1981 and in London in April 1982, the Indian mission organized tea receptions for this purpose, without involving the host country. Sharda Prasad finalized guest lists of around 20, in collaboration with our envoy in that capital. Held at the PM's hotel or place of stay, no one from her delegation or mission, besides Sharda Prasad, joined these. The guests were seated at tables of five or six, with one place left vacant, so that the PM could move from table to table, spending some ten or fifteen minutes with each cluster. Was that effective, or might it have been better for the PM to spend an hour with a smaller number of distinguished guests?[39] I do not know who thought up that particular format; underlying it was Indira Gandhi's hunger for intellectual stimulus. In the background was surely her awareness of having missed out on a university education, and a memory of how her father Jawaharlal had been a magnet for outstanding figures from around the world, when she served as his companion and hostess.

Of all the travels that Indira Gandhi undertook in my time in the PMO, those to the US, UK, France and Saudi Arabia were clearly the most important. Consider the evolution in her attitude

---

37 In the normal course, the PM met a wide range of Indians, including scientists and others, but I do not know if a special effort was made to meet authors or other intellectuals. But as noted earlier, she wanted her guest list at official dinners and lunches to be as varied as possible.

38 Even Sharda Prasad, a fine guide on other matters, did not mention this, and of course, there was no job description or suggestions furnished by predecessors.

39 That was the method employed by PM Narasimha Rao, on his visit to Berlin in February 1994.

to Washington DC. Travelling to Cancun, she was emphatic that her aircraft not make a refueling stop in the US. At Cancun she fended off attempts by the US TV channels to get her on their morning shows. But once she satisfied herself that President Ronald Reagan was open-minded, an extended charm offensive towards the US followed, culminating in her July 1982 visit. In the case of Margaret Thatcher, she found an easy bond. France, long neglected by India, became another key partner. With all three, the goal was not only to improve bilateral economic and political ties, but also to secure support for multilateral aid, via the World Bank, IMF, and the Asian Development Bank. Saudi Arabia, neglected in the past, became important for the economic investments it could furnish.

Some Incidents

The return leg of the PM's visit to Saudi Arabia in April 1982 produced an incident that affected my PMO assignment. That four-day trip ended with a visit to Dammam, the industrial and education center, one of the country's showpieces. We flew to Dammam that morning on a special Saudi aircraft from the capital Riyadh, and were to take the Air India special flight home in the afternoon, after a succession of visits to industrial plants and institutes, with a quick lunch in between. After the last engagement, the entire entourage traveled by motorcade, directly to the airport, a journey of 30-odd kilometers.

The Saudi princes and ministers who had accompanied Mrs. Gandhi saw her off; while the plane was taxiing to the takeoff point the Air India Director came to my row of seats. Seated next to me was the head of the Press Information Bureau (PIB), responsible for about 15 Indian journalists taken on this trip; he said that a journalist who had been left behind had now reached the airport. While the PIB official kept silent, I remarked: 'I guess it is too late now to turn back'. I did not realize that Air India had not reported the problem to anyone else, perhaps on the principle that bad news should be conveyed to the lowest level tenable. I assumed that the Principal Secretary, seated two rows ahead, had been informed.

Once in the air, this news reached PC Alexander who took me to task for not informing him immediately. I explained the situation to him. I also tried to reason that it was hardly feasible for the PM's aircraft to turn back after a ceremonial farewell, but he rightly asserted that this was not for me to decide; nor was it valid to assume that he had been informed. On reaching Delhi, I was told that the PM wanted a written explanation. I wrote out a short note that my failure to inform the Principal Secretary was a major lapse of judgment, and conveyed my sincere apology. I thought it irrelevant to add that the PIB official also bore responsibility.

The PM's travels produced other incidents. Air India brought up a new issue several weeks before the July 1982 visit to the US and Japan. The airline's Regional Director in Delhi, who traveled on the PM's aircraft on all overseas trips, met me with his team, to suggest that a Boeing 747 aircraft should be used for this journey, as this was 'safer'. I knew that this point had come up earlier, but the PM was clear that using such a large plane was ostentatious and needlessly expensive. I told the Air India team that the issue was too important to be tackled in a conversation with me; if it was their professional advice that it was unsafe to make that round-the-world journey (US-Hawaii-Japan) on a 707 aircraft, they should write directly to the Principal Secretary. I also told them that notwithstanding the PM's preferences, they had the right and obligation to give their best professional advice on such a vital matter.

They promised to get back after internal discussion. Some days later they returned to say that in their reconsidered view the 707 was safe, but it needed some additional navigation aids, which they were in the process of installing. Naturally, I reported these exchanges at each stage to the Principal Secretary. One might add that the US President continued to use a 707 aircraft as Air Force One for his travels right up to the mid-1990s.[40] When Rajiv Gandhi came to power in November 1984, he switched to a 747 aircraft for his foreign travels.

---

[40] It may also be noted that the US 'Air Force One' planes—actually more than one 707 aircraft—have been continually modernized and refurbished during this long period of service.

Another incident comes to mind. Indira Gandhi had limited knowledge of economic terminology—despite her clear gut understanding of economic issues. For instance, she sometimes said that the only decision she regretted was the devaluation of 1966, just after she assumed office. She implied that she had not fully examined that proposal and acted on erroneous advice—but she did not say this explicitly.

At a rare internal meeting in early 1982, attended among others by PC Alexander, Economic Adviser Arjun Sengupta and Information Adviser Sharda Prasad, where I was present, she remarked: You people keep telling me that inflation is going down, but I see prices rising all the time![41] None of the worthies present pointed out to the PM the distinction between the inflation rate and price rise. I thought perhaps someone might offer this correction privately, but evidently that did not happen. Some days later, meeting a foreign dignitary, she repeated that remark, and I kept silent. When it happened a second time with another visitor, perhaps a European foreign minister, I stayed back at the end of the meeting, and said to the PM: 'May I mention something? Economists use words in a complicated way; when they speak of the rate of inflation what they mean is only that the rate of price increase has slowed.' She replied: 'Fine,' and I left. In retrospect, that was an act of *lèse majesté*, but what was one to do? Loyalty to the PM did not mean blind followership. Surely service values require speaking up, of course as tactfully as possible.[42]

Departure from PMO

In May 1982 PC Alexander summoned me to his office. With a stern face, he told me that I would have to return to MEA, adding the reason: 'The PM does not like you'. There had been straws in

---

41 Both these officials held the rank of 'Secretary to the Government'.

42 Writing on the Emergency (1975-77) when the government assumed extraordinary powers, Natwar Singh, an uncritical admirer of Indira Gandhi wrote of the PM's style: 'Even a mild form of *lèse majesté* was not permitted.' (*Walk with Lions*, 2013, p. 73). I have subsequently discussed this episode with IFS colleagues. Some felt that I was foolish to stick my neck out, while a minority sympathized with the dilemma, and felt that my action was right.

the wind, and I was not taken by surprise. I replied that for any civil servant it was a unique privilege to work in the PMO, the more so under a leader such as Indira Gandhi. I was ready to go back to my Ministry whenever released, and would await further instructions.

For all my brave words, this came as a shock. At one level I was astonished that the PM had formed such a dislike. Besides the events narrated above, I had made mistakes. One was a faux pas in the early months of my job, using stenciled cover letters to Indian embassies, when forwarding the PM's national day greeting messages. Drafts of such messages came from the MEA; I made amendments as needed, obtained the PM's approval, and sent the text to the Indian embassy concerned via telex, while the signed copy went to the embassy via the diplomatic bag. The stenciled cover note was used for this signed copy, for what was a routine cover message to an Indian embassy. One day in early 1982, PC Alexander asked if I had been sending the PM's messages in this fashion. He added that Natwar Singh, leaving his post as High Commissioner in Islamabad, had shown my cover note to the PM (probably with which went the message for Pakistan's national day) and told the PM that unlike 'in my days' when the PM's messages were treated with reverence, shabby methods were now in use. Alexander said: Natwar Singh's motive was to show the incompetence of his successors at the PMO. I agreed that my action had been unwise.

It did not strike me that I should have given to the Principal Secretary an account of the positives I had accomplished. For instance, a small change had been made at my suggestion some weeks after I joined the PMO in relation to the PM's correspondence with foreign leaders. Noting that most messages from leaders came encased in elegant folders, I had suggested to Dhawan that we should do the same, using handmade paper. He had swiftly implemented this change. I had not thought to showcase this to anyone to claim credit.

Another possible error: around that time, I had developed a friendship with Joint Secretary Vijay Tripathi, sometimes spending time in his office to chat over a cup of tea. Possibly this was seen as a personal alignment, especially as little of my work intersected with Tripathi's remit. I should have realized that such actions at the PMO attracted notice, and became subject for interpretation in a politically charged atmosphere.

Around May, another incident placed me in difficulty with the MEA. Principal Secretary Alexander told me to send a note to the Foreign Secretary asking for a draft on some matter. I replied that such a message from me to the Foreign Secretary would be seriously misunderstood as an act of arrogance, and that I would put up a note to Alexander, which he could sign. For some reason, Alexander was adamant and said he had no time, and I should do what he wished. I took care in writing that note to the FS, emphasizing that I acted on instructions, and that the requested draft was to be sent direct to Alexander. My big error was that I did not walk across to the FS's Office and explain the background to him. As it turned out, Foreign Secretary Rasgotra took umbrage, and discussed this with the other secretaries, including Natwar Singh, at their then customary daily morning meeting.

I waited for over three months for my replacement, Gharekhan, in a kind of strange limbo. I did not join the PM's nine-day trip to the US, which covered New York, Washington DC, the West Coast and Hawaii, with a subsequent half-day stopover in Tokyo, to meet Prime Minister Suzuki and attend a dinner. The usual routine of the PMO work continued, including hectic logistics for that extended US journey, but I was not involved in substantive pre-visit discussions.

Looking back, I mainly blame myself for that fall from grace at the PMO. I had not heeded the trenchant advice Foreign Secretary Sathe had given when I joined, and failed to understand the nuances of its inner working. When things went wrong, some officials greased the skids, but is that not that the way events play out in highly charged Indian establishments? Once an official is in difficulty some others—not all—will try to profit from that, to improve their own standing. That is human nature; the PMO was a fairly ruthless place.

On my final day at the PMO, in mid-September 1982, I had a brief meeting with the PM. I thanked her for the privilege she had given to me to serve in the PMO. The Prime Minister responded by saying that my move back to the MEA 'does not mean that there was anything personal against you'. I replied that it might be good if that message could be conveyed to my Ministry. She surprised with her response: 'I will tell the Foreign Minister and the Foreign Secretary that you are not to be humiliated on your return.' She understood accurately that some of my own colleagues would want to settle scores with me. And that was precisely the reception given to me by a few IFS colleagues, though many were sympathetic, even supportive, including Foreign Secretary Rasgotra. It was the PM's assurance that then helped me to overcome some issues. I was determined to hold my head high, and remain on a path of professionalism and rectitude.[43]

The Larger Picture

How did India's foreign policy appear as seen from the apex of Indian governance? Even while I was not involved on matters relating to high policy, it is worth recounting some impressions.

Foreign aid was a high priority, and shaped especially the Prime Minister's travel agenda. Alas, immediate neighbors were below the radar for Indira Gandhi, which for too long has been a weakness in India's foreign policy. One should remember that SAARC as a regional group did not exist at that time.

What were the priority countries as seen from the PMO? Major Western powers figured prominently, but Germany was a strange omission. The Soviet Union received special attention; she made a six-day visit in 1976, and her final visit to Moscow was in October 1982. In contrast, Asian states received scant attention—consider the one-day visits to Indonesia and the Philippines, in contrast to longer stays at Fiji and Tonga, to say nothing of East Europe. The MEA had a minor role in visits; the Foreign Secretary may have offered suggestions to the PM and to the principal

---

[43] In April 2015 when I showed a draft of this chapter to former foreign secretary MK Rasgotra, he very kindly offered the following comment: 'A day or two after you quit the PMO, at my morning meeting with the PM she had asked what I planned to do with Rana and I had told her that Rana was a most competent IFS officer and I needed a few days to rearrange placements in MEA to have him with me to assist me in administrative work. Her one-word response was: "good"; and we moved on to another topic.'

secretary, but the decisions came directly from the PM, especially the duration of each visit. Indian ambassadors guided the visit content, but were subject to intense personal scrutiny by the PM, usually conveyed through the PMO joint secretary. I recall well the intense exchange of telex messages and phone calls with our ambassadors in the weeks before each journey. This was not an ideal method, in terms of visit prioritization and sequencing, to maximize foreign policy impact.

One conditioning element was the legacy of the Emergency, and Indira Gandhi's desire to move out of its shadow. Consider the effort made to avoid a stopover in the US on way to Mexico, and the huge sense of relief after the first Gandhi-Reagan meeting at Cancun in October 1981, which led swiftly to an extended, multilayered journey to the US in July 1982.

Overall, the MEA was sidelined in my time at the PMO. Things changed after Rasgotra took over as the Foreign Secretary in April 1982, but PC Alexander retained his primacy as the key adviser on external issues, the more so with a decline in G Parthasarathi's role.

Concluding Observations

Once, Vijay Tripathi consulted me on a major appointment. When I told him that as best as I knew, the person being considered was competent and clean, his insistent query in response was: that is all very well, but is this person 'reliable'? This was a revealing insight into how those in power look for the like-minded, as their political acid test, to ensure that those in high offices conform to the prevailing political ethos, and will not rock the boat. If each administration tries to appoint those that are intrinsically oriented in their favor, i.e. cast in its own image, how will the country achieve good governance? If we interpret 'reliability' in such a narrow, self-preserving context, how will those that are straight and honest, but not given to conformist sycophancy, ever gain traction? And who will be the loser when those in high office do not speak truth to power? This is a major problem for Indian governance.

I had long admired Indira Gandhi for the extraordinary leadership she provided to India, and her deep personal commitment to the country's advancement. I have no first-hand knowledge of all that transpired during the Emergency, i.e. India's dark night from June 1975 when she shocked India and the world, right up to to March 1977 when she lost the general election, even losing her Parliament seat. Like many of my generation, I lamented the excesses of the Emergency, but saw little of those days, having left for Algeria in September 1975. But even in those first two months in Delhi when I was immersed in winding up my affairs and preparing for a first head of mission assignment, I saw the climate of palpable fear and ultra-caution among civil servants. Close friends spoke in lowered voices and eschewed customary banter about political figures. Some ripples of the Emergency even reached Algeria. My personal setback at PMO has done nothing to diminish admiration for the extraordinary leadership that Indira Gandhi provided to India.

In my view, Indira Gandhi's years in the wilderness were punishment enough. They did not warrant the mindless actions of a vindictive Janata regime that jailed her in early 1979. That gave her hero status, which became her path to re-conquering the heart of India, to win re-election in December 1979. My 13 months on Indira Gandhi's staff have only enhanced my admiration for this charismatic figure. Her net contribution to India is greatly in excess of her shortcomings.

India's need for external economic support underlay India's foreign policy in 1980-84, as witnessed in the restoration of the relationship with the US, new fecundity in India-UK ties, and a real opening in ties with Paris, much neglected in the past. But she and her advisers failed to read the tea leaves in relation to Asia. The very first foray into restarting discussions with China in December 1981 was mishandled.[44] In South-East Asia, nonaligned India paradoxically showed how deeply it was a legatee of the Cold War, in exhibiting little interest in the region and acting without mindfulness towards the key ASEAN countries.

In her economic policy, Indira Gandhi was surrounded by a phalanx of advisers who were steeped on old-think, rigid statist

---

[44] See the Oral History record of Ambassador Eric Gonsalves; he led the Indian delegation to the first round of India-China talks in Beijing, December 1981, www.icwa.in/pdfs/Ohericgonsalves.pdf

policy that paid lip service to socialist shibboleths and failed to comprehend its failure. Perhaps she lacked self-confidence in her own instinctive understanding of the country's economic needs, and perhaps she was also a victim of her own political posturing in the *Garibi Hatao* actions. But some easing of economic policy and opening to foreign investments did take place in that final term, after 1980. That is a story that is waiting to be told, especially the interplay between Indira Gandhi's instincts and her timorous advisers.

Indira Gandhi, despite foibles and small weaknesses, was a towering personality, profoundly committed to serving India. The good that she did, and the leadership she provided to our nearly ungovernable country far outweighs the lapses of the Emergency, that detour from democracy. She paid the price for that, and returned to office in January 1980 with renewed commitment, initiating the huge political and economic consolidation that India achieved in the ensuing years. The roots of Narasimha Rao's Economic Reforms of 1991 are traceable to that period, partly carried forward by Rajiv Gandhi in 1984-89, even though Rajiv's innate decency and sincerity did not match his administrative acumen. That is another story that begs to be told.

9

A Final Sojourn

Ministry of External Affairs (1982-83)

Returning to the MEA from the PM's Office was bittersweet. For about two weeks, I felt adrift, without a real assignment or clear work designation, suffering from the blunt reality of being ejected from a prime job, for all my fine words about willingness to return to my parent ministry. Snide comments from a few colleagues also hurt a bit. But then I was appointed to a professionally rewarding job, and could throw myself into new tasks.

On my first day at the MEA, the senior colleague to whom I reported was brusque: While in the PMO you had suggested the creation of a unit in the MEA to handle matters relating to Overseas Indians. Why don't you take this on, and head our first Overseas Indian Cell? By offering a minor position in a unit to be created from scratch, clearly he was settling an old score; while I was at the PMO he had felt slighted when his wife was dropped from the PM's banquet for a visiting prime minister, though she was the 'Lady Accompanying' that dignitary's wife.[1] He did not believe my explanation that the PM finalized her guest lists, and frequently struck off names from drafts. I guess it was hard to believe that a PM went into such detail.

---

[1] He was not the only one at the MEA to derive satisfaction at my exit from the PM's Office, but such a reaction is natural. We are all programed towards a degree of *Schadenfreude*. And I had been less tactful than I ought to have been while working at the PMO.

I barged into Foreign Secretary MK Rasgotra's office and requested him to find a suitable job for me, in keeping with the PM's assurance that I 'was not to be humiliated'. He promised to deal with this, and give me a worthwhile assignment. For a few days, I had no job. I spent time at home, rather despondent, sitting on the lawn of our C-I residence on Humayun Road (I had inherited that choice four-bedroom house, a stone's throw from Khan Market, from PMO predecessor Kamal Bakshi, retaining it till my departure from Delhi at the end of 1983). For several days I handled the work of Joint Secretary (UN) who was away in New York for the UN General Assembly session. That was temporary, covering a subject of which I knew little. In early October I was appointed Joint Secretary (Administration), traditionally one of the key jobs at the MEA.

This chapter mainly covers personnel administration, a subject not known for reader appeal, even less for glamor. Yet, in any foreign ministry, people management is a central task, since it deals with the only real resource that this entity possesses, i.e. its personnel at all levels. It became a great opportunity to understand better the working of the MEA.

Administration Division

The Indian system of financial control is unique. It originated in the 1920s, when the colonial administration saw that the progress of gradual transfer of power in India meant that some ministries and official agencies would be under Indian control. The system deployed was intended to give the Finance Ministry tight authority over the utilization of funds, thorough its Department of Expenditure. Thus, all expenditure, even in relation to the budget of ministries that has been approved by Parliament, requires a second round of approvals from the Department of Expenditure. Finance Ministry officials attached to each Ministry carry this out; money cannot be spent without the approval of what is called 'associated finance', and they send major proposals for further examination by the Expenditure Department. They enjoy extraordinary power. In few other countries does the Finance Ministry have such stranglehold over the entire government. (Compare this with the situation in most African states, where the permanent secretary is also called 'chief accounting officer' and bears personal responsibility for ensuring that his ministry keeps within the sanctioned budget; he is then left free to act, while conforming to financial regulations).

The head of the MEA's Finance Division is traditionally an additional secretary brought in from the IAS or one of the central services. An IFS Director assists him; he too has to follow the line set by the Department of Expenditure. Frequently, the Additional Secretary (Finance) overrules the Foreign Secretary on matters such as visits abroad by MEA officials. As one former foreign secretary told me, from time to time the Finance Division needs to be 'hammered down'; foreign secretaries have adequate latent power to overrule them, but few are willing to do this. The reason? Apprehension that this will blot one's copybook, in relation to the post-retirement assignment now perceived as a 'right' of every secretary-rank official. The political leadership dispenses this favor at will. Many officials are thus inhibited from doing the right thing for fear of displeasing the political masters.

The MEA's administration work was split mainly between two joint secretaries, one handling all personnel issues, and the other the 'establishment', meaning the drawing up of rules and overseeing their application, plus the provision of all the MEA services including those to missions abroad, property related issues, as well as inspection of missions carried out on an ad hoc basis.[2] Lalit Mansingh (1963 batch) was the Joint Secretary (Establishment). Additional Secretary JR Hiremath (1934-2014) supervised both the joint secretaries, as also some other units such as Vigilance and 'Personnel' (which meant security, at MEA and at missions). Further, at that time, this Additional Secretary also worked with Ambassador Samar Sen, appointed in mid-1982, chairing a committee reviewing the working of the MEA;

---

2 From 1956 to 1958, the MEA had an 'inspection unit' which visited all embassies and consulates, but thereafter, this task, vital in any diplomatic service that has a substantive spread of missions, has only been carried out on an ad hoc basis. An Inspection Unit was established in the mid-2000s, but works fitfully; the time is ripe for this unit to focus on mission performance.

Sen chose to focus initially on the functioning of embassies.[3] At the end of 1982, Foreign Secretary summarily decided to remove JR Hiremath as head of administration, re-assigning him to work full-time with Ambassador Sen. The FS probably had his reasons, which he did not share with me when he told me to issue an office order to this effect. I said one could not act in that fashion towards a senior colleague; fine, he responded, I will issue the office order. I urged that a senior colleague deserved to be told of the reassignment to his face, but the Foreign Secretary was adamant that he did not need to do this. In the Indian system, the Foreign Secretary has a special role, as the head of the IFS, and cannot delegate administrative authority to anyone; this circumscribes the role of a secretary or additional secretary heading the Administration.

This meant in effect that for a year, during 1983, the MEA unusually had no one at secretary or additional secretary rank to supervise the administration; Lalit Mansingh and I worked directly under Foreign Secretary Rasgotra. That worked well, mainly because of the latter's confident work style and willingness to delegate. For us as joint secretaries, it meant a wider field of ambit than usual. Rasgotra preferred to deal with issues across the table, rather than read lengthy notes on file. That led to efficient work; daily, I could take to him personnel matters on which I needed approval, especially those relating to senior colleagues; he would give decisions across the table. In no instance did he later question the action taken, even when senior ambassadors wrote to him appealing against a decision I conveyed on the MEA's behalf.

I commenced work with a major legacy issue. In the earlier period 1979-81, the MEA's Administration, under Additional Secretaries NP Jain and SK Singh, mainly at the initiative of Joint Secretary Kiran Doshi, implemented a number of important reforms, which were essential especially for embassy personnel

[3] This was the MEA's second foray into comprehensive reform, after the 1966 Pillai Commission (Chapter 3). Alas, the effort ended badly, owing to indecision in the MEA. The Sen Report, produced at the end of 1983 was filed away, neither published nor examined in detail. JN Dixit gave first pubic airing to its major findings in his book, *The Indian Foreign Service: History and Challenge* (2005).

posted abroad, which had been delayed for many years, owing to resistance, even intransigence, from the Finance Ministry.[4] An example: children's education facilities for officials posted abroad were dismal; right up to 1980, embassy officials, diplomatic and non-diplomatic, received ₹200 per month as 'children's education allowance' for children at local schools; for children that stayed back in India, the allowance was ₹100, but they also received each year a 'children's holiday passage', allowing children to join their parents during long school holidays. At one stroke, the Singh-Doshi team implemented a long pending proposal, permitting all India-based officials, regardless of rank, to send children to the cheapest English-medium school, at government expense. This permitted families to be together, and on average did not cost much more than the annual children's holiday passage. Similar actions were also implemented in the use of staff cars and other basic amenities that were vital for embassy personnel. Other reforms covered the medical scheme for all grades of home-based officials, payment of daily allowances, foreign allowance payment in US Dollars at places that had non-convertible currencies and other actions of this genre. These reforms ended what had been a particularly anomalous situation in which the unattractive posts abroad (those classified as 'C' or 'C-' in the MEA's five-step system), were also the places with the poorest allowances. A major consequence to the improvement in allowances and benefits at hardship posts has meant that the relative attractiveness of all categories foreign assignments is now fairly even.

Most of the above was done with the knowledge of the Finance authorities, but some actions were implemented unilaterally by MEA, when the Department of Expenditure delayed matters endlessly. By the time I came on the scene many of these issues had been resolved with Finance, but it had left the Department of Expenditure with a sense of resentment towards the MEA.

---

[4] Kiran Doshi had a degree of understanding of the MEA administration issues that was unmatched, having served as Deputy Secretary (Establishment) in 1975-76, plus a second spell from 1978-81, starting as Director (Finance), and ending as JS (Establishment & AD). He also steered the MEA's major overseas embassy property acquisition program that commenced in 1980, which has been of inestimable value to the country.

Consequently, I ran into a problem within the first few weeks. I unilaterally approved action, involving the baggage of an official who had served as Consul General at Medan, on a strong recommendation of the under secretary concerned, putting aside my doubt that the matter needed Finance approval.

True enough, when Finance came to know of this, I received a written summons, to meet the Additional Secretary CG Somaya, a particularly fine official (who later served as Comptroller and Auditor General). He asked me to explain our action; I replied that it was an error of judgment not to have taken Finance approval, and such action would not be repeated. His rejoinder: 'That is a glib response.' I then explained that it was not my practice to give excuses, but if he wanted to know how we came to act as we did, I was glad to explain the logic of our action, which was correct in substance, but wrong on procedure. The conversation then took a cordial turn; he understood that we had acted in conformity with rules. We parted on good terms. But we also saw that after the SK Singh-Doshi reforms, we were on a tight leash.

Personnel Administration

I commenced this 15-month spell with a small step, maintaining an 'open door' to all members of staff, allowing anyone to meet me, without appointment. It made for interruption most of the day, but it also provided much needed access for troubled the MEA personnel, plus insight into their problems. I took swift action where needed, also giving short shift to those with unreasonable demands. Coming in to work at 0900 hours each morning, I had over an hour for quiet work on major issues, including files put aside the previous day for reflection. This allowed me to end the workday at 1730, contrary to the MEA practice for officials, especially for heads of divisions, to linger till late hours.

The MEA's 'Senior Establishment Board' (SEB), handles transfers of section officers and private secretaries (both take rank of attaches abroad, but are not treated as 'representation officials'), and personal assistants.[5] This is an important cluster

[5] What attaché rank means in the Indian system is that the official is included in the embassy diplomat list, but does not receive a representation grant (i.e. an official entertainment allowance).

of officials; Joint Secretary (AD) chairs this SEB, with other administration officials as members. Typically, non-diplomatic staff in the MEA alternate between headquarters and embassies; personal assistants and private secretaries are the only officials, (other than executive level diplomatic officers) that go directly from one embassy to another, before returning on a home posting. The change I brought about in SEB was to eliminate a pre-cooked 'slate' of transfer proposals; that was usually the way those with influence massaged choice postings for themselves. The new method: the meeting would commence with examining the list of officials 'ripe' for transfer, and broadly earmark the category of posts to which they might be sent (i.e. under the MEA five category formula: 'A+, A, B, C, and C-'); thereafter, we would look to the openings available, and fit the earmarked officials into these. I ignored all scraps of paper on which a wide range of colleagues, including senior ones, sent in their recommendations in favor of particular individuals. (The only exception was requests sent on medical grounds; the Indian system has always been soft in accommodating these, leading to exploitation by a few). That meant slightly more work for the Board, but no one could manipulate things in advance; board members were free to suggest individuals for particular posts, provided they could justify this in open discussion. This change worked well, improving both fairness and credibility.

The 'Foreign Service Board' (FSB) decides on appointments of diplomats to embassies, i.e. those at ranks of third secretary (IFS probationers), up to consul general and deputy chiefs of missions. Ambassador appointments are handled differently. The Foreign Secretary chairs FSB, and the other three MEA secretaries are members; the Commerce Secretary joins this Board, as the appointments include those to commercial posts at embassies. JS (AD) acts as an aide to FSB, putting up the proposals.

Typically the FSB meets three times per year, and each meeting takes up around 40 appointments, including transfers from embassies to the MEA. While the custom was that the Under Secretary (FSP), Vivek Katju, a fine colleague, would prepare a slate of proposals; I applied here the same method used at the SEB, and prepared my list of suggested appointments, in Katju's presence. Thereafter, I would compare my list with the one he had prepared, and make such changes as needed, taking into account his advice. I ignored all the *shifarish*, or requests, received from interested parties. That rough draft of proposals was then discussed with the Foreign Secretary, who generally went along with the suggestions. The next stage was to circulate the draft proposals to the members of the FSB. The Board meetings typically were smooth; the majority of our proposals were accepted, with a few changes suggested by the members. I recall only one instance where Foreign Secretary Rasgotra insisted on a direct mission-to-mission transfer that went against the rotation principle. We managed to make this process equitable and relatively transparent.

I did not have the imagination to completely open up the transfer process, by asking officials to 'bid' for the posts they wanted. That is practiced in many modern foreign ministries, and was implemented in the MEA around 1995. It works surprisingly well; though everyone cannot be satisfied in terms of their chosen assignments, it delivers a high degree of satisfaction. Moreover, it reduces the scope for manipulation, and improves credibility. We have found that officials are willing to go on tough assignments, for their own reasons, sometimes to preserve their claim to an A+ post (i.e. an English-speaking Western country), when their children are ready for university education; sometimes they prefer to serve at hard locations which give generous allowances.

Appointment of ambassadors is the exclusive preserve of the Foreign Secretary; he makes recommendations directly to the Prime Minister. The MEA's 'NGO division' (handling top secret documents and records of IFS officers) sends him a list of posts falling vacant over a block of about six months; he then draws up recommendations, which typically go to the Principal Secretary to PM. In practice the Foreign Secretary usually discusses these proposals with the External Affairs Minister (EAM), but the slate that goes to the PMO does not need the Minister's formal approval. That unusual system originated with PM Jawaharlal Nehru who held personal charge of the MEA, i.e. during 1947-64 (at times assisted by a minister of state); this remained unchanged under Indira Gandhi. The exception was 1977-79, Janata Party rule under PM Morarji Desai, when Atal Behari Vajpayee was

EAM; he decided on ambassador appointments.[6] During my time in the Administration, Foreign Secretary Rasgotra sometimes consulted the other secretaries, especially if he did not know well the officials under consideration; once in a while he mentioned to me a few names, and asked for suggestions.

The Administration Division also handled promotions, but typically a joint secretary did not play any role in promotions to his own level, or promotions to the more senior ranks of additional secretary or secretary. In those days, very little selectivity was applied, except that a few unfit were left out. Other promotions, to the ranks of first secretary and counselor were automatic at that time, depending only on years of service. That has now changed and promotions have become slightly more selective. But as before, the merit principle is not applied in the sense of giving fast-track promotions to the very best. Across the civil service, little faith exists in India that merit can be applied with objectivity; it is safer to take up promotions batch by batch.[7] The exceptions were the appointment of Shyam Saran and Shivshankar Menon as Foreign Secretary in 2004 and 2007, when they jumped over two and one batches respectively; such deep selection has not since been applied in MEA. Those actions were exceptional in terms of Indian public service practice.

A major task we handled in 1983 was a 'cadre review', which was carried out at intervals of several years. Our chief aim was to create additional posts at senior levels, so as to accommodate more officials for promotion to our highest grades, as additional secretaries and secretaries (i.e. Grades II and I for those stationed abroad). In retrospect I realize that this method was misguided, because it perpetuated a system of very little selectivity in promotions for IFS officials to the highest ranks. The simple fact

---

[6] Later, when IK Gujral was EAM in 1996-98, he played a similar decisive role on ambassador appointments.

[7] It is interesting that in the armed forces, and even in the judicial system, the seniority principle prevails for the highest appointments, even while the merit criterion is applied to the seniority list, for promotions at middle-senior ranks. Reluctantly, I have modified past views and now recognize that without a rigorous system of determining merit, a simple application of the merit criterion would lead to abuse.

is that if we had fewer top-level posts, we would be compelled to choose with much greater care.

The cadre review hinged on obtaining approval from the Finance Ministry's Department of Expenditure, and thereafter steering the proposal through the Committee of Secretaries, chaired by the Cabinet Secretary. Foreign Secretary Rasgotra handled this personally, first visiting the Expenditure Secretary, and carrying out informal discussion with the key players. I accompanied him to the Cabinet Secretary's meeting, in what became an object lesson in handling senior officials that have been among the MEA's frequent critics. That morning, a secretary heading a major ministry commenced the hour-long session with a long tirade against the MEA, saying that this Ministry did not know the meaning of inter-ministry cooperation, and that it always behaved in a manner that was arrogant and self-centered. He went on in this vein for about five minutes. Neither the Cabinet Secretary not Rasgotra responded, and when all that harsh criticism had been vented, the meeting proceeded with a point-by-point discussion, as if the tirade had not taken place. In effect, extreme criticism became self-defeating. Our cadre proposals were approved with minor changes.

Other Reform

Some reform actions were implemented, though not all of them actually delivered the expected results. I should not overlook a major *mea culpa*, in terms of a possible initiative that was not attempted, owing to my lack of vision.

Some moves were simple. In 1983, we attempted to ensure that all transfers, especially of non-diplomatic staff, took place in May-July, to minimize dislocation for the children of officials that were at school. Many other foreign ministries apply a similar method, and in our case, it worked reasonably well, but subsequently this lapsed and we were back to a round-year pattern of transfer moves, mainly because of our failure to implement this method in disciplined fashion.

In early 1983, we carried out complete revision of the schedule of financial powers delegated to embassies. This was essential to simplify administration, reducing needless correspondence between embassies and the MEA; it gave embassies freedom to purchase and replace office equipment, within set parameters and standing regulations, without need for prior the MEA's authorization. When it came to publication of the new rules, I insisted on a red cover for the 50-page compilation, against the advice from administration colleagues that government publications should not feature bright covers. Since, that handbook has gone through much iteration, while retaining that cover. It is known as the 'Red Book' of delegated financial powers.

A more ambitious effort, started in mid-1983, sought to revise the entire set of basic MEA administrative regulations, known by its title: 'IFS (PLCA) Rules'. These cover issues typical to a foreign ministry in relation to its embassies abroad. It carried forward a process that Doshi had launched, as narrated above. Lalit Mansingh, supported this; the task involved several officials under his charge. We used a 'collegial' method for this revision; drafts of the intended changes for each chapter were discussed by our administration team, with a Finance Division team, led by Director (Finance), in an informal setting, often meeting over lunch in my office—I did not join the discussion but was available to help resolve issues that came up. Two under secretaries were especially helpful in this effort, Deepak Bhojwani and Bhaskar Mitra. The process was non-binding for our finance colleagues, in that we listened to their advice and accommodated this as much as possible, to produce our near-final text. But that did not prejudice the Finance Division's right to re-examine the proposals, when our draft formally went to them. In net terms, we made them partners in the proposed changes, without tying them down. All this involved careful negotiation with the Additional Secretary (Finance), attached to the MEA, to get his approval to this exercise. It helped that SC Mahalik, a fellow-Stephanian and old friend held this office.

The work went smoothly, and a quasi-approved draft of the entire 300-page publication was prepared after some months of work. I left the MEA at the end of 1983 for Nairobi, just as this was completed, and heard later that when a new Additional Secretary (Administration) was appointed in 1984, he asked for all the papers, and that was the last anyone heard of that particular exercise. The moral: Indian institutions are collections of individuals; teamwork and continuity are all too often absent. Many officials commence new assignments on the assumption that everything done by predecessors was of little value, and that they must hew their own new path. Successors are held in similar low esteem. The MEA often exemplifies these traits, as colleagues may attest.

Around early 1983 we received word that the PM wanted us to examine the idea of establishing a foreign service training institute. The MEA had managed for all these years without such an entity, and we in the Administration took a conservative view that a training institute was not needed. The Foreign Secretary agreed initially, but we were overruled by the PM, who insisted that a training entity be created. Accordingly, colleagues in the division and I drafted the 'Cabinet Note' that was a pre-requisite for any creation of posts in the government. The Cabinet duly approved this around mid-1983. The Foreign Service Training Institute became reality in 1986.[8] We were late in realizing that it was not sufficient to train officials at entry into the Service. This showed Indira Gandhi's vision.

The major issue I failed to take up was the increasingly critical shortage of IFS personnel. Each year, the MEA sends in a 'requisition' for new recruits for the IFS to the Union Public Services Commission (UPSC), typically based on a simplistic survey of the likely vacancies, calculated in terms of those due to retire from the Service in the coming year, adding a tiny percentage to cover deaths and voluntary retirements. No one had considered a need for real expansion in the Service, because we all failed to understand that the MEA headquarters in particular required significant expansion. Clearly, I had forgotten a recommendation our reform group had made in 1975 that: 'A stronger Headquarters set-up is essential for improving our professional efficiency'.[9] In the 1970s or even later, expansion in the size of the IFS did not figure in discussion at the MEA, even at lunch or tea sessions, where all kinds of issues were thrashed threadbare. We had not

8 Around 1995, the word 'Training' was dropped from the title, and it became our 'Foreign Service Institute'.

9 Details are given in Chapter 13.

attempted comparison with other diplomatic services, and the notion of 'benchmarking' ourselves was unfamiliar. In retrospect, it was both a personal and collective failure of imagination.

Other Actions

I did not join any of the inspection teams that visited embassies on episodic basis, to fix allowances, resolve practical issues facing them, and where possible, carry out staff cuts—that was exclusively the prerogative of JS (Establishment). We had not at that time moved to the more modern method of using the inspections to evaluate the performance of missions. But I made two visits to Indian embassies to attempt staff cuts, as part of an ad hoc effort to reduce staff in embassies. The first was to the Embassy to Kabul in early 1983. Ambassador SK Singh was always graceful and hospitable (he insisted that I stay at the Residence); he was loath to see major reduction, though clearly, the Indian aid program in Afghanistan had been scaled back after the 1979 Soviet invasion and cuts were warranted. After much discussion we agreed to cut a couple of posts at the level of non-diplomatic support staff.

The other visit was to Washington DC, where the effort was mainly to reduce staff at our 'Supply Wing'. That agency, like a similar entity in London, was an extraordinary anachronism carried over from World War II (in the 1940s a 1000-strong India Office functioned at London, functioning as a liaison unit to the colonial capital; an Indian 'Agent General' was appointed in Washington DC around 1942; at Independence in 1947 that office became the Indian Embassy). The task of the Supply Wings was to procure equipment needed in India, at a time of World War II shortages). I met US and Canadian business representatives who supplied aircraft spare-parts, and machine components needed mainly for our defense production establishment. Reciting from a common song-sheet, they told us that India saved a great deal of money by routing orders through these Supply Wings. It became a bizarre spectacle—commercial enterprises interested in maximizing their own profits, pleading for an expensive Indian arrangement, which they described as cost-efficient for India, as if that was their concern. I suggested some staff cuts, but that did not resolve the basic issue. It took a decisive personal initiative in 1987-88 by Prime Minister Rajiv Gandhi to close down these anachronistic entities in both these capitals.

In Germany in 1992 I was to encounter another 'attached office', a 'Railway Wing', also dating to the old days, whose raison d'etre was inspection of equipment ordered by the Indian railways. We carried out a detailed analysis, and showed that the cost of a set of resident railway officials in Bonn (there were a total of 4), was more than the total cost of sending from India 90 railway engineers and inspectors, on one-week inspection tours. That too begged for abolition, but the vested interest of the railway establishment was to retain such outposts (there was another one in Paris) to be able to send favored officials on foreign assignments. Foreign Secretary JN Dixit was initially favored our proposal, but then abruptly turned it down and told me not to pursue this further. I guess he had been 'spoken to' by someone in high authority.

The other glaring, continuing anomaly is the maintenance of 'Audit Offices' in London and Washington DC. I do not know if anyone has attempted a comparative cost analysis, between retaining these large establishments with over 15 officials at each place, and sending out teams of audit inspectors from Delhi, to perform audit inspections of Indian missions in Europe and the Americas. No one wonders how Indian embassies in Africa and Asia are audited perfectly well out of New Delhi. Perhaps one day the Comptroller and Auditor General of India may turn attention to this, or it might be better for a parliamentary committee to do this, avoiding any possible conflict of interest?

End of Assignment

Approaching two years in Delhi, in mid-1983 I sought an overseas appointment. I asked Foreign Secretary Rasgotra for Kenya, and also mentioned this to Principal Secretary Alexander, who remarked, 'You are not asking for much.' I explained that after Nairobi, it was my intention to seek a posting to the US; by that time, Ajit and Priya would be ready for university. That was readily approved. At the end of December 1983, Kris Srinivasan (1959 batch) took over from me, and I left for Nairobi, ending my final spell at the MEA.

10

Out of Africa

Kenya (1984-86)

My family and I reached Nairobi in the first week of January 1984. It was a privilege to step into the large shoes of Apa Saheb Pant, India's first 'Commissioner to East Africa', a charismatic figure who was based in Nairobi for several years commencing 1948, much before independence came to Africa.

Kenya and East Africa

Kenya was the true jewel of East Africa, though some gave that appellation to Uganda for its agricultural wealth and beauty. Kenya was the region's economic hub, with industrial infrastructure far ahead of the others. But the country was riven by tribal rivalries, between the Kikuyu, representing around 35% of the population, who had thrived under Jomo Kenyatta, and were natural economic entrepreneurs. Their principal rivals were the Luo, represented in politics in the early years by Tom Mboya. Kenyatta's successor was Daniel arap Moi, ruling as President since 1978, belonging to a small tribe, the Kalenjin, from the highlands region of North-central Kenya. The country's immediate neighbor Tanzania provided a stark contrast; Julius Nyerere's singular contribution there had been to eliminate tribalism, even while his experiment with socialism had brought economic ruin.

Though outwardly stable, Kenya was a tinderbox. An abortive coup attempt against President Moi by the Kenya Air Force on 1 August 1982 had produced vast upheaval; the Indian community was a major victim. That event, the first of its kind in Kenya, shaped some of the thinking among Indians, who numbered around 70,000 when I reached Nairobi in January 1984. It was my first experience of a country with a sizable Indian diaspora, and that helped to develop my ideas about the role of overseas Indian communities.[1] The principal lesson was: the presence of a large diaspora gives the home country a permanent stake in maintaining smooth and cooperative relations with that foreign country. Regardless of the citizenship of diaspora members, the home country retains a permanent interest in their safety and wellbeing. The August 1972 expulsion of the Indian community from Uganda by President Idi Amin had symbolized the acute crisis that overseas Indians might suddenly face; India had watched helplessly at that time.[2] This taught us to politically manage relations in ways that insulated our diaspora, to preclude such calamities.

The Nairobi Scene

President Moi was in firm command of the government, with Vice President Mwai Kibaki in a subsidiary, subdued role; the latter had a reputation for enjoying the good life.[3] It used to be said that while the first president, Jomo Kenyatta had collected property, Moi was a silent partner in a number of industrial and other ventures, building great wealth for himself. He acted as a patron to many, and dispensed monies liberally to his supporters and to different tribal communities. Just as Kenyatta had carried a ceremonial flywhisk as his personal symbol, Moi carried in public a gold crested swagger stick, much like a field marshal's baton. He policy slogan was *Nyayo*, i.e. 'following in the footsteps' of the first president.

---

[1] See Rana, 'India's Diaspora Diplomacy', *The Hague Journal of Diplomacy*, Vol.4 No.3 (2009), pp.361-372.

[2] The irony was that the expulsion of around 60,000 'Asians' from Uganda gave impetus to the entrepreneurial genius of these people, who mainly migrated to North America and the UK, achieving much greater prosperity. Since the mid-1990s they have been welcomed back to Uganda, and have had their properties restored to them; around 10,000 have come back.

[3] Mwai Kibaki served as President from 2002 to 2013.

When I reached Nairobi in January 1984, the public trial of former Attorney General Charles Njonjo was underway. He had been a powerful figure, close to Moi, and had fallen from grace; that produced a charged public atmosphere, with the newspapers, showing a remarkable degree of independence, full of stories and reports on the days proceedings at the trial court. In the end Njonjo was acquitted and left for London, which cooled down the situation. In those years some judges for the Kenyan Supreme Court were imported from the West Indies; owing to a pervasive tribal ethos, since Kenya's independence this was the preferred way for keeping balance in the judicial system.

Permanent Secretary Kiplagat headed the Foreign Ministry. A highly efficient and elegant professional, he has remained a good friend over the years, including the time of my teaching visits to Nairobi in 2008-12. After he retired from the foreign ministry he played a special role in Kenya's peace-building activities in Sudan, Somalia, and Mozambique. He spoke of this in detail at a 2009 symposium on Kenyan diplomacy held at Nairobi. The other ally at the Foreign Ministry was Assistant Minister Philip Leakey, of whom I write below.

It was easy to meet ministers and permanent secretaries, though I would not say that this really helped as much as one might have wished, in advancing our work with these partners. India enjoyed a good reputation and this was always an asset. Indian community friends sometimes helped in facilitating meetings.

A small rump of the formerly numerous white community remained in Kenya, keeping low profile, but owning large farm estates, as well as industrial holdings, living in secluded areas such as the Karen suburb of Nairobi. Philip Leaky and his elder brother Richard Leaky, wildlife conservationist, were the only ones to play a prominent public role.

The High Commission

The High Commission Chancery was (and has remained) in downtown Nairobi, on the 3rd and 4th floor of a building owned by the Life Insurance Corporation of India, a short walk from the Foreign Ministry and many major government offices.

Fortuitously, Chitra Narayanan (1975 batch), elder daughter of KR Narayanan, my mentor at MEA in 1965-67, was the senior first secretary, in effect the deputy HC. At what was for India a medium-sized mission, we worked together as a team. The military attaché at Addis Ababa held concurrent charge for Kenya.

The Nairobi mission had been inspected in 1983, and the inspectors had recommended small reduction in the support staff. While I was preparing to leave Delhi, colleagues in the personnel division had asked with a mild sense of mischief, that I would 'presumably' not want them to implement these cuts. I replied that they should go ahead with the cuts—I had long held that it was better to have a mission that was slightly over-worked than one where the personnel had an easy life; that helped to keep us out of petty squabbles and misdemeanors.

With around 3000 young Kenyans going to India for studies each year, and the Indian community, holding passports of varied hues, principally Kenyan, Canadian, and UK, visa issue was a major consular activity. This was my first experience with consular services visible to the public as the mission's efficiency barometer; colleagues at Nairobi readily understood that they had to maintain high standards to build our reputation.

The Indian Community

Most of the Indians in Kenya and East Africa were from Gujarat, with substantial numbers also from Punjab and other parts of India. They came originally as indentured labor and as petty shopkeepers, *dukawalas* that ran stores that sold a variety of products in the interior of the country, a kind of buffer between the colonists and the African majority. Winston Churchill, Under-Secretary of State for the Colonies, who traveled to East Africa in 1907-08, praised the 'Asiatic' for '...his industry, his thrift, his sharp business aptitudes (that) give him the economic superiority'. Churchill noted that the Indian trader had gone to places where no white man would go, and had opened up both trade and communications; Indian bankers had supplied a large part of the capital, and even helped the whites; and it was Indian labor that had constructed the vital railway line; he also astutely noted that these Indians were in an invidious position between Africans and Europeans.[4]

Indians had prospered, taking advantage of economic opportunities, and had become leading industrialists, bankers and entrepreneurs in virtually all fields of activity, be it tourism or wholesale and retail business. They were mainly Kenyan nationals, but within their families most had a multi-nationality situation, with wives often retaining Indian citizenship, and their children nationals of different Western countries, including Australia, Canada, the UK and the US. This was seen as a safeguard, a parachute, against possible adverse developments, which might force them to leave Kenya.

Of the 70,000 Indians, about half lived in Nairobi, with the rest spread over almost all the towns, except the arid north. The only occupation they did not pursue was agriculture; for the rest, they were traders, industrialists, shopkeepers, professionals in different walks of life, and service personnel. The three major families were the Mehtas and the Madhvanis, both originating in my hometown, Porbander in Gujarat, and the Chandarias from the Jamnagar area, also in Gujarat. My parents had known well Seth Nanji Kalidas Mehta, who had traveled to what became Kenya, as a boy and worked in a tea-stall. I have vivid recollections of meeting Seth Nanji in the 1950s at the residential girls school that he had founded, on the outskirts of Porbander; in those years he stayed in a small cottage in the sprawling school compound. Sometimes I joined my father at a simple meal with Seth Saheb; he ate just five items at meals, typically, rice, dal, a *sabzi*, *papad* and salad, but for his guests a couple of dishes were added. The principal Mehta residence was a palatial home on the corner of Uganda Road. (The Madhvanis also had a big house on that road, but did not live there.) My mother was a good friend of Sethji's wife Santok Ben, to the point that all their children called her *Masi*. In Kenya I met often Mahendra Mehta, the youngest son of Seth Nanji, and several members of the Madhvani family. Manu Chandaria was the outstanding business leader in Kenya.

There were many other Indian families of distinction, from Punjab and other parts of India, those that had made a successful

[4] Churchill, *My East African Safari*, pp. 31-7.

transition as industrialists, owners of hotel chains, banks and insurance companies, realty magnates and the like. Indian professionals working as bankers, doctors and businessmen, many of them recent arrivals, leavened this migrant community, and added to its reach and influence. None were active in politics.

The expulsion of Indians from Uganda under Idi Amin weighed heavily on the minds of the Indian diaspora in much of Africa. That did not deter them from enjoying the good life that Kenya or other countries offered, despite a situation of varying difficulty in terms of personal security. In Kenya, a rising crime rate, including attacks on homes of the wealthy by armed gangs was a problem; the security guards hired by those who enjoyed prosperity, in Nairobi and other cities, did little to prevent this. This has remained one of the paradoxes in Kenya, right up to present times.

Indians and Africans as ethnic communities kept each other at a distance; few stepped across the racial divide in their social and cultural engagement. Mixed marriages have always remained a rarity. Business partnerships did exist, but the successful ones were not many. India's message to these communities, reflected in the early speeches of Jawaharlal Nehru both before and immediately after Independence, to 'identify' themselves with the local citizens, was seriously misunderstood. It was taken to mean that India recommended 'integration'. In much of Africa, this community is known as 'Asians'—because the religious or other affiliations of the subcontinent have never interested the local population. These 'Asians' have remained on the fringes, lacking direct political power, but exerting influence through their wealth, which has always given them strong connection to politicians and bureaucrats.

The Hindu Council of Kenya brought together all the 140-odd associations of the Hindus of the Indian community, representing some 75% of the Indians. The sizable and dynamic Sikh community, divided in its different affiliations, worked with the Hindu Council at times, but was not formally part of it. The Muslim community included the relatively orthodox Dawoodi Bohras, under the strict religious and social control of their leadership based in Mumbai; the Ismailis, loyal to the Aga Khan, always a well-knit community, and some smaller groups. To Kenyans, all of them were 'Asians', called *mohindis* in Swahili. Affiliations of religion and of other kinds among this community mattered little to most Africans. When there was a breakdown of law and order, this entire cluster, regardless of internal classifications, became a target of mobs and malcontents.

Fragmentation in the overseas Indian community is near universal. In part it is the result of a strong Indian individualistic steak, as also an inability to work to advance collective interests. The personal ambition of individuals to be recognized as leaders contributes to this. For example, the Goan community of Kenya, numbered in those days at just over a thousand, and used to be much larger before youthful members migrated to Canada, Australia and elsewhere. They had three associations or 'institutes', each with its splendid hall and entertainment facilities—at least one had a dance floor on springs, which could be 'tuned' as needed to give varying degrees of bounce. They held rival celebrations for their festivals. That pattern of division was repeated across each community cluster.

I thought hard about how to work with this important diaspora community, with its heterogeneity and divisions. The lessons learnt in Hong Kong from Commissioner PS Kotdasangani were invaluable. The only viable method of establishing credible connection was to throw oneself into this community, to be receptive to all, and attend all manner of functions, personal, social, or large community events, putting aside one's own convenience. That meant frequent travel to different towns and regions, often over weekends. Mimi was an extraordinary asset, going to all the different community groups that invited her, Hindu, Sikh, Muslim or Christian. She established her own circle of friends, who with their husbands also became our allies. Mimi also developed friendship with Wanjiri Mathai and other African ladies. She also kept up with tennis and won a trophy, also in the process cultivating a different circle of friends.

I attended many executive committee meetings with the Hindu Council, though I was not a member, and met with different community groups and their leaders. Ramesh Desai,

Hindu Council President, was a frequent interlocutor. Dharam Prakash was another community leader and a source of support. Over the years, Indian envoys had tried to promote greater unity among these groups, and I walked that same path. I frequently urged the Hindu Council to reach out and build on common ground with the other Asian segments, especially to undertake local welfare activities for the benefit of Africans, which might improve the reputation of all Asians; there was a crying need for such actions. The key argument in support was: if our disparate groups could come together in times of distress, as most recently during the riots at the time of the Air Force coup attempt in 1982, should it not be feasible in good times to work jointly on projects that burnished an Asian reputation?

These themes were pursued over time in countless conversations, small meetings and even social functions. We also reached out to some of the Muslim groups, especially the Bohras and the Ismailis. Presented in varying language, the response was fairly similar: not enough mutual trust exists among different groups to undertake joint projects, but when crisis erupts, we have always come together; in those situations, every person and local cluster that can help has reached out to all victims of Indian origin, without asking about affiliations. That was the case during the Uganda crisis in 1972, and during the abortive coup in Kenya ten years later.

These ideas produced protracted discussion, but no meaningful result. It seemed that in times of normalcy, there was simply no motivation to overcome customary mutual inhibitions and resentments. Ideas of the kind that we as official Indian representatives espoused were seen as idealistic and impractical. At the same time, I found that the very act of dialogue produced positive waves among them for India, and deeper commitment among the community towards Indian actions.

It should cause no surprise that over time, in the three decades since I served in Nairobi, things have not changed, even after further spells of civil unrest in which the *Mohindis* were a principal target of mobs, as happened during the civil strife that followed the 2007 elections in Kenya. Lifestyle of these Kenyan Indians remains unchanged.

Far-sighted people, such as the Chandaria family, among the most enlightened in Africa, implement welfare activities of their own, aimed benefiting the African majority. For instance, Manu Chandaria has long run a quiet program that rewards policemen that have rendered outstanding public performance. In 2012, this family donated K. Shillings 100 million (US $1.5 million), for a children's wing at a major Nairobi hospital. Some other leading Indians in Kenya have done the same, and won recognition for their social, educational and development activities. The Ismailis have long been charity pioneers in Kenya, under the leadership of the Aga Khan, among the most enlightened religious leaders anywhere. Nairobi's Aga Khan Hospital, now a medical university, stands in testimony. Other community segments have tended to be insular; they contribute to African causes, often under local pressure, but could do much more.

Many religious figures from India came to Kenya to meet their followers. Indian envoys had the opportunity to meet them at religious and social functions organized by different Indian clusters. The major personalities I met included: the Pramukh Swami heading the leading Swaminarayana sect, as also the *dadis* of the Brahma Kumaris; and Morari Bapu who came to deliver *katha* and religious discourses. Other visitors included Seyadana Saheb of the Boharas; the Aga Khan made an annual visit. We also worked with local groups that invited the more secular among such personalities, such as Swami A Parathasarathy of the Vedanta Academy. Where appropriate, I tried to probe them on the guidance they gave to their followers, and the utility of some joint activity by Asians. In discussion with the Aga Khan I suggested stronger welfare-oriented actions in India; at the time he did not often visit India, but that has now changed

The Indian community in Kenya reflected good cheer, optimism and tremendous dynamism. This might seem a paradox, but one should not overlook their ease of life, based on the key conditions: the exceptional fertility of the land, a salubrious climate and the economic growth opportunities the country has provided. Government policy favored business, and was non-discriminatory. The one area from which the Asians of Kenya have kept away is politics, as they simply do not have the numerical strength to mobilize electoral appeal. On the African continent, South Africa is the sole country where overseas Indians have the numbers to permit an active political role.

Here is a small example of working with Indian groups. After about a year in Nairobi, I met one Ratubha, a modest businessman who was the undisputed leader of a small Rajput community from Gujarat that numbered a few hundred. We found an easy connection and had a long chat, at the end of which Ratubha exclaimed in Gujarati: I have made a big mistake. When I pressed him to clarify, he said: Soon after I reached Nairobi, he had sent the Chairman of the Rajput Association to meet me; on return, he told Ratubha that the new HC was 'arrogant' and did not care for his own community. I recalled that meeting, but had seen it in a different light. When the Rajput Association head met me and spoke of their pride that a fellow-Gujarati, and that too a Rajput, now represented India in Nairobi. I had thanked him for coming, and had explained that an Indian representative dealt with and connected with all communities from India on an equal basis; I could not act on the basis of my own regional or community affiliation, because that would undermine this wider outreach. Ratubha went on to say that he had finally understood my words and actions! Ratubha and I became good friends, and on visits to his home at Kajiado, some 150 km from Nairobi, deep into the Masai region, I saw the respect in which he was held by those splendid and proud tribal people. Once while traveling together, the High Commission's combi-van broke down with a minor mechanical fault. Ratubha's small rotund figure was so well liked that every vehicle passing stopped to ask him if any help was needed.

Work Environment

It would take much space to list all those that we came to know and worked with in Nairobi, and in other places such as Mombasa, on travels to towns that had an India-connection. Many became good friends, Indians and Africans. We took care to mix with different groups, without suggesting that we had exclusive friendships with any. This probably helped in widening our contacts. It was clear from the outset that the diplomatic community was not going to be more than an adjunct in our outreach, though we worked closely with these colleagues in relation to affairs of the increasingly important international agency UNEP (see below). We readily accepted all the Indian community and African invitations we could accommodate, to functions, religious or secular. That left limited free time, but that went with the job. It built enduring friendships, and gave deeper insight into the country. Ajit and Priya, who were entering their late teens, paid a price; I ought to have been much more involved with their final high school years.

TV and radio were under government control, but the print media was independent and feisty. *The Nation* had the largest circulation, with *The Standard* closely behind, besides Swahili journals. They reported with freedom, but exercising discretion, steering clear of direct criticism of the President. But ministers and officials agencies were fair game.

A unique feature of life as an Indian representative was invitations the *Harambee* public meetings that took place in the interior, almost always on Sundays, where people came together for a worthy cause, i.e. 'working together' as this Swahili word implies. Meeting had to be licensed by the District Commissioner (Kenyan district officials all wore uniforms that indicated their rank, a good model for a developing country). Several hundred or even thousands of people gathered around a makeshift stage from which elected officials and local worthies made their speeches, interspersed with traditional music and dance; the finale was the public collection of funds from the dignitaries and common people, with each contribution announced, the name and amount. I typically attended one or two such meetings each month, usually to help students going to India, or for medical treatment; it was gratifying that even a small amount of around K Sh.1000 to 2000 I usually gave received generous applause.

It became evident that to be effective in Kenya, one needed direct contract with the country's President. I established a 'back channel' arrangement through a leading member of the Indian community. My first private meeting with President Moi took place in 1995 at the State House at Eldoret, in the Highlands. I went alone, and conveyed to the President India's interest in working closely with Kenya, and our commitment to deepening economic relations. He welcomed this and we discussed some ongoing activities, including our actions in small-scale industry (see below). He welcomed this and added that he would not stand on protocol to receive me. He seemed pleased with my response that whatever he did as President would naturally be in accord with protocol. After that first encounter, Permanent Secretary Kiplagat told me with a twinkle in his eye: I hear that you have recently met 'His Excellency'. I replied in the affirmative and added that at all times, I would report to him any substantive discussion; it was vital to keep in good repair the main communication link with the Foreign Ministry.

Thereafter I met President Moi regularly at intervals of a few months. Some extended meetings took place at his farm estate, not far from the town of Nakuru; other times I met him at State House in Nairobi, where the meetings were brief. His farm estate sprawled over some 6000 acres of fertile land, and included an airstrip, several villages and two residential schools, which he had funded. I typically flew into this estate in a small aircraft, in the company of a leading member of the Indian community. We would sit with President Moi, who might be accompanied by three or four others, for informal conversation, in what amounted to a kind of *diwan-e-khas*, quasi-private audience. Refreshments would arrive as appropriate to the time. Sometimes Moi would say: let us go for a drive; we would pile into a Volkswagen microbus, with Moi occupying the front passenger seat; he would show us some of the agricultural experiments undertaken, or we might drive to one of the schools to see a new lab or building, or meet an assembly of students. I used such occasions to speak of our interests, be it small-scale industry or other projects on which we were working. Political issues seldom came up.

For an Indian representative, the situation in Kenya was an education. It demonstrated the limits to India's influence, in that country and with our diaspora. As a 'bird of passage' an envoy could not presume to understand better the circumstances and the interests of a community of Indian origin than that community itself, whose members lived their daily lives and faced existential threat in a complex environment. They saw events as per their own logic. Regardless of our motivation, we could not step beyond the role of friendly wellwishers. What we could do was to sustain close links with the government, and be responsive to the diaspora's needs. Sure, the Kenyan governance system had its flaws, but unlike Western states that engaged in finger wagging, and in later years criticized in an increasingly sharp manner Kenya's situation of corruption and authoritarianism, we had no interest in such preaching. As fellow developing states, we had to be aware of our own limitations. And the presence of the diaspora required us to be discreet.

India-Kenya Relations

The first Indian representative in Nairobi, Apa Saheb Pant, 'Commissioner to East Africa', was one of our finest diplomats of the first generation. I was privileged to meet him in Nairobi in 1985, when he came as a board member of Kirloskar (Kenya), a joint venture, and saw the respect in which Kenyans held him, nearly four decades later. Other leading envoys in Kenya, remembered well, included Marshal of the Air Force Arjan Singh, and Prem Bhatia, leading newspaper editor. Over time, it is the reputation that envoys leave behind in a foreign country of assignment that often provides a trustworthy indicator of the quality of their work.

India-Kenya political relations were in good repair, though no major exchanges of high visits took place in my years. We had no bilateral disputes to overcome, and cooperation along varied fronts proceeded well. The examples given below illustrate this. We did receive Indian ministers from time to time. One was Natwar Singh, then a minister of state, accompanied by an influential MP, KP Singh Deo. I accompanied them to a number of meetings, including a call on President Moi. Despite our past history, Natwar took note of our local contacts and influence, and remarked: 'You do us proud in this country.' ND Tiwari, then Minister of Industry, also came at the head of an economic delegation.

Several Indian companies had important investments in Kenya. GP Birla (now CK Birla) was the lead investor in Pan African Paper Mills, regarded by the World Bank as one of the most successful joint ventures in Africa. Another leading investor was Vijaypat Singhania of the Raymonds group, with a fully-integrated woolen mill that processed Kenyan wool to produce suits for the likes of Moss Bros. in the UK; the Life Insurance Company of India, was a major shareholder in a joint venture in Nairobi, in which a Kenyan parastatal also had a large share. Another half-dozen Indian investments were also thriving, and the number rose steadily. Bilateral trade was also on a rising path. That made Kenya our leading economic partner in the region.

We achieved singular success in promoting small-scale industries out of India. This happened in a serendipitous manner, as recounted in my first book.[5] President Moi saw the value of simple micro enterprises as a means of providing employment to a large and growing population of unemployed Kenyans. Micro enterprises of this kind in *Swahili* are called *jua kali* ('open air') manufacture. This is one area in which India's experience that is enormously relevant in Africa; several other countries, including Ethiopia, Tanzania and Zambia have shown equal receptivity to Indian small-scale and micro industry technology.

Some weeks after I had reached Nairobi in January 1984, the dynamic head of our state enterprise National Small Industries Corporation (NSIC), JS Juneja happened to pass through Nairobi on the way to Dar-e-salaam; on an impulse, I sought a meeting with Assistant Foreign Minister Philip Leakey, and we walked across from the Chancery to the Foreign Ministry. At that time, Philip Leakey, youngest son of the great anthropologist Mary Leakey, was active in politics and was the only white member of the ministerial council. That sparked mutual interest in bringing to Kenya India's small-scale industry experience, and the rest, as they say, is history. Our small-scale industry actions culminated in an exposition organized in 1985 by NSIC where machinery for about 25 micro units was displayed in working order, as a practical demonstration. At the end of the event, we gifted this equipment for training small industry technicians. President Moi visited this display, and was much impressed, giving this activity his personal support. One net consequence: just after I left Kenya in mid-1986, a 'Ministry for Small Industry and Appropriate Technology' was created.

5 Rana, *Inside Diplomacy*, pp. 116-7.

Western companies, operating from their position of strength as the leading and often exclusive sources of machinery and technology, treated Africa as their economic preserve. That placed them in opposition to India's market entry. This was paradoxical as in many instances Indian technology was based on Western sources, and a more enlightened view would not have hurt the West. I suppose one fear for them was that Indian machinery and equipment was far more relevant to Africa, compared with their offerings. Further, as a developing country, we were traversing a concurrent path to economic growth that was parallel to Africa's, which made the Indian experience more relevant. The instances given below illustrate the way this jousting played out in Kenya:

- Tractors and farm equipment supplied to African states was often ill-suited to local soils, the more so when European tractors were principally in the high-horsepower category, suited to Europe's frozen and heavy soils. They simply did not manufacture the kind of 20 and 30 HP tractors that were suited to local conditions and small farms. If we look into the backyards of large farms, most African countries are a graveyard of large sophisticated machinery that cannot be repaired locally. Consequently, we faced much opposition in introducing our farm machinery into Kenya and other countries.
- Indian pharmaceuticals faced a similar challenge in Kenya as elsewhere, in that registration and market entry formalities posed obstacles, but the fact of a huge price advantage made Indian exports very attractive. We made a small start in this sector, which gained momentum subsequently, especially in the late 1980s under the energetic actions by one of my successors, Kiran Doshi.
- In 1985, The Netherlands implemented an interesting triangular project, a textiles training center, where they brought in an Indian textile machinery manufacturer as the principal operating partner. As recounted in *Inside Diplomacy*, we also learnt the hard way the pitfalls of such a deal, in that Indian machinery suppliers simply did not have the documentation and detailed drawings on their equipment of

the kind that this European partner saw as a prerequisite.[6] It showed the distance that Indian exporters had to travel in order to gain acceptance in global markets, and meet the standards that were a basic requirement.

- Trucks manufactured by Tata Motors made a modest entry—we helped them to get acceptance for trials by the Kenyan Army. Visits to Kenya in 2008-11 showed that our vehicles were struggling with a reliability problem. An Indian price advantage has to be supported by the requisite quality standard.

In 1985, an Indian state-owned education technology consultant, EdCIL won a contract to provide the master plan for a new Moi University at Eldoret, but it failed to leverage that into further assignments for Indian enterprises, as it ought to have done. Part of the reason was that at the time, Indian education enterprises were not active in world markets, and lacked the savvy that is required. Indian state-run educations establishments have never had an incentive to go overseas, and in those years, private institutions, such as Manipal and DPS Schools, had yet to enter foreign markets. Education technology is a major latent asset that India is yet to exploit in a comprehensive manner.

Another story, which relates to events after I left Nairobi, illustrates the way in which India and its technology are relevant in Africa. In the 1970s, Kenya had given to Italy the privilege of operating a space station on its equatorial coast, in the vicinity of Malindi; such locations are highly desirable for space research and for the operation of satellites. Former Foreign Ministry Permanent Secretary Kiplagat gave an account of Kenya's with the renewal of that agreement with Italy in the early 1990s; he narrated this at a Nairobi symposium on 16-17 September 2009, on 'Kenya's Early Diplomacy: 1963-1993' (I was the only non-Kenyan invited).

> The Italians were keen to have Kenya sign the agreement without studying it. But the government refused to sign the agreement and instead decided to make its own cost analysis. The government contracted nuclear physicist from the University of Nairobi who went to India for a week to study space exploration. India was

[6] Rana, *Inside Diplomacy*, p. 111.

> willing to share information at no cost and this helped Kenya in making a decision which upheld the integrity of the nation. Hence, despite the fact that Kenya is lacking in resources, it is important for government to be firm on national issues.[7]

This episode symbolized the quality of our South-South cooperation, and the confidence that animated India-Kenya relations.

UNEP and Habitat: Multilateral Diplomacy

UNEP and Habitat are the only two autonomous entities of the UN family that are headquartered in Africa, though neither is a full 'agency'—UNEP, the larger of the two, is a 'Program'; efforts to expand it to an agency have not succeeded. When UNEP was to be established, Nairobi, New Delhi and Vienna were in the running as possible locations. Some Western countries had calculated that the two developing countries would slug it out and Vienna would be the default choice. At the 2009 symposium on Kenya's early diplomacy (mentioned above), I heard for the first time that to break this impasse, Kenya made a direct approach to India and persuaded it to withdraw in their favor. At our High Commission, which doubled as India's permanent mission to these two UN entities, we had no memory of this. This is an instance of our poor institutional memory, even in relation to an issue that was locally important.

An Egyptian, Mostafa Tolba, headed UNEP; he seemed rather beholden to the West and did little to advance developing country interests, to the point where Egyptians were exasperated with him. A senior Indian civil servant, V Ramachandran, headed HABITAT; a fine professional who acted with grace, he was widely admired. Work at these two, especially at UNEP, expanded considerably during my time, in keeping with rising global awareness of the need for united action to deal with the challenge of environment degradation, but this was still the early phase of our engagement. It was the West that dominated these discussions; India was at

[7] Extract from the report on the symposium 'Kenya's Early Diplomacy: 1963-1993', held at Nairobi on 16-17 September 2009, published by the Kenya Foreign Service Institute.

the phase of building its domain knowledge. We received little technical support, and usually no one from Delhi came for these UNEP meetings.

The group of permanent representatives, consisting of the 70-odd envoys in Nairobi oversaw UNEP affairs, and met frequently. The G-77 group was active, and in my first year at the assignment, a particularly effective Mexican ambassador headed it. In 1985, I became the group convener. I was also elected to chair a UNEP committee with a very long title, which was established by the UNEP Governing Council to interface with the Commission on Sustainable Development, an independent body created that year, headed by the Norwegian Environment Minister, Gro Harlem Brundtland.[8] Consequently, in 1985 and 1986 I traveled to Jakarta and Ottawa respectively, for meetings with this Commission. The Jakarta meeting, my first encounter with Mrs. Brundtland and her group, was important because of a minor misunderstanding that had arisen between them and our UNEP committee, before I took charge. It did not take much effort on my part to assure the Brundtland Commission that we fully respected their mandate and autonomy. That won me appreciation from the Commission, especially the Japanese representative; Japan was the leading funding source for this Commission. The visit to Ottawa took place just a few months after the terrorist bombing of Air India's *Kanishka* aircraft in the Irish Sea; I have never received more security protection than what the Canadian Mounties provided during that three-day stay.

In contrast, work at Habitat was in low key, but it did involve me in very pleasant travel to Gabon in 1984 and to Jamaica in 1985, for annual meetings of the World Habitat Conference. Apart from joining in some drafting groups and helping with the political aspect of resolutions, I had little to contribute to these events.

Overall, multilateral activities at Nairobi added an interesting layer our work, though environmental issues had not acquired in the mid-1980s anything like the salience they now enjoy. For instance, once in 1986 at a UNEP meeting of permanent

---

[8] The Report of this Commission, *Our Common Future*, was published in 1987. See: http://conspect.nl/pdf/Our_Common_Future-Brundtland_Report_1987.pdf

representatives I spoke of how Canada had taken long grass strains from Kenya, crossed these with wheat plants and produced out of this new wheat varieties that did well in their short growing season. My information came from a TV documentary and some reading on this subject. I told our group that this raised the question of genetic diversity, and how rich countries had taken germ plasma from developing states, a key resource, without giving any compensation to them—that evoked no support from other developing countries, not even from the Kenyan delegate who was clearly unaware of this issue.

Some Events

I heard the news of Indira Gandhi's assassination on a BBC broadcast, stepping out of a shower that 31 October 1984 morning. We were shocked; so many images of that extraordinary person were fresh in memory. I had walked with the PM on that short path, which linked her residence and office, where she was killed. The High Commission's conference room became our memorial room, with its condolence book; Mimi joined me in standing for hours to receive an endless stream of Kenyans and Indians, besides the diplomatic corps and government representatives.

That tragedy, and the subsequent killings of Sikhs in Delhi, brought to the High Commission local threats and led to strains in relations with the local Sikh community. The Kenyan authorities gave me an armed escort for a short period, and we also had to deal with telephoned threats to the Chancery. I received a few nasty phone calls at home, which were reported to colleagues, but did not call for action. On one occasion the Special Branch visited our Chancery on a Sunday afternoon to check on a bomb threat; I waited outside till they gave an all clear.

For several months thereafter I received no invitations to Gurudwara functions, but gradually, contact with moderate elements among the Sikh community resumed, including visits to the Sikh temples, i.e. those that were not under the control of radical elements. The Kenyan authorities made it clear that they would not tolerate any local echoes to the events in India, and that tough line perhaps helped to ensure that there were no violent incidents.

A different set of issues came up when President Yoweri Museveni seized power in Uganda in January 1986, overthrowing the government of Milton Obote, and an interim leader, after a prolonged armed struggle. At that time there were about 2000 Indians in Kampala and other parts of that country. When that takeover was imminent, I was in India on home leave; we feared that the Indian community would become scapegoats during that regime change. From MEA we kept up telephone contact with the acting HC in Kampala, via the new-fangled direct international dialing system that had just been introduced in India. When Museveni's troops were about to enter Kampla, I interrupted home leave and returned to Nairobi to help with a possible exodus of Indians across the Uganda-Kenya land border and railway line, as had happened when Idi Amin had expelled Indians in 1972. The Hindu Council of Kenya activated itself and we made arrangements to receive an Indian community in flight. In the event, Museveni's soldiers maintained tight discipline, and there was no looting or plunder. A trip I made to the Kenya-Uganda border post, and the precautions we had taken proved to be unnecessary, but we reasoned it was better to be alert than sorry.

The Third World Conference on Women met in Nairobi in 1985, and India sent a 20-strong delegation that was led by Minister of State Maragatham Chandrashekhar, and included a diverse group of women politicians and leading personalities, including Sheila Dixit and actor Smita Patil. Our Minister had no notion on handling such a diverse group; the daily morning delegation meetings became a farce, with temper tantrums by the minister that reduced some delegates to tears. Perhaps the Minister felt insecure in the presence of delegates that had substantive achievements to their credit. New Delhi heard of this fracas and during a consultation visit, I was asked by the PMO to give a verbal report of what had transpired. That episode contributed to the sacking of this minister from the Rajiv Gandhi government.

In those days, Kenyans needing heart surgery mainly went to the UK for treatment at great expense, since these facilities were not available in Kenya. A minister contacted me in 1985 and asked us to check on options in India, for one of his constituents, a young boy needing a heart valve replacement. Apollo Hospital had opened in Chennai, and Dr. Prathap Reddy's team offered fixed price heart surgery, that included all incidentals. We contacted him directly, and on receiving confirmation sent this young Kenyan boy to India, accompanied by his father. A week later, the minister asked me to go with him to the airport to receive this boy. At the airport, we saw him descend the aircraft steps—no aero-bridges in those days—and laughingly reject the wheelchair that had been brought for him, as he walked to greet his family and friends. Press correspondents who had assembled for the event interviewed me and I spoke my mind on the fact that this surgery had cost one-tenth of the typical cost in the UK. *The Nation* prominently carried my comments, accompanied by an editorial titled 'Listen to the Envoy', arguing that for too long African nations had looked to the West, and needed to work with fellow-developing countries.

The Kenya-India Friendship Association (KIFA), which has existed for long, brought together Kenyans who had studied in India and others. Education cooperation was an important track in our exchanges, and around 3000 young people traveled to different Indian universities, especially in Pune, Chandigarh and South India for higher education. Agriculture Minister Omamo, a product of one of our agriculture universities, headed KIFA and he cheerfully came to the High Commission for its bimonthly meetings. In 1985, KIFA established a fund for Kenyans students in India facing personal or family hardship, and entrusted the annual income from this fund to the Kenyan High Commission in New Delhi to disburse, since they had the best picture of those that were in need. KIFA also took another initiative, to sponsor the legendary distance runner Kip Keino, to spend a month in India to coach Indian athletes. Keino gave one piece of advice that remains relevant even today: as with the highland regions of the Horn of Africa that produce world-class distance runners, India should look to the inhabitants of the Himalayan region and other hill regions, because they have high lung capacity that is the hallmark of such athletes. We have not heeded this wisdom.

The outstanding Indian jurist and public intellectual Nani Palkhiwala visited Nairobi towards the end of 1985, for a world convention of Giants International, a service club, much like Rotary, established out of Mumbai, very active among the Indian community of Kenya; it also had Kenyan members. Palkhiwala was the lead speaker at an evening commemorative dinner; looking to a largely Indian audience, Palkhiwala treated them to one of his typical lectures, highly critical of the India system and its governance failures. As always, he was witty and eloquent, drawing repeated rounds of laughter and applause. The next morning the Special Branch police met the Giants Chairman in Kenya and warned that Palkhiwala would be expelled for publicly ridiculing friendly India. The organizers explained that the speech was designed to entertain, and that the Indian High Commissioner, seated at the high table, was among those that had applauded the speaker. The policemen were mollified up to a point, but warned that they would monitor the second public lecture that Palkhiwala was to deliver the next day. This was reported to Palkhiwala, who took the hint and proceeded to deliver a scintillating address on the theme of India's glorious heritage.[9] This appeared to please the Special Branch officers, visible among the 1000-strong audience at the Premier Club. This incident cemented an enduring friendship with Nani Palkhiwala.

I was lucky in one particular respect in that an Indian godman, who had visited Kenya frequently right up to 1983, did not come to Nairobi in my time; I refer to Chandraswami, of whom I wrote in *The Contemporary Embassy* (2013):

> In India we saw a strange period in the 1970s and 1980s when 'godmen' favored by Indian leaders traveled to different countries, among them Mauritius, Kenya and Peru, bullying embassies into obtaining for them access to the leaders of these countries, surely not in pursuit of any national objective. Even Margret Thatcher, as Leader of the Opposition in 1975, received at her office and subsequently sought the counsel of this particular godman, Swami Chandraswami; he predicted that she would become prime

[9] The full text of this set of ideas is in a 35-page publication of *Bharatiya Vidya Bhavan India's Priceless Heritage* (1980).

minister in three or four years, and would serve for seven, nine or eleven years.[10]

The particular numerology notion that Chandraswami 'sold' to President Moi was that some numbers were especially lucky for him and using these would protect him. Thereafter, Moi would order officials to establish schools to accommodate a specific number of children; initially, some officials opted to round off the number upwards, and incurred presidential wrath. Very quickly the message went home that the number set by the President had to be respected scrupulously.

Our Life

In Nairobi, and later in San Francisco, my mother, who had mainly made her life with my brother Nirmal Jhala and his family after my father's demise in 1972, blessed us with a six-month visit. She lived in Kolkata or wherever Nirmal's IAS assignments took him in West Bengal. She also stayed with us for some months when we were posted in Delhi. In Kenya, my mother found herself in her element, and in a matter of days had established her own circle of friends. At her departure, she was hosted to a round of farewell parties that might have driven any envoy to envy. My sister Dilhar has carefully preserved a Gujarati poem that one of her friends read out as a tribute at a farewell event.

Mimi was active as always in the affairs of a local welfare body; in Nairobi it was the Indian Women's Association, which was headed by custom by the wife of the Indian High Commissioner. They organized a host of activities that raised funds for the welfare of Kenyan organizations. The Indian community was generous, and sizable amounts of money were raised through charity bazaars, music evenings, commemorative dinners and other activities.

Kenya was also attractive for friends who came to visit in good numbers. We also hosted two visits by Gaj Singhji, the former

[10] Natwar Singh, former Indian diplomat and former external affairs minister has recounted this extraordinary episode in 'Margaret Thatcher, Chandraswami_and I', *Walking with Lions: Tales from a Diplomatic Past*, Harper Collins, 2013, pp. 173-9.

Maharaja of Jodhpur, though he did not stay with us. Pandit Jasraj came twice and we organized public concerts as fundraisers, besides musical soirées at the Residence. These visitors added to our local connections and friendships. A less attractive visitor was the wife of the then Foreign Secretary who stayed with us as a matter of right, and was a thorough nuisance. On her final evening she threw a temper tantrum at me, during a dinner at the home of good friends. Occasionally swallowing such discomfort was part of the job!

An exceptional visitor to Nairobi was Mother Teresa, whose organization 'Sisters of Charity' ran orphanages, children's homes and hospices in Nairobi and other places. They were of course a major priority in our fundraising activities. Once, when my wife and I went to the airport to receive Mother Teresa, she flitted about birdlike, handing out little metal medallions to all the staff, customs officials and others. She spoke of the branches of this organization in Rwanda, Burundi, and other places in Africa, with around 3000 people working around the world. This prompted me to ask her a naïve question: 'How many were with you at the outset of your activities?' I guess she had faced such queries many times before; she replied simply: 'Jesus Christ and I.'

We traveled extensively in Kenya, and also made two private trips to neighboring Tanzania, once to see Ngorongoro, the fabulous game park sheltered in an extinct volcano cone. We probably traveled to all the Kenyan game parks, except to the ones in the distant north. Masai Mara was head and shoulders our favorite, but we never got to see the migration of the wildebeest.

The diplomatic community in Nairobi was fairly active, the more so as we worked together at the two UN entities based there, though it was not my priority field of action, as mentioned above. In those days, Western embassies were not as obsessive about issues of local corruption, democratic values and human rights, as they became in later years, when a few of their envoys gained notoriety for their activist postures, in what amounted to interference in Kenyan political affairs. Such actions would be more credible in the eyes of developing countries if they were not selectively applied; one does not hear of these universal principles being applied in autocratic countries that are closely allied with the West. Around the time I left Nairobi at the end of my assignment there occurred an unusual incident when a Western envoy retired from his post and immediately took up an assignment as an adviser to President Moi; such crossing over is rather unusual in our profession.

End of Assignment

By 1986, Ajit had graduated from high school and Priya was in her final year. I looked around to the available options and found that the post of consul general in San Francisco was to fall vacant just around the time I was due for transfer from Nairobi. I put my hat into the ring and this was accepted. A colleague—I forget who—told me: some might advise that you are too senior for that assignment, but don't listen to them; San Francisco is among the best that our service offers, and you should not miss this. Things did indeed play out the way he had indicated, and I stuck to my choice. When I had transited through London, on the way back from Ottawa, PC Alexander, by then the High Commissioner in London asked me to come to London as Deputy HC; it would have been a high-profile assignment, but I opted to stick to San Francisco.

Visiting President Moi at his farm estate around April 1986 I mentioned that I would be ending this assignment in a couple of months. His immediate response was that he would tell my government that if we were interested in continuing close relations, I should not be moved out of Nairobi. That was unanticipated. I then explained my need to be at a place where I could afford to give our children high quality university education. He thought for a moment and said that in those circumstances, he would agree to my departure, since he knew I would not leave Nairobi unless I had to. Later that morning I accompanied the President on a drive. We stopped at the largest of his schools and he asked the Principal to assemble the children. Returning to the school half an hour later, Moi delivered an impromptu address: pointing to me he spoke about the work I had done and added that he was giving me permission to leave Nairobi only for the sake of my children's education. He went on then to speak of the importance of education and how parents had to make sacrifices for this.

Several weeks later I went to the State House for a formal farewell call on the President. In those days, the ritual was unusual; the departing envoy stood in the corridor outside the President's personal office, flanked by the Foreign Minister and the Permanent Secretary, facing the assembled media representatives. The President would then emerge and make some remarks, before bidding farewell to the envoy. As it turned out, Moi remembered our earlier conversation, and he repeated at some length the points he had made to the schoolchildren, namely that he was giving me permission to leave Nairobi only because I had explained the education needs of my children. He also had some kind things to say about my work. The next day's newspapers carried this story at some length. I debated whether to report this to New Delhi and opted not to do so. Colleagues at Headquarters have a healthy disregard for anything that smacks of self-promotion.

Attending a customary round of farewell parties, which tended to be numerous, I requested my hosts to make a contribution to KIFA's Kenyan Student Fund, rather than give us presents. We managed to collect around K Sh.300,000 in this fashion. I left directly from Nairobi to San Francisco in July 1986, while my family went to India to spend some time at home before joining me at the new post.

11

West Coast Story

San Francisco (1986-89)

San Francisco (SF) turned out to be far more worthwhile professionally than I had imagined, for two reasons: first, our Consulate General (CGI) covered 17 states, some of the country's largest, stretching from California to Texas, Oklahoma, and Nebraska, all the way to Alaska and the Hawaii islands; second, developments in India transformed our work profile, adding salience to economic work, without reducing the value of other activities. That meant I traveled extensively, spending several days each month on visits to different states. Engagement with the Indian diaspora permeated our work. It was good to be at this post when India's diaspora and economic outreach was shifting gear. In 1986, India had three consulates in the US, in San Francisco (SF), and at New York and Chicago.[1]

Consular Diplomacy

The traditional raision d'être of a consulate general is consular services, the more so at a location that is a significant source of tourists, business visitors and an ethnic community, all of whom need visas and passport services. At San Francisco consular work was just the tip of the iceberg, but a very visible tip. When I reached SF, consular services were in a mess, a blot on our reputation. The problem was graphically underscored via four articles in the

[1] Now India has five consulates in the US, including two more in Atlanta and Houston.

largest circulation ethnic weekly, *India West*, the first coinciding with my arrival. The series title was: 'Is the Consulate General of India really inefficient?' Yet, the intent was not hostile, but urged remedial action. That became our priority.

In our region, 'clients' for consular services lived in three time zones, which meant that even before the office opened at 0900 in the morning, the six-line telephone rang continually. The receptionist could only handle one caller at a time, and other calls were unanswered. The remedial measures, were straightforward, not demanding rocket science expertise:

- We installed a recording that guided callers with basic information, including a voicemail box for visa form request.
- For the first three hours each morning two persons attended to the phone.
- Visa and consular service application forms were distributed widely to Indian associations and cultural groups, travel agents and others, to be photocopied liberally.
- Colored plastic bins were used for our processing throughput, to distinguish the applications received each day of the week, to easily track the work process; our aim was a three-day turnaround.
- Applicants coming in person were advised, through notices prominently displayed in the waiting room, that applications received up to noon each day would be processed the same day and could be picked up at 1600 hours.
- By paying a 'rapid processing fee' of $5, those in a hurry could pick up their visas within one hour. Our consular regulations did not specify this, but urgent services were chargeable; we stretched that provision. After I left SF, I heard that our auditors had objected to this action. The MEA was apathetic—it neither approved nor disputed our action. This was a pity, because the method was effective, customer-friendly and raised revenue.
- I explained to the consular staff, including those locally engaged who played a key role, that for a foreign national, a visa was imperative. If we maintained our claimed three-day turnaround, they would not hassle us, nor make abusive phone calls; efficiency lightened our workload.[2]

---

[2] I later used the same arguments in Germany, another place with high consular demand.

It took some months to fully implement this system; it transformed our performance. The MEA regulations permitted hiring temporary staff to meet urgent demand, and that was done. Our staff understood our objectives, and cooperated fully; it ended the daily ire they had faced, via phone calls, letters and personal visits; they enjoyed the new atmosphere.

In a short while, the CGI won kudos from the Indian community and from American visa applicants. It became a living demonstration of the strategic value of efficient consular services. Our relations with the ethnic media and with the Indo-American community were transformed, to the envy of colleagues working in other parts of the US, as became clear during our biennial meetings of the heads of consulates and Embassy colleagues.

Two other consular issues deserve mention. The US is an 'El Dorado' for migrants, those with legitimate documents and those without, Indian and others. An entire industry exists, with tentacles in different corners of the globe, to exploit them, in their dream of economic betterment. In the 1980s, thousands poured into the US from India, via travel routes that showed ingenuity. At that time, porous controls and an abundance of bogus Social Security cards meant that many of them lived and worked in cities and townships, including agricultural farms owned by prosperous Indians in North California and elsewhere. As with illegal migrants that headed for Germany narrated earlier, whenever undocumented migrants were apprehended, the US authorities stamped their passports as 'invalid' for subsequent entry into the US. Consequently, many destroyed their own passports, applying for new ones. Our regulations mandated that only one-way travel documents could be issued to those expelled, if they were verified as Indian citizens; they did not want that. Consequently, their applications for replacement passports took many months to process; often, the home addresses they gave were false, defying verification in India. That produced anger; the applicants felt that we were not helping them with replacement passports. Such consular issues were insoluble, though a few did eventually opt to return to India. Others disappeared into the pool of the undocumented.

Within the thriving Sikh community on the West Coast, agitation over Khalistan was acute when I reached San Francisco;

it tapered off gradually. In my first few months, the CGI received some threats over the telephone, which we reported to the police authorities, who undertook discreet but effective surveillance; the problem did not escalate, beyond a couple of demonstrations held outside our office. On a few occasions the federal agencies providing diplomatic protection also stepped in, but most of the time they remained in the background. That meant also that I could no longer visit gurdwaras, as had been customary in Kenya.

There is a footnote. Just when we began to implement consular improvements, in late 1986, our Embassy in Washington DC decided to raise the visa fee from $5 to $5.90 (or some such figure), to take into account currency fluctuations. We wrote back that it would be impossible to apply this change because it involved additional correspondence with applicants, just to get $0.90, at a time when we could not cope with our consular demands. It was far better to wait a few months and put into effect a new visa fee, in a rounded figure. Further, asking for this additional payment cost us more than the money we sought. We did not hear anything further, but later our auditors objected to this notional revenue loss. Audit objections usually come some time after the event; it is customary to write to the official concerned, for information that successors may not have, given short memories of administrators. For some reason, this was not done. In 1996, over a year after leaving the Service, I received a strange letter from an MEA under secretary, surely directed by someone else; I was asked to pay about ₹96,000, to make up for this revenue loss. I wrote to the Foreign Secretary K Raghunath, detailing the facts. He wrote back immediately, expressing outrage, said he would deal with it; that was the last I heard of this issue.

Outreach, Diaspora Diplomacy & Software Promotion

On the US West Coast, rising awareness of Asia led to the buzzword 'Pacific Rim'. This covered China, Japan, Korea and much of SE Asia, but not India. I argued that 'the Rim also has a Hinterland', that India should be included in that priority region. Later in the 1990s the phrase 'Asia-Pacific' gained currency, though it was not always clear, at least initially, if India was included. Today, the better term is the 'Indo-Pacific' region, linking the states on the two oceans. Behind these words was the reality of India in the American mindspace; we needed to match and partly offset fascination with China. In SF, those were the early days of a slowly rising interest in India.

It was exhilarating to see that across the country, our countrymen—and women—were active in community affairs and engaged with mainstream US groups, engaged in politics, raising funds and organizing actions, many in partnership with the mainstream American community. The Festival of India, held from the end of 1985 to the autumn of 1986 had provided a springboard, in its exceptional, open-minded decision to permit any group of people, or association, to organize its own cultural activity, and use the Festival logo, calling these, be it dance, or music, or a even a simple book display in a local library, an 'associated event of the Festival of India'. That produced a deluge of activity, giving visibility to Indian-Americans and to friends of India, raising their morale. In those days life was relatively uncomplicated, with no threat of terrorism or narrow politicization of ethnic communities; it was risk-free. We return to Festival issues below.

India's diaspora outreach had moved into an active phase. On the flip side, we did not fully see the potential dangers of that new priority, as elaborated below. But it was clear to some of us that the pursuit of 'non-resident Indians' (NRIs) should not supplant our engagement with the mainstream US entities, businessmen and others.[3] Sadly, at some places Indian missions began to treat the diaspora as their principal action target. In New Delhi a major business organization said in a group discussion held in 2001, attended by over 20, that when Indian business delegations travel abroad, the guests invited by some Indian missions to their receptions consist almost exclusively of NRIs.

In the late 1980s the number of Indian Americans in the US was around 800,000.[4] The SF Bay Area was home to about 60,000

---

3 See: Rana, 'India's Diaspora Diplomacy', *The Hague Journal of Diplomacy*, Vol. 4, No. 3 (2009), pp. 361-72.

4 Dramatic change in the Indian presence in the US is testified by the fact that by 2014 that number has grown to 3.2 million. That makes it a significant factor in bilateral relations.

of them; many were technocrats and information technology (IT) specialists, working in major US companies. An increasing number were venture capitalists, besides those in business and in academia. This produced a profusion of Indian associations and cultural groups; on visiting different cities we met the office bearers, and attended community functions. Los Angeles (LA) was a special concentration point, home to 70,000 persons of Indian origin. I traveled frequently to LA, virtually once every month, mostly on day visits from early morning to late evening, or staying over for a single night.[5]

Major US cities vie for consular representation; in some states, inter-city competition is intense. One example is Houston and Dallas in Texas. In California, SF was the old established metropolis, with wealthy families dating to the mid-19th century, rejuvenated by the emergence of Silicon Valley, and the merger of surrounding towns into the huge Bay Area sprawl. SF was locked in tight competition with that brash upstart LA, with new money, industrial strength, Hollywood and associated glamor, in effect a much larger, dispersed metropolitan entity. The number of consulates in LA had overtaken those in SF; a country taking a fresh decision on California representation almost automatically opted for LA as the more vibrant commercial and cultural center, but those already established in SF, did not move out. This produced a strong SF-LA rivalry.

Whether it was in SF, LA or at places such as Dallas, Houston or Oklahoma City, among every set of activists in the Indian community, small and large rivalries played out through competing associations, and programs guided by different personalities; elections produced sharp contestation. This was an inevitable consequence to community activism; I had seen this in even more acute form in Kenya. Other diaspora groups, notably the Jewish community, also have their internal rivalries, but these are mostly kept behind the scenes. We Indians are too individualistic, and poor team players. I had developed personal guidelines to minimize imbalance or charges of partisanship in engagement with the Indian community as narrated earlier.

---

5 A relatively small ethnic weekly published out of Los Angeles, *LA Times* wrote an editorial on my departure and ferreted out that I had made 37 official visits to LA in just over three years.

The only Indian state enterprise with a toehold in SF was the Bank of India, with a 'representative office', well located in the Bank of America Tower. Its manager was an enterprising individual who readily agreed to host a monthly discussion meeting on Friday afternoons, bringing together leading businessman of Indian origin, as well as visiting Indian personalities. For instance, Ratan Tata, who came to SF for business meetings, joined us twice. One young participant was Prakash Chandra, an IT engineer with a leading US enterprise. After one meeting, Prakash and a couple of his friends asked if CGI would work with them if they were to set up a group of young activists promoting stronger India-US exchanges. I welcomed this, as fitting closely with our objectives. In a matter of months, the 'Silicon Valley Indian Professionals Association' (SIPA) was formed in 1987. It grew rapidly to a membership of 1000, organizing monthly meetings to discuss developments in India and meet with Indian business entrepreneurs visiting the US.[6] They developed networking connections among themselves, and acted as CGI's brains trust for organizing an annual series of 'Software India' conferences, the first of which was held in October 1987, bringing together a dozen Indian software enterprises, to meet with potential American clients, other software companies and the IT industry majors. It was the first time that Indian software was marketed jointly in sustained and comprehensive fashion; for example, the initial encounter between Microsoft and Indian companies took place at the 1987 Software India event, held at Seattle.

We thus stumbled into software promotion. The 1987 Software India conference met at Palo Alto, and then at Seattle, LA and Dallas—before it moved to Chicago, New York and Washington DC, the very first such marketing anywhere, and a prototype for similar actions in other parts of the world. Thanks to the ready support given by Ambassador PK Kaul, the Commerce Ministry provided seed funding from its 'market development fund', but that was the limit of official support from Delhi. We obtained the participation of a software promotion body in India and then Indian companies joined the show. The likes of NR Narayana

[6] SIPA later went into a low-key phase, but is now more active and has a membership of 5000. See: http://www.sipa.org/about/

Murthy, Nandan Nilekani and others, set to become big names, attended. Consider: in 1986 India's software exports were around $15 million; for 1990 we set ourselves a target of $100 million, which seemed far out.

In those days small, emerging Indian companies typically offered that they could handle all kinds of work, in any machine language; they found it hard to grasp the advice offered by Indian Silicon Valley engineers, that they would be more credible with potential US customers if they offered specialized expertise. Their main selling point was that they were inexpensive; it was a vice-president at Oracle that made a prescient observation, telling us: today your selling point is price arbitrage, but in some years your real strength will emerge, your quality arbitrage.

These promotional activities led to a miscue of the kind that sometimes happens. A major US enterprise, disregarding our advice that they should enter into collaboration with Indian counterparts, opted to 'poach' experts from Indian companies, luring them with high salaries. Several months later, somewhat sheepishly they told us that their program had not worked well; they brought a dozen talented individuals, but none had previously lived overseas; some could not adapt to the work environment, or the climate. That company, and others then went on to build genuine partnerships with Indian enterprises.

Texas Instruments (TI), based in Dallas, was the pioneer in setting up its first software development center in India, in early 1986. Even before I made my first of a dozen journeys to that dynamic business hub, we were contacted by one of their vice-presidents, an Indian, with a request for exemption from an industry-wide power-cut that the Karnataka state government was to impose; their fledgling Indian venture then employed 30 software engineers. I sent a fax to the Chief Secretary at Bangalore and was delighted to receive a reply within a day, saying that the state government was cognizant of the importance of the software unit and that they would not suffer any power disruption. TI was very gratified. In mid-1987, a senior TI representative told me that two of their engineers had quit; they saw this as a setback. I replied that TI deserved congratulations, as it was actually serving our larger objective, as an incubator for Indian engineers to start their own ventures. He was not much amused, but that was the reality.

In 1987, thanks to good friend Prof. WM (Mac) Laetsch, one of the four vice-chancellors at UC Berkeley, a periodic discussion group was established. Going beyond academia, it reached out to Indo-Americans and others, helping the University widen its outreach. It provided us with one more platform to discuss stronger India-US cooperation. Around 1988, at one of these bimonthly events, the chief executive officer of a major American chip design company told this group how they had set up an Indian joint venture in which their Indian employees held 60% ownership, taking advantage of market access that India provided to such NRI companies. Someone asked him what would happen if these Indian shareholders left employment with them; he replied that this was no problem, because they trusted them to work for the success of this venture. I did not encounter that kind of open businesslike attitude in Europe.

A few years after I left San Francisco, SIPA waned in influence and membership, but another group, led by successful venture capitalists and technologists came into existence, 'The Indus Entrepreneurs' (TiE). It gained in strength during the 1990s, and today is a global entrepreneurship network of over 13,000, with 61 chapters in 18 countries.[7] It has successfully mentored young engineers to develop business ventures of their own; living up to its carefully chosen name 'Indus', it has opted to reach out to all South Asians, including Bangladeshis, Pakistanis and Sri Lankans. It is a unique model of diaspora activism.

Life in San Francisco

San Francisco is among the most pleasant cities in the world, with a year-round salubrious climate and splendid living conditions. The winters are mild and the summers pleasant, even unexpectedly cool, especially on the small peninsula on which the city is located. The Consul General's residence is in the tony Presidio Heights, wisely purchased in 1981, during the MEA's drive to acquire properties abroad.

The Consulate General is located about two km from this residence, in an unfashionable location, some five km from the

---

[7] See: www.tie.org

downtown area, but easy to access, with good parking space for the many applicants that come by car for consular services. We own the building and a few months before I left, we completed the process of obtaining city permission for expansion, adding a floor to the building. That kept up a personal tradition of steering property projects, but not staying on to enjoy the benefits.

A group of leading Indo-Americans, consisting of businessmen, bankers and academics had established a monthly lunch club, with membership traditionally offered to the consul general. I joined in good cheer, and coined for it the label 'No Name Lunch Club'. It was a forum for useful conversation and contacts. Such networks are essential in diplomatic work, highly productive as long as one is not locked into an exclusive set of friends, which might alienate others, or gives an impression that diplomats are not accessible. Such impressions, even if inaccurate, spread easily among the diaspora.

The Bohemian Club of San Francisco is a unique, grand institution, established in 1872. It's motto is 'Weaving Spiders Come Not Here'; members are not supposed to discuss business at the Club, or pursue professional interests, but it is great for networking. It leans towards the Republican Party; many Republican US presidents have been members, as also some of the biggest US business magnates. Foreign consuls general are welcomed, but on the Club's terms. The screening involves visits to about a dozen executive committee members, who assess if the individual should be admitted—not all are accepted. I did my rounds and joined a few months later. The Club owns a massive downtown property, occupying a large section of a block, with two principal entrances, including one used for the limited number of functions that women can attend; it adjoins a small theatre. Otherwise, the club is exclusively 'men only'. It has a valuable library collection, a massive dining room, a long bar, elegant smoking and reading rooms, reception halls, lodgings for members, and other facilities.

What distinguishes the Bohemian Club from other exclusive institutions created by the rich for the rich—such as the even more exclusive, small Pacific Club opposite SF's iconic Fairmont Hotel—is that from inception it has welcomed a different class of members, artists, entertainers, musicians and authors, who give it a distinct flavor. The Club owns the 'Bohemian Grove', 2700 acres of virgin redwood forest purchased in 1899, in what turned out to be a prescient act of environment conservation. Its redwoods are up to 1000 years in age, rising to a majestic 300 feet. That forest is awe-inspiring.

This forest is the locus of an extraordinary summer camp held over three weekends and two weeks in mid-July, an event the Club calls 'the Grove', an all-male affair, extending to the service staff. About 160 acres of this forest are used for this, and members and their guests stay at 120-odd 'camps' scattered in the undulating terrain, with rustic wooden huts and chalets, offering communal ablutions and basic comfort, but no TV; in those days the only phone was at the gate office. Membership of individual camps, highly coveted, in effect creates closed groups within the club, often profession-dominated; thus 'Owl's Nest' has heavyweight Republicans, including several former US presidents, another consists of bankers. Each levies its own charges, often heavy, and has traditions and rituals. The summer camp holds two iconic events, 'High Jinks', a one-time performance of a play, usually written by a member, performed just once; it is a tradition for lots of people to take on minor, walk-on roles, becoming a 'spear-carrier' in the Club's idiom. In contrast, 'Low Jinks' is a lively medley evening of music, especially jazz, song and dramatic skits, heavy on humor; one year I attended, after stagehands had shifted the props, their names were announced; one was Clint Eastwood.

Each day at the Grove has its featured attractions, and most camps put up their own entertainment, in the shape of receptions, lunches and dinners, as also music and impromptu jam sessions. Eminent speakers deliver lectures at a lovely meadow around a small lake, with attendees sprawled on the grass or seated at log benches. No vehicles are allowed within the Grove, other than a fleet of open bodywork Ford buses, built to replicate designs from the 1930s; they traverse several routes that link the camps. Another quaint tradition is for people to relieve themselves at the base of a redwood, i.e. 'water the trees'. All in all, the Grove is a return to one's youth, shedding worldly care—there is even a ceremony on that theme, to mark the start of each year's Grove.

The SF consular corps was active and met at monthly lunches. In a fashion typical at many consular cities, it did not make a distinction between career and honorary consuls, so that the corps had 70+ members. The City of San Francisco, like many large US cities, had its chief of protocol, a retired State Department official, and through him some minor privileges were enjoyed by the corps, including support from a city volunteer group that organized events to make foreign consulate personnel welcome. Los Angeles, Dallas, and other cities had similar arrangements.

Political Outreach

In the US, Indian consulates were not involved in political activities, which were handled by the Embassy in Washington DC, with two exceptions. (I was to find later that in Germany the situation was rather different, in that political outreach could be undertaken in that exceptionally 'federal' country, at the level of their *Landers*). First, in coordination with the Embassy in Washington DC, the consuls general were asked to meet congressmen and senators who were particularly influential from an Indian perspective, or were opposed to us on major issues. The notion was that these politicians might be more amenable in their home constituencies, but things often did not work that way. I found it hard to see them, though one did meet with their aides. Those strongly opposed to us—like some Republican congressmen from the farmer-dominated constituencies in North California, simply would not meet me; their sizable Sikh constituencies made them politically sympathetic to the Khalistan cause. In those years the mainstream Indian community was not sufficiently politically mobilized to exert constituency pressure on such politicians. That lay in the future.

Second, it made sense for us to approach Governors and their staff, to get them interested in India, to sponsor business delegations and other visits, to prospect for stronger economic links. That worked well in states such as California, Colorado, Texas, and Washington. Some individual politicians developed a keen interest in India and worked with us for better exchanges. California's Lieutenant Governor Leo McCarthy became a valuable contact, and I developed a friendship with his aide Jock

O'Connell. Similarly we developed friendships with some state congressmen in Washington State. But one problem persisted: most states did not have a mechanism for external contacts. Some states and the larger cities had designated protocol officers, but they could offer little practical support, beyond facilitating local visits. An exception was Texas, where the Mayor of Dallas hosted an annual event for ambassadors based in Washington DC, who were flown in on chartered planes for a two-day promotional tour; major companies in that city offered fine hospitality. By virtue of good friendships in Dallas I was twice invited to this event, the only Consul General so included.

Our diaspora facilitated some of our political and other outreach; that in turn empowered and in a fashion 'legitimized' them. It also fed the local political ambitions of the diaspora, and brought them into closer engagement with the political process at city and county levels. The phenomenon of the Indian diaspora contesting state and federal elections on a large scale had not yet begun. They became active through their own networking across the US; a 'Federation of Indian Associations' played a pioneering role in those years. Other clusters of Indo-Americans pursuing national level recognition also emerged, sometimes affiliated to professions such as medical doctors, or different regions in India. An Indo-American was appointed in 1988 in Washington DC to an assistant secretary of state level post, which required Congressional approval. Sadly, some members of his regional Indian community opposed that nomination. The Indian diaspora was on a political learning curve.

Los Angeles had a 'sister city' relationship with Mumbai, and like virtually all such twinning arrangements operated by Indian cities, it simply did not work. Unlike in most parts of the world, Indian mayors enjoy no executive or financial powers; they typically hold their ceremonial offices for a single year. In consequence, India misses out on this useful device for 'sub-state diplomacy'. Later, I witnessed a like situation in Stuttgart in Germany, which was also twinned with Mumbai. Possibly Prime Minister Modi, who wants to encourage city-level cooperation, may succeed in reworking local governance arrangements in India.

Engaging Academia and Thinktanks, Marketing India

We had extensive contacts with major universities throughout our vast territory. Two priorities were the leading universities in the Bay Area, UC Berkeley, and Stanford. We helped these institutions to connect better with the Indo-American community; Prof. Mac Laetsch, Vice Chancellor, hosted UC Berkeley's first outreach through a dinner for leading Indo-Americans he hosted in 1988. My successor, Satinder Lambah, built on these connections; he persuaded leading NRIs to fund full professorships at both universities. At Stanford, Prof. Krishna Saraswat ran a visionary IT research center that opened my eyes to the way iconic business enterprises that were fierce competitors in the marketplace could work jointly to a time horizon of five years or longer.

Our priority in these academic contacts were institutions that had centers for South Asia or Indian studies, but during every trip to different cities, a visit to a university was an invariable feature. It made me aware of their deep scholarship; we urged them to intensify connections in India. UT Austin, Rice University in Texas and the University of Washington in Washington State were important, as were a clutch of universities in and around Los Angeles, including UCLA, USC and others. Small colleges, a vital element on the US academic landscape were no less important; we depended on an academic contact to develop a visit program; that added to our network.

Visiting UC San Diego in late 1986, I saw its computer center with several Cray supercomputers—a remarkable sight, a high temple of technology—I learnt of a network that linked together academic institutions, called 'Arpanet'. In my tour report, I suggested that Indian institutions should join this new network, because this would give them an improved international profile. Alas, as was the unfortunate norm, I received no response from the MEA and the other official agencies that were addressed, including the Department of Science & Technology. Little did I imagine that Arpanet was the forerunner to the internet; I had glimpsed, very dimly, the future.

It was also in San Diego that two major contacts were developed. On a visit to the Salk Institute in October 1986 I met Nobel laureate Dr. Jonas Salk, and learnt about the remarkable work on biotechnology that they were conducting. Dr. Salk made an important observation: he felt that India's decision to rely exclusively on injection-based polio immunization (based on French technology) was a serious mistake, and the oral vaccination method that he had developed should not be abandoned. For him it was an immense tragedy that 'hundreds of thousands' died or were crippled needlessly by polio each year in India. He had written to the Indian authorities, and as a gesture of protest, he had decided to stay away from the Indira Gandhi Award jury, of which he was member. I reported this to the MEA, and to a senior member of the Prime Minister's Office, with no result. Some months later, when I accompanied Ambassador PK Kaul to meet Dr. Salk, he repeated these points. Possibly the Ambassador reported this to Delhi, though I doubt this; in any event, no action resulted. It was only 15 years later that India came back to the oral vaccination method. In retrospect, I should have continued to badger New Delhi, though I did not know enough about the subject. In those days NGOs or civil society agencies that could take up such issues did not exist. Perhaps Dr. Salk should have gone public, but that was not his style.[8]

The other great contact at San Diego was Prof. MC Madhavan, on the economics faculty of San Diego State University. Taking the help of leading Indo-American businessmen, he had developed a remarkable annual series of 'Mahatma Gandhi Awards', modest sums of a few hundred dollars given to the best high school students graduating from the school district. Remarkably the awards went to the toppers, not to Indo-Americans; leading schools and elected personalities of the city or country made the selection. Prof. Madhavan's dream was that if such awards could be instituted in other cities, they would bring alive the memory of Mahatma Gandhi, to a young generation of Americans, as the very first recognition they had received. Prof. Madhavan has continued with his pioneering education and social work.

---

[8] In the late 1990s, as a member of the governing council of the Ranbaxy Science Foundation, I got to know from Prof. Jacob John the dynamics of India's polio immunization policy, and the high relevance of the position that Dr. Salk had taken.

We also focused on leading thinktanks. In the San Francisco Bay Area, SRI International was a prime target; getting them to pay greater attention to India produced result. RAND, at Los Angeles is a major autonomous thinktank, given its reputation and its connections with the Department of Defense. They had not done much work on India; I visited them early during my assignment, and kept up frequent contact. Ambassador Kaul also visited them and gave an upbeat assessment of India's prospects. RAND's response was tepid; the only concession they offered was that they would undertake a 'project' on India, subject to locating a funding source. The situation underwent gradual evolution, but real transformation in the attitude of RAND and others in the scholar community came only after the launch of India's reforms in 1991.

In the Bay Area, two entities deserve mention. The Electrical Power Research Institute (EPRI) at Palo Alto is funded by all the US power utilities; they contribute a fraction of their revenues in what is a model of privatized industry-wide research, something that has never existed in India. At the very first meeting at EPRI, facilitated by an Indian who worked there—this was a frequent mode to initiate contacts—the vice-president who received me asked plainly: you seem keen for us to develop cooperation in India, but how do we know that your successors will show the same interest? I replied that by then, I hoped they would have sufficient contacts in India to not need our assistance. We discussed prospects for exchanges in high-voltage transmission, which did indeed move forward with BHEL and others. Contacts were also established with the American Electronics Association (AEA), based at Santa Clara; with 3000 member companies, it was one of two major information technology industry representatives (in 2008 it merged with the 'Technology Association of America' to form 'TechAmerica'). We urged CII to partner them, but at that stage CII had established cooperation with another Washington DC based body covering the same industry, and nothing came of that, except that AEA invited us to a couple of their conferences, giving us an opportunity to market India as a software partner.

In 1988, it occurred to us that it would be worthwhile to reach out to an electronics industry journal, and persuade them to write about developments in India. Friends at SIPA suggested that *Electronics Business* was a fine target. It took just two phone calls, to their LA office and then to their editorial office on the East Coast, to persuade them to send a special correspondent to India; all we provided was help to meet Indian officials and business enterprises. That produced five articles in this journal. Not all the publicity was positive; one headline sticks in memory: 'Hello...crackle...crackle...this is India calling...' They wrote not only on software but also on the emerging electronics and telecom industry, and helped to raise awareness of India opportunities. It was a lesson on how a simple action, at a ripe moment, could produce comprehensive result.

Outreach to US companies produced interesting consequences. The Consulate General established a business-friendly reputation. A big-name IT company that had its US headquarters in New York sent a team of representatives to meet us; I asked them the reason for this. Their reply: we have heard that in the US it is your mission that is attuned to working with technology companies, and may help us best. Often it was Indians within these companies that acted as internal evangelists, which was a byproduct of diaspora outreach.

Not every initiative worked as intended. In a 2012 publication I narrated the following:

> Our Silicon Valley friends urged that Indian companies should consider making strategic investments in high technology start-up enterprises, in the manner in which South Korea and Taiwan had done, with the aim of gaining access to technology, and giving an impetus to home production. Based on their advice, we carried out soundings. Vinod Khosla, one of the founders of Sun Microsystems, and recognized even in 1988 as one of the leading figures in the emerging venture capital industry (he was and has remained a partner with Kleiner Perkins Caufield & Byers), expressed interest in helping us, and we learnt that even a relatively small corpus fund of around $10 million would suffice for several investments at the first and second financing rounds of startups. But after consultations with our industry leaders, and with the Department of Science & Technology, we realized that the idea was ahead of its time for our businesses, and government entities, in our system, and simply could not sustain the kind of risk

> that such investments would entail, where the success rate is barely two or three in a dozen investments—even if these successes would probably more than wipe out the losses.[9]

Another failed initiative deserves mention, because it has produced long-term consequences for India. Energized by PM Rajiv Gandhi's efforts to modernize India and his efforts to unshackle the Indian economy, six outstanding IT and electronics industry savants, led by Prof. Kumar Patel of Bell Labs, initiated dialogue with the Prime Minister in 1987. They were asked by the PM to draw up a plan for chip design and manufacture in India. The group included Prof. Krishna Saraswat of Stanford University, who was a good friend and guide. After several months of brainstorming, they drew up a detailed proposal for what would have provided a foundation for design and fabrication of chips, the vital base for an electronics and telecom manufacturing industry. The aftermath is unclear, but no action resulted. That plan has not seen the light of day and this episode has been forgotten; the initiators of those ideas have remained silent. The facts of this episode are locked away in the archives of the Indian Department of Science and Technology and in PMO. In 2014, India began work to establish chip manufacture, playing catch up in a technology race where it might have had a headstart. If only...

I attended conferences and seminars organized at different institutions, including thinktanks, on India-related themes throughout the region served by CGI. Such events drew participants from different institutions from the US and from India. One also observed a clear trend—those invited from India were primarily those that were critical of Indian policies, and rather few among them offered balanced perspectives. It was almost as if criticism of the Indian government was a precondition to their invitation.

Behind that trend lay a dominant US assessment of India, typical of the time. US West Coast institutions were fascinated by China, but the attitude towards India was different. These

[9] See Rana and Chatterjee, co-editors, *Economic Diplomacy: India's Experience*, (CUTS, Jaipur, 2011), Chapter 19, 'Networking with Local Partners: Experience in Silicon Valley, Mauritius, and Germany'.

scholars, many longtime specialists, seemed obsessed by India's shortcomings, and were generally pessimistic of its future. A frequent refrain was that India had undergone 'de-institutionalization', in that governance was weak, and that Indira Gandhi, who had been succeeded by her son Rajiv Gandhi in November 1984, had undermined the legal system and key national institutions. Prof. Paul Brass was one leading scholar whose name sticks in memory, but there were others of that ilk. Beyond that network of specialists, one did not find much interest in India; the focus of business and politics was on the Pacific Rim.

When we now look back to the five years of Rajiv Gandhi's prime-ministership, 1984-89, as also to Indira Gandhi's preceding four years when she returned to office in 1980, we can trace some early steps that led to the Economic Reforms that PV Narasimha Rao launched in 1991, which have produced a paradigm change for India. Alas, during the 1980s, few saw the prospects for deeper change that these early first steps heralded. Our effort from San Francisco, to argue the Indian case to business audiences and political leaders, was rudimentary public diplomacy. My refrain, that the Rim also had a hinterland, did not find many takers. During two visits to the US in my time, PM Rajiv Gandhi confined himself to visiting Washington DC and New York. Most Indians were fixated that the East Coast metropolitan areas epitomized the US, and the other regions mattered little. This was especially true of Indian business.

The only significant political visit to our region was by External Affairs Minister ND Tiwari to Los Angeles, barely two weeks after I reached San Francisco. I failed to take proper advantage of that visit. The Minister was in the city for a full day but our program, prepared under the Embassy's guidance before I reached SF, consisted exclusively of meetings with leading NRIs, and functions hosted by different Indian associations. We should have used the visit for outreach to mainstream American institutions, including the *Los Angeles Times*. I failed to exercise imagination to amend it.

Worse, in executing that precooked program, lacking understanding of the vast spread of LA, I took at their word the travel time estimates given by different Indian hosts; each was an underestimate, which taken collectively, produced cascading delay. Even though a dozen super-efficient motorcycle outriders of the California Highway Patrol (the famous 'CHiPs' of an iconic TV series) escorted the minister's car, we ended the day traveling 350 km on the freeways. That produced huge delay; at the end of a full day, the Minister returned to his hotel well after midnight. I was mortified that time management experience at the Prime Minister's Office had not been put to good use. ND Tiwari, whom I got to know better while serving at Mauritius, was graceful, voicing no criticism. On reaching the hotel, he lingered at the entrance for a few minutes, to shake hands with and thank each of the escorting outriders.

Economic Diplomacy

With the help of an energetic Consul (Commercial), BK Ghosh, we analyzed the trade figures for Indian exports to the US West Coast, especially to California, and found that India's market share in the total US import basket, miniscule as it was, at around 0.7% of the country's gross imports, was even smaller in our region, at below 0.5%. It revealed that there was untapped potential, which our businessmen had not fully exploited. This was also a mindset issue: when we look outwards from India, most Indians would say that the US lies to the west; few realize that the US West Coast is actually closer to India travelling eastwards, across the Pacific.[10] This meant that when most Indian businessmen traveled to the US, their focus was on New York and its neighboring regions, with perhaps a few going on to Chicago. The West Coast and Texas were simply not on their radar.

Against this background I advanced the notion that the US should not be viewed as a single market, but as a collection of regional hubs, with the boundary line between them depending on the products and the pattern of importers, distributors, and customers. For instance, garments or shoe imports for California were handled primarily through Los Angeles and San Francisco.

[10] We are prisoners of both habit and of images imprinted in our minds: maps in Indian textbooks, place Europe at the center, with Japan and the Americas at the two extremes. Even today, maps placing Asia at the center are not common.

Seattle in Washington State was also an important center. Similarly, Dallas, Texas was the hub for the US Southwest region. Trade shows held at Chicago, Dallas, Houston, Las Vegas, Miami, New York and other cities, focused on specific product lines and markets; this mapped the regional zones. This meant segmenting the country for targeted marketing.

Texas was case in point. The 'Dallas Market Center' built by property magnate and billionaire Tramiel Crow, consisting of a dozen huge exhibition halls, hotels and related trade-show facilities, totaling about 10 million sq. feet of exhibition space, was a major hub. By good fortune, Tramiel Crow and his wife were Indophiles, and a leader of the Indian community at Dallas, Kris Murthy, had good contacts with him. We sought to interest Indian enterprises to join the two dozen major trade shows held at Dallas each year, and had some success in attracting participation. Today, a number of Indian exporters are based at this Center; the number of business events, and show facilities there has grown exponentially.

Dallas and Houston were in sharp competition to attract foreign consulates. Houston had the advantage that it is the state capital, and the center of the oil industry, but Dallas is the hub of diversified business, and more dynamic. Dallas has been chosen by many countries as more relevant to economic promotion especially owing to the role of the Dallas Market Center. In 1989, when the MEA was at the point of choosing a location for its fourth consulate in the US, I urged Dallas over Houston, but this was not accepted; India's consulate in Houston opened in 1991.

Among the Indian associations of business, CII was dynamic in prospecting the US market and in developing economic connections. CII was also receptive to my arguments about treating the US as a collection of regional markets, more than any official agency.[11] In both 1987 and 1988, CII brought high-level 'CEO missions' to the West Coast and to Texas, consisting of about eight major Indian business personalities. I traveled with them throughout my region, covering SF, LA and Dallas. These visits

[11] My experience, at different assignments, has been that few in Delhi, including the MEA, have time for such quasi-philosophical arguments, if they are not presented with an actionable proposal.

raised awareness of India among US business decision-makers. They did market their companies, but primarily spoke of India as an economic destination. CII was visionary, undertaking generic promotion much before the 1991 Reforms; today we would call this 'public-private partnerships' to market India. The most vivid example was their sustained pursuit of the legendary Jack Welch, CEO of General Electric, which produced the transformation in GE's India engagement, including establishment of one of the world's largest, diversified research centers, at Bengalaru.

Trade shows and exhibitions in our region drew some Indian companies. At times, the promotional body ITPO, brought Indian exporters in a cluster, for higher visibility.[12] This was an effective method, as testified in several other accounts as well.[13] In 1988, ITPO tried another track, with less convincing results. It organized a standalone Indian exhibition at San Francisco, with about 60 Indian companies presenting products ranging from garments and shoes to handicrafts. We quickly learnt that the biggest problem with such a single country event is to attract buyers and local businessmen. While such 'Made in India' events work in developing countries, where the aim is also to raise the country profile, in developed markets it is far better to stick to the established specialized shows.

Cultural Work

The first major event when I reached San Francisco was the closing of the Festival of India, set for November 1986. Pupul Jayakar, the presiding deity of the entire series of Festivals since the first one in the UK in 1982, visited SF and we were told to organize for her a meeting with leading Indo-Americans to obtain their support for the grand closing event, as a full-day celebration in a major public park. I invited 25 leading personalities to the Residence to meet her, including Ali Akbar Khan Saheb, and other Indian artistes of the Bay Area teaching classical music and dance, and

---

[12] 'Indian Trade Promotion Organizations' was a useful device for motivating and assisting exporters to go to new markets and develop new products. In the 1990s the 'Trade Fair Authority of India' was merged with it.

[13] See Seshadri, 'Accessing US Footwear Market', *Economic Diplomacy: India's Experience* (2011) p. 85-94.

community leaders. Pupul gave them an outline of the program, featuring six different groups from India. We offered to organize a food fair to complement this, taking advantage of the seasonal salubrious weather. Ali Akbar Khan suggested that Indian and American artistes that had studied music and dance might also perform during the day, to fill out the program and give it a real participatory character. Pupul Jayakar objected, declaring that the high-class talent being brought from India could not be mingled with local students who were not of the same grade. This produced an emotional outburst from a young Chitresh Das, then a struggling Kathak dancer and teacher who also lived near San Francisco; he was anguished that a recommendation from Ali Akbar Khan was so easily dismissed. A compromise was then worked out that the young local artistes would also perform, but in the central plaza of the park, and not on the main stage; Pupul was adamant that the main stage be reserved for the professionals from India. Her attitude was symptomatic of disdain for amateurs among high Indian culture priests; they failed to value cultural exchanges, where the goal is to spread awareness and build relations.

Pandit Ravi Shankar, Ali Akbar Khan Saheb and Ustad Zakir Hussain and were just three among major Indian musicians that had settled on the West Coast. Pandit Jasraj visited us each year as our houseguest and gave several concerts. Others came regularly from India, some spending weeks and months teaching Indians and Americans from temporary bases. A heavy seasonal influx of other great Indian musicians and dancers has become the norm, with both the Indian community and Americans supporting them. Official Indian agencies do not now need to support Indian artistes for programs in North America and West Europe. US foundations, official and private, also now support such activities.

An outstanding Indian art historian and scholar with an international reputation, Dr. Pratapaditya Pal makes his home in Los Angeles; he was a senior at St Stephen's College and an old friend. In the 1980s he headed South and SE Asian art at the LA County Museum. Pratap helped me to understand the art scene on the US West Coast, and the value of art and museum exchanges. He took me to the Norton Simon Museum at Pasadena (located in the LA sprawl), and told me about a cultural issue. In 1984 that Museum had acquired two 11th-century bronze *Natarajas*, which turned out to have been stolen from a temple in Tamil Nadu. When sent to London for cleaning, the Indian government filed a case, contesting ownership, and won this, under an ancient British law dug up by some smart lawyers. That resulted in an agreement between the Museum and the Indian government to return the art objects to India. One clause provided that thereafter, India would consider the loan of some art objects to the Norton Simon Museum. They sent a formal request in 1987, which I forwarded to our Department of Culture, pointing out that this Museum received large streams of visitors, attracted by its Impressionist art, including van Gogh paintings, bronzes by Degas. They also held a small collection of Indian bronzes; objects loaned by us would inspire visitors to travel to India. That fell on deaf ears; I was told that India had considered their request as mandated, and rejected it. Sadly, Indian museums are not habituated to international exchanges, which cripples cooperation.

Embassy-Consulate Relations

The Ambassador in Washington DC was the captain of the Indian team, and as a Consul General, I showed him full respect. Others in the embassy, starting with the deputy chief of mission, were Foreign Service colleagues, and we worked closely together. For most of my time, the Ambassador was PK Kaul, former Cabinet Secretary, providing good leadership. At the end of my assignment, Dr. Karan Singh, former cabinet minister and former Maharaja of Kashmir arrived, but I saw him only briefly.

Soon after reaching SF, I had urged that the Ambassador and senior officials, and the CGs should meet regularly. For the first time, six-monthly meetings were instituted in 1987, rotating between different locations. This provided information-sharing and harmonization in our activities.

I accompanied Ambassador Kaul on his visits to states and cities in our jurisdiction. That gave me additional insight, plus a chance to meet useful people; I also helped the Ambassador with my contacts. I enjoyed an easy relationship with him and felt free to offer ideas. I once mentioned that he had in the Embassy some of the finest IFS officials, but it was necessary for him to trust them and use them fully, rather than rely on just a couple of IAS (Indian Administrative Service) officials posted at the Embassy, as his close advisers. That fell on deaf ears. PK Kaul belonged to the IAS, which has long seen itself as a rival to the IFS. In 1982-83, when he was Commerce Secretary and a member of the Foreign Service Board, I had seen his antipathy to the IFS. It should be added that some of my ilk reciprocate this sentiment towards the IAS.

Ambassador Kaul preferred to deal with Indo-Americans and was perhaps a little uncomfortable in reaching out to Americans, a serious drawback for one in his position. For instance, I suggested that he hold a dinner in honor of Tramiel Crow of Dallas at his Washington DC Residence; Mr. and Mrs. Crow would bring their Texas friends to such an event, permitting the Ambassador to widen his contacts. He claimed to like the idea, but he did not act on it. On another occasion at SF, I saw his discomfort in speaking with the head of a major US law firm; after that meeting my contact told me: you are positive on attracting US business to India, but your Ambassador does not seem so keen. In essence, this underscored a typical problem with 'political' appointments, including officials from outside the IFS. Some were lazy or pursued personal agendas; that was not an issue with Ambassador Kaul. A deeper problem was that some were uncomfortable in social discourse with Americans.

Managing a large embassy is a demanding task, the more so in a capital such as Washington DC. The presence of multiple 'wings' often produces internal division and parochialism. A non-career ambassador finds it difficult to manage relationships within the mission; the more so if real harmony does not prevail between the ambassador and his deputy, usually an additional secretary rank official, who may have been an ambassador at a couple of assignments. Embassy management is always much more difficult at comfortable posts, and the problem is compounded if officials are underworked. That engenders extra-curricular activities, and internal squabbles based on half-real or imagined slights. Embassy heterogeneity, in terms of official Indian agencies represented, aggravates this danger.

A Distant Island

In mid-1988, when I had barely completed two years at SF, I received a phone call from Foreign Secretary KPS Menon, the first time I heard from him directly. He said that I was specially selected for Cuba; the PM directly decided on appointments to barely a score of countries, and Cuba was in that cluster; the PM felt that at a time when the world was evolving rapidly, I met the requirement for an ambassador who might reach out to Fidel Castro to help in Cuba's transition to a more open policy. Looking back today, the wishful thinking implicit in that boggles the imagination; I am sure such a notion could not have originated with someone of Foreign Secretary Menon's international acumen. Taken aback at the abruptness of the proposal and its unreal assumptions, I replied that both my children were at university and that I could only afford to keep them there if I stayed at SF for the full three-year term. Foreign Secretary Menon, as the kind person he has always been, did not press the point.

Perhaps someone remembered that refusal. Around May 1989 I was informed that I would be moving to Mauritius. That did not seem fair, on the face of it, and I wrote to Foreign Secretary SK Singh, a good friend, if I could be sent elsewhere. He replied with his customary sagacity that I would find Mauritius rewarding and that after getting there I should write and tell him if he was right. It seemed futile to argue further. And on reaching the new post I did discover that SK Singh had been entirely correct.

12

Paradise Island

Mauritius (1989-92)

Mauritius welcomed me in unusual fashion. On my first working day in Port Louis in September 1989, an editorial in the ruling MSM party newspaper, *The Sun*, addressed some nice words of welcome and then declared bluntly: the new High Commissioner should not make the mistake of treating Mauritius 'as India's 25th state'. That unprovoked warning seemed strange, but reflection led me to understand that though gratuitous, it made a kind of sense, from a Mauritius perspective.[1]

Consider the context. About 70% of the island state's 1.1 million people, now grown to 1.2 million, are of Indian origin; Hindus account for 51% of the total. Muslims are around 20% of the total, mainly of Indian origin, though many among them identify themselves with Pakistan. Creoles made up the balance, descendants of slave labor brought by the Dutch and French from Mozambique and West Africa.[2] Finally, around 3% are of Chinese trader descent; the wealthy Franco-Mauritians number barely 1%, including the 14 families that own 50% of the sugar plantations,

1 Returning in August 2014 on a private visit to the 'Emerald Island' with my wife, I checked with a some old friends; a few remembered that incident, and thought it may have been the work of an over-zealous editor, but I remained of the view that it was a deliberate gesture, sanctioned by someone in authority.

2 This Indian presence among the Creoles is submerged in Mauritius, but is more notable in the neighboring island of La Réunion, which has continually been under French control and is now part of France.

the old mainstay of the economy. The country is thus intimately linked with India.

Mauritius has had mixed experience with Indian envoys, and with Indian actions. My immediate predecessor, Kant Bhargava (1958 batch), is a modest person, unassuming and gentle; he had given no offence. But others were cast in a different, assertive mold, individuals who had toyed with local politics to suit official and even personal agendas, at different times. Why did this happen? That is a complex story. In part it speaks of laxity in envoy oversight from New Delhi. Some are tempted to play Indian politics in the environment of a small country whose outward 'Indian-ness' is deceptive, as my story may show. For Mauritius, it was not unreasonable to warn a new Indian envoy against overreach.

I chose to ignore that public warning. It seemed wise not to raise this with anyone in authority, even while I felt strongly that such a message was unnecessary. Interference in this island-state's internal affairs was not my official mandate, nor remotely a personal objective. It seemed better to respond through actions; that would demonstrate India's intentions more cogently than words could. As events played out in the two years and eight months I spent in the country, my mission did not give cause to anyone to seriously question our conduct, with a small exception described below. Nor did we attract media criticism, even in the customary Mauritian frenzy of a general election that took place on 15 September 1991. For me the assignment became an extended object lesson in bilateral relationship management, how to work closely with, and respect a small neighbor.

The Mauritius Scene

Mauritius was an uninhabited island when the Dutch discovered it in the 16th century. They and the subsequent colonizers, the French and then the British, initially brought in slaves from Africa, followed by indentured Indian labor, to work in their sugar plantations. The UK gained legal title to Mauritius from France as part of the 1815 Treaty of Vienna, under which it agreed to safeguard the island's French heritage, protecting the small number of French settlers. Immediately thereafter, Britain stepped up induction of Indian workers, who were lured by false promises of a prosperous life. These migrants arrived with just the clothes on their back, besides their personal values and work ethic; some brought a precious copy of the *Ramayana*, which became the anchor of their faith. They landed at what is now *Aapravasi Ghat*, with its stone steps leading up to a quay and its two small stone tanks; it is now a national monument. Here, the indentured laborers, men and women, bathed for the first time after their arduous journey battened down in the holds of sailing ships; their names were entered in bulky registers, for apportionment to different estates. Fathers and sons, brothers and sisters were separated; even on the small island, bullock-cart journeys north to south took up to two days. The Mahatma Gandhi Institute, Mauritius, carefully preserves the photographs of these migrants, taken after 1870; the simple virtue and determination in their faces sometimes bring tears to viewers.

Others that came included small numbers of traders from China, mainly from venturesome South Chinese communities such as the Hakka, with their maritime traditions, plus some from India; the latter included Gujaratis, some of them Muslims (from minorities like the *Bohras*, *Ismailis* and *Mamen*, who were also active in the Gulf region and East Africa). That varied ethnic legacy makes Mauritius 'a rainbow nation', a land of pluri-diversity: it has a multitude of languages, with English as the official language, French the preferred language that dominates the print media, and Creole as a shared lingua franca. Example: the state radio network broadcasts in eleven languages. The religions practiced include many shades of Hinduism, Islam, Christianity, and a smattering of other faiths. Each community is socio-culturally self-contained, but lives in mutual tolerance, not through integration or inter-marriage, but respecting differences. For an Indian, Mauritius is a picture of our old customs and ways of life, frozen in time, as brought by the first generation of migrants, largely unchanged thereafter. Examples: the Tamil festival of *Cavadee* produces many processions where hundreds of devotees parade with their bodies, faces and tongues pierced with needles, nails and small lances, culminating at South Indian temples with fire-walking. Among the Hindus of Bihar and UP descent, rich or poor, the marriage feast is a simple vegetarian meal for all guests, consisting of the same seven items, served on a banana leaf.

Mauritius gained Independence in 1968, its freedom movement led by Sir Sewosagar Ramgoolam, the first Prime Minister. The constitution is based on the British parliamentary model, with a ceremonial head of state, and executive power in the hands of a prime minister. Uniquely for Africa, Mauritius opted to retain the British Queen as the symbolic head of state, with an appointed governor general. It was only in March 1991 that Mauritius declared itself a republic with the Governor General, Sir Veerasami Ringadoo becoming the first President.

The 70-member Parliament is elected through an ingenious system calculated to generate ethnic and political equity. Mauritius is divided into 20 constituencies, each electing three MPs (the small Creole-inhabited island of Rodrigues, 500 km away, elects two MPs). In each, citizens cast three votes, which must go to different candidates, so that each party presents a three-person slate, usually with an ethnic mix. For most of its history, the country has had three major parties, and the outcome hinges on a coalition among two of them. It thus happens often that a coalition wins all 60 seats; such a clean sweep is tempered by a supplementary formula under which eight more seats go to 'best loser' candidates, i.e. those that have lost by the narrowest margin. That ensures the presence of an opposition in the Parliament. The people of Mauritius view politics as a quotidian vocation, practiced with passion. The print media is independent, feisty, and combative—the radio and the only two TV channels in my time were state-run.

By the late 1980s, the Mauritius economy had begun to rise phoenix-like, bringing to mind its traditional sugarcane harvest method of burning fully grown cane crop, to remove the undergrowth and leaving behind an ash residue to nourish the soil.[3] This economic surge was based on diversification, a vibrant new textile industry, and first steps in an offshore financial center;

---

[3] Such harvesting methods are unknown in India, also a major cane grower. One reason may be a shortage of labor in Mauritius, and a need to speed up harvesting.

by 1990, per capita income had risen to $2000, and the hard-headed economists of the World Bank and the IMF had begun to speak of an 'economic miracle'. Two transformative actions underlay the island's success in moving out of its colonial monoculture inheritance. The first was the 1975 Lome Convention, framing the economic relationship between the European Community and the Africa-Caribbean-Pacific (ACP) states. Prime Minister Ramgoolam had astutely negotiated a 'sugar protocol' on behalf of the producers; he persuaded them to accept a guaranteed purchase price formula, at around half the price prevailing at that time; he reasoned that the boom of the mid-1970s would not last forever. Consequently, when world prices slumped heavily, the ACP sugar producers gained windfall profits. The second key action was taken by Anirood Jugnauth, after he swept Ramgoolam out of office in the 1981 elections, namely, calculated diversification of the economy, focused on the textile preferences given by the European Community to the ACP states. By the late 1980s the results were in full flow, thanks to the entrepreneurship shown by the Franco-Mauritians, and some businessmen of the Indian and Chinese communities. Consider: of all the garments imported by the European Community under ACP textile preferences, about 90% were from Mauritius; 75 other ACP states had simply not utilized this opportunity.

By the early 1990s, a third phase had commenced. The garment and knitwear manufacturers of Mauritius had begun to establish manufacturing subsidiaries in places such as Madagascar, to take advantage of cheaper labor. At home, the government had guided the establishment of an offshore banking center, and a start had been made towards implanting the knowledge industry, especially software centers and a nascent IT industry. All this reflected the government's foresight. Today, Mauritius companies own textile centers in Bangladesh, India and several African countries. A vibrant 'cyber-city' symbolizes change.

Mauritius wisely opted from the outset to have no armed forces, much like Costa Rica in Central America. It has a special armed unit in its police force, called 'Special Mobile Force', a kind of para-military unit; it also established a Coast Guard, with an aviation wing, to police its huge exclusive economic zone. India has been its partner of choice in providing key personnel and equipment for this Coast Guard.

Indian Interests

My wife and I traveled to Mauritius directly from San Francisco, in part because the post had been vacant for some weeks. After presenting credentials to the Governor General, we proceeded to India. That early spell on the island-state gave me time to reflect on Indian objectives in that country. I wrote out a three-page note, in bullet-point fashion, as a personal guide on India's tasks. Unknowingly, this replicated a format that is long customary in France, known as 'Ambassador's Instructions'.[4] The difference was that this was a personal exercise; no one at the MEA took any notice of this effort, setting out 'country objectives'. I did not retain a copy.

After I left the IFS, I had occasion to publicly set out reflections on Mauritius, commenting on a 2003 incident, when the Indian High Commissioner was withdrawn at short notice. Perhaps through excessive zeal, he had attempted to play politics. In an article published in *The Indian Express* of 7 June 2003 (reprinted some weeks later in the popular Mauritian daily *L'Express*), I said:

> This heady heterogeneity could easily have fractured into a divided country, or simmering ethno-religious discontent. Instead, it has nurtured a modern state that is remarkable for its ethnic-religious accommodation and economic progress. The different communities work together, but lead separate social lives, celebrating with great verve their own festivals without outward rivalry or envy. Its only post-Independence aberration in the shape of inter-community clashes occurred in 1998, resulting from inept handling by the police of localized Creole resentments. Since 1981 (coinciding with the Prime Ministership of Jugnauth), the island moved to a high growth track, abandoning its excessive dependence on sugarcane (though it remains important, for employment and exports, benefiting from the continuing ACP preferences extended by the EU, that are now threatened by WTO regulations). In many ways Mauritius has become a developing state exemplar, with agile

[4] See, Rana, *The 21st Century Ambassador* (2005), pp. 129-30; *The Contemporary Embassy* (2013), p. 90.

public-private partnership in economy diversification covering textiles, manufacture and now knowledge industry, and a per capita GDP of $4000. The World Bank hails it as a development model.

India's interests in Mauritius are straightforward. It is a near neighbor with strong connections. First, as a nation of stability, harmony and accommodation, in its self-image as a "pluri-cultural" and "rainbow" state, it serves as a counter-point to other countries where old migrant Indian communities face tension and resentment. Second, as a prosperous state, it is an interesting if small economic partner, and a multiplier for wider economic partnerships in its region of Southern Africa and the Indian Ocean Rim. Third, in the past, when apartheid ruled South Africa and the memory of mercenary-led attack on the neighboring state of the Seychelles in the mid-1980s was vivid, India also extended a measure of discreet security support. Happily that situation has passed and the region is free of tension. India retains a residual interest in the stability of the region.

In the past, India manifested direct political interest, when at the time of the 1983 elections the country's founding father and Labor party leader Sewosoor Ramgoolam was challenged by Jugnauth's MSM, the Indian envoy adopted a partisan role in support of the latter, at New Delhi's behest. Thereafter, we learnt fairly quickly that this did not produce any special advantage; we also understood that any government in Mauritius would see it's self-advantage in a cooperative relationship with India, so it does not pay to get too involved. This has broadly remained the official policy track for almost two decades, but it faced an internal Indian challenge.

A few in India, often belonging to the *sangh parivar*, transport the Indian political experience to Mauritius and mis-apply this to its political scene. It is indeed relevant for India to urge unity among the regional sub-groups of the population of Indian origin, but not to the point of choosing between their political parties, or their power-sharing formulas involving other ethnic communities... It is hard to imagine any government in Mauritius that would be inimical to Indian interests, given the web of mutually beneficial connections that exist...In essence, the vital Indian interest in Mauritius remains in the continuing welfare and advancement of its entire people, including the large community of Indian origin.

> We also have a stake in continuing trade investment and other economic activities, none of which are of exclusive character, or under threat from third sources, beyond normal competitive forces. The India-Mauritius treaty that has funneled foreign investments into India from third countries, taking advantage of local tax-exemptions for such offshore investments, is a minor issue, but useful from an Indian perspective of attracting FDI.
>
> There are two other tasks that few in India have considered. First, the main local challenge for the ethnic Indians in Mauritius is that too few of them have moved from worker and professional status to entrepreneurship, especially the majority Hindus. We encounter the same phenomenon in the other lands originally peopled by indentured labor from India. India can offer practical help, like the entrepreneurship development training program that we had organized in 1991, with the help of IDBI. We can also urge the different associations of the Indian community to develop such economic orientation and practice mutual self-help. Second, while the Indians of Mauritius are our natural friends on that island, we also need better ties with the other communities that we have tended to ignore—whether it is the Creole or the Franco-Mauritians. My experience has been that this can be done without any local alienation.
>
> Put another way, this is no more than the message of secular diplomacy, centered on a true reading of our long-term interests.[5]

India has learnt from such episodes, and has sent competent professional diplomats to represent India. By including Mauritius with the cluster of SAARC heads of government invited to his inauguration in May 2014, Narendra Modi underscored the special value attached to this country.

A word on the profile of the majority Hindu community: originally they were mainly small farmers, cultivating sugarcane, often on marginal land. Their children took up jobs in the textiles and garment industry, and those with better education sought government jobs, and some went into the professions, be it medicine, law or technology and engineering.

---

[5] First published in *Indian Express*, 7 June 2003.

A persisting weakness in this community was lack of entrepreneurship. There are, of course, exceptions, and they are slowly inspiring others to entrepreneurship. I discussed this often with the members of the executive council of the Hindu Council of Mauritius, which I attended from time to time as an invitee. They agreed with this socio-economic diagnosis, but seemed resigned to the situation. We made efforts at the High Commission to provide entrepreneurship training, through a course run by one of the Indian institutes that specializes in this field, also taking care to include Creoles and others in that training course.

Swami Krishnanandji (1900-92), established the 'Human Service Trust' in Mauritius, with branches in India and Africa; they ran an old peoples home for destitute elders of all communities, which has continued its fine work as we saw on a visit in 2014. A visionary, he guided some young followers towards public service, including active involvement in Mauritius political leadership. His goal was to sensitize them to look after their interests, overcoming prevailing political apathy. Many Hindu Mauritians that took to politics in the 1970s were from that first generation that he had mentored. His able lieutenant, Dhandeo Bahadur, remained committed to this Trust, and was one of the key community leaders in our time.

Krishnanandji was born and brought up in Jodhpur, and was a friend of Mimi's grandfather before he took sanyas. At a small function held for us soon after we reached Mauritius, he had evoked that old Marwar connection, addressing Mimi as *Champawat Baisa*, which had brought tears to her eyes. Some months after we left for Bonn, we received an unexpected phone call from Swamiji on 23 August 1992, when he spoke of plans to visit Koln, to be with some of his followers there, and he gave us his blessings. Barely two hours after that a weeping Dhandeo phoned to say that Swamiji had passed away, and that we were the last persons with whom he had spoken.

At Swami Krishnanandji's inspiration, Bombay Hospital annually brought a full team of heart surgery specialists, nurses and support staff to Mauritius to carry out operations at the leading government hospital for those that could not afford to travel abroad. This was human service in action, which also added to India's reputation.

Bilateral Relations

I maintained close exchanges with Prime Minister Jugnauth. It became a practice to exchange dinner visits with him every three months or so; Mauritius ministers were always accessible. I did attract one adverse comment. When our External Affairs Minister visited Mauritius in mid-1990 the Leader of the Opposition Paul Berenger called on him and complained that they found the Indian High Commissioner too close to the government. The Minister asked me to respond. I replied that it was my job to work with the government in office, but this was not at the cost of inaccessibility to any other political group. Anyone who wanted to see me was welcomed with cordiality, and I accepted invitations to a wide range of local functions. If any specific partisan action could be identified, I would respond to that charge as well. As it turned out, a couple of months later Berenger joined the government as Foreign Minister, when Sir Satcam Boolel, leader of the Labour Party and Deputy PM, broke away from Jugnauth. That brought into the government Prem Nababsingh as Deputy PM, who became a close friend.

One opposition leader, not active in politics in my time, that asked me through an interlocutor to meet him 'secretly'; he was annoyed when I refused, and probably complained to his friends in Delhi. My simple position was that in that open society; clandestine meetings were not in my remit. I also suggested that he was most welcome to meet me whenever he wished. As it turned out we met at a marriage function several months later; when he took me aside for a private chat, he seemed to accept my explanation.

India has always treated Mauritius as a close partner, meriting special treatment, a sentiment that was reciprocated. The Indian Navy helped it to establish its Coast Guard, providing the vessels, training and Indian officers to man the higher command levels, while Mauritian officers were trained to assume charge. During the South African apartheid era, when Mauritius perceived a threat of mercenary attack from foreign rogue groups, India stepped up naval patrols in the region, and established a program of annual friendly visits by Indian Navy ships. Helicopter pilots and technicians for the Coast Guard were also seconded from India, while Mauritians pilots and engineers were trained and mentored.

Around the mid-1990s, a few years after I left, taking advantage of the generous provisions of a bilateral Double Taxation Avoidance Agreement signed in 1983, especially its' liberal treatment for capital gains, Mauritius became a favored transit route for international companies making investments in India. This has been a consequence to India's 1991 Economic Reforms, which enhanced the FDI flow into India. This is now a difficult issue, a subject of prolonged bilateral discussions, and remains unresolved. India wants to revise the treaty, but Mauritius has refused; India has little option but to work out a mutually acceptable resolution.

Over the years, India has provided considerable technical aid, especially through training facilities. Hundreds of scholarships have been given. In my time around two thousand students went to India each year, on a 'self-financing' basis. With the expansion of university education facilities in Mauritius, this flow has tapered off. India played a small role in this, through its state enterprise EdCIL, though this company could have been more proactive. It failed to convert a first contract in 1991 to plan the expansion of the University of Mauritius, into follow-up assignments. Since then, private Indian universities have stepped in to establish affiliates. They show dynamism compared with our public universities, whose hands are often tied with onerous regulations, and have little incentive to go abroad. Consequently, India misses out on overseas projects, which can be vital connectors between countries.

Indian aid projects in Mauritius produced mixed results. A major 200-bed Jawaharlal Nehru Hospital, long in gestation, was inaugurated in 1991, during a visit to the island by Vice President SD Sharma. That project, handled under ITEC, our aid implementation agency, was in its final stage by the time I reached Mauritius, but that does not absolve me from failing to anticipate a problem that arose, which dented our reputation. While the standard of the civil construction, India-financed and supervised was good, the quality of hospital equipment supplied was poor, to the point that the Mauritius authorities replaced much of it immediately after the project was handed over to them. The Indian Health Ministry had little experience with implementing an overseas project; this was the result of the 'lowest bidder' method for purchasing operation theater equipment, beds and ancillary material, coupled with inadequate quality control.

In 1990 Mauritius asked us to take up a politically important project for the rehabilitation of its tea industry, which consisted of small farms located in hill terrain, mainly owned by holders of Indian descent, struggling to maintain quality and output. A dynamic tea expert who knew the industry well, Basant Dube, took up this difficult challenge, in full knowledge that at best, our contribution might prolong that source of livelihood for a decade or so. Our project produced limited result. Today, the Mauritius tea industry is almost extinct, but that delay gave some small farmers a chance to valorize their land holdings, thanks to new housing estates in that booming economy. That experience also made me aware of a fine tea project that Dube and his friends were pursuing in Keonjhar district of Odisha; when we visited it in 1991, during a Bharat Darshan tour. Mimi and I saw how this 600-acre plantation, producing quality tea, had come up in a region long devastated by *jhum* (shifting) cultivation endemic to that region. That was part of a larger project to extend tea cultivation to new regions.

Other projects were executed well. Among these was a radio telescope, established over a large tract of rocky soil in the north of the island, which gave Mauritius a place in pure science research. India also maintained a satellite tracking station at one of the high points overlooking Curepipe; it was of considerable value for monitoring and controlling the satellites launched from India that were placed in polar orbit. Indian personnel ran this station for many years, while Mauritian technicians were trained and gradually took over its operation from 1992 onwards.

About a score of Indian experts from different fields were deployed in the country, under the ITEC program. That set of technical exchanges added luster to India's image. Under the same program, we also provided training in India to hundreds of Mauritian experts in professional disciplines. Nominally, MEA assigns a 'quota' of training slots to the countries that benefit from this program, but in practice it gladly accommodates any reasonable request, the more so from a priority country such as Mauritius.

Some project ideas withered on the vine. Mauritius has a single airport, with only one runway. In the 1980s, when a mercenary force had attacked the Seychelles, using Apartheid era South Africa as its support base, Mauritius agonized over its own vulnerability, and made soundings with India on building a second airport. They identified a possible site in the north of the island, but even in that low fertility, rocky region, with scattered farms, it would have diverted land from sugar plantations, affecting small Indian-origin farmers. The Indian government expressed general support, but I felt that it was not viable for us. Several factors militated against it; the initial cost estimate (I do not recall the figures) seemed inadequate; a full service airport was much too expensive for us. It might also place us in the middle of controversy, since the farmers would be against takeover of their land. Finally, and most important, it was unclear if the Mauritius government was serious about it. I took a non-committal stance and advised New Delhi accordingly. Fortunately, apart from a few scattered news reports, this issue did not figure in the Mauritius press; nor was it pursued in bilateral discussions.

We became indirectly involved in a dramatic industrial action, which reflected the quality of our relations. Electricity workers on the island-state went on a flash strike around noon, on 21 March 1990, within two hours of PM Jugnauth taking off for the Namibia Independence celebrations at Windhoek. The island-state had never before suffered such industrial action and no one had standby power generation equipment. I received a phone call from the Governor General at about 1600 hours; he said that Acting PM Boolel was with him, and would shortly come to India House to seek help. When he arrived, I explained that the simplest way of obtaining Indian aid would be for PM Jugnauth to mention this to the Indian PM, who was also attending the Windhoek celebrations. At the same time I phoned Foreign Secretary Muchkund Dubey to alert him about the likely request for engineers from India, who would have to be sent on the regular Air Mauritius flight that would be leaving Mumbai some hours later. New Delhi has a fine crisis response mechanism in the Cabinet Secretariat, and that procedure worked well, with several phone calls exchanged between experts on the two sides to identify the technical parameters of the diesel power generation equipment used on the island. Thus a 20-strong team of Indian experts landed in Mauritius within 24-hours of the strike action.

News of the arrival of the Indian engineers percolated soon after their arrival, though no announcement was made. Within hours, Mauritius labor leaders renewed discussions with the government, and consequently, before they could be deployed, some strikers resumed work and full power supply was restored on the island on the following day. We had stood by a friendly state and helped in a crisis. That should have been an unmixed blessing, but once the strike was over, we encountered a curious attitude among some Mauritian officials, who even suggested in conversation that the strike was already on the way to resolution, and that Indian help had not really been necessary. We let that pass, but that aftermath had one moral for me: among friendly states, acting on verbal request and trust is fine, but even in times of urgency one should seek written confirmation, to preclude after-thoughts.

Economic Diplomacy: Trade & Investments

Bilateral trade underwent major growth during the years I served in Mauritius; the High Commission played an active role, assisting Indian exporters. The flow of investments from India into Mauritius also increased. We helped with major contract offers made by Indian companies, through discreet discussion with ministers and officials, also organizing social entertainment for business visitors to meet local counterparts. In 1991, our Commerce Ministry's ITPO held a major trade exhibition on the grounds of the Mahatma Gandhi Institute, that gave us new visibility as a supplier of quality products. CII brought a strong business delegation the same year. For the first time, we also reached out to Franco-Mauritian companies, getting them interested in India as both a source for imports and as an industrial partner. In 1990, the leading Mauritian business association took a delegation to India, again for the first time.

A key development was a contract won in 1991 by the state enterprise TCIL, specializing in telecommunications. That first contract, for laying a cable network, overcome blocking moves by Western enterprises that resented entry by a new player; they disseminated false reports on TCIL's competence.[6] In *Inside Diplomacy* (2002) I wrote about a personal assurance I gave to Prime Minister Jugnauth (who held the telecom portfolio). TCIL lived up to its solid reputation, and performed well. It won more contracts in subsequent years. Hero Motors established an assembly operation for their motorcycles. Ashok Leyland won tenders for the supply of buses and acknowledged in personal discussion that the island's demanding hill terrain had pushed them to improve their vehicle quality. Gradually the message went home to Indian companies that Mauritius was a demanding market, and a notion that second-grade products could be offloaded in Africa was misplaced. That message needs constant reinforcement, as colleagues that have served in Africa will affirm; supply of sub-standard Indian products remains a recurring problem.

I have long held that India's economic ties with any foreign country should be measured in terms of our market share in that country's total imports. At one glance, this reveals ranking; year-on-year comparison demonstrates Indian export performance, discounting the vagaries of that market. Consider: India's global share in world exports was barely 0.52% in 1990, before Economic Reforms; now, in 2015, the figure has risen to over 2%. In a small neighboring country it is to be expected that our market share should be fairly substantial. The focus of our promotion work has to be to make that figure grow. In November 2014, Indian External Affairs Minister Sushma Swaraj declared that India had become the largest trading partner of Mauritius. Those seeds were sown in 1990.

I was in the middle of my term when Economic Reforms launched by PM Narasimha Rao in July 1991 produced paradigm change, and started our process of expanding foreign economic partnerships horizons. Noted economist and former Deputy Governor of the Reserve Bank of India, Rakesh Mohan, then

6 See Rana, *Inside Diplomacy* (2000) p. 110.

Economic Adviser in the Industry Ministry in New Delhi sometimes tells the story of how they found in 1991-92 that among the keenest of response to the Reforms from among Indian missions came from was for him at the time an unknown island called Mauritius.[7]

Culture & Education and the Diaspora

In *Inside Diplomacy* (2000) I had written:

> Our cultural work in such an environment took on special characteristics. The first task was to help the Mauritius Hindus in the study of the Hindi language, for which there has always been a strong demand. For the High Commissioner and his colleagues in the mission, it meant an endless round off participation in religious ceremonies and gatherings of socio-cultural character in the rural areas, and the towns. These ranged from the festival of *Maha Shivratri* when tens of thousands of pilgrims would walk up to 60 or 70 km each way, to bring holy water from *Ganga Talao* in the hills of the South), to the festival of *Kavadee* and it's ritual body piercing and fire-walking by hundreds of Tamils. It was possible to do this, and at the same time pursue contact with the other communities, especially the Muslims and the Creoles, even if not with the same intensity. Educational linkages, in the shape of opportunities to study in India, was the secular tool of wider contact, with some two or three thousand coming to India each year for higher studies.[8]

The Indian Council of Cultural Relations (ICCR) had established a cultural center in Mauritius in 1986, naming it after Indira Gandhi; it functioned from modest rented premises in my time. Mauritius gave a valuable four-acre plot of land in Vacoa township, not far from the Indian Residence, and elaborate plans construction plans were drawn up. Satish Gujral, noted sculptor and artist, was chosen as the architect. His design was for a massive building, with music classrooms that measured 30′ 40′. On his visits to the island, I urged him to scale down the

---

7 Based on conversations; I got to know Rakesh Mohan well in 1993-94 in Germany, while he was on a sabbatical at Maastricht University in the Netherlands, and traveled often to the Bonn region.

8 Rana, *Inside Diplomacy*, (2002), p.157.

building; MEA agreed with this. I left the country much before work on the project commenced, and he paid little heed. We thus ended up with an Indira Gandhi Center for Indian Culture (IGCIC), which is large to the point of surpassing requirements, and rather impractical to boot, with exposed corridors that are awash with water during the rainy season. With its grandiose deep red cupolas big and small, some call it the 'Red Elephant' of Mauritius.

A fine academic, Dr. Parasnis, headed IGCIC; though lacking in experience in running a cultural center, he made up for that with determined effort and active engagement, traveling across the island to different institutions. We brought in music and dance teachers from India in a continuous cycle; while most of them preferred to come on regular contracts of two years (bringing their families), we saw that it was more productive for IGCIC, and cost-effective, to deploy experts on short contracts of four or six months. This is a key issue in the way we deploy cultural experts across the world at our cultural centers, which have now grown to over 30. IGCIC also played a useful role in guiding those going to India for university education.

Our Life

The Indian High Commission had about 10 diplomatic level officials, plus another 20 India-based personnel, and around 30 by way of local staff, making it one of our large missions. Our team worked with a sense of purpose and unity. An outstanding senior colleague, Sharat Sabharwal was the Deputy High Commissioner for most of my assignment. I was equally fortunate in the other officers on the team, especially Ambar Sen and M Ganapathy, counselor and first secretary respectively.

The Residence, called 'India House', is at a salubrious location, in the township of Vacoa, located on a plateau, with a slightly cooler microclimate, compared with Port Louis. Wisely, in the mid-1960s the Indian government had bought this property, located on three acres, when European families began to leave the island. When funds sanctioned by MEA fell short by a small amount from the final price demanded, some leading local families like the Currimjees made up the shortfall.

In late 1991, we decided to shift the Chancery from its cramped location in the Life Insurance Corporation building, to the new Bank of Baroda building, whose construction commenced in 1991, also in downtown Port Louis, overlooking the port. The Chancery shifted to these fine new premises two years after I left the country; a small downside was that we were no longer right next to Government House; it used to be a 50-meter walk to the PM's Office and the Foreign Ministry.[9]

Mimi established an Indian Women's Association, based on her Kenya experience. In an article published in Mauritius in 2014, she described this:

> I got some ladies together in Mauritius, and shared my ideas. Their response was great and within days 'The Indian Women's Association of Mauritius' was born in early 1990. In the ensuing two and half years that we spent in Mauritius, apart from our monthly meetings, with some demonstration or a talk by a guest speaker, we conducted a number of other activities.
>
> Our biggest achievement was the TV program carried out with the support of the Mauritius Broadcasting Corporation, called 'Rasoyi', a cooking demonstration exercise, where we showed the regional foods of India to the viewers. It was a huge success: against an initial plan for 6 episodes, it ran to 24 episodes, telecast at primetime. At the end of the entire series, we organized a *Mela* at India House, offering some of the varied foods that had featured in Rasoyi. The money collected was donated to Swami Krishnanandji's ashram for the elderly at Calebasses. The recipes of the Rasoyi program were also compiled in a book, copies of which I believe are still available at the Indira Gandhi Centre of Indian Culture (IGCIC).
>
> Another event, which has remained memorable for me, was the participation of IWA at the *Ganga Talao* during the festival of *Shivaratri*. Our ladies cooked and served food to hundreds of hungry and tired pilgrims for two days at the Human Service Trust camp. That was a rewarding experience.

It paid to be open in social engagements, accepting as many invitations from different local groups as possible, also going

[9] In 2014 work was to commence on the construction of a new chancery on a three-acre plot of land obtained in the Cyber-City area. This would give us our own building complex, purpose designed, with room to house some essential staff as well.

to Muslim and Creole community functions. Weekends were taken up with small community celebrations, anniversaries and religious functions in villages across the island. At many, speeches were delivered in Hindi, and I frequently crisscrossed path with different Mauritian dignitaries, including the PM, going to several of these.

The diplomatic corps was small and well-knit, with 18 resident missions. The French Ambassador Phillipe Coste, and I established close rapport; at my first courtesy call, he brought up a point that resonated with me. Saying that our countries enjoyed close friendship he asked if it was logical that we should be seen as rivals in Mauritius. I agreed, and we decided to meet every two or three months. The Franco-Mauritians and others noted this; as for the Indian majority, our ties with them were so comprehensive that there was little room for them to misinterpret such actions. This widened the High Commission's action ambit.

We received friends that came and stayed with us; India House had but one guest room, but it was good to put it to use. KR Narayanan came, staying with his London School of Economics friend, Sir Veerasamy Ringadoo, the Mauritius head of state; he spent much time with us. Usha Narayanan had come earlier and stayed with us. Swami A Parthasarathy, great teacher and head of Vedanta Academy, whom we had got to know at Nairobi and received as a guest in San Francisco, also stayed and delivered lectures at the Mahatma Gandhi Institute. A special blessing was the final overseas journey of the founder of India's emerald industry, Jaipur's Kailshankar Durlabji, and his wife, parents of my College classmate Rashmi, and his brother Yogi; he passed away two years after that visit. Pandit Jasraj came twice; at one of his concerts he framed in a classical raga the famous verse of a leading Mauritius poet, Somduth Bhuckory, *Aai kahan se janani meri?* (From Whence Came My Motherland?).

High Level Exchanges

During my term, the Mauritius PM paid two official visits to India, the first one in January 1990 as Chief Guest at our Republic Day celebrations and again at the end of 1991. In the reverse direction we received Vice President Shankar Dayal Sharma in mid-1991, and Prime Minister PV Narasimha Rao in March 1992.

The Mauritian visits to India were successful but politically uneventful. Official talks covered the usual subjects, with Mauritius supporting us on most issues; the double taxation agreement had not yet emerged as a contentious issue. Bilateral programs covering aid and technical cooperation were finalized smoothly. An event that stands our in memory from the 1990 visit is PM Jugnauth's visit to Satya Sai Baba at Whitefields, near Bangalore.

PM Jugnauth was not known for public expression of religious ritual, but someone prompted him to visit Satya Sai Baba. Flying into Bangalore, we went from the airport to Whiltefields, accompanied by his wife and the delegation, which included his chief adviser and head of civil service Bhinod Bacha, media adviser Nando Bodha, plus both the high commissioners, with their spouses. We were taken to a small lounge; in the distance we glimpsed Sai Baba walking among the devotees, in his public audience. We were in the midst of an elaborate 'high tea' when Sai Baba came into the room; after initial courtesies, he turned to Bodha and asked him to describe his work; told that he was the media advisor, Sai Baba asked: do you always give honest advice? Or do you give the advice that will be acceptable to your PM? Bodha explained that he did his best to offer advice with integrity. Sai Baba persisted with his questions to Bodha, and ended that grilling by saying that an official's foremost duty was to consistently offer honest advice. Sai Baba ignored both Bacha and Mauritius HC Anand Newoor, directed a couple of innocuous questions to me, and then 'materialized' a tiny glass *Shiva-linga* for my wife, saying that he knew she was a devotee of Shiva. For the Mauritius PM he materialized a ring with nine colored gemstones. Then, he took the PM and Lady Jugnauth to a private meeting. Clearly, Sai Baba's intent was to convey a warning to Jugnauth against self-centered and motivated advisors. It was a remarkable performance, full of political nuance, showing understanding of the situation on the island.

Following that, I traveled in the PM's car to the hotel (Lady Jugnauth went separately on her program); Jugnauth spoke candidly of his audience: Sai Baba seemed to know some of his innermost secrets, including events in his personal and political life, and health issues that he had not even shared with his wife. He added that he could not explain how the Sai Baba knew so much. Some months after return to Mauritius, in a public speech Jugnauth gave a detailed account of that encounter with Satya Sai Baba. I was struck by the honesty of that statement, because he repeated some of what he had told me on that car journey.

Prime Minister Narasimha Rao's 3-day visit to Mauritius in March 1992 was a landmark in several ways. He was invited as chief guest to the celebrations marking the proclamation of Mauritius as a Republic, held on the National Day, 12 March. He also decided on my next assignment during that visit.

I had been to Delhi in on consultations two months earlier, and was told that PM might choose to extend his stay by a day, undertaking no additional official program. He would decide only after reaching Mauritius; I should not officially inform the host government about this. I replied that was impossible; we had to alert our hosts, the more so because after spending a night at *Le Reduit*, the Mauritius head of state's official residence, PM was to shift to the Royal Palm Hotel; any extension of stay required advance arrangements. I was then told to act as needed, as long as no official commitment was made. On return I alerted Prime Minister Jugnauth that his guest might decide on the final day, either leave for India directly after an official dinner, or stay that night and leave the next day around noon. Jugnauth replied: they would be delighted with an extended stay and would make provisional arrangements. That plan worked. On the morning of the third day, PM opted to stay, enjoying a rare morning of leisure, walking on the beach and relaxing with a book. I spent some time with him, going over French language newspaper coverage, and discussing his local impressions.

That visit was notable in three ways. I had been warned in Delhi that PM's travel to Latin America a few months earlier had been a disaster in terms of food arrangements; he was a vegetarian, and preferred almost exclusively his native Andhra cuisine. On travel abroad, it was his habit to have his meal prior to any official banquet. My wife, taking the help of our close friend and neighbor Lakshmi Reddy, put into effect a full operation to prepare at our home all his meals in the best Andhra tradition, as narrated in the first chapter.

Acting on my own, I took the help of leading businessman Bashir Currimjee to rent eight mobile phones for the duration of the PM's visit. That first generation model which had just gone into operation on the island resembled a small brick in size and shape, but was a technology leap that India had only heard about. We supplied one to each senior member of the delegation, and they were delighted at the convenience, especially as any activity in Mauritius involves long road journeys; delegation members isolated in their own cars could keep in contact. It was PMO's first exposure to this technology, and may have contributed to India's early decision to bring mobile phones to India.

PM Narasimha Rao had brought with him, unusually, a strong group of Indian Members of Parliament, which included KR Narayanan, and Ram Jethamalani. Noted journalist Ved Pratap Vedik told me many years later that it was at the end of an Indian community reception at India House that PM informed KR Narayanan that he had been chosen as the Congress party candidate for the election to the office of India's Vice President.

Towards the end of 1991 we organized an unusual tour to Rajasthan for Lady Sarojinee Jugnauth and some others. It grew out of a visit to Mauritius by several nephews, nieces and their spouses from Mimi's side of the family. They organized a fine Rajasthan soirée featuring traditional attire and the *ghoomar* dance by the young ladies; PM Jugnauth and his family were among the 40 guests. Some months later, that evening's discussion developed into a plan for Lady Jugnauth, her son, his fiancée and her mother to travel across Rajasthan by car. Some diplomat spouses were also to join, but in the event only the US Ambassador, Penny Korth went on the trip (paying her way, while the others were official guests of the Indian government). Mimi traveled to India and met the group at Udaipur and then escorted them to the Ranakpur Jain temples, Rohet Garh (her family home, now a splendid heritage hotel, where the entire group stayed as our guests), a night at Umaid Bhawan Palace at Jodhpur, and finally to Jaipur, traveling via Ajmer for lunch at Mayo Girls School and a visit to the *daragah* of Ajmer Sharif. At Udaipur, Jodhpur and Jaipur they were hosted to social functions by the former maharajas, making this 'one of our most memorable trips' as Lady Jugnauth told us when we met her in August 2014.

My Next Assignment

In early 1991 I learnt that CV Ranganathan, ambassador at Beijing was to move to Paris. I requested Foreign Secretary Muchkund Dubey to consider me for China; that would have served as a capstone to my earlier work there. That was not to be, because Haider, then Deputy High Commissioner in London refused a major assignment in SE Asia and insisted that he be sent to Beijing or Paris. At a time when a minority government led by PM Chandra Shekhar survived with Congress party support, Haider had the political connections to make that happen, and I lost out. It was a setback, but such things happen in any career. On a visit to Delhi at the end of 1991 I found that colleagues at the Ministry of External Affairs much junior to me were vying for Bonn; I placed my hat in that ring, mentioning my interest to the PM. He was non-committal. It was his style to decide in his own time.[10]

On the last day of the Mauritius visit the PM's Private Secretary Ramu Damodaran told me that PM wanted me to choose between Beijing, Bonn and Tokyo. I rationalized that when I had been keen to go to China, this was denied to me; I did not want the kind of delay faced in 1978-79 for a New York assignment. Tokyo demanded someone who knew Japan well; I did not fit that bill. Germany, especially after unification would be a real challenge; I requested PM to send me to Bonn; he readily agreed. It took another two weeks for the Ministry of External Affairs to issue formal orders, and start the process of obtaining the *agrément* (to make that happen, I had to invoke the PM's personal authority, overcoming a gentle blocking move by senior MEA colleagues who had their own agenda). I left Mauritius in the last week of

[10] Some years after I retired from Germany, Narasimha Rao indicated in a conversation with me that he wanted someone in that job to take advantage of opportunities for economic diplomacy and felt that I had performed to his expectation.

May 1992, traveling directly to Germany, without going to Delhi for the customary briefings, to take charge in Bonn on May 26.

One last action was left for me. I heard through the grapevine that the PM was thinking of appointing a politician from North India as my successor. I believed that might cause a setback to all we had achieved, building credible and forward-looking relationship, with no baggage of domestic Indian politics. I wrote directly to the PM, to urge that a career diplomat be sent. In the event, Shyam Saran, a highly regarded colleague who went on to become foreign secretary was nominated, and served with great distinction.

Mimi departed for India some ten days before I left directly for Bonn, on receiving urgent news that her mother was gravely ill; she was then our only surviving parent. Sadly, she reached home just after her mother's funeral. It has weighed on us that neither of us could see our parents in their final days, much less attend their last rites. This is a price that working abroad sometimes extracts of us, for all the glamor of diplomatic life.

I used those first weeks in Bonn for quiet reading of all the bilateral dossiers and other embassy papers; and starting the process of calling on diplomatic colleagues. I traveled to Delhi immediately after presenting credentials to the German Federal President at the end of June 1992. Such a direct move to a new embassy may seem strange, but it works well, especially if there has been a long gap between incumbents, or if there are urgent issues to be tackled. At four assignments, Prague, San Francisco, Mauritius and Bonn, I went to my new post in this manner. It ensured that at the new job, after gaining initial familiarity with issues, one could credibly solicit MEA's help, particularly on administrative problems. Some foreign ministries now allow new envoys incognito familiarization visits to the new assignment, which also works.

13

Rethinking the Ministry of External Affairs

In earlier chapters I described actions taken at the MEA, and at missions, to improve the working of the Indian diplomatic system. It is worthwhile to collate these, adding detail, since this theme is today central to improving the performance of foreign ministries. My interest in this subject was sparked by a Quakers seminar I attended at Geneva in September 1967. Many IFS colleagues have worked on reform; Kiran Doshi's contribution in 1979-81 was exemplary; Leela K Ponappa is another colleague that worked long on change from within the Establishment Division. Satinder Lambah's 2002 report on MEA improvements has been a valuable guidebook. Many others have pursued improvements, while posted abroad or at MEA. What has been missing in India is a coherent, comprehensive examination of the changes needed, study of best practices in other foreign ministries, and analytical writing on diplomacy process issues. That is beginning to change, and some colleagues have begun to work on this, especially after ending their Foreign Service careers. Some currently in the Service also pursue these issues.

The MEA's biggest reform effort was the Pillai Committee, set up in 1965. After Nehru's demise in June 1964, some in New Delhi wanted to cut the MEA to size; it had been Nehru's ministry in 1947-64, favored with the PM's personal direction as none other. Former Secretary General NR Pillai produced an outstanding, visionary report; it is the only major published examination of the MEA. I recall extended and sometimes heated IFS Association meetings where we discussed our submission to this Committee. In 1982-83, Samar Sen headed another committee that looked at Indian diplomacy, initially focusing on the working of our embassies. It submitted a report in 1983, which has not been published, though JN Dixit produced in his final work a summary of its conclusions.[1]

In 1974 and 1975, I was involved with two comprehensive reform actions, via notes submitted to Foreign Secretary Kewal Singh; they produced little action, but they helped to develop my ideas. They shaped some actions taken when I worked as head of personnel administration in 1982-83, though I missed that opportunity to address the grossly inadequate size of the IFS. Of course, over time much reform has taken place in the Indian system. Most changes have come gradually and incrementally, without a master plan. Yet even these have given hope that those pursuing improvements have not been tilting at windmills.

It was after 1995 that I began to look closely at how foreign ministries all over the world function. This coincided with the emergence of such comparative study among a few specialists. My career experience and later work of the past two decades has produced a conviction: the Indian diplomatic system is of high quality, and possesses some of the finest personnel in the world. Yet it consistently under-performs, and operates much below its potential. Some will say that is true of the entire Indian body politic. Perhaps, but my preoccupation here is with that one segment of the Indian governance system of which I have the closest familiarity.[2]

Joint Efforts of 1974 and 1975

In 1972-75, while I worked in the MEA as a deputy secretary and then as director, lunch clubs were active as they have always been. At these daily sessions that brought together some six or eight colleagues, we often debated professional issues, though light-hearted fun and gossip was never absent at those sessions.

---

1 See: JN Dixit, *Indian Foreign Service: History and Challenge* (2005).

2 For a succinct account please see: Rana, 'The Glass Gets Fuller', *Foreign Service Journal*, Washington DC, June 2014.

Around a fairly fixed core that attended regularly, other colleagues that happened to be in Delhi were always welcomed. We sought an outlet for our ideas on how the working of the MEA might be improved, and found ourselves impatient at what we viewed as ossified mindsets among the top hierarchy; we were keen to work for transformation. I have written in Chapter 5 how Saad Hashmi, Kewal Singh's confidant, told us that we could produce a set of actionable ideas on MEA improvements. Our group included Kamal Bakshi, Kiran Doshi, Surinder Arora, and a couple of others; I became an informal convener. In early 1974, we wrote up a short note.

This is reproduced below, in its original form, bad grammar and errors included.[3] On some points we were ahead of our time; a few of these ideas remain relevant even today.

MEA Reorganization

In an increasingly vocal and assertive environment, foreign ministry officials who have traditionally observed a disciplined silence are likely to be demoralized when they find that their professional competence and service interests are being ignored. If this happens, the loss will not only be theirs, but also of the country they have sought to serve. The following paper sets out some suggestions for improving the functioning of the ministry and missions abroad.

Headquarters

1. The utilization of Junior Officers

Strongly motivated junior officers whose professional skills are carefully nurtured would take greater interest in their work than is the case at present. Greater involvement by deputy secretaries and under secretaries should be encouraged through better indication of responsibilities, involvement in decision-making, and travel opportunity to their territorial areas. Heads of divisions have a special responsibility for this.

[3] I did not make it a habit to retain documents from my Service career, and this is one of the very few that I hold with me. It was not an official document, and for that reason, it was unsigned and undated. The original was handed over to Saad Hashmi, and what I retained was a carbon copy.

2. Coordination among divisions

A weekly division heads meeting taken by FS (perhaps a half-hour 'standup' gathering each Monday at 9:45 AM) would enable purposeful policy direction and information flow. A 'task force' approach should be used in tackling special issues, using Director (Coord) as the main link.

3. Senior direction

Appointment of a young IFS officer as PS may assist the Foreign Secretary. Possibility of redistributing work and decision-making among the secretaries may be considered, to reduce some of the burdens on the FS and enable concentration on issues of policy and over-all direction.

4. New type multi-functional territorial divisions

MEA would improve its foreign policy role vis-à-vis other ministries if territorial divisions handle political and economic work.

Given the nature of MEA territorial functions (which concentrate on analytical and decision oriented fields in which there is little repetitive work) it would be useful to reorganize divisions making the branch officer (under secretary or attaché) as the key unit, assisted by a PA, one assistant and a diarist-dispatcher LDC. This unit would keep its own files and cover all aspects of a given group of countries. Accommodation would also be reorganized. Section officers would also function as branch officers with reduced responsibilities. On an experimental basis the system could be tried with two divisions.

5. WANA and the Southern divisions

Enhanced political interest in the Gulf region, opening of new missions, oil diplomacy and the importance of Iran and Afghanistan make it necessary that WANA should be split into two divisions; one concerning Iran, Afghanistan, Iraq and the Gulf area, and the other the rest of the region, including pan-Arabic issues.

Importance of Ceylon and Burma necessitate that they be covered by a separate division, while the rest of SE Asia, including Indo-China and Australasia form another division.

6. Economic division

Basic economic work for different regions should be transferred to territorial divisions, which can follow this in an integrated manner and represent the ministry with authority in dealing with other ministries, rather than the present situation in which the work is either covered in an uncoordinated fashion, not handled at all.

The Economic Division's territorial officers should work within territorial divisions. The Economic Division would then handle multilateral economic work, as also represent MEA viewpoint, and carve out a greater role on ECAFE, UNCTAD, IBRD, and similar fields. It would also handle economic coordination.

7. Bilateral talks

Institution of annual bilateral talks has proliferated but lacks focus. Before any talks are held the territorial division head and his counterpart concerned with that country through other divisions should evolve a strategy for (a) projecting specific Indian positions for that country and (b) pinpointing issues on which we want information or elucidation. Generalities and statements of known positions at such talks be curtailed through pruning of the opening tour d' horizon.

8. Relations with other ministries

Active efforts needed to regain for MEA central role in foreign policymaking. This involves a tougher line on encroachments by other government agencies and special efforts at placing IFS personnel in other ministries. Commerce must be made to accept more our people and through suitable personnel selection, convinced that we are not dumping difficult cases on them. Same applies to building expertise on economic affairs (Finance Ministry and Planning). Would be worthwhile to send some officials to the Defense Ministry.

9. Miscellaneous

(a) *Missions should be more actively involved in policy formation than is the case at present. Also, territorial divisions have the responsibility for implementing this.*

(b) *Probationers on training are placed with territorial divisions, in some cases, to work as attachés for several months. Perhaps some can be placed in the same way with Commerce, Finance, and Defense.*

(c) *Means devised for streamlining our communication with missions with more telex and wireless links. Evolve special procedures to prevent logjam of telegrams at headquarters during emergencies.*

(d) *Branch officers and deputy secretaries be attached as liaison officers to major visitors to India to enable them to cultivate useful contacts among foreign officials and to give them an opportunity to see the economic, social progress in the country.*

Missions Abroad

1. Staff reductions

Some of foreign missions, particularly in Europe, are larger than our requirements warrant. By combining information work with political duties at some posts, staff could be reduced (Austria, Poland, San Francisco, Netherlands). In some others, political and commercial work could be combined (Switzerland, Czechoslovakia, Sweden), while elsewhere posts can be cut back (Bonn, New York). The posts can be transferred here to improve the missions-headquarters ratio, which stands around the low figure of 4:1.

2. Projection of image

Massive economic difficulties and internal problems, as also our inevitable concerns after 1971 with sub-continental problems, have led to an image of India which is immersed with immediate issues and is unable to lift its head to wider horizons. A dynamic external policy is needed to correct this. Publicity and daily teleprinter transmissions should be concerned with positive developments and less with news. Teleprinter links to be provided to all Posts.

3. Political reporting

Monthly political reports should be written strictly by the excellent instructions issued in 1971 on brevity, analytical approach. Missions be encouraged to write in depth (but brief and readable) special dispatches on major issues, rather than engage exclusively in episodic correspondence. Scrap annual reports. Abolish system of routine acknowledgments but encourage constructive Mission-Ministry dialogue.

4. Commercial work

Commercial work is the responsibility of the mission, particularly HOM. Conscious efforts needed by heads of missions to give experience in commercial work to all young officers, even when they are not primarily engaged in this task. Some of the foreign exchange saved in reducing posts abroad could be diverted to a fund, disbursed at the discretion of FS, to missions which have done exceptionally well in export sales, to be used on their promotional activities (entertainment, tours, etc.).

5. Postings

A fair and performance-oriented postings policy would strengthen morale. Special care needed in selection of officials who are to occupy number 2 positions in important missions. To resist missions being burdened with special attachés from other ministries (Scientific, Educational and Defense) which does not yield commensurate results, and frequently reduces the actual effectiveness of missions.

6. Neighboring countries

We all acknowledge the importance of neighboring countries but incentives are basically insufficient for these posts. Hard station allowance (recommended by Pillai Committee) should be reconsidered. Restrictions on extra leave credits for these posts be scrapped. Foreign exchange (perhaps Pounds 30-20 p.m.) be allowed to officials at these posts.

7. Probationers training

Under current policy all probationers go abroad after about 3 years training in India. Unless special efforts made in missions to give all-around experience, they lose valuable opportunities. Not all Missions Heads fully cognizant of this problem.

8. Miscellaneous

(a) *As a matter of policy, there should be about a weeks overlap between officers on transfer.*

(b) *Representation grants at most stations are basically adequate but firm supervision needed, not on details of claims but on effectiveness of spending.*

Rather little came directly from this effort. An under secretary (i.e. staff officer) was appointed in the Foreign Secretary's office. As authors we did not even get to meet the FS to discuss our paper, much less receive feedback. All we knew from Saad was that the Foreign Secretary had 'appreciated' our paper.

A year later, immediately after the Emergency was declared on 25 June 1975, the External Affairs Minister, like other ministers, received PM Indira Gandhi's letter, demanding an improvement in government work. The FS set up a committee under Jagat Mehta, Additional Secretary (AD & PP), and they prepared a set of recommendations. The FS also asked our group, again through Saad, to come up with suggestions. We held several meetings and re-hashed some of our suggestions, and added new ones.

Without reproducing that second note in full, since many themes from 1974 were repeated, let me summarize the new points.

- Probationers should be sent abroad on their first language assignment within 18 months of appointment, rather than wait for almost three years: 'Prolonged training at Headquarters teaches them little and generates demoralization.' [This was also a key recommendation of the 2010 Abid Hussain Report, which was eventually implemented by the MEA.]
- The debate between specialization and generalization 'is essentially the result of low valuation being placed on specialization…the key to this problem lies in encouraging specialization in one or more fields' (emphasis in original).
- 'A stronger Headquarters set-up is essential for improving our professional efficiency'. [This is one of the major actions undertaken by the MEA in 2015, by Foreign Secretary K Jaishankar.]
- 'We need to examine the possibilities of computerization, both for information storage as for personnel management…'
- 'FS may find it of advantage not to have any territorial divisions directly under his charge so as to concentrate on overall direction…' [This was a bold assertion to make to the MEA head. That problem, an overworked foreign secretary, placed alongside other secretaries nominally of equal rank that are underworked, persists to the present day.]
- 'The efficiency and public-spiritedness of Regional Passport Offices is of vital importance to MEA, since this is MEA's only point of contact with the general public.' [This was public diplomacy in concept, though we did not then know that term.]

- '...a regular Foreign Service Inspectorate charged with the task of regular inspections of missions is essential.' [Created in 2006, later abandoned, this Inspectorate has been resuscitated in 2015.]
- 'We should consider the possibility of setting missions specific tasks and objectives, and their performance should be judged in relation to these assignments.' [Shades of performance management, again a topical issue.]

I discussed this note with Jagat Mehta in his office in July 1975, in the presence of his Administration Division team. His attitude was dismissive ('you seem to be trying to teach old grandmothers how to suck eggs...'). The problem was institutional, not personal; Jagat Mehta was always cordial to young colleagues.

Our notes of 1974 and 1975 are relevant today on the limited point that we partly anticipated the future, and set out prescriptions that are today the norm in most foreign ministries. I come back to this point later.

Other Actions

Another old document, of which I retained a copy is a 10-page letter written on 11 September 1979, from Algeria, to Joint Secretary (Administration), old friend and batchmate, IP (Munna) Khosla. The MEA had sent out to missions a copy of the 29th Report of the Estimates Committee of Parliament on the working of Indian embassies, asking for responses to the recommendations made by this important committee. Some extracts from my letter:

- 'Instituting a system offsetting the periodic objectives for each mission (paragraph 2.45 of the Estimates Committee Report): I would endorse the suggestion of the Estimates Committee wholeheartedly... After the WANA (West Asia and North Africa) heads of missions meeting in January 1977, I had prepared a detailed note setting out specific targets for this mission for the year 1977-78. I must confess that some of the targets erred on the optimistic side. However, the exercise helped considerably in setting priorities and served as a reminder in terms of matters left undone. It should be possible and practical to require each mission to prepare, as an annual exercise, a note setting out specific targets, goals, or objectives in different fields (economic, cultural, technical cooperation and even political, in terms of exchanges of visits, meetings of all the joint commissions etc.)... Naturally the objective would be to set practical and attainable goals...' [Such 'Action Plans' became an official norm in 1980, but applied in desultory fashion.]

- Review of performance of missions and inspections (paragraphs 2.462 2.81 of the report): '...it should be possible to institutionalize and improve the system of performance assessment. One means would be the annual target plan of each mission. Another method would be to ensure that whenever senior officials of the Ministry visit missions abroad, they would be required to submit their impressions on the performance of the missions.'
- Training of IFS probationers: 'For the past 20 years we have continued to tinker with the training programs, but the only effective result has been a progressive prolongation of the period which probationers spend in India... there is near zero absorption by probationers...'

In 1979, these ideas were ahead of their time. The first two are still not implemented in the MEA, though around the world, both annual planning and performance management is the nub of supervision and efficiency management in foreign ministries. The third point recommending abbreviated training programs for new Service entrants became a core recommendation of the Abid Hussain Committee report of January 2010.

Actions After 1995

After leaving the IFS, I taught at the Foreign Service Institute and worked on diplomacy-related themes for about 14 years. By 1998 I had written out three chapters for a memoir when in September that year, on a train journey from Stuttgart to Essen, on the route that winds through the spectacular Rhine valley, an idea took shape that a survey of the working of the MEA might be a better option.[4] That led to my first book, *Inside Diplomacy* (2000), partly

[4] I wrote out the skeleton of that book over three hours during that journey. Mimi has photographs of my immersion in that task, against that scenic backdrop.

based on a survey I had carried out in 1999. It had some impact and led to the MEA asking senior officials and ambassadors to suggest possible improvements, which were examined by colleague and friend Satinder Lambah, who gave a report to the MEA in 2002 on the changes needed.[5] Some of those suggestions were gradually implemented.

In 2000, I came across a fine book edited by Brian Hocking, that compared the foreign ministries of a dozen countries.[6] This prompted me to commence work on *Asian Diplomacy: The Foreign Ministries of China, India, Japan, Singapore and Thailand*, (DiploFoundation, Malta and Geneva, 2007); owing to lack of published material on the diplomatic systems of these countries, I relied on interviews and collation of data, with very limited institutional support for such a project.[7] That took eight years and involved over 160 interviews. This book has the flaw that I did not know nearly as much about the four foreign countries studied as I did of India; but unlike multi-author works, i.e. all the other published works on MFAs, my book pursues a consistent analysis line, with sharp comparison. That work guided me towards further studies.

In 1999, following a chance encounter with Dr. Jovan Kurbalija at Malta, I became involved with distance teaching through the internet, via a small international non-profit entity, which rapidly grew into DiploFoundation.[8] That sustained my interest in distance education, and produced spinoffs, including

---

5 The Lambah Report has not been published.

6 Hocking, Brian, ed. *Foreign Ministries: Change & Adaptation* (Macmillan, London, 1999).

7 I approached an Indian agency, and potential German, Japanese and UK funding sources, with no success. The Institute of Chinese Studies, Delhi gave me a visiting fellow position and helped me to make two trips to China, partly for data collection. In 2005, the Woodrow Wilson Center at Washington DC gave me a two-month 'public policy scholar' appointment that helped greatly with desk research, data collection and writing the bulk of the book *Asian Diplomacy* (2007); they also re-published the book in 2009, jointly with John Hopkins University.

8 This entity was initially called 'Diplo Projects' (see: www.diplomacy.edu). DiploFoundation has won many awards for its teaching work and for its advocacy of sound internet governance. It was set up in 2002 through a memorandum between the governments of Malta and Switzerland.

three self-learning distance courses developed in 2002-05 for the Canadian Foreign Service Institute, one of which was picked up by the British Foreign Office; I also became involved with the UK adaptation of that course, working with my old friend from Hong Kong days, Sir John Boyd. At DiploFoundation I also organized two conferences on the working of foreign ministries, at Geneva in 2006 and at Bangkok in 2007 (the latter in partnership with the Thailand Foreign Ministry); foreign ministry representatives from over 30 countries attended each of these.[9] In 15 years with Diplo, I developed five courses, and have had the privilege of teaching about 700 participants in these courses, mainly diplomats from Latin America and the Caribbean, and Africa, and smaller numbers from Europe; we are now beginning to draw participants from Asia; about 10 from MEA have attended our courses.[10] The guiding goal in Diplo's distance teaching has been to help developing country foreign ministries to improve their human resource capacity.

Abid Hussain Committee (2008-10)

In 2008 I was appointed to a committee set up by the MEA to examine the working of the Foreign Service Institute (FSI). Remember, FSI was set up in 1986, on a decision taken by Prime Minister Indira Gandhi. I taught at the FSI from 1995 to 2008; in 2001 the FSI named me professor emeritus.[11] It was a special privilege to serve under widely respected, senior IAS colleague Abid Hussain (1926-2012); he was a mentor to all those who fell under his spell. He had observed MEA affairs closely, as Commerce Secretary, and as envoy to the European Union and to the US. The decision to set up this committee originated with Foreign Secretary Shivshankar Menon, and was implemented

9 The Geneva conference also led to an edited book in which the papers presented at the conference were published. See, Rana, Kishan S, and Kurbalija, Jovan, eds. *Foreign Ministries: Managing Diplomatic Networks and Optimizing Value* (DiploFoundation, Malta and Geneva, 2007).

10 Around 70% of our course participants are working diplomats, with the balance made up of international officials, students and others interested in international affairs.

11 I gave up that honorary appointment in 2009, after my teaching activities at FSI came to an end.

by Dean, FSI, Surendra Kumar; former foreign secretary Lalit Mansingh was the other committee member. Dean FSI, and his deputy, a joint secretary, served as ex-officio members.

The Abid Hussain Committee produced a total of 29 recommendations in a short report that was presented to the Foreign Secretary in January 2010. I drafted the text, but it is truly a collective document, since the Committee went over the draft line by line, and many sections were rewritten more than once on the basis of our collective discussion, always guided with wit and charm by Abid Saheb.

Abid Saheb wrote the preface, and he forbade me from changing a word; he graciously said:

> Kishan Rana remained a real source of strength and donated all his knowledge to the subject of training which was the sum total of his many experiences in this field both at home and abroad. He developed several pertinent ideas which have been incorporated in the report. He displayed immense capacity for understanding subtle nuances whether relating to the large panorama or of minor details which are reflected in the report. His superb quality of work won him the unqualified admiration of all involved.

Lalit Mansingh left the committee some months before we completed the work, perhaps owing to an impression that our work did not enjoy the full support of the MEA hierarchy. He was probably right in that estimation. It was after four months that Foreign Secretary Menon found time to receive Abid Saheb and I in May 2010, for our final meeting to discuss the report. I urged that it be made public (the MEA has traditionally been reluctant to publish such documents; the Sen Committee report of 1983, and the Lambah report of 2001 have not seen the light of day). Our report was published two months later, tucked away in a hard-to-locate section of the FSI's webpage. By 2013 it had disappeared from that webpage.

The 31-page Abid Report does not incorporate an executive summary, but its 29 recommendations are numbered, making easy reading. These include:

- FSI is one of the 'key resources of MEA', shaping personnel at all levels. It has MOU (memorandum of understanding) cooperation relations with 34 counterparts across the world, and works closely with counterparts within the country.

- It needs more desk officers and in-house faculty; it also needs to develop a research track (recommendations 2 and 6).
- FSI's international engagement capacity should be strengthened (recommendation 5).
- Entry-level training for probationers should be shortened, with the total time spent in India before the first posting abroad 'may not exceed 12 to 14 months' (recommendation 7).
- Training programs for heads of missions and posts, and for deputy chiefs of missions need to be developed (recommendation 9).
- MEA 'should consider re-ranking service seniority on the basis of marks obtained'; this would raise the value of training and bring the process in line with the practice in other civil services (recommendation 12).
- The interview process at the Union Public Services Commissions needs to be strengthened, given the importance of communication skills and mastery of English in the IFS; this entails dialogue with UPSC and improved English training for those that sit for the exam in regional languages (recommendations 13 and 18).
- Mid-career training is of special importance in foreign ministries, and e-learning is a key option (recommendations 19 and 20). There is also a need for training programs for heads of missions, and use of scenario planning, and our own case studies (recommendations 21 and 22).
- Training for IFS B personnel is no less vital (recommendation 23), the more so to implement the advice of the 1966 Pillai Committee, to permit MEA to shift to a system of desk officers and desk assistants.
- Courses for foreign diplomats, run successfully by FSI should involve some payment by participating countries that can afford to do so, rather than have FSI cover all costs including airfare (recommendation 24). Besides organizing special courses for foreign diplomats from select countries, FSI should also conduct *in situ* courses in the concerned capitals (recommendation 25).

- FSI's website should be continually updated and used for wide outreach (recommendation 29).

In late 2012, I was asked to join an informal group that worked at preparing MEA's response to an initiative by PM Manmohan Singh to get all ministries to update their master training plans. Joint Secretary (AD) sent me a copy of an 'Approach Paper' they had written, and in response, on 7 January 2013, I sent to him and others a framework for a 'master plan' for training in MEA. A few of those ideas were incorporated into MEA's final document on training.

Other Public and Private Actions

In the years 1995-2015 I have written about 100 articles in Indian and foreign publications, of which more than half have been on the working of Indian diplomacy. Many have been published in the newspaper *Business Standard*. Both former editor (and now publisher) TN Ninan, one of the giants of Indian journalism, and editor AK Bhattacharya, have been hospitable to me in accommodating these, for which I am grateful.

Within a few months of starting lectures at the Foreign Service Institute, New Delhi in the second half of 1995, Kamal Bakshi and I teamed up, and jointly presented our lectures on diplomacy-related themes right up to early 2008. I gradually produced several teaching modules, covering bilateral diplomacy scenarios, negotiation simulations, role play, crisis management, drafting of resolutions, and writing of records of discussion, which were fine-tuned with Kamal's suggestions, and we ran these over a decade and more at the training programs for foreign diplomats and Indian probationers.[12] I also used these modules in the training programs I ran at the foreign ministries, diplomatic academies, and universities at: Argentina, Armenia, Bahrain, China, Iran, Kenya, the Maldives, Malaysia, Namibia, the Netherlands, Oman, Russia, Serbia, Singapore, South Africa, Suriname, Thailand and Trinidad & Tobago. I delivered lectures at Jawaharlal Nehru

[12] Kamal Bakshi and I are delighted that some of those teaching materials have been adapted and developed by the next generation of lecturers at the FSI, New Delhi.

University, New Delhi, and the London School of Economics. In 2010 I was appointed to the guest faculty of the Diplomatic Academy at Vienna, the world's oldest training institution in this profession, where I now annually offer a weeklong course of six lectures.

I have carried out dialogue with a succession of foreign secretaries in the past 20 years, mostly through notes offering suggestions. A few of these produced outcomes.

- In 2006, when the Public Diplomacy Division was created, Foreign Secretary Shyam Saran told me in a conversation: 'Well, your suggestion has been accepted.' In 2013 that Division was folded into the External Publicity (XP) Division; it was relocated in 2015 into the Policy Planning Division.
- In 2008, on the eve of MEA's first conference of all its ambassadors, Foreign Secretary Menon told me that this was a product of one of my suggestions. That conference is now an annual staple.[13]
- Since 2002, Kamal Bakshi and I wrote to a succession of foreign secretaries on the need to improve the working of the Foreign Service Institute. In particular, the MEA needed to assert 'ownership' of the FSI, and treat training as an investment in the future and a core MEA management responsibility. That might have contributed, in 2008, to the setting up of the Abid Hussain Committee.

One idea that figured in these suggestions was the setting up of a 'Foreign Service Inspectorate'; even the 1966 Pillai Committee had recommended this. I have also pushed for this in published writing and in correspondence with foreign secretaries. On reflection, this now appears to be both outdated and unnecessary. The IFS is too small a service to afford the luxury of a full-time inspectorate, with a staff of at least two or more

[13] While most foreign ministries hold such conferences as a regular activity, insisting that ambassadors combine the event with their annual leave (which does not happen as yet in India), the UK has been another latecomer to this practice, holding its first full conference around the same time as the MEA. I should add that the MEA has long held regional conferences, mainly at foreign locations, where envoys from say, Africa or West Europe, are assembled for a couple of days, but that serves a different purpose.

senior and mid-level officials. The network of some 120 Indian missions and 40+ consulates is large enough to warrant a need for regular inspections, but the same task can be accomplished by building in a 'distance inspection' function into the MEA process, supplemented by a requirement for senior MEA officials that visit different foreign capitals on other tasks, to devote a half to full day for such inspections.

Such inspections are not financial audits, which are mandatory in every system and go on in the MEA and other ministries, all the time. The two key aims of inspections are to assess performance, and identify man-management issues. In relation to the latter, Germany uses a method that is very relevant: all their home-based officials at embassies submit an online annual survey on their seniors, including the ambassador; these numerical and descriptive assessments are homogenized and averaged out, by a special unit at the Foreign Office in Berlin. This report, where comment is rendered anonymous, goes back to the ambassador, who is required to discuss this in a meeting with all his staff. At the same time, Foreign Office officials examine this set of responses from embassy staff, to identify potential problems and breakdown situations.[14]

Basic Need for MEA

At heart, what the MEA needs is to radically improve its *capacity* for diplomatic engagement with foreign countries, regions and on global issues, and at the same time, to improve its organizational method to supervise and enhance *performance*. Capacity hinges on personnel, in terms of numbers, location, motivation and ability to deliver. Thus the obverse side of manpower numbers is the quality of their performance.

The single most important reform move by the MEA has been the decision, announced in mid-2007 to double the strength of the IFS. The MEA has opted for a slow-track method to implement this, relying mainly on stepped-up annual intake, from an average of 15 per year, now to 40 per year. This has meant that from 2007 to 2014, the strength of the IFS has crept up from 650

[14] See Rana, *The Contemporary Embassy: Paths to Diplomatic Excellence*, Palgrave-Macmillan, 2013, pp. 79.

to 850, and it will perhaps take 10 more years to reach the goal of 1300. An alternate method might have been the one used by Brazil in 2003, under the Lula presidency when it greatly expanded its embassy network, to step up recruitment from around 40 per year to 100. That has brought in needed diplomats, but also created a manpower bolus that will be hard to digest, in terms of future promotions and cadre management.

The other excellent related measure that the MEA has implemented is to open its doors to in-placements from other branches of government, as also the private sector, especially for the new Development Partnership Administration, another outstanding innovation, implemented in the face of resistance from a Finance Ministry that seemed to lack vision in blocking this move for some years. These moves, and a decision to accept placement of some 25 more officials from the Commerce Department into Indian embassies, will raise the effective manpower strength. The next related move in the pipeline for 2015 should be to expand the number of science counselors at embassies from the present five to at least a dozen or more; this too seems to have the backing of PM Modi.

In implementing the above, the MEA will be tackling what has been overdue since the 1960s, a significant expansion of its Headquarters, in relation to embassies abroad and in absolute terms as well.[15] In 1999, the ratio of executive level officials at the MEA, in relation to its embassies was 1 to 4.3. By 2007, it had improved, reaching 1 to 3.3. In 2014, it improved further to a ratio of 1 to 2.7. I have argued that an ideal ratio for a foreign ministry is around 1 to 1.5 to 2.[16] Foreign ministries that are understaffed in comparison to their missions abroad cannot digest their output, nor guide them adequately. When the foreign ministry is too large (e.g. with a ratio that approaches 1 to 1), this produces micro-management of embassies, and undermines embassy initiative.[17]

---

[15] In the early 1960s it was realized that MEA Headquarters was understaffed because even in those days the Finance Ministry was open to sending more staff to embassies, but opposed to adding to MEA manpower. YD Gundevia, who retired as one of the secretaries at MEA, has written about this in his outstanding account of life in the Ministry in the Nehru years in *Outside the Archives* (1984).

[16] See Rana, *Asian Diplomacy* (2007), Chapter 8, comparing five foreign ministries.

[17] Ibid.

As for performance enhancement, in 2015 MEA is finally considering some new measures. According to press reports, in December 2014 it carried out brainstorming at its most senior levels to identify tasks for 2015. If that is implemented rigorously, it would be possible to fold into that process the old annual plan method that has been a requirement since 1980, but has been implemented in desultory fashion. On the plus side is a determination in the Government of India to apply performance management across the entire public service. The government that took office in May 2014 has given new impetus to this, given Prime Minister Narendra Modi's track record with good governance methods in Gujarat as Chief Minister.

What about empowering officials to come up with actionable, needed measures that would improve the working of the MEA? This connects with what some of us had tried to do way back in 1974-75, as set out above. Two examples are available, from the UK and Germany.

Final Thoughts

As this is written, in June 2015, under Foreign Secretary S Jaishankar, the MEA is embarked on change. This is along several tracks. First, a number of officials have been brought back from missions, to strengthen headquarters. Second, the French method of Ambassador's Instructions is to be introduced, despite some resistance. Third, the Policy Planning Division is to undergo transformation, with many more staff, and with some of the public diplomacy functions fused into it. Fourth, academic scholars are to be brought into the new Policy Planning Division, on contracts, which would further open up the MEA, though this does not for now represent a lateral entry into the IFS, as they are to be on contracts. This process may be the tip of the iceberg, with more change in the pipeline. Much of this is along the lines of what I have supported, but an apprehension remains that the changes may not endure, without deep institutional support. The coming months will show how this plays out.

Those officials working within organizations that seek internal change in India need a personal foundation of optimism and perseverance. They should be able to deal with setbacks when their ideas receive little attention, a sense of humor to keep in perspective their own roles, which all too often, are rather modest. Any illusions they may have for transformative actions are bound to come a cropper. Their strongest hope might be to infect others with the notion that it is worthwhile to seek improvement, even if the particular ideas they espouse may or may not be all that important. Further, evolving circumstances usually demand adaptation in reform concepts. Though some friends may disagree, I do not take myself too seriously, even while I continue to harbor expectation that change will come. The key is to attract more IFS colleagues to work on systemic issues, centered on the vital requirement to strengthen India's diplomatic capacity.

14

Career Conclusions

For Winston Churchill, history was a guide to understanding contemporary issues and anticipating the future. Churchill said: *The farther backward you can look, the farther forward you are likely to see.*

I deeply believe that the diplomatic profession has much to learn from 'mining' and examining knowledge embedded in the collective memories of its alumni, including institutional knowledge, and analysis of experiences. It is amazing how little attention most organizations pay to their own past. Foreign ministries can do this via organized discussions with diplomats of their first generation (as Kenya did with its 2009 conference on its early diplomatic experiences of the first three decades after independence), and through oral history accounts, i.e. interviewing former officials and political figures, to create an archival database of one's experiences.[1] The Americans do this well. No less powerful is the method of capturing new insights from everyday events, though this seems banal. How many institutions, especially foreign ministries, ask their officials that have participated in a bilateral negotiation or a conference, an overseas visit or some other significant event, to add to their reports

---

[1] In September 2009, the Foreign Service Institute attached to Kenya's Foreign Ministry organized a two-day conference on that country's early diplomacy, where those that had served in the Ministry in its early days immediately after independence gave their accounts of those experiences. I was the only non-Kenyan to attend this conference. The conference record is on the Institute's website as a PDF file.

a short note on the new things learnt from that experience.[2] Most foreign ministries require officials, especially heads of missions, to compile 'handing over notes' prior to departure. Is this monitored? My impression is that presently, barely half of Indian ambassadors bother to write these; some comply in perfunctory fashion.[3] Added together, and effectively cataloged in a digital archive, such bits of observation, perhaps not always illuminating in themselves, add up to a powerful body of practical knowledge, and an effective guide for the future.

The internet has transformed the working of foreign ministries, especially those that effectively use *intranets*, or virtual private networks; those that still do not, due to cost or indifference, pay a big opportunity cost. Such intranets become a huge information exchange. The British FCO uses it to interview all candidates for embassy assignments. One method especially attractive is the US State Department's 'Diplopedia', a collaborative tool, essentially using a wiki method of crowdsourcing, to produce basic guides and tools for handling tasks typical to diplomatic work.

Out of my 35 years in the IFS, I spent just over eight years at Headquarters, including 14 months at entry-level training, and 13 months in the PM's Office. Thus total time spent working in the MEA barely came to six years, much as I valued each such opportunity at the nerve center of the Indian diplomatic system. In my final 11 years, I was continually overseas. Perhaps this has engendered for me an embassy perspective, i.e. empathy for the official posted abroad, reflected in my writing. That experience is in stark contrast to IFS colleagues that have spent much longer at Headquarters, including a few that have even served continually at MEA for six or more years at a time. Generally speaking, those professionals that spend a long time at their capital tend to do

[2] In the immediate aftermath of the hijacking of an Indian Airlines aircraft to Kandahar in 1999, and its controversial aftermath in which India released some highly dangerous terrorists, I had suggested to an MEA colleague directly involved in this event, if he could write on what he had learnt from that episode. He did not do this, I guess in the apprehension that an honest narrative of this kind would be seen as critical of powerful individuals that had acted in a distinctly unwise fashion.

[3] See Rana, *21st Century Diplomacy* (2011), Chapter 15, Annex I, for a template for what I recommend as a comprehensive handing over note.

better in their careers than those that spend more time abroad—out of sight, out of mind, one might say.

I have written enough about myself. Let me devote this final chapter to the experiences of others in the diplomacy profession, in the shape of broader lessons skimmed out, which might be of utility, especially for young officials commencing work in foreign ministries and embassies, and those contemplating a foreign service career. It may also appeal to the general reader, in terms of the challenges faced in the public services. True, this chapter departs from a memoir format, but it offers reflections that flow from my experience and that of others.

These thoughts are summarized in eight simple conclusions. A keen reader may find that my narrative supports these lessons.

1. Expand the envelope for action, be proactive

More than ever before, the task of advancing the country's external interests is vast, holistic and multi-faceted. Senior officials typically closely supervise the young official working in a foreign ministry. On the face of it, the latter have limited latitude for autonomous action. But in today's hectic work environment, where a multitude of state and non-official actors jostle, with varied, urgent issues to be tackled, there is no dearth of opportunity for initiative. One of the simplest methods is to reach out to thinktanks and academia, engaging them in discussion, attending seminars or conferences, and widening one's knowledge base. That also applies to cultivating contacts in other ministries and official agencies that are involved in, or relevant to the regions and countries that are in one's charge, to understand wider thinking. A larger goal is to build domain expertise, focused on themes that are relevant in foreign affairs, especially at a regional or global level. Do young officials do this as well as they might?

For those working at embassies and consulates, the arena for personal initiative is large, even for the junior official. The scope for outreach is almost endless, and seniors can provide guidance. In most capitals, young embassy colleagues come together in their own clusters. An example is 'OECD Sneakers' in Paris, a network of young officials. Information technology facilitates actions, via Facebook and other social media tools. Some ambassadors give latitude to juniors, recognizing that they bring a degree of personal commitment that can produce remarkable results. Example: in the 1960s, when Egypt was host to many Arab nationalist movements, a young Ranjit Gupta, language probationer at Cairo cultivated leaders of the South Yemen independence movement. When the Yemenis were to go to Geneva in 1968 to negotiate the terms of independence with the UK, they requested Indian Ambassador Apa Pant that Ranjit should accompany them; Ambassador Pant agreed and persuaded the MEA to endorse his decision. New Delhi then dispatched the MEA's head of the Legal and Treaties Division, SP Jagota, to act as a behind-the-scene advisor, assisted by Ranjit. The Yemenis accepted this arrangement, but made it clear that they would treat Ranjit as their principal Indian interlocutor; I do not know another instance where a third secretary from a foreign country played such a role in major negotiations.[4]

For a head of mission, the arena for proactive action is large. Consider two examples from Africa. When Kenya's Bethwell Kiplagat arrived in Paris in the late 1970s as his country's envoy, putting aside protocol dictates that the first call in the diplomatic corps should be to the dean, he chose to visit the Somali Ambassador, telling him that this bilateral relationship was the most important one for his country.[5] That led to friendship, through which the two envoys helped start a bilateral dialogue at home, that in turn dramatically improved their fraught inter-state relations. Kiplagat went on to play a key role as a pan-African peacemaker in his subsequent assignment as permanent secretary in the Kenyan Foreign Ministry; he remains active in domestic public affairs. The other story concerns Namibia's High Commissioner in London in the mid-1990s, Veccoh Nghiwete, who asked the British Foreign Office to help him make a visit to Northern Ireland, at a time when the 'Troubles' were at their height, to understand the situation; few envoys visited that part

---

4 Source: Ambassador Ranjit Gupta's Oral History record, under publication by the Indian Council of World Affairs. I was in Geneva at the time and witnessed the role that Ranjit played in South Yemen's negotiations with the British.

5 Panel IV, 'Diplomacy of Peace: Peace and peace processes in Kenya's Early Diplomacy 1963-1993', *Kenya's Early Diplomacy: 1963-1993*, Foreign Service Institute, Ministry of Foreign Affairs, Nairobi, 2009, pp. 71-7.

of the UK, least of all from Africa. That gesture of empathy won him approbation from the British authorities, and may have contributed to a very rare dinner invitation at Windsor Castle from Queen Elizabeth. These actions reflected imagination and finesse, plus a willingness to act out of the box.[6]

2. Manage risk, exercise judgment

Working at foreign assignments, the diplomat, especially a head of mission, faces situations of opportunity that call for initiative, where risk has to be balanced against potential gain. Sometimes time is too short to consult headquarters. A decision to act often hinges on understanding the local situation, which means that it is the person on the spot that must decide, and take the consequences if the decision turns out to be erroneous. Such opportunity can also come at the foreign ministry, but a hierarchy chain is usually available for consultation, though exceptional situations may require an individual official to act urgently. This is obviously not a prescription for rash action; the consequences must always be weighed, to decide when and how to act.

Example: In September 1994, MPM Menon (1942-2013), was to present credentials to the ruler of the United Arab Emirates, President Sheikh Zayed, at a time of crisis for India, when erroneous reports of a 'plague' in Gujarat had produced panic reactions in some countries. UAE had suspended all India connections, including 150 weekly flights, shipping services, even receipt of letters and parcels; this had produced deep unease among the country's then 1.2 million strong Indian community. Ambassador Menon was told that as four other envoys due to present credentials, he would get just five minutes of conversation time with the head of state, and should stick to pleasantries, avoiding substantive issues. Ambassador Menon nevertheless went ahead to speak of that crisis, pointing out that the disease outbreak in Gujarat was being tackled and that no European

[6] Recounting this story in 2000 when I was a Commonwealth adviser to the Namibia Foreign Ministry, Ambassador Nghiwete added that when the Court Gazette published his dinner encounter with the British monarch, his diplomatic colleagues in London, including Arab envoys that had served there for two decades and longer, quizzed him how he had wangled this rare invite.

country had imposed such bans. Sheikh Zayed promised to look into the issue. Compounding his action, Ambassador Menon then briefed the local press on his démarche, which was against UAE custom. Some foreign ambassadors warned Menon that he risked expulsion for that impulsive public diplomacy. But a week later, the UAE acted on his démarche; all the restrictions with India were rescinded.[7] A calculated risk had paid off, perhaps because no one had brought to the notice of the UAE head of state the consequences of those restrictions.

Another example: In the 1980s, the British Ministry of Defence criticized Sir Brian Barder, High Commissioner in Nigeria, for failing to promote sales of fighter aircraft and tanks to the Nigerian army. In a trenchant reply copied to all the key departments in Whitehall, he pointed out that pushing defence equipment into a country where similar equipment sold earlier was rusting away unused, contradicted Britain's advice to Nigeria on sound economic management, as also its aid policy, that was aimed at economic development and poverty reduction. Against a past Nigerian record of failure to keep up payments for defense equipment, the effect of new sales would be that the UK Export Credit Guarantees Department would end up paying for British defence sales that Nigeria did not need. Barder's deputy congratulated him on 'such an eloquent career suicide note'. Barder heard nothing further, and found later that his forthright missive had produced an inter-department impasse, and in effect a policy reversal.[8]

At a 2015 training workshop organized in an Asian country by the Asia Europe Foundation, DiploFoundation and New Zealand's National Center for Research on Europe, a senior Swiss diplomat gave a fascinating account of the way Presence Swiss, an organization created for outreach to Swiss people abroad, and for public diplomacy prepared for a key event. In 2009 a national referendum was held under that country's unique constitutional system, whether new mosques with minarets could be built—a

7 See Rana and Chatterjee, eds, *Economic Diplomacy: India's Experience*, CUTS, (2011), pp. 114-5.

8 See, Sir Brian Barder, *What Diplomats Do: The Life and Work of Diplomats*, Rowman and Littlefield, 2004, pp. 126-9.

Turkish mosque under construction had triggered intense debate in the country. It became a test of how far the Swiss were willing to go in multicultural expression. For Presence Swiss the challenge was to carefully anticipate the result and discreetly alert friendly Islamic states that a ban on new minaret construction did not mean hostility to Islam, and that the issue was a narrow one framed in a specific Swiss context. Swiss embassies were mobilized to contact important friends in major Islamic states to explain the full background and emphasize that the country was not abandoning its open policy and respect for all religions. In the event, the risk taken in acting ahead of a vote result paid dividends, and reactions in these countries were muted; they did not engage in 'Swiss-bashing' as some had feared.

3. Diplomacy is a process, not a discrete set of events

It is easy to view major events, be it a visit by a head of government that produces a long-sought dramatic outcome, or an agreement that resolves a long-pending issue, as transformative occasions. The reverse may apply to an unfavorable development in a foreign country, or some other kind of setback, which can produce despondency, especially when that partner country is not willing to make amends. The reality is that countries are in the business of managing external relations for the long haul. It is the continuum that is of lasting worth, within which discrete events may be seen as stages or chapters; it is that long saga that will count for the future. A related way is to look not to particular events, such as a ministerial visit, which can be described as *process*, but rather to concentrate mainly on the *outcomes* from such events.

Example: Consider the value of summit visits, comparing the frequency of visits by heads of Indian governments to Africa, with how China tackles that important, fast-growing continent. Why are summit visits important? A clear answer to that comes from the manner in which PM Narendra Modi has reached out to countries, neighbors and to those afar, in his first year in office. Each of his 18 overseas visits (a remarkable tally compared with previous Indian prime ministers), has been carefully crafted, with multilayered actions that engage different segments, governments, business, the media and the Indian diaspora. The

Modi Government seems to understand well that each relationship is located in a continuum; summits permit shifting the quality of relations to an entirely new level. Intrinsic to that is a realization that the summit is not a one-shot event. In the past, say in Africa, India tended not to follow any logic or master plan in wooing states big or small. For instance, only two Indian prime ministers have visited the continent's largest country, Nigeria: Nehru in 1962 and Manmohan Singh in 2007. Contrast this with China, which each year sends one of the top two leaders, its President or Premier, on an extended tour that covers up to 10 countries each time. China does the same in Latin America. That ensures close tracking of major projects in each country, integral to China's massive new economic commitment to Africa and Latin America. It also tells these states that they are valued as long-term partners.

The issue goes beyond high-level exchanges, and leaches into the management of important bilateral relationships. With a few exceptions, most countries, prominent among them the developing states, tend not to handle these as a process that should be part of a master matrix. Consider some exceptions: each year Canada identifies two or three countries as deserving of intense cultivation, especially for purposes of trade and investment enhancement, and organizes a series of overlapping actions for this purpose, aimed at lifting that relationship to a new plane. Thailand, during the years of Prime Minister Thaksin Shinawarta (2001-06), carried out an intense examination of what all of its key ministries sought in their ties with some 25 priority countries, looking to a five-year horizon; it then produced a master plan for each, monitored closely for implementation. France does this across the board with its 'Ambassador's Instructions' method, applied each time a new envoy takes up assignment in a foreign capital.[9] In many countries such intense *focused strategizing*, even in relation to major foreign partners, simply does not occur. Example: the Indian Department of Commerce identifies some foreign countries as 'focus markets' but does not consult the Economic Division of the MEA before this is finalized; often, the Indian embassies in the selected countries are also not in the picture. This goes against the reality that very many agencies of government are today involved in trade and

[9] See Rana, *The Contemporary Embassy* (2013), p. 91.

economic management, which requires joint actions, in a holistic perspective.

4. Non-state actors are increasingly important in managing foreign relations

The notion that non-state actors are legitimate, active elements in the 'national diplomatic system' of countries is today a given; it has even become a truism. Yet understanding of all that this implies, has been slow in coming; in some developing country foreign ministries, the needed actions for domestic outreach are either not undertaken, or lack sufficient rigor. Legacy thinking, an attitude that 'this is not the way we work in our foreign ministry', inhibits action.

Example: India is a late mover on this, but the Ministry of External Affairs is beginning to accept new methods; but unlike say Mexico, we do not as yet have a unit to manage outreach to non-state actors. This task is bundled into the work remit of the Policy Planning Division. In recent years, some enlightened territorial divisions directly engage academia and thinktanks, but this is episodic. A suggestion that a regular forum be established to guide such actions withers on the vine. Similarly, a regular mechanism for consultation with business associations, on a periodic basis does not exist; it could examine the support business requires from embassies, plus make for more effective economic promotion. In China leading thinktanks—mainly funded by the government—are not only treated as legitimate interlocutors by the Foreign Ministry and other entities, but even the country's apex foreign policy decision-making body, the 'Leading Small Group on Foreign Affairs' (headed by the President, with some members of the Politburo Standing Committee joining him), regularly meets the heads of the key thinktanks.[10]

Another example: Engagement with non-official agencies often goes together with 'outplacement' of officials, sending them to work with different kinds of entities that deal with international affairs. Germany allows its Foreign Office officials to work in thinktanks and in political party organizations. That degree of openness results from a conscious decision after WWII,

[10] Information obtained in confidential discussion in 2013.

and that prescription may not work in other countries. The British Foreign Office, practicing more traditional civil service separation of from politics, nevertheless encourages its officials to work on deputation in NGOs and similar organizations, as well as companies, to bring in wide experiences; at any time some 20 officials are to be found under such secondment. We do this in India, but episodically, partly because our work culture does not recognize that outplacement broadens the individual's personal horizons and also serves the institution; placement in non-official organizations is rare.

5. Issues are interconnected, call for holistic action

Developing mutually beneficial relations with a partner country, or managing a problem relationship, or pursuing regional cooperation, or handling a global issue in which one's nation has a strong interest—all these are today complex tasks that call for unified action across a range of themes and sectors. The fact that many different agencies deal with subjects that have an international footprint also makes it essential that such actions follow a comprehensive action plan. The foreign ministry is naturally cast in the role of coordinator, partly because it has no sectoral agenda (unlike line ministries that have their own zones of competence), and partly as it is the manager of the diplomatic machinery, i.e. the overseas embassies and consulates. Sometimes the office of the head of government may perform this role, either because the issues are too important to be entrusted to others, or to impose unity among conflicting stakeholders.

Ministries often work to cross purposes, or pursue agendas that do not conform to real national interest, as we have seen in the experiences I have narrated. For a foreign ministry, this usually means finding a domestic compromise, after intensive consultation. For those in embassies abroad, it involves locating a safe path that focuses on real interests in the country of assignment, while working with different home official agencies. Either way, the net objective is a 'whole of government' and a 'whole of nation' policy, easy to describe but hard to achieve.

Example: Amar Sinha has written about a sharp commercial dispute that emerged in an unnamed country, following which an Indian software company's executives visiting that country were sent to jail, because their local partner was influential.[11] The Embassy and the Ministry of External Affairs mobilized a range of contacts in that country, taking care not to adopt the standpoint that the Indian company was necessarily in the right, but urging that the issue be seen in the broader perspective of the excellent relationship with that country; they also urged that commercial disputes needed to be resolved through due process. That found an echo with the local administration, which agreed to release the Indian company executives, and accepted an arbitration process, which subsequently produced a mutually satisfactory settlement. A jingoistic reaction to the original indefensible action would only have exacerbated the problem.

Another example: In a 2015 report, the German Foreign Office has acknowledged that it was slow to react to the Ebola crisis, though it recalled an ambassador based in Latin America and appointed him as commissioner for coordinating a German response.[12] The Foreign Office is now to create a new directorate-general as a center for crisis response, with a focus also on negotiation, UN peacekeeping, and professionalized deployment of civilian crisis experts. The objective is for the Foreign Office to lead from the front, while working closely with other official and non-official agencies. This is a fine model for our times.

6. Practice teamwork; utilize young officials, shed hierarchy mindsets

That organizations need teamwork is an established nostrum. It warrants reinforcement because senior officials heading foreign ministry units and embassies tend not to delegate, not nearly as much as they might. This may have something to do with the potential damage that might result from mismanaging an issue with a foreign country. It may also result from the fact that diplomacy is a conservative profession. If we look closely into the work ethos of reputed diplomatic services, we may find that despite their outward reputation for excellence, young officials

[11] See Rana and Chatterjee, eds, *Economic Diplomacy: India's Experience*, CUTS, (2011), Chapter 9, pp. 95-102.

[12] See *Review 2014: A Fresh Look at German Foreign Policy*, http://www.aussenpolitik-weiter-denken.de/en/topics.html

are often not utilized nearly as well as they might be. It would be impolitic to name them. Examples of the reverse kind are Singapore and the UK, among others.

An antidote does exist, as one Service colleague put it: even if you believe that others may not do as well as you might (which is typical thinking among 'Type A' personalities), that difference might usually be one of a few percentage points. Why not then ease up and let others run the show? Young officials have a natural urge to prove themselves, and are unburdened by memory, which is often a load that experienced officials sometimes carry. Guide the youngsters, but with a light hand.

Example: During the Libya crisis of 2012, when countries that had workers and engineers stranded in oilfields and other installations were obliged to carry out emergency evacuation.[13] The Indian Ambassador in Cairo Navdeep Suri decided to entrust the task to three young officials, two third secretary language probationers, Manusmriti and Sanjay Kumar Muluka, and second secretary Rakesh Kawra (plus an attaché from the High Commission in London, GS Uprari). Ambassador Anil Trigunayat, who had just completed an assignment in Libya coordinated actions from Malta (where he had held concurrent charge) by mobile phone, dredging up his past contacts in Libya. The evacuation was completed successfully.

Another example: When in 1999 Robin Cook as British Foreign Secretary was persuaded to use Foreign Office officials to come up with reform ideas that would give a new edge to UK diplomacy, he also agreed that this could be done through intranet-based teams that invited ideas from young officials, at home and abroad, in what could be called a version of 'crowdsourcing'.[14] That produced in six months a far-reaching set of suggestions for transformative reform, put together in a document titled 'Foresight 2010' (alas, not published), which had a major impact on the working of the British diplomatic system. The German Foreign Office used a like method of harnessing young diplomats, through its intranet, for the second generation of reforms, after

---

[13] See detailed report in *The Telegraph*, 1 Jan 2015: http://epaper.telegraphindia.com/paper/7-11-01@01@2015-1001.html

[14] See John Dickie, *The New Mandarins: How British Foreign Policy Works* (2004).

the changes that were put into effect on the basis of the Paschke Report of 1999.

In embassies abroad, teamwork takes a special character, given the heterogeneity in representation in large missions, where officials from different ministries and agencies rub shoulders. Large missions may host representatives from a dozen or more entities, including those from cultural, defense, environment, finance, intelligence, tourism, and other agencies. Forging them into a team, even when they are answerable to diverse masters, and may not share a common agenda, is never easy, but good heads of missions manage this, through leadership and a blend of trust and exhortation. All diplomatic services have experience of this, both through their exemplars and their failures. The key seems to be to practice balance, inclusiveness, and fair treatment for all. In particular, if diverse officials can be made to work in a single team working to a precise set of tasks, that joint effort produces outcomes that permeate into the group as a whole. Denmark adds a twist to this, by appointing the junior officials as team coordinators; this simple method gives those nominated a confidence boost, and teaches them leadership skills. Such task-force methods have wide application, the more so when crosscutting issues are at stake. Singapore typically sends young officials on overseas delegations, even leading such teams, which helps to build experience, getting over the notion that such tasks are the prerogative of seniors. We live in an age in which such practices help us to overcome some of the inhibitions of hierarchy.

7. **Advocacy, trust and credibility remain at the core of diplomacy; despite the rise of public diplomacy and the revolution in information technology, the classic tasks of relationship building and bilateral management remain unchanged.**

This may be the hardest 'old' lesson to absorb, because each generation in diplomacy (as in other fields) views its own age as one of paradigm transformation; older diplomats tend to resist change ('that is not how things were done in my time').

Technology continually modifies organizations and their working methods. When the telegraph was invented, some thought it marked the end of diplomacy as it had existed in the past, since the instant transmission of messages and instructions eliminated the penumbra of incertitude between the dispatch of a set of instructions, and their receipt by the destination embassy for action. Reports sent from the field to the center, i.e. the foreign ministry similarly faced a period of limbo, though receipt at Headquarters did not always require or produce action. Now, with virtually instantaneous transmission of almost all kinds of messages, that cushion of delay and inaction is lost.

One consequence is message overload. It is routine to re-transmit (or directly send out) reports that one embassy addresses to the Headquarters, to many other missions. That keeps them in the information loop, but it also tests their attention span. A new method, not known in the past, is for a cluster of embassies to collaborate in writing a joint report on a complex situation; that is a far sight better than having single missions offer their assessment, to be challenged by sister embassies that bring in a different perspective, producing needless, sometimes senseless, debate. New interlinked communication networks—especially 'intranets'—permit holistic analysis.

ICT permits more refined, purposeful advocacy, but the core skills are unchanged, and predate new technology. Example: *The Little Red Dot: Reflections by Singapore Diplomats* (2005) carries a fine essay by Lee Khoon Choy, former senior minister of state at the Foreign Ministry, on how as Ambassador to Egypt in 1969 he handled Singapore's decision to recognize Israel.[15] He explained the action in advance to Egyptian interlocutors, drawing attention to the security situation his country faced after the 1965 break in Singapore's union with Malaysia, affirming also that their position on occupation of Arab territory by Israel would remain unchanged. In this fashion, Singapore showed respect for Egyptian sensitivity, and kept open the communication lines. The result was that Cairo reacted to Singapore's public announcement with equanimity, unlike in the case with Romania three months later, when it broke off relations with Bucharest following the latter's

[15] Lee Khoon Choy, 'Solving Two Diplomatic Challenges', Koh, Tommy, and Chang Li Lin, eds. *The Little Red Dot: Reflections by Singapore's Diplomats*, (World Scientific, Singapore, 2005), pp. 71-5.

recognition of Israel. The simple lesson: handling friendships between countries is not different from the way individuals ought to treat one another; it pays to put oneself in the shoes of the other, and act with care and 'mindfulness', using this word in its wide Buddhist connotation. In South-East Asia this might be called the 'ASEAN style of diplomacy'. A long-term perspective is always of value.

Representational entertainment is another professional activity that can be utilized to foster old-fashioned virtues, especially credibility and trust. Diplomatic entertainment involves the use of official funds to organize social functions where the host and guests meet, network, and get to know one another in informal settings. The manner in which such activities are organized, and supervised, speaks to the good or inefficient use of this method. In well-ordered diplomatic services, such funds are allotted to officials as a 'grant', meaning the money has first to be spent for the designated purpose, and is reimbursed after a supervising officer is satisfied that it has been applied to the intended purpose of building relationships with those that are helpful to the embassy in its official objectives. For diplomats, this entails maintaining an 'entertainment register' in which names of guests, the purpose of the event and the details of its organization (including usually the menu at a meal served), are set out. The head of mission's entertainment narrative goes to the foreign ministry, which may vet this and as needed, advise this senior official to apply the money in optimal fashion, or widen outreach in terms of the persons invited.

Such supervision over detail is intended to ensure that the relatively modest sums provided help embassy officials build deep as well as extensive networks of contacts, to 'transform acquaintanceships into relationships'.[16] Many colleagues from different diplomatic services I have interviewed over the past 17 years have testified to the effort entailed in building relationships, for instance, spending time at functions that may not be glamorous or well-attended, often going to two and three receptions in a single evening, even at far-flung locations, after

[16] This language comes from a Schumpeter column, *The Economist*, 14 March 2015.

a full working day. Not everyone does this. It is much easier, and less boring, to go only to glittering events hosted by major powers or the socially well connected. It is for this reason that at most capitals, the adept diplomat reaches out much beyond the 'beautiful people', and utilizes entertainment funds to build deep and productive relations with those that will help to enhance beneficial friendships, be they in bilateral or multilateral settings.

As the noted US TV broadcaster Edward R Murrow said: 'The really critical link in the international communications chain is the last three feet, which is best bridged by personal contact —one person talking to another.'[17] This old truth remains at the core of relationship building. One of the victims of Wikileaks was the US Ambassador in Mexico, Carlos Pascual. The leaked cables disclosed that he had reported to Washington DC on the situation in Mexico with sharp adverse comment, and had thoroughly criticized the Mexican army. This caused much embarrassment for the envoy when his reports were splashed on newspaper front pages; he found himself isolated and ostracized by the Mexican authorities. Responding to a *Washington Post* question as to whether Mexico had lost confidence in him, Mexican President Felipe Calderón said: 'Trust is hard to earn and easy to lose.' In March 2011, Ambassador Pascual resigned, citing personal reasons.

8. Build a learning organization that also encourages innovation.

Continual learning and innovation have become central to all organizations, as a path to success. The challenge is to manage these processes in ways that sustain and advance organizational objectives. A variety of methods are today being applied, and these call for examination and wider replication. In particular, foreign ministries need to look at one another and apply borrowed ideas, of course seasoned with judgment and adaptation, to suit their own circumstances. For instance: annually, EU heads of foreign ministry administration met for the past 20 years, to discuss mutual experiences. Should not other regional groups consider

[17] William F Burns, '10 Parting Thoughts for America's Diplomats', *Foreign Policy*, 23 October 2014.

such methods, given the fact that the bulk of foreign ministry work is similar?

Personnel management is especially important for diplomatic services, as are evolving methods of foreign representation. For instance, the UK initiated a process about 15 years back to entrust more embassy tasks to locally engaged staff and cut back on home-based personnel, including junior diplomats. That worked well to save money, but had an indirect consequence: it left too few overseas job openings for new service entrants, which meant that they could not gain vitally needed field experience. The FCO also found that its 'one-man' embassies, where everyone other than the ambassador was locally engaged, led to difficulty, overloading the ambassador and leaving no one in charge when he was away from the assignment capital on leave or other duties.[18] They are now altering that to ensure that at least two home officials are assigned to each embassy. The moral: good ideas may also have a downside that might take some time to manifest itself; it pays to be flexible and modify methods as needed.

The Dutch 'Advisory Council on Foreign Affairs' is one method for wide consultation with outside experts. Such mechanism has multiple advantages, not the least of which is that it demonstrates to publics that the official machinery is open to outside ideas. The Indian MEA tried this for a few years in the 2000s, but the scheme ended when the Minister of External Affairs who had experimented with this, left office. Such a mechanism should be institutionalized, not left to the whim of high office personalities. All foreign ministries stand to gain by consulting representatives of academia, business, industry chambers, the media, thinktanks, and others, through such advisory groups.

Training is of course the classic learning mechanism. This goes beyond holding of programs for skilling of officials at different levels. Experience sharing also takes place via discussion seminars, joining short courses at institutions of excellence at home and abroad, and sabbaticals. But too few foreign ministries have a clear program for sending officials on sabbaticals that focus on subjects that match their expertise requirements.

---

[18] See 'Modernizing Dutch Diplomacy', Final Report 2015, p. 65.

A Final Word

The eight conclusions suggested above are intertwined; they reinforce one another. They are not unique and would probably also apply to other fields of activity, especially to the business world. In putting these forward, I suggest that we need to frequently examine our own actions, to draw from these relevant learnings. That keeps the organization and its personnel alert and refreshed. And it helps professionals enjoy their chosen career.

Finishing this memoir completes a project long in gestation. It has been enjoyable to revisit the past, reconnect with old friends, and challenge one's memory, enlisting also the help of my family, to fill out gaps. I hope this work transmits to readers, including new diplomatic service entrants some of the passion that this profession can engender, and encourage others towards this career choice. Humility and humor are among the attributes that work for diplomats, blending well with strong personal commitment, providing a delightful cocktail that can keep one refreshed till the end of a service career and beyond. And yes, there is a life even after one's public service comes to its natural end. Prospects for further service in different fields and pursuit avenues for one's interests increase all the time, offering a cornucopia of choice.

Index of Personalities

Index of Subjects